INSIGHT **CITY GUIDE**

MOSCOW

Discovery
CHANNEL

APA PUBLICATIONS   **L**
Part of the Langenscheidt Publishing Group

⚓ INSIGHT GUIDE
MOSCOW

Editorial Director
Brian Bell
Editor
Jason Mitchell
Art Director
Klaus Geisler
Picture Editor
Hilary Genin
Cartography Editor
Zoe Goodwin

Distribution

UK & Ireland
GeoCenter International Ltd
The Viables Centre, Harrow Way
Basingstoke, Hants RG22 4BJ
Fax: (44) 1256-817988

United States
Langenscheidt Publishers, Inc.
36-36 33rd Street, 4th Floor
Long Island City, NY 11106
Fax: (1) 718-784 0640

Australia
Universal Publishers
1 Waterloo Road
Macquarie Park, NSW 2113
Fax: (61) 2-9888 9074

New Zealand
Hema Maps New Zealand Ltd (HNZ)
Unit D, 24 Ra ORA Drive
East Tamaki, Auckland
Fax: (64) 9-273 6479

Worldwide
Apa Publications GmbH & Co.
Verlag KG (Singapore branch)
38 Joo Koon Road, Singapore 628990
Tel: (65) 6865-1600. Fax: (65) 6861-6438

Printing

Insight Print Services (Pte) Ltd
38 Joo Koon Road, Singapore 628990
Tel: (65) 6865-1600. Fax: (65) 6861-6438

© 2006 Apa Publications GmbH & Co.
Verlag KG (Singapore branch)
All Rights Reserved

First Edition 2006

ABOUT THIS BOOK

The first Insight Guide pioneered the use of creative full-colour photography in travel guides in 1970. Since then, we have expanded our range to cater for our readers' need not only for reliable information about their chosen destination but also for a real understanding of the culture and workings of that destination. Now, when the internet can supply inexhaustible (but not always reliable) facts, our books marry text and pictures to provide those much more elusive qualities: knowledge and discernment. To achieve this, they rely heavily on the authority of locally based writers and photographers.

How to use this book

The book is carefully structured both to convey an understanding of the city and its culture and to guide readers through its sights and activities:

◆ To understand Moscow today, you need to know something of its past. The first section, marked with an orange bar, covers the city's history and culture in lively, authoritative essays written by specialists.

◆ The main Places section, marked with a blue bar, provides a full run-down of all the attractions worth seeing. The main places of interest are coordinated by number with full-colour maps.

◆ A list of recommended restaurants is included at the end of each chapter in the Places section.

◆ The Travel Tips listings section at the back of the book provides a point of reference for information on travel, hotels, shops, nightlife and all the other practical travel information

you'll need. Information may be located quickly by using the index printed on the back-cover flap – and the flaps are designed to serve as bookmarks.

◆ Photographs are chosen not only to illustrate geography and buildings but also to convey the moods of the city and the life of its people.

The contributors

Insight Guides have maintained a guidebook to Moscow since the fall of the Berlin Wall, but with *City Guide Moscow* we felt that this remarkable, ever-changing city needed a completely new book.

Leading the way is **Michele A. Berdy**. An American-born columnist for the *Moscow Times*, Berdy has lived in Moscow on and off since 1978, developing a passion for this

metropolis as if it were her own. She is your guide in the Places chapters of the book, covering all the city's major attractions as well as hidden gems off the beaten track.

Berdy also wrote the history of the city and has gone a long way to explaining the challenges facing Moscow today. And, like a true Russian, she explains the country's passion for food (and drink) and its love of fairy tales and magic. But Moscow is not Moscow without the arts, and Berdy has also provided an insightful guide to the city's literary and artistic heritage.

Carl Shreck, a colleague of Berdy at the *Moscow Times*, wrote the Muscovites chapter, and to tackle the interlinking worlds of Russian religion and architecture, the leading scholar **William Craft Brumfield** wrote two illuminating chapters.

The Travel Tips section was expertly put together by **Brian Droitcour** and **Marc Bennetts**. Droitcour freelances at *The Moscow Times* and wrote the Accommodation and Activities sections. Bennetts, who runs an English-language academy, contributed the Transport and A–Z sections. The restaurant reviews were written by **Jillian Ong**. The vivid photography of **Richard Nowitz** appears throughout the book.

Invaluable editorial assistance was provided by **Roger Williams** and **Clare Griffiths**. Additional research was provided by **Lydia Strong**. Proofreading was by **Neil Titman** and the index was compiled by **Helen Peters**.

CONTACTING THE EDITORS

We would appreciate it if readers alerted us to errors or outdated information by writing to:

Insight Guides, P.O. Box 7910, London SE1 1WE, England. Fax: (44) 20-7403 0290. email: insight@apaguide.co.uk

www.insightguides.com
In North America:
www.insighttravelguides.com

Contents

Maps

Travel Tips

THE BEST OF MOSCOW

Setting priorities, saving money, unique attractions...
here, at a glance, are our recommendations, plus some
tips and tricks even old spies won't know

MOST AMAZING MOSCOW

Religion, espionage and politics all have their
monuments in Russia's enigmatic capital.

● **Red Square.** Even
before you stand on
this vast courtyard
you'll have an image
of it in your head, per-
haps with tanks rolling
past Stalin's perch
atop the Lenin Mau-
soleum. Nevertheless,
the view is timeless –
and most magical at
night *(see page 91)*.

● **The Kremlin.** Layer
upon layer of history
has been laid down
inside these

brick walls. From con-
taining the original city,
the fortress became the
seat of religious power,
tsarist rule and then
Soviet might. It is still
the centre of power
today *(see page 81)*.

● **Museum of the KGB.**
Only open to trainees
of the FSB (the KGB's
latest incarnation) and
foreign tour groups,
the museum highlights
the technology of espi-
onage during the Cold
War *(see page 160)*.

● **Sergeev Posad
Monastery.** A refuge
for Peter the Great
and a site of pilgrim-
age for Orthodox
believers, a beautiful
rival to the Kremlin
(see page 200).

● **Museum of Wooden
Architecture, Suzdal.**
The handiwork of
some of Russia's
finest craftsmen is
on display here, in the
form of wooden
cathedrals and cottages
(see page 206).

ANCIENT ATTRACTIONS

● **Golden Ring.** Long
before Moscow was
the undisputed ruler
of Russia, numerous
principalities sur-
rounded the city and
rivalled its influence.
Today the kremlins of
Vladimir and Suzdal
still survive and are
the highlights of a
tour of the Golden
Ring *(see page 203)*.

● **Old English Court.**
A concise documen-
tation of England's
long-standing
economic ties with
Russia *(see page 101)*.

● **Chambers in
Zaryade.** The life
of medieval traders
and boyars is well
preserved in this
tiny museum *(see
page 102)*.

LEFT: a fine balancing act between the old
and the new. **ABOVE:** the unforgettable domes
of St Basil's Cathedral. **RIGHT:** antique stores
sell vintage editions of Russia's best authors.

SOPHISTICATED SHOPPING

- **Vernisazh, Izmailovsky Park.** This old flea market in the eastern suburbs has become the city's premier location for souvenir shopping. Whether you're looking for dolls, old maps, busts of Lenin or genuine icons, you'll have plenty to choose from.Don't forget to haggle *(see page 190)*.
- **GUM.** No longer Moscow's most prestigious shopping mall, but the corridors of GUM are still lined with the finest names in European fashion, jewellery and cosmetics *(see page 94)*.
- **Okhotny Ryad Underground Mall.** Moscow's latest shopping addition is your standard mall experience, made unique by the ornamentation of Zurab Tsereteli, Mayor Luzhkov's favoured artist *(see page 110)*.
- **TsUM.** Moscow's first department store, and an old favourite of Chekhov and his family *(see page 151)*.
- **Yeliseev's Food Emporium.** Yeliseev's has long been the place to find the finest imported groceries and rare cheeses and chocolates. Even during the darkest days of economic depression, its elaborately decorated counters were ready to serve *(see page 147)*.
- **Petrovsky Passage.** A smaller, more elite version of GUM, and especially popular with those looking for more intimate service – and even higher prices *(see page 152)*.

ABOVE: nouveau cuisine and Communism's final fling. **BELOW LEFT:** though landlocked, Moscow has some of the best and most affordable sushi in the world. **BELOW RIGHT:** the airy corridors of GUM, Moscow's famous shopping mall.

MORE THAN CABBAGE AND CUCUMBERS

- **Sushi.** Moscow has quickly become one of the best places in the world to enjoy raw fish – and remarkably, it's reasonably priced.
- **Caviar.** Perhaps it is Russians' love of caviar that has developed them into such sushi gourmands. There are several types to choose from, and all taste best on fresh blini with a shot of chilled vodka to wash the taste down.
- **Black Bread.** Russia prides itself on the wholesome, hearty loaf, and the best product of its bakeries is the heavy, rye-based *chyorny khleb*.
- **Georgian Cuisine.** Moscow's favourite ethnic food – it is flavourful, spicy and vegetarian-friendly. Plus it is usually accompanied by a fine bottle of Georgian wine.
- **Vodka.** Russia's national drink is as various as the wines of France. Any barman will recommend their favourite. Don't forget to have plenty of *zakuski* (salads and pickles) with which to follow the shots.

GILDED CATHEDRALS

One could never see all of Moscow's churches and cathedrals, but here are a few not to be missed.

● **Cathedral of Christ the Saviour.** Russia's largest cathedral, its history is complicated: built to commemorate the defeat of Napoleon in 1812, destroyed to make room for the Palace of the Soviets under Stalin, and then rebuilt by the mayor-builder Luzhkov just in time for the new millennium to stand as a symbol of the resurgent city *(see page 120).*

● **Dormition Cathedral, Kremlin.** Once the cathedral used for the coronation of the tsars, this is still the Kremlin's finest house of worship *(see page 85).*

● **St Basil's.** No one will believe you've been to Moscow without a picture with this church as the backdrop. Famous and fabulous on the outside, skip the tour inside if you're short of time *(see page 96).*

● **Church of the Intercession at Fili.** A fantastic example of Russian baroque, which somehow remained intact through the Soviet attack on religion. Even the

gilded tsar's box and large iconostasis are still preserved *(see page 142).*

● **Church of St Nikolay the Wonderworker in Khamovniki.** Built by a community of weavers, this Christmas-cake-coloured cathedral is one of the finest neighbourhood churches in the city *(see page 125).*

● **Novodevichy Convent and Cemetery.** The peace and tranquillity of this fortress monastery is a must see for photographers. It once housed unwanted brides of state, but is now the final resting place of some of Russia's most famous people, including Khrushchev, Chekhov and the circus star Nikulin *(see page 126).*

A WEALTH OF MUSEUMS

● **Armoury Palace Museum and Diamond Fund.** During the height of imperial Russia, the wealth of the state compared with any country in the world. The elaborate fittings of state, from silk ball gowns to enormous jewels and Fabergé eggs, are preserved in the Kremlin's two finest museums *(see pages 88–9).*

● **Tretyakov Gallery.** The home of Russian art, the Tretyakov traces its development from the beginning with a fine collection of icons, including rare works by Rublyov *(see page 176).*

● **Gorky Museum.** You don't have to be a fan of Maxim Gorky's work to enjoy this museum. It's one of Moscow's finest examples of *style moderne* archi-

tecture – and accessible to the public *(see page 133).*

● **Pushkin Museum of Fine Arts.** The Pushkin's collection of Impressionist art is second only to the Louvre's, and it boasts a fine antiquities collection *(see page 116).*

● **New Tretyakov Gallery.** The finest collection of Russian artworks from the early 20th century *(see page 185).*

● **Museum of Private Collections.** Moscow's first international standard museum, the collection highlights non-conformist works saved from destruction during the days of Socialist Realism *(see page 119).*

● **State Historical Museum.** Documenting the history of the Russian Empire from early Russians to the tsars *(see page 93).*

LEFT: Pavel Tretyakov stands guard outside the gallery he founded. **ABOVE:** surrounded by fortress monasteries and crowded with old churches, in Moscow colourful onion domes seem to sprout from almost every street corner.

THE CONSPICUOUS NEW RUSSIANS

- **Tretyakov Passage.** Exactly what New Russians want in a shopping centre – ample room to park your armour-plated SUV, ostentatious pop music to make sure people are looking, and plenty of places to whimsically spend six-digit sums *(see page 100)*.
- **Rublyovo-Uspenskoye.** This has become some of the hottest real estate in town, as New Russians quickly take over the old Soviet dachas in the area, replacing them with their "cottage" communities – "cottage" being the Russian word for a four-storey stone house with turrets and towers, a six-car garage, swimming pool and tennis courts. Of course there are also nearby upscale shopping malls, chic

restaurants and health clubs *(see page 208)*.
- **Casinos.** Of course, with New Russians so eager to impress others with their money, casinos are very popular. Covers of US$200 are common, and New Arbat has become the city's answer to Las Vegas *(see page 137)*.

REMNANTS OF SOVIET RUSSIA

- **Lenin's Mausoleum.** Where else are you able to enjoy a private audience with a major world leader and be allowed to do all the talking? Don't miss this opportunity *(see page 95)*.
- **Memorial Museum of Cosmonautics and the VVTs.** You can relive the days of the Soviet space race at the Cosmonautics museum and see the first two astronauts to return from space: Belka and Strelka, two intrepid canine explorers. The VVTs contains some of the best surviving Socialist statuary in the city *(see page 165)*.
- **Mayakovsky Museum.** This whirlwind of a museum recreates the heady optimism of the Soviet Union's early days, which are so often overlooked *(see page 162)*.
- **Muzeon Sculpture Gardens.** Following the Berlin Wall like a stack of dominoes, statues that once glorified the Soviet regime were pulled down by angry Muscovites. Rather than be destroyed, they are now on display here alongside works commemorating those who died in famines, purges or Gulags *(see page 188)*.

ABOVE: shopping for admirers on Old Arbat. **RIGHT:** holding onto the past with both hands.
BELOW: you don't have to sell the family silver to enjoy a trip to Moscow.

MOSCOW ON THE CHEAP

Dine Carefully. It is possible to enjoy a high quality of life on a backpacker's budget in Moscow. Look for good Georgian cafés serving freshly grilled *shashlyk*, and you can get a decent meal for 5 dollars or less. On the other hand, go to a lavishly decorated New Russian-style restaurant and you can spend 50 dollars or more on essentially similar food. Sushi bars are all the rage, but can be good value.

Drink Cautiously. Nothing is cheaper than vodka in Moscow, but that only goes for bad vodka bought from a kiosk. Almost all restaurants serve beer and wine, and often at a very reasonable price that is less than half of what you would expect to pay at home. Venture into a hotel lounge bar or sophisticated nightclub and even the smallest glass of wine can set you back nearly 10 dollars, and this is after paying a large cover just to enter.

Haggle. Moscow's official economy is just like that of anywhere else – what you see is what you get, and at the price marked on the label; but when Muscovites spot tourists outside the official economy (taxi cabs, souvenir shopping and even some hotel rates), the quoted price is often double what the vendor actually expects to be paid. Even a novice haggler should be able to save at least 20 percent.

A CAPITAL REBORN

While it still retains its legendary enigmatic aura, Moscow has re-wrapped itself in the familiar cloak of a grand European capital

For generations in the West, Moscow has conjured up images of red stars and black limousines, grey apartment blocks and dowdy citizens, tanks on parade and tanks on the attack, and lately – disorder and confusion. Leave all those old stereotypes at the border. Moscow today is a vibrant European capital, lit by neon and filled with cafés, clubs and casinos. Once again graced by golden cupolas and pastel-coloured manor houses, its streets are crowded by beautiful young people in the latest fashions.

It is a city with something for everyone. For art lovers, it has some of the world's finest collections of painting and sculpture, from European masterpieces to Russian avant-garde and monumental Socialist Realism – not to mention cutting-edge contemporary art. For music lovers, there are magnificent 19th-century halls where the world's most celebrated musicians perform (at budget prices), along with sublime Orthodox church choirs. For lovers of the performing arts, local dance and theatre still define these arts throughout the world. For lovers of architecture, glorious cathedrals, palaces and emporia illustrate many styles, from the vaulted halls of medieval Muscovy through Classicism, *Style moderne* and Constructivism.

Museums let visitors relive European history on battlefields, in palaces and in the homes of artists. Gourmets can look forward to fabulous cuisine from virtually all the nations of the world, accompanied by hearty local beers and flavoured vodkas. And for those who wish to step out of the hustle and bustle, there are quiet crooked streets shaded by ancient trees, where you can catch glimpses of fur-clad women slipping into courtyards, catch the scent of incense drifting from a brightly coloured parish church, or hear the doleful sound of a cow bell ringing on the breeze from a kitchen garden.

Moscow is reinventing itself, as it has done so many times before, after fire, invasion, and shifts in power. It's not easy, or smooth. There is a gaudy jumble of epochs and styles, a sometimes-uneasy mix of rich and poor.

But that is the way Moscow has always been: flashy and dowdy, ancient and modern, Eastern and Western, elegant and kitsch, spiritual and vulgar, with twisting lanes and broad avenues, one street a cacophony of sound, the next so silent you can still hear the nightingales sing. ❑

PRECEDING PAGES: living it up on Tretyakov Passage; remembering the past on Red Square.
LEFT: snow covers the tranquil Novodevichy Convent.

CITY OF TUMULT

Built and rebuilt in the image of ruling prince, tsar, general secretary and mayor, Moscow has grown from a small wooden settlement on a bluff between two rivers to a metropolis that rules the world's largest nation. Its past has been a glorious struggle between state and religion that has kept it in the spotlight on the world stage

Come to me, brother, in Moscow… These words – written by Prince Yuri Dolgoruky of Suzdal to his ally Prince Svyatoslav in 1147 – are the first known mention of the city that has charmed, terrified, awed and captivated the world for nearly 900 years. Archaeologists believe this fertile area of woods, bogs and rivers has been inhabited for much longer, perhaps as far back as the 5th century BC. Hence, the Prince didn't see the need to send any directions along with his invitation.

At the time that the princes met to consolidate a base in the city, Moscow was only a small trading settlement in the vast Kievan Rus Empire, albeit a strategically placed one. This empire began in the 9th century, when a Viking (Varangian) leader named Rurik had consolidated what is now the western part of Russia with a capital in the southern city of Kiev. In 988 Prince Vladimir of Kiev accepted Christianity and baptised his subjects.

At its peak, Kievan Rus stretched from north of Lake Ladoga on the borders of Finland to the Caucasus on the Black Sea. When the Kievan ruler Yaroslav the Wise died in 1054, the kingdom was divided among his sons, and only briefly united under Vladimir Monomakh from 1113 to 1125 before it dissolved once more into internecine conflicts.

LEFT: an 18th-century view of the Kremlin from across the Moscow River.
RIGHT: the 12th-century illustrated manuscript in which Moscow was mentioned for the first time.

Suzdal, Vladimir, Novgorod, Chernigov, Tver, Rostov and other cities all became separate principalities, sometimes working together, sometimes vying for power.

The Tatar-Mongol Yoke

In 1156 Prince Yuri Dolgoruky, considered the founder of Moscow, built the first wooden walls around the Kremlin to enclose and protect the small settlement. But walls would not protect Moscow. In 1224 a Russian chronicler wrote: "For our sins, unknown tribes came. No one knows who they are, nor whence they came, nor what their faith is, but they call them Tatars." These Mongolian horsemen from the East appeared like a bolt from the blue, pillaged and plundered, and then reigned over Russia for nearly 250 years. At the height of their conquest, their territory stretched from Poland to the Pacific Ocean and from the Arctic Ocean to the Persian Gulf. This period, called the Tatar-Mongol Yoke, began when Batu Khan attacked Moscow in 1237; from then until the 15th century the khans appointed the Moscow grand princes, who were expected to pay tributes to them, by taking the Bolshaya Ordynka road from Moscow to the Golden Horde, the Tatar khanate set up by the Volga River and named after their glittering tents.

Russians still argue about the impact of the Tatar-Mongol Yoke on Russia. Some maintain it kept Russia fettered to Eastern traditions, away from the main trends of development in Western Europe. Others point out that the Tatars were relatively benign conquerors; the Church was left untouched (and paid no taxes), and judging by the Russian language, the Slavic people picked up some skills from their Eastern overlords: the Russian words for customs, treasury, some monetary units and many other administrative concepts come from the Tatar language.

In 1328 Ivan Kalita (called "Moneybags" for his practice of skimming the other princes'

tributes paid to the Tatars) was designated Grand Prince by the Khan. In 1340 he built sturdier oak walls around the Kremlin and reinforced them with stucco. Dmitry Donskoy started to build white stone walls in 1366, expanding the Kremlin territory. In 1380 he defeated the Tatar Khan Mamai in Kulikovo Field on the Don, giving him the name Dmitry of the Don. The Tatars took revenge in 1382, burning the city to the ground once again, and launching damaging raids in 1451, 1455 and 1461 during the reign of Tsar Vasily II.

The "Third Rome"

During the early centuries of the Moscow principality, the Church maintained contacts with religious leaders and councils in the West. Moves to return the Orthodox Church to Roman Catholicism were violently rejected by Vasily II, and when Constantinople, spiritual home of the Orthodox Church, fell to the Turks in 1453, Moscow claimed the mantle of the "true Church". A chronicler wrote: "Two Romes have fallen, but the third stands. And a fourth there shall not be."

Moscow was also loosening the grip of the Golden Horde (followers of Islam since the 14th century) by gathering the small principalities around it under its rule and assuming its mission as the leader of the Christian world. The idea of Moscow as the "Third Rome" has held the imaginations of rulers and thinkers in Russia ever since, and has recently been felt more strongly in Russian politics.

Ivan III (Ivan the Great, r. 1462–1505) is credited, along with his successor, Vasily III (r. 1505–33), with "the gathering of the Rus", the folding of the many Russian principalities under the rule of the Moscow Grand Prince – sometimes voluntarily, sometimes through violent struggle.

When Ivan III married Sophia Paleologue, niece of the last Byzantine emperor, Constantine XI, he cemented the tie that bound Moscow, the Third Rome, to the previous centres of the Orthodox Church. In 1480 Ivan III renounced allegiance to the Khan, and in 1493 had himself crowned as the Sovereign of All Russia, adding the double-headed eagle of Byzantium to the image of St George as the ruling symbol. The prince among princes, the Grand Prince, was now an autocrat, served by noblemen called boyars. As Moscow grew in importance, so did the Kremlin: Ivan III invited Italian builders to help construct enormous churches in Cathedral Square, expanded the territory of the Kremlin, surrounded it with high brick walls, and moved the traders out of the fortress to what is now Red Square. From 1508 to 1516 workers cut a moat 36 metres (120 ft) wide and 12 metres (40 ft) deep along the Kremlin walls on Red Square.

The first tsar

The city continued to grow and be fortified under Ivan IV, who has gone down in history as Ivan the Terrible (the Russian name really

unfettered autocratic power. He also successfully conquered the Tatar city of Kazan in 1552 and, four years later, the Golden Horde in Astrakhan, which he celebrated by commissioning the Cathedral of the Intercession by the Moat (St Basil's Cathedral) on Red Square.

In 1584 Ivan the Terrible died suddenly while preparing for a game of chess. The throne went to his eldest surviving son, Fyodor, a religious but simple-minded man. The city of Moscow had grown, and during Fyodor's reign Kitai-gorod and Bely Gorod, the White City named after the stone it was built with, were enclosed with walls, forming a

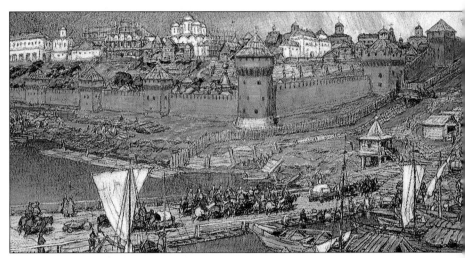

has the sense of awe-inspiring). He assumed the throne as a small child in 1533 and had himself crowned "Tsar (the Russian for the Roman *caesar*) of All Russia" in 1547. The first part of his reign was relatively progressive and productive: Tsar Ivan oversaw the building of the Kitai-gorod walls, established local governments, codified military service, formed the first *streltsy* (musketeer) regiments, and formed a council of boyars that offered some rudimentary checks on

LEFT: a 16th-century miniature depicting combat between Russians and Tatars in 1238.
ABOVE: the Kremlin as it looked in 1584.

THE FIRST SECRET POLICE

After his beloved first wife Anastasia Romanova died, Ivan IV came unhinged. Suspecting his boyars of poisoning her, he left the city in 1564 and announced that he would step down from the throne. Fearful of being leaderless, the people of Moscow begged him to return. He did, but on the condition that he be allowed to form a special force to protect him – the *oprichniki*: a force of 6,000, dressed in black and riding black steeds, who carried out a reign of terror on boyars, citizens and towns – anyone the insane tsar accused of treachery. Later, in a fit of anger, he struck and killed his eldest son; this event is immortalised in a famous painting by Repin *(see page 179)*.

large arc stretching beyond the Kremlin, beginning and ending at the Moscow River and following what is now the Boulevard Ring. The walls were dotted with 27 towers, of which 10 were entrances, many elaborately decorated in tiers. Fyodor's main adviser was the boyar Boris Godunov, who mended the rifts caused by Ivan the Terrible, and during his reign. The Church in Moscow became independent, with its own Patriarch in 1589.

The "Time of Troubles"

When Fyodor died in 1598, there were no heirs – his brother Dmitry had been killed in the city of Uglich with his throat slit – so the to be Dmitry invaded Russia with an army from Poland. Gudunov died suddenly, and the false Dmitry was greeted as the true heir to the throne. The Poles took over the Kremlin, and another reign of terror began, ending with the false Dmitry being denounced, killed, burned and fired out of the Tsar Cannon in the direction of Poland. For another eight years the country went through a number of leaders (including another false Dmitry); armed bandits roamed the countryside; and the Poles launched waves of incursions. It wasn't until the volunteer army led by Minin and Pozharsky drove the Polish invaders from the Kremlin that peace returned.

council of boyars elected Boris Godunov, whose family was Tatar in origin. Before accepting the crown, he went to visit his sister, the tsar's widow, in Novodevichy Convent to ask her blessing, and when the people of Moscow turned up at the convent to beseech him, he accepted. But his reign was marred by crop failures and famines that took more than 100,000 lives in Moscow alone. Rumours swept the populace: Boris Godunov was responsible for Dmitry's death; the crop failures and famines were a sign of God's disfavour.

The Poles decided to profit by the instability in Moscow. In 1604 a young man claiming

This period of chaos and lawlessness is called the "Time of Troubles", and has remained a haunting memory for Russians. It is still invoked today to support a strong, even autocratic leader: for their history shows that a strong hand is better than no hand at all.

The first Romanovs

In 1613 a gathering of boyars, clergy and ranking service gentry met to decide on a new leader. They finally agreed on a young boyar named Mikhail Romanov, the first in the dynasty that would not end until 1917 with the abdication of Tsar Nicholas II. Moscow in the

17th century enjoyed a period of relative calm. Around the Earthen City wooden walls were built along what is now Sadovoye Koltso (the Garden Ring Road), enclosing the small settlements of merchants and craftsmen that had grown outside the White City walls.

The city impressed foreign visitors as prosperous and grand, filled with churches, taverns and markets, its bearded and pious citizens clothed in long kaftans trimmed in fur. Markets were filled with the chatter of dozens of foreign languages. Noblewomen, however, did not appear on the streets; they were secluded in *terems* and left their houses only to attend church services and visit their families. Moscow was decidedly part of the East.

And then came the Romanov who would be called Peter the Great. When Tsar Fyodor III died in 1682, the council of boyars decided to bypass his feeble-minded son, Ivan V, and name his bright and active half-brother, Peter, as tsar. The conservative *streltsy* regiments rebelled, attacked the Kremlin and killed much of Peter's family. Peter's older sister Sophia whisked him off to the monastery at Sergeev Posad (*see page 200*), and eventually became regent of the two boy co-tsars. When Sophia seemed ready to grasp the throne for herself in 1689, she was incarcerated in the Novodevichy Convent.

Peter largely grew up on the outskirts of the capital, learning boat-building and trades, and playing war games with his "toy regiments". Curious and energetic, he set off to Europe incognito to study the crafts, arts, sciences and state institutions of his European neighbours, studying shipbuilding in London and Amsterdam. He rushed back to Russia in 1698 when it appeared Sophia had arranged yet another *streltsy* rebellion, executing thousands of officers (some in view of Sophia's convent windows). Peter took control of Russia; he crowned himself emperor and began a series of reforms that would infuriate the Church (demanding that men cut off their beards, the Orthodox sign of piety), terrify the population (demanding that the kaftan be replaced by Western dress)

and change Moscow for ever. In 1703 he expanded Russia to the north, building a port in the boggy land straddling the Neva River. In 1712, he moved the court to this port – now St Petersburg – and declared it the capital of the Russian Empire.

Moscow as second city

Moscow was no longer the centre of the Russian Empire. Tsars and tsarinas regularly came to Moscow for coronations, weddings and state visits, and built residences in the Kremlin and pleasure palaces outside the city. Some minor nobility remained, some retired to Moscow manors. But Moscow,

with its winding streets and medieval walls and towers, was relegated to the Byzantine and Tatar past that Peter and his heirs wished to forget and overcome. For most of the next two centuries, the court, government, high culture and the arts would flourish in the Western-style city on the Neva. Moscow flourished, too, but as the centre of the Orthodox Church and the capital of commerce. By the 1780s, the decrepit White City walls had been torn down and an elegant, tree-lined boulevard built in its place. Moscow may have been "a big village", as the residents of St Petersburg called it, but it was not without grace and charm.

LEFT: Poles occupy the city in the "Time of Troubles".
RIGHT: Peter the Great, with St Petersburg – his new capital – in the background.

But another catastrophic invasion ruined the city once more – this time from the West. In 1812 Napoleon attacked Russia with the largest army the world had ever seen, and after the indecisive battle of nearby Borodino *(see below)* moved into the capital. Governor General Rostopchin had ordered the city to be abandoned and set ablaze, destroying nearly three-quarters more – this time from the West. The French plundered the Kremlin's churches and palaces before they had to admit defeat.

Moscow underwent an extraordinary renovation over the next decade. The wooden walls that protected the Earthen City were torn down to make what is now the Garden Ring Road. The moat that separated Red Square from the Kremlin was filled in and the Neglinnaya River put underground, so that the Aleksandrovsky Gardens could be laid on the western wall of the Kremlin. Stone houses and churches replaced wooden structures.

By the end of the 19th century Moscow shone once again. The merchant kings of this commercial capital funded the arts, theatre, music and dance. They built schools, hospitals, orphanages, train stations, clubs and churches. There was an explosion in the arts, as the poets of the Silver Age (so called because they followed the Golden Age of the

THE BATTLEFIELD OF BORODINO

On 7 September 1812, Napoleon's armies and the Russian armies under General Kutuzov met on the battlefield near the village of Borodino 120 km (75 miles) west of Moscow. It turned out to be one of the bloodiest battles of that war: the Russians lost 42,000 of their 112,000 men; the French lost 58,000 out of 130,000.

The next day Kutuzov retreated, allowing the French into Moscow, but Muscovites had torched and abandoned the capital, leaving the French to freeze in the harsh Russian winter with few provisions. Again, in 1941, a battle raged here for six days, as Russians held off the German armies' assault on the capital.

The battlefield of Borodino covers 1,000 sq. km (400 sq. miles) and includes fortifications of both 1812 and 1941 and an excellent museum (*Gosudarstvenny Borodinsky voenno-istorichesky muzey-zapovednik*; village of Borodino; tel from Moscow: (8) 238-51-546; admission charges; suburban train from Belorussian station to Borodino Station and then by bus to "Borodino" or "Poreche" to the museum stop; Patriarshy Dom, *see page 227*, also arranges tours to view the mock battle). On the first Sunday in September, thousands of military-history enthusiasts don home-made, historically accurate French and Russian uniforms and enact the battle once more.

realist prose writers in the mid-19th century) and the innovations of the Moscow Art Theatre thrilled the public.

Russia also exploded geographically over the 19th century, its borders extending from Afghanistan to China and the Pacific Ocean. The port city of Vladivostok opened up trade in Asia, and the Trans-Siberian Railway, completed in just 14 years in 1905, linked Europe with the Far East. Russia's industrial development was rapid; by the turn of the century it was one of the fastest-growing economies in Europe.

But there were explosions of a different kind. The reforms of Alexander II, called the

The last tsar

Nicholas II, by all accounts a kind man but an utterly ineffectual ruler, inherited the throne at a critical time in the country's history. Had he possessed greater vision, or been more resolute, or made more concessions to the demands of the population, the course of Russian history might have been less brutal. He barely survived the uprisings of 1905, but with a few further political concessions, including the establishment of a parliament, the Duma, maintained the monarchy for a few more years.

The celebration of 300 years of the Romanov dynasty in 1913 was the last hurrah

Tsar Liberator for emancipating serfs in 1861, did not go far enough. Absolute power remained in the hands of the tsar and his advisors; vast wealth and property were possessed and flaunted by a small aristocracy, while the poor barely managed to eke out a living in the countryside and cities. Writers and painters protested in their art; young revolutionaries protested with bombs, assassinations and uprisings. Alexander II was killed by a terrorist; his son Alexander III died unexpectedly in 1894.

LEFT: the battle of Borodino, 1812.
ABOVE: coronation of Nicholas II in Moscow, 1897.

of the Russian throne. When Russia entered World War I in 1914, its overtaxed citizens were pressed further. Hungry and demoralised soldiers and sailors responded to new cries for change and revolution. In February 1917 the tsar abdicated the throne and a temporary government attempted to take charge. But it was too late. In October 1917 Vladimir Lenin, leader of the Bolsheviks, led a coup in St Petersburg. Most of the aristocracy that had not already fled the country now struggled to escape. Civil war rent the country, abetted by foreign powers helping the "Whites" overcome the "Reds", lest revolution burst over the borders. Fearing that the tsar and his family, held as prisoners in the Urals city of Yekaterinburg, would rally the opposition, Lenin ordered them killed. The Russian Empire was no more.

The capital of the USSR

In 1918 Lenin moved the new Bolshevik government to Moscow, although the city was only officially proclaimed the capital of the Soviet Union after the Civil War ended in 1922. Moscow's palaces and manor houses were expropriated and turned into communal apartments; dozens of families lived in partitioned rooms, sharing kitchens and bathrooms. Emptied of their sacred vessels and

verged on insanity. At least as paranoid as Ivan the Terrible, he consolidated his power through purges and repressions, imprisoning or executing purported "enemies of the people", clearing villages of rich peasants and forcibly collectivising the rest. An estimated 8 million people were executed, sent to labour camps, or died in prison; at the height of the Great Terror in 1937, at least 650,000 people were killed. Industrialisation, fuelled by convict labour, proceeded apace; the price was enormous, but the country began to recover from the devastation of revolution.

Moscow changed dramatically under Stalin. With the first General Plan for Reconstruction

icons, churches were turned into warehouses, dormitories, offices and studios. War Communism – draconian methods to expropriate food from the peasants and keep the labour force at work – was nudging the beleaguered population towards rebellion once again; the Soviet authorities responded with the New Economic Policy. NEP permitted limited free markets of food and consumer goods, which brought the country and city back from the edge of starvation and desperation.

Lenin died in 1924. After an internal power struggle, he was succeeded by Joseph Stalin, a former seminary student who embraced the Revolution and power with a fervour that

approved in 1935, the Sovietisation of the city began in earnest. The city's meandering lanes were cleared of houses, broad avenues laid, the famous markets of Sukharevka and Khitrovka closed and emptied, main streets widened and new highways built leading out of the city. What are now called "Stalinist classical" apartment houses went up in the centre of the city for the Party faithful, the buildings trembling as the first metro line rumbled under the streets. Tenements and shanties fell, but so did churches, taverns, shops and palaces. Moscow was to become the Model Soviet City, designed more for parades of armaments and workers than for the comfort of its citizens.

The Great Patriotic War

Work halted abruptly on 22 June 1941 when Hitler launched an attack on the Soviet Union. Stalin was unprepared, having ignored the warnings of spies and diplomats, and insisting that the Non-Aggression Pact signed with Hitler in 1939 would hold. He ordered his commanders to "ignore the provocations" from the German army and not return fire. By the time the order came to defend themselves, the majority of the armed forces' aircraft had been destroyed by Nazi bombs and entire divisions encircled. Many of Moscow's citizens and most of its artistic treasures were evacuated from the city. Although the city suffered from bombing raids, the advance of the Germans was halted at the outskirts of the city, not far from the main international airport today, in November 1941, and the city survived with only moderate damage. The country, however, was devastated: an estimated 20 million people died during what Russians call the Great Patriotic War.

Large-scale reconstruction resumed only in the early 1950s when the great "Stalinist skyscrapers" went up over the city, heralding, Muscovites hoped, a new era of prosperity and peace. Khrushchev, who came to power after Stalin's death in 1953, loosened some of the controls on the arts, denounced the atrocities of Stalin, and promised Moscow's citizens that he would finally solve the "housing problem" that dogged the city. New neighbourhoods were built of five-storey, yellow-brick apartment buildings: the apartments were small, but they were one-family dwellings, set in communities with stores and services. These buildings – called *khrushchevki* after their initiator – still dot the city. They have aged badly and are to be torn down, but they once represented a modicum of comfort to millions of Muscovites who had lived in communal apartments or worker's barracks.

Under Khrushchev and his successor, Leonid Brezhnev, the city centre was little changed; most of the building went on at the edges of the city. Apartment buildings sprang up around Moscow that were taller, usually made of white-cement panels and sometimes decorated with mosaics or coloured stone. They were more spacious and comfortable than the *khrushchevki*, but monotonous in their similarity.

Sprawling estates

Moscow at the end of the Brezhnev era was a huge, sprawling city surrounded by housing estates. There were no slums, but neither were there ethnic neighbourhoods, business districts or private dwellings. There were few restaurants and clubs, and cultural life was staid, but entertainment was affordable and the

streets were safe. The city and country had settled into a relatively predictable, stable monotony. There were no repressions or purges, but dissent in the arts or government was punished by imprisonment or exile. There were no large-scale wars, but the Cold War seemed destined to last indefinitely. After the triumphs of the Soviet weapons and space programmes in the 1940s–60s, there were no technological breakthroughs, but industry and agriculture produced the bare minimum to feed, clothe and house the population. Soviet power seemed unbreakable, the Soviet republics joined for ever. There was nothing that hinted of the changes to come. ❑

LEFT: Lenin in Red Square on 16 October 1917.
RIGHT: Soviet stars replace tsarist eagles on the spires of the Kremlin in Red Square, 1935.

REVOLUTIONARY TO ROMANTIC: THE ART OF PROPAGANDA

The Revolution affected more than just politics, it nurtured some of the 20th century's greatest avant-garde artists – until their work was thought less than ideal for the Party line

The 1917 Revolution not only overthrew the social and political system in Russia – it revolutionised the arts. Avant-garde artists such as Kazimir Malevich, Alexander Rodchenko and Vasily Kandinsky, who were all sympathetic to the cause, suddenly found themselves in favour, heading art schools and studios.

Throughout the 1920s they splintered into a bewildering assortment of unions and associations, such as *Komfut* (Communist Futurism), *Proletkult* (Proletarian Culture) and *Lef* (Left Front of the Arts). Often mutually antagonistic, they joined forces with the new Soviet government to proclaim, "Long live the art of the Proletarian Revolution!" and "Only Futurist art is the art of the proletariat now!"

These artists created cinema advertisements and public service posters, decorated agit-prop (agitation and propaganda) trains that brought the message of Soviet power to the masses, designed workers' clubs, books, china, workers' clothes and public monuments. For the Russian Telegraph Agency (ROSTA) the poet Vladimir Mayakovsky teamed up with artists Mikhail Cheremnysh and Ivan Malyutin to make witty cartoon posters on subjects ranging from personal hygiene to the evils of capitalism. The "bourgeois" art of the upper class disappeared, and Moscow was filled with a new art for the new age: angular, expressive, jarring and in enthusiastic service to the new regime.

ABOVE: a vintage poster by photographer Alexander Rodchenko (1925) shouts the need to read. Many avant-garde artists embraced the new society, and work by Rodchenko and Mayakovsky *(right)* was to define international poster and book design until the 1980s.

ABOVE: poster campaigns during World War II played upon the emotions of patriotism and fear to motivate the citizens. Left is their version of "Uncle Sam Wants You", while on the right women are told that "Fascism is the worst enemy of women" – calling on women to join the battle against the invaders.
LEFT: "Keep Quiet!" Other poster campaigns during the war reminded people not to give away state secrets carelessly.

THE ROMANCE OF SOCIALIST REALISM

Radical innovation in the arts came to an end in 1934 when Andrey Zhdanov, secretary of the Communist Party of the USSR, made a speech to the First All-Union Congress of Soviet Writers that defined what art would be acceptable to the political leaders. Called "Socialist Realism", it consisted of *ideynost* (ideology), *partiynost* (Party loyalty) and *narodnost* (national character, or rather the positive portrayal of the masses). This was first applied to literature and then to all the arts.

It called for a romanticised depiction of Soviet reality: kindly but authoritative leaders, healthy and prosperous workers, and peasants joyfully engaged in the great work of building the new Soviet state. Abstraction and critical realism were out. The image of a young woman at the wheel of a convertible tooling down a sun-dappled Moscow street was in.

Socialist Realism remained state policy until the 1980s, although its strictures were loosened in the post-war years. Some artists, temperamentally attracted to realism, created masterpieces; others tossed off paintings of milkmaids and metalworkers for their Union of Artists contracts while privately experimenting with other genres. Today, there is a modest revival and appreciation for classics of Socialist Realism. It may be unsophisticated sentimentalism or slavish propaganda, but at least you can tell the girl from the goat.

RIGHT: Original propaganda posters, such as this one printed in 1920 by Vladimir Mayakovsky, are very rare these days. Many early works were produced during a frenzy of artistic activity that took place against a background of political intrigue, World War I, the Revolution and finally the Civil War. But disillusionment set in, and while some artists chose exile, those who remained were brought down by Socialist Realism.

BELOW: this painting (1935) depicts an ever-smiling Stalin inspecting works at a hydroelectric plant in Ryon. Any Socialist Realist artist worth his salt knew that works should celebrate Party leaders, show the new heroes of proletarian society and illustrate enormous agricultural or industrial projects. This style was mocked and parodied as the Soviet Union disintegrated, but is gaining a real, if kitsch, value among collectors.

TOP RIGHT: *The Soviet Republics* (1930) by Karpov celebrates the country's agricultural achievements in an impassioned work.

RIGHT: this famous painting by Pimenov, *New Moscow* (1935), may seem a straightforward landscape, but it takes a more subtle approach to Socialist Realism by displaying an idealised world that the workers of the world should unite to create. Such pieces do show great skills – of both painting and optimism.

THE NEW LAND OF THE FREE

The breakup of the USSR was one of the defining events of the 20th century. Moscow, centre of power of the vast Soviet Empire, was at the eye of the storm that followed. For many citizens, optimism was soon superseded by bankruptcy and deprivation. Yet somehow they survived

By the 1980s the USSR was in a period of stagnation: economic development, funded by high world prices on oil and gas and carried out on a wave of post-war enthusiasm, had slowed catastrophically. While the country was able to maintain most basic services – free education and medical care, pensions, transport and basic consumer goods – outside the major cities ration cards were issued for such necessities as meat, sugar, tea and coffee. Suburban trains leaving Moscow stations were called "sausage expresses", filled with people hauling meat and staples they could no longer find even 100 miles from the metropolis.

Leonid Brezhnev died in 1982 and was quickly succeeded by two ancient and ailing Party officials, Yuri Andropov (1982–4) and Konstantin Chernenko (1984–5). And then Mikhail Gorbachev, at age 54 the youngest General Secretary of the Communist Party since Stalin, was chosen to lead the country.

The lid pops off the boiling pot

Gorbachev immediately showed himself to be a different kind of Soviet leader. Determined to reform the ailing economy and moribund political system, he announced a policy of *glasnost* (public disclosure of economic and social issues), *perestroika* (restructuring of the economic and political system) and acceleration of social and economic advancement. He

LEFT: many older Russians believe Putin's strong hand in domestic affairs is better than no hand at all.
RIGHT: crowds regularly took to the streets during the chaotic 1990s.

tried both to put an end to behaviour that inhibited economic growth (crackdowns on alcoholism and income from moonlighting) and to encourage a spirit of economic and political innovation, allowing co-operatives (small private enterprises) and joint ventures with foreign companies. In 1988 he supported an amendment to the Constitution that allowed real competition for seats in the Congress of People's Deputies, the first time that more than one candidate had stood in an election since 1917. What had once been a rubber-stamp parliament became a real parliament, which elected Gorbachev to the newly created post of President of the Soviet Union in 1989.

But the process he unleashed proved impossible to control. Ethnic and economic tensions in Kazakhstan, Armenia, Georgia, Moldova and elsewhere erupted into uprisings and wars. The Baltic states of Latvia, Lithuania and Estonia demanded secession from the Union. Freedom to travel and access to foreign news and culture showed Soviet citizens how far their living standards lagged behind the developed world, and they took to the streets in demonstrations of hundreds of thousands, banging pots and demanding food and consumer goods in the stores. Spurred by the changes in the USSR and their own democratic movements, the citizens of Eastern and Central European countries

Russian Federation. Their competition, fuelled by personal animosity, competing visions of the country's development, a worsening economic situation, strikes and continuing wars in the republics, jerked the country between greater freedom and crackdowns. And the media, which had thrown off the strictures of censorship, showed everything – strikes, Congressional debates, corruption, poverty – all day, every day, to a fascinated nation.

In August 1991 a group of hardliners within the Communist Party staged a coup while Gorbachev was on holiday in the south. Boris Yeltsin and his government were not arrested and became the de facto leaders of the three-

rebelled at elections and on the streets. In November 1989 the Berlin Wall, the symbol of the Cold War, fell. By March 1991 the Warsaw Pact was dissolved. In this heady atmosphere of change, the republics of the Soviet Union declared various forms of "sovereignty" within the Union. In Russia, still a constituent part of the USSR, a new Congress of People's Deputies first elected Boris Yeltsin its Chairman in 1990 and then created the post of President, which Yeltsin won by a landslide in 1991.

This was a critical year. There was an untenable situation in the country: two centres of power, held by Gorbachev as President of the USSR and Yeltsin as President of the

day resistance, eventually drawing the military to their side. The coup leaders capitulated on 21 August (one of them, the head of the KGB, shot his wife and then himself to avoid arrest), and Gorbachev returned to Moscow. But he returned to a different country. The Baltic states seceded from the Union, followed by virtually every other Soviet republic.

While daily life did not immediately change (in fact, even the coup went unmarked in all but the largest cities), the USSR ceased its existence. In early December the leaders of Ukraine, Belarus and Russia – the three republics that had founded the Soviet Union – signed an agreement that established the

The Cost of Change

In 1991 a one-room apartment cost 5,000 roubles; by 1993 a cup of strawberries cost 60,000 roubles.

Commonwealth of Independent States. It was then signed by the rest of the former republics (except the Baltic states and Georgia) on 21 December. On 25 December, Mikhail Gorbachev resigned as President of the Soviet Union. That evening, with little ceremony, the red Soviet flag was lowered over the Kremlin and the Russian tricolour was raised.

Towards a second coup

Boris Yeltsin inherited a country that was bankrupt, economically backward and corrupt, with a population of 145 million exhausted by six years of turmoil and deprivation. His "shock therapy" to release fixed prices and jump-start the economy did put food and goods back in the shops, but at prices that were hundreds of times higher. Families lost their entire savings; factories closed or laid off workers; collective farms folded. Another state crisis was brewing, caused by internal dissent within the government – reflecting both differing visions of the future and thirst for power – and facilitated by a state system that had been cobbled together in haste without clear lines of authority within the branches of government. The Russian Congress of People's Deputies took a turn to the right and attempted to wrest power from the presidency.

In a move still debated, in September 1993 Yeltsin defied the Constitution and disbanded Congress. The deputies retaliated by declaring Alexander Rutskoy, then Vice-President, acting head of state. At the beginning of October, the Congress was well armed and barricaded in the White House. The leaders launched attacks on the Moscow Mayor's Office, the Ostankino TV Centre and a number of strategic sites throughout the city. The army and militia, also divided in its loyalties, did not immediately respond. Finally the army entered the city and tanks fired on the White House as the world watched. After two days of fighting, more than 140 were dead and nearly 1,000 wounded. The

leaders of the second Russian coup surrendered. A new Constitution was quickly passed that focused power in the hands of the President. The White House was renovated by Turkish workers in record time, a tall fence was placed around it, and the country, once again, tried to put dissension behind it and move forward.

The wild '90s

There is probably not a soul in all of Russia who would disagree: the 1990s in Russia were hell. There was nothing in the country to facilitate or even permit private enterprise: no wholesale or retail distribution systems or infrastructure, inadequate financial institutions,

insufficient transportation and communications systems, no advertising and marketing resources, few office buildings, virtually no commercial space. Regulatory laws were contradictory or simply non-existent. The voucher system of privatisation, intended to give citizens a share of economic wealth, proved to be a sham; practically the entire industrial wealth of the country ended up in the hands of a few individuals. Fortunes were made overnight out of nothing. No one paid taxes. Pensions and salaries were not paid for months and even years. The basic services in medical care and education deteriorated catastrophically. Street crime and prostitution soared. Drugs, casinos

---

LEFT: food shortages bring queues in 1990.
RIGHT: Yeltsin rallies for democracy.

and HIV appeared, while high culture all but disappeared. Mafia groups divided up the economy and controlled sectors; protection rackets solved disputes through contract killings. People switched professions or invented new ones, like "shuttling" to Turkey and China to buy goods they could sell at outdoor markets. War broke out in Chechnya. Pyramid schemes wiped out savings of unsuspecting investors for a second time. Media outlets owned by oligarchs played politics instead of reporting the news.

Although Yeltsin's approval ratings were 8 percent in January 1996, a skilfully run campaign and unabashed media support landed him 53 percent of the vote in the July run-off

elections. Then, in August 1998, the bubble finally burst: the government defaulted on its debts, causing the rouble to plummet from 6 to $1 to 25 to $1 virtually overnight. The freedom and democracy that people had longed for under the Soviet Union and fought for in the 1980s and early 1990s brought year after year of suffering and chaos.

And yet somehow, under the outward manifestations of corruption, crime and confusion, people adapted, established businesses, taught in schools, made movies, built houses, graduated from universities, found jobs and muddled through. Somehow people began to build the foundations of a functioning political

system and economy, however inadequate or malformed. Towards the end of the century, Russia was teetering, but on her feet.

All the same, when Yeltsin surprised the nation on 31 December 1999 with his resignation, few rued the day. His time was over. If no one knew what to expect from Vladimir Putin, the former head of the FSB and Prime Minister for only a few months, people were ready for change.

The new millennium

Putin was elected in 2000 with 52 percent of the vote, and again in 2004 with over 71 percent; his approval ratings are consistently between 70 and 84 percent. He is credited with the relative stability and order that Russia has enjoyed in the new millennium, and absolved of responsibility for the dogged problems of corruption, escalating war in the Caucasus and terrorism. Some criticise him for limiting press freedoms, curbing political diversity and repealing direct election of governors; others say these are unfortunate but necessary measures to maintain order in a country where control was slipping away.

If you ask Russians what they think of their country's recent history, almost no one will disagree about what's wrong; but you'll hear dozens of fascinating answers to what Russians call "the cursed questions": who's to blame and what is to be done.

The Russian capital today

The price was high, but Russia and its capital city of Moscow survived. Under the stewardship of Mayor Yuri Luzhkov, building contracts may have been awarded with dubious objectivity, and reconstruction plans satisfy few – but Moscow has emerged as a bustling, modern European capital, the centre of the Russian government, culture and business.

But under the new façade, you can still find ghosts of the past: the quiet courtyard of a manor house; the statue of Lenin forever pointing to a bright future; the tiny parish church dwarfed by skyscrapers; the narrow lanes, winding down hills to the Moscow River, as placid today as it was nearly 900 years ago. ❑

LEFT: despite calls for more democratic reforms, Putin has restored respectability to Russia's global image.

The Russian Federation

The Constitution of the Russian Federation, ratified in 1993, declares that the country is a multinational federation: a democratic, secular, federal state based on rule of law and a republican form of government, in which "man, his rights and freedoms are the supreme value". It consists of 89 constituent parts, called republics, regions *(oblasts)*, territories, cities of federal significance (similar to the District of Columbia in the US), one autonomous region and autonomous areas. It recognises private, state, municipal and other forms of ownership, including of land, and mandates ideological diversity.

Although the Constitution stipulates three main branches of government – executive, legislative and judicial – the power to make decisions and policy is concentrated in the executive branch. The President, elected by popular vote for up to two four-year terms, appoints the Prime Minister and Cabinet, determines the main foreign and domestic policies and can initiate legislation. The 89 constituent entities have been divided into seven large regional groups headed by a presidential envoy. A large Presidential Administration and Security Council wields considerable power and oversees much of the day-to-day running of the state.

The legislative branch, called the Federal Assembly *(Federalnoye Sobranie)* is bicameral. The upper house, called the Federation Council *(Soviet Federatsii)*, is made up of appointed representatives from the 89 constituent parts of the Federation, and is largely tasked with issues related to relations between the constituent parts, although it also approves laws passed by the lower house, appoints judges to the higher courts, and can dismiss the President with a two-thirds majority vote. The lower house, called the State Duma *(Gosudarstvennaya duma)* is the main law-making body in the country, and also approves the President's appointment of Prime Minister and other executive appointees. The Duma can give a

vote of no confidence in the Cabinet, but in response the president may either dismiss the Cabinet or dissolve the Duma. Half the 450 seats in the Duma are single-member mandates; the other half are filled by representatives from political parties that have won at least 5 percent of the vote.

New election laws passed in 2005 have raised the percentage of votes needed to pass the party barrier from 5 to 7 percent and eliminated single-member mandates, as well as changed direct election of governors to presidential appointments.

In 2005 a new body, called the Public Chamber, was established by the Presi-

dent; it will consist of 126 "respected citizens". The Chamber is meant to be a kind of clearing house to funnel concerns, initiatives and problems to the President, but it is not clear how this advisory board will contribute to better public representation.

The judicial branch consists of lower courts and the Constitutional Court, Supreme Court and Arbitration Court, presided over by judges appointed by the Federation Council (on presidential recommendations) for life. Although the judicial branch is theoretically independent, independence varies with each judge and case. ❑

RIGHT: Russia's parliament in progress.

Decisive Dates

500 BC First neolithic settlements established in the region.

AD 500–1000 East Slavic tribe called Vjataichi occupies the area.

879 Death of Rurik, leader of the Varangians, or Vikings, after founding the empire of the Kievan Rus.

988 Prince Vladimir of Kiev accepts Orthodox Christianity.

1147 First written mention of Moscow, by Prince Yuri Dolgoruky, considered the founder of Moscow.

1054 Death of Kievan ruler Yaroslav the Wise leads to division of Kievan Rus into multiple principalities.

1113–25 Vladimir Monomakh briefly reunites Kievan Rus for final time.

1156 First wooden walls built around the Kremlin by Yuri Dolgoruky.

1237–8 Moscow plundered and burned by Tatar Batu Khan. Khans begin practice of appointing Moscow Grand Princes.

1340 Under Ivan Kalita, "Moneybags", oak walls are built around Kremlin, reinforced with stucco.

1366 White stone walls built around the Kremlin.

1380 Dmitry Donskoy defeats Tatars at the battle of Kulikovo Field.

1382 Tatars burn Moscow to the ground.

1427 Church of the Miraculous Icon of the Saviour completed, the earliest surviving architecture in the city.

1453 Turks take Constantinople, and Moscow claims the mantle of the "true Church" of Eastern Orthodoxy.

1462–1505 Reign of Ivan III (the Great), who reconstructs the Kremlin and moves traders to Red Square. More importantly, he begins the process of uniting all Russian principalities under the crown of Moscow. The Dormition Cathedral by Italian Aristotele Fiorananti is completed in 1479.

1480 Ivan III renounces the state's allegiance to the Tartar Khans.

1485–95 Current brick walls built around an enlarged Kremlin.

1493 Ivan III crowns himself Sovereign of All Russia. Moscow is its capital.

1508–16 Moat cut along the Kremlin walls on Red Square.

1533–84 Reign of Ivan the Terrible, who establishes council of boyars.

1561 St Basil's Cathedral built to commemorate the routing of the Tatars in Kazan (1552) and Astrakhan (1556).

1563 First book printed in Moscow.

1585–93 The White City walls built (current Boulevard Ring).

1604–13 The "Time of Troubles", in which the country searches for a strong leader and Poles occupy the city.

1612 Moscow liberated from the Poles by troops led by Minin, a butcher, and Prince Pozharsky.

1613 Mikhail Romanov elected tsar, ending the "Time of Troubles" and beginning the Romanov dynasty.

1659 Wooden walls built around Earthen City (current Garden Ring Road).

1682–1725 Reign of Peter the Great.

1689 Peter's sister Sophia incarcerated at Novodevichy Convent after her attempt on the throne.

1702 First public theatre opened.

1703 Russia's first newspaper, *Vedomosti*, is printed.

1712 Peter the Great moves the capital to St Petersburg.

1755 Moscow University founded.

1780s White City walls torn down.

1812 Moscow set alight and abandoned to thwart Napoleon's troops, who enter the city on 2 September. They retreat, suffering heavy losses, on 6 October.

1816–30 Earthen City walls torn down and Garden Ring Road built.

1819–22 Neglinnaya River forced underground and the Aleksandrovsky Gardens laid by the western Kremlin walls.

1825 Bolshoy Theatre opened.

1861 Tsar Alexander II liberates the serfs.

1866 Moscow Conservatory founded.

1869 Tolstoy publishes *War and Peace*.

1882 First telephone system established in Moscow.

1883 First electric streetlights established.

1898 Moscow Art Theatre founded.

1902 Yaroslavl station completed by Fyodor Shekhtel, leading *style moderne* architect.

1905 Moscow torn apart by strikes and worker uprisings. Trans-Siberian Railway completed.

1912 Futurist Vladimir Mayakovsky publishes *A Slap in the Face of Public Taste.*

1914 Russia enters World War I.

1917 In February Tsar Nicholas II abdicates throne. Civil War begins. On 3 November Soviet power is proclaimed in Moscow.

1918 On 12 March the Soviet government is transferred to Moscow.

1922 Civil War ends. At the First All-Union Congress of Soviets the USSR is established with Moscow as its capital.

1924 Lenin dies. Stalin rises to power.

1935 First metro line opened. The first General Plan for the reconstruction of Moscow approved.

1941 On 22 June Nazi Germany invades the USSR and reaches Moscow.

1945 On 9 May Germany capitulates.

1951 The Second General Plan for the reconstruction of Moscow approved.

1953 Khrushchev comes to power after the death of Stalin.

1957 The 6th World Festival of Youth and Students is held in Moscow.

1980 The Summer Olympics are held in Moscow, but boycotted by the US after the invasion of Afghanistan.

LEFT: Ivan the Terrible (reigned 1533–84), who routed the Tatars. **RIGHT:** Vladimir Ilyich Lenin, first Premier of the Soviet Union.

1985 Mikhail Gorbachev becomes leader and declares a policy of "*perestroika, glasnost* and accelerated social and economic development".

1989 Berlin Wall falls.

1991 Boris Yeltsin elected President of Russian Federation within the USSR. August coup of hardliners against Gorbachev. On 21 December the former Soviet republics declare the dissolution of the USSR and the establishment of the Commonwealth of Independent States. On 25 December Gorbachev resigns and the Soviet flag is lowered over the Kremlin.

1993 Russian Congress tries to unseat Yeltsin, but fails.

1996 Yuri Luzhkov elected mayor of Moscow with 95 percent of the vote; re-elected in 1999 and 2003.

1998 Default on government debts; rouble collapses.

2000 Prime Minister Vladimir Putin is elected President after Boris Yeltsin resigns.

2002 129 hostages and 41 Chechen fighters die when Russian troops storm Palace of Culture theatre.

2004 Putin elected for second term with more than 71 percent of the vote.

2006 Russia temporarily cuts off the supply of gas to Ukraine because of a conflict over rising prices. Record low temperatures hit the city. ❑

THE MUSCOVITES

In the world's billionaire capital, where wealth
is publicly paraded, daily life can still be very
hard for the average citizen. Even so, the city remains the
promised land for Russians from every corner of the country

In any discussion of the country's wealth disparity, Russians will inevitably point out that "Moscow is not Russia", a remark that brings the conversation to an end with nods and shrugs of agreement.

While parts of the country are economically depressed, Moscow stands out as a bustling bastion of opportunity and decadence. It is a city of frenetic consumerism, where streets are lined with expensive foreign cars, where posh restaurants and cafés spring up almost daily and where exclusive clubs are playgrounds for the country's richest and most beautiful.

Like characters from a Chekhov play, millions of Russians dream of moving to the capital. Keenly aware of this, Moscow's authorities have kept in place a draconian, Soviet-era registration system to prevent the masses from flooding into the city. Unlike outer regions blighted by unemployment, there is plenty of work here, from building to banking, and it's the place to make a stellar career. It is, after all, the billionaire capital of the world. According to a recent survey by *Forbes* magazine, out of a declining national population of around 144 million, a quarter of Russia's wealth is concentrated in the hands of just 100 people, most of whom either reside in, or made their fortunes in, Moscow. In late 2005, the city had 33 billionaires, two more than runner-up New York.

If you've got it, flaunt it

Flaunting wealth in the form of luxury cars, clothes, eating out and entertainment is a favourite pastime among Moscow's rich, many of whom earned their fortunes in murky fashion during the violent, turbulent 1990s following the collapse of the Soviet Union. Hummers, Mercedes and Lexi are common sights on the perpetually jammed streets of central Moscow, as are burly men in expensive suits with ostentatiously dressed women in tow.

In the 1990s, many of Moscow's more deep-pocketed residents were Western expatriates who flocked to cash in on economic opportunities offered by the nascent capitalism of the

PRECEDING PAGES: young soldiers enjoy a shooting arcade. **LEFT:** the courtyards of Moscow become a winter wonderland once the snow begins.
RIGHT: Russians are huge fans of *morozhenoye* (ice cream), even during the winter.

Wild East. Consequently, foreigners were valued patrons of the city's most expensive clubs and restaurants, as were "New Russians", a class of nouveau riche as notorious for their extravagantly bad taste as for their filthy lucre.

The rouble crash of 1998, however, sent many expats fleeing Moscow with their bank accounts all but wiped out, while millions of Russians were left to start from a financial Ground Zero. Since then, buoyed by high world oil prices, the country's economy has steadily grown. Expats have slowly been trickling back, and a new generation of wealthy Russians has been making its money as legitimately as it can in a country rife with corruption. In order to sur-

vive financially as well as physically, many of these New Russians who managed to ride the rouble crash – and threats from rival businessmen – have made strides to "get out of the game" and make their fortunes legitimately.

The poverty gap

The wealth disparity between Moscow and the rest of the country is mirrored within the city itself, providing daily scenes worthy of the most exaggerated Soviet portrayals of victims of capitalism. It is not unusual to see the city's wealthiest residents strutting their stuff past drunks and beggars in states of extreme human degradation, begging for spare change or sprawled out unconscious awaiting removal to the drunk tank.

The relative lack of such scenes during Soviet times even inspired one famous New Russian joke. A New Russian walks down the street and sees an old classmate begging. "Vanya, how are things going for you?" the New Russian asks the homeless man. "Not so well, Sasha," the beggar answers. "I haven't eaten for three days." "You should look after yourself, Vanya. *Force* yourself to eat."

More bizarrely and far less tastefully, wealthy Muscovites in search of entertainment have recently turned to "extreme tourism" agencies. These dress their clients as homeless people and organise for them to go begging on the streets for a day.

An emergent middle class

Between these economic extremes, however, a middle class has begun to emerge, made up of small-business owners, employees in Western companies, marketing specialists, lawyers and middle-managers in an array of industries.

Steady economic growth has given this social group the chance not only to make ends meet but to patronise mid-priced clubs, restaurants and fitness clubs, and take holidays abroad. Turkey, Egypt and Cyprus are popular destinations, due to bargain travel packages and the relative ease with which Russians can obtain visas for these countries.

Buying property has also become increasingly accessible to the middle class, as a mortgage industry has begun to emerge. Despite comparatively high annual interest rates (between 10 and 15 percent), taking out a mortgage is gaining in popularity in the quest for quality living space that has consumed Muscovites since the days of the dreaded Soviet-era *kommunalki* – communal flats where whole families were forced to share because of housing shortages.

The ethnic mix

As the capital of a country with more than 130 ethnic groups, Moscow is hugely diverse. Many different nationalities came to the city in Soviet times, and, in spite of the tough registration systems, many others flocked and continue to flock to the capital following the collapse of the superpower. Officially, at least, the Soviet Union promoted the Friendship of Peoples, a phrase enshrined in the title of a Moscow university named after Patrice Lumumba, the first Prime Minister of the Democratic Republic of the Congo, who was assassinated in 1961. The Friendship of Peoples concept was also the inspiration for an enormous golden Soviet-era fountain at Moscow's All-Russia Exhibition Centre that features a giant wheat sheaf in a granite bowl surrounded by statues of young women in the national costumes of the Soviet Union's 16 republics *(see VVTs, page 165)*.

Today, Moscow houses representatives of almost every ethnicity in the Russian Federation, as well as hundreds of thousands of

The Russian government estimates that between 500,000 and 800,000 immigrants live in Moscow, while more than 96,000 work permits are issued annually to foreign workers. A majority of these were issued to migrants from former Soviet republics, known in Russia as "the near abroad" because of historical links, though tens of thousands were also issued to migrants from the "far abroad", including Turkey, China and Vietnam.

Popular xenophobia

Internationalism and the Friendship of Peoples received much lip service in official

migrants from former Soviet republics. Moscow's official population hovers around 10.5 million, but unofficially the number is estimated to be as high as 14 million including illegal migrants and commuters from the sprawling suburbs. A majority of Moscow residents are ethnic Russians, Tatars, Ukrainians and Belorussians, but Moscow also has large ethnic communities from the former Soviet Union's Central Asian and southern republics, including Kyrgyzstan, Moldova, Uzbekistan, Tajikistan, Armenia, Azerbaijan and Georgia.

LEFT: wedding party at Victory Park.
ABOVE: a photo stunt on the city streets.

UNITY TAKES A HOLIDAY

In 2005 the government scrapped the 7 November holiday celebrating the establishment of the Soviet government in 1917, replacing it with a new holiday on 4 November called People's Unity Day. At the inaugural People's Unity Day in 2005, a demonstration of around 3,000 nationalists gathered near the Chistye Prudy metro station in central Moscow for what they called "The Russian March". Demonstrators carried signs that read "Russia against the Occupiers" and yelled chants such as "Moscow is a Russian city, we'll chase out the occupiers" and "Russia for Russians, Moscow for Muscovites".

Soviet policy, and Russia today still has the country's multi-ethnic make-up enshrined and honoured in its Constitution. But the influx of different ethnic groups, particularly Russia's dark-skinned neighbours has provided fodder for nationalistic politicians and xenophobic, Fascist organisations demanding that their country halt this "invasion".

In the ideological vacuum following the collapse of the Soviet Union, xenophobia has proved to be a violent, deadly and disturbingly popular doctrine, especially among young adherents to neo-Fascist groups. Beatings of non-Russians, particularly those with dark skin, have been common in the past few years,

Snapshots of typical citizens

If central casting were to conduct a reconnaissance mission to determine the type of extras needed for a Hollywood film shot in Moscow, the casting agency's more observant scouts would quickly realise that there are several characters without whom it would be impossible to portray accurately life in the Russian capital:

The Gypsy Cab Driver. The ubiquitous "gypsy cab" is a phenomenon in Moscow and often a full-time or part-time source of income for its driver, who is usually eager to discuss, among other things, domestic and global politics, the weather and the precarious sanity of other drivers. The Gypsy Cab Driver is not nec-

and the authorities have largely ignored the problem, despite several high-profile deaths by beatings from skinheads. On the anniversary of Adolf Hitler's birthday in 2001, skinheads attacked and killed a young Chechen man. Africans and Asians have been victimised in similar attacks.

Many of the migrant workers from the "near abroad" work for miserly wages at construction sites and sell produce at outdoor markets in order to send money home. Slowly, the authorities have begun to concede that these guest workers are beneficial to the local economy, but many Muscovites have trouble accepting this reality.

essarily a Romany and can vary in shape, size and nationality. Regardless of how long he has been in Moscow, he is quick to boast his knowledge of short cuts and daily traffic trends. As if adhering to a script issued by a secret gypsy cab drivers' union, he will inevitably initiate a conversation with a foreigner by asking, in Russian, "And where are you from?" As a rule, gypsy cabs charge less than registered yellow taxis, and brawls have been known to break out in Moscow between the two groups in establishing their respective turf.

The Traffic Cop. Patrolling the streets for violations, the Traffic Cop is the mortal enemy of the Moscow driver, quick to flag him down with his baton for even the slightest infraction of the law, and prone to extorting bribes in exchange for scrapping protocol. The Traffic Cop is known as one of the most corrupt members of a police force notorious for its crooked officers, and his department's Russian acronym – GIBDD – has spawned a saying among drivers using each of the letters to spell out: "Hand the inspector the dough and drive on."

The *Dyevushka*. Far from her Soviet-era reputation in the West as a burly, androgynous builder of Communism, the *Devushka*, or "young woman", is one of the prides of the Russian people, known for her beauty, femininity and resourcefulness. Two world wars and political purges left the Soviet Union and Russia with a distinct deficit of males, creating cut-throat competition among women to find a husband. The *Dyevushka* can be seen flaunting her beauty on Moscow streets much to the delight of her potential suitors, but she is not just another pretty face: though living in a patriarchal society, the *Devushka* often acts as a breadwinner after marriage in addition to raising children and managing the household.

The Golden Youth. Moscow is a party town, and few Muscovites are as dedicated to the city's nightlife as the so-called *zolotaya molody-ozh*, the *jeunesse dorée*, the decadent children of Moscow's nouveaux riches. Sticklers for the latest European fashion trends, the Golden Youth can be seen in their element in Moscow's *elitny*, or "elite" clubs, while their chauffeurs wait outside in Mercedes, Bentleys and Landcruisers, reading science-fiction novels or nodding off. The Golden Youth's taste in drugs and music is constantly changing, and the strict face control of the clubs they haunt make it difficult for the hoi polloi to keep up with their trends.

The Cashier. Dealing with the Cashier can be one of the more frustrating experiences in Moscow. Whether at kiosks, grocery stores, flower shops or corner convenience stores, the Cashier, typically a heavily made-up, middle-aged woman wearing a blue smock, is generally indifferent to a customer's desire to purchase goods from her establishment. This indifference is best epitomised by her common refusal to allow a customer to pay in large notes due to her inability to produce any change. The Cashier, however, can be resourceful. Given a lack of small change in her register, she has been known to offer gum in lieu of a few roubles. She will not, however, accept gum as payment in lieu of roubles.

The *Babushka*. Weary, intrepid, and capable of aggressive outbursts unexpected from a woman of her age, the *Babushka*, meaning "grandmother" or "old woman", is simultaneously one of the most feared and respected figures in Moscow. The *Babushka*'s withered face, resembling that of a figurine carved from

a dried apple and ensconced in a scarf wrapped around her head, reveals the wear sustained in a century of war and social upheaval in her motherland. But while the *Babushka* can be seen begging for change to supplement her meagre pension and is entitled to a seat on any form of public transport, she is not exclusively a figure of pity. She is also prone to angry outbursts over certain aspects of the new Russia, including public displays of affection between young lovers and Moscow drivers' general disregard of pedestrian crossings. But anyone who helps the *Babuskha* carry her small cart up a set of stairs will usually garner kind words such as, "May God grant you health." ❏

LEFT: beards were once banned under Peter the Great, but are still treasured by clerics and eccentrics alike.
RIGHT: *babushkas* sell everything from roses to dill to supplement their income.

AT THE RUSSIAN TABLE:
BEYOND BORSCHT AND BLINI

The popular belief is that most Russians survive on a diet of potatoes and beetroot supplemented with a few cucumbers and all washed down with vodka. It's an image that's soon shattered in Moscow

Today in Moscow you can find almost every kind of food, and there are venues to suit every pocket, from street stalls selling *sloyki* (cheese-filled puff pastries) to elegant dining halls serving haute cuisine at prices that will make you gulp.

Russian cuisine was originally based on simple ingredients that could be farmed (or caught) in northern climes. In the 18th century it was strongly influenced by French cookery, which explains the penchant for thick meat sauces, complicated salads and the huge range of cream-filled *tortes*. Today, most restaurants offer a varied menu, from simple peasant soup to the most elegant French-influenced dessert.

Breakfast and snacks

At *zavtrak* (breakfast), start the day the Russian way with one of the varieties of *kasha* (porridge) or *syrniki*, thick pancakes made with *tvorog* (curd cheese) and *smetana* (sour cream) and served with jam. If you are still hungry, have some smoked fish and meats or fruit and *kefir* (Russian lassi). In the unlikely event that you need a mid-morning snack, head to a *kofeynaya* (coffee shop) or *gastronom* (grocery) for a *pirozhnoe* (pastry). *Khleb* (bread) is available from the *bulochnaya* (bakery). It is almost obligatory while in Russia to try *chyorny* or *rzhanoy* (black bread), a dense rye bread. Look for *Boroditsky*, a black bread dusted with dill.

LEFT: Moscow's markets may seem a bit rough around the edges, but they can be a gourmand's dream.
RIGHT: a sophisticated snack – caviar and chilled vodka.

Lunch and supper

Obed (lunch) is the largest meal of the day and consists of *zakuski* (starters) and *salaty* (salads), *sup* (soup), *vtoroye* (main course) and *sladkoe* (dessert). In Moscow, more modest versions of the traditional heavy Russian lunch include the ubiquitous *biznes-lanch* (set-price business lunch). At home, the evening meal, *uzhin*, is often much lighter than a traditional lunch and comprises salads or *buterbrod* (open sandwiches). This is in contrast to celebratory dinners and meals in restaurants where guests sit at the table for hours, slowly making their way through plates of *zakuski* and main courses, all accompanied by vodka, toasts, stories, jokes and singing and dancing. And at the end of the meal, it is traditional to take *chay* (tea), usually with lemon and sugar, and, if you have room, a rich *tort* (cake).

Zakuski and salads

The glory of the Russian table are the *zakuski* – appetisers that include salads, sliced smoked meats, smoked and salted fish, fresh and pickled vegetables, salted and marinated mushrooms and *pirozhki* (a yeast or puff pastry filled with meat, potatoes, mushrooms, sautéed cabbage or fish). Loading the table down with *zakuski* is part of traditional Russian hospitality and the main feature of the meal. Ingredients for salads

include cucumbers and tomatoes (or radishes) seasoned with a dill and sour cream dressing. *Vinegret* is a salad of beetroot, potatoes, carrots and pickles. The classic Olivier salad is made of potatoes, onions, pickles and thin strips of meat, and is dressed with mayonnaise. For something lighter, try a fresh *kvashenaya kapusta* (sauerkraut), mixed with cranberries and carrots and drizzled with oil.

Russians are very good at preparing fish, and it is a main element to any feast. *Selyod*, pickled herring served with fresh onions and boiled potatoes, or *selyodka pod shuboi* – translated as "salted herring in a fur coat" – made of beetroot, potatoes, boiled egg and sour cream, are included on most tables. Russian smoked fish is excellent (sturgeon, salmon, trout or cod) along with servings of *shproty* (sprats) or *ryba zalivnaya* (fish in aspic). If you're feeling flush when you're eating out, order blinis (pancakes) with *ikrá* (caviar). The delicate bluish-grey, lightly salted Beluga caviar, *malossol*, is the finest. Other, less expensive caviar include *ossetra,* which has smaller grains and a stronger flavour, *sevruga*, which has even smaller grains and a strong, nutty taste, or *krasnaya ikra* (red salmon roe), which has large grains that pop in your mouth in an explosion of flavour.

Meat starters include *studen* (or *kholodets*), veal or beef in aspic served with horseradish, and a variety of smoked meats and sausages. For vegetarians a classic hot appetiser is what Russians call *zhulen* (from the French *julienne*), which is a dish of sliced mushrooms served in a white sauce topped with cheese and served in small pots bubbling straight from the oven.

Soups

The famous borscht (beetroot soup), actually a Ukrainian dish served with hot rolls called *pampushki* drizzled with garlic sauce, can be found in nearly all Russian restaurants. For a lighter soup, try *gribnoy,* made with fresh or dried field mushrooms; *ukha*, a simple fish soup made with potatoes, carrots and onions and sprinkled with dill; or *kurinaya lapsha*, a clear chicken broth served with noodles. *Shchi* (cabbage soup) is made with fresh cabbage or sauerkraut in broth and seasoned with a dollop of sour cream. *Pokhlebki* are hearty soups that nearly cross the line into stews, and can be made from meat, poultry or fish with onions, potatoes and carrots.

VODKA IS NOT THE ONLY DRINK

If you only drink vodka while in Moscow, you'll miss a wealth of other options. *Sbiten* is a fermented drink made of honey and spices and served hot. *Medovuka* is a spiced honey wine. *Nastoika* is a flavoured, vodka-based liqueur. Armenian cognacs are often drunk straight, like vodka with a slice of lemon. *Kindzmariuli* and *Khvachkara* are Geogian sweet red wines not to be missed, while *Mukuzani* and *Saperavi* are red and dry. The best dry whites are *Tsinindali* and *Yereti* wines. *Shampanskoe* (champagne) is most commonly *polusukhoye* or *polsladkoye* (semi-dry or semi-sweet), but you can also find *brut*. Try *Sovietskoye, Nadezhda* or *Novi Svet*.

The pride of Russian soups is the rich and piquant *solyanka*, made of mushrooms, fish or meat and seasoned with pickles, olives, capers and lemon and topped with sour-cream. In summer, try *okroshka*, a light soup of *kvas* (a mildly alcoholic drink made from black bread) ladled over diced vegetables, or *svekolnik*, a clear beetroot soup served over a salad of potatoes, cucumbers and radishes dressed with sour cream and seasoned with dill or parsley.

Main dishes

After the glory of the starters and soups, traditional Russian main courses tend to be simpler and are usually a *myaso* (meat) escalope or grilled lamb or beef. You can also try beef Stroganov in a rich sour-cream sauce, or pre-Revolutionary dishes made of venison, boar, sucking pig, goose or duck. You may want to order *golubsty*, stuffed cabbage usually served in a tomato-based sauce, or *pelmeni*, the Russian version of ravioli served in a broth or baked under a hearty spoonful of sour cream.

You might also try *kutlety pozharsky,* cutlets made of minced and seasoned chicken, or chicken *tabaka,* a young chicken pressed and fried to crispness. *Treska, forel, karp, sterlyad* and *osetrina* (cod, trout, sterlet – a small sturgeon – and sturgeon) are traditionally baked in a white sauce or sour cream, fried in batter (*v klyare*) or grilled (sturgeon is especially good this way) and served with *tkemali* (a piquant sour-plum sauce). In most restaurants you make a separate order of *garnir* (garnish), which is usually a choice between baked or fried potatoes, rice or buckwheat oats (*grechnevaya kasha*).

If you can fit a dessert in, you might like to try *kisel*, a traditional soft jelly made of fruits and thickened with cornflour, or splurge on a Napoleon, which involves layers of puff pastry with a rich cream filling (so called because it was originally triangular and reminiscent of the traditional French three-cornered hat).

Table drinks

In general Russians have a huge capacity to drink alcohol, but they do also drink non-alcoholic drinks with their meals. *Minerálnaya vodá* (mineral water), *mors* (fresh berries mixed with sugar and water) or *kompot* (a fruit drink made of simmered fresh or dried fruit and berries) are favourite beverages. Starters are traditionally accompanied by chilled vodka drunk straight: try one of the flavoured vodkas such as lemon or pepper and honey. The trick to staying on your feet is to take a mouthful of salad or appetiser immediately after the gulp of vodka. Russia also produces excellent *pívo* (beer).

Ethnic food

Apart from the usual international cuisines, Moscovites are mad for *Gruzinsky* (Georgian)

food. The city has its fair share of places that sell delicious *shashlyk*, a kebab of marinated lamb, beef, chicken, seasoned minced meat or sturgeon grilled on skewers and served with a sour-plum or spicy tomato sauce. If you're eating in an ethic restaurant, the meal includes an array of salads and starters: chicken *satsivi* (an onion-walnut sauce); *farshirovannye baklazhani* (aubergines stuffed with walnuts); *lobio* (spicy, stewed beans); *basturma* (spicy dry-cured beef); *khachapuri* (puff pastry filled with a sharp cheese); and *khinkali* (dumplings filled with lamb served with fresh black pepper). Don't forget to order a carafe or two of excellent Georgian wine (*see box opposite*). ❑

LEFT: fine wines – whether Georgian or imported – are easy to find. **RIGHT:** a medley of spices give cuisine from the Caucasus a hearty flavour.

LITERATURE AND THE IMAGINATION

Literature from and about Moscow is perennially popular. From the pages of Muscovites' favourite books come the images of the city they love – an idealised place which can be more real to them than the busy streets themselves

For some, Moscow is a city of brilliant musicians and singers; for others, it's a city of exquisite dance; for others still it's a city of avant-garde art or magnificent architecture. But for Muscovites, it's a city of literature: a city of poets and writers who lived in its houses, walked its streets and recreated their city in poetry and prose so well-known and beloved that the boundaries between the imagined city and the real city have become hopelessly smudged and blurred.

Here Pushkin's Evgeny Onegin flew down a snow-covered Tverskaya ulitsa in a sleigh. Here Moscow's white stone walls turned red in Mayakovsky's poems of the Revolution. Here Tolstoy's Anna Karenina went to the horse races in the same place where the Hippodrome stands today, and the Rostov family of *War and Peace* lived in a manor house on Povarskaya ulitsa and walked along the little Arbat lanes.

The tour guides at the battle of Borodino panorama say that the question they are asked most frequently by both Russian and foreign guests is: "Where did Pierre Bezukhov stand?" They say they are always a little sad when they remind visitors that Pierre was a character in a novel, as if they were telling a child that fairies don't exist.

The apartments and houses where writers lived have been lovingly preserved and are a wonderful introduction to Moscow. Even if you know little of Anton Chekhov, Lev Tolstoy or Marina Tsvetaeva, visit their homes. You'll see Moscow as it was in another era, with all the delightful details of home life: a

basin for washing by a narrow bed; poems scribbled on a wall; knick-knacks in a curio cabinet. The older women who work in these apartment-museums know their long-gone housemates the way they know their neighbours in the next flat, and they will happily tell you all the family gossip: about playwright Anton Chekhov's marriage to the actress Olga Knipper (they disapprove; she wasn't kind enough to him); or how the Tolstoy children would slide down the staircase on pillows and slip out into the garden through the window (they consider them naughty, but charming).

They will also, if you ask, quote from memory page after page of prose and verse about

Moscow, like this exalted description of the city by Mikhail Lermontov:

Moscow is not just a big city like thousands of others. Moscow is not a silent giant of cold stone laid in symmetry. No! She has her own soul, her own life. Like in ancient Roman cemeteries, each of her stones preserves an inscription engraved by time and destiny, an inscription that is indecipherable to the masses, but rich with meaning and filled with thoughts, feelings and inspiration for the scholar, the patriot, the poet. Like an ocean, she has her own lan-

And it's absolutely true. All of Moscow has been captured on the page, from the majesty of the Kremlin walls in Lermontov's poetry to the huts and hovels of Khitrovka in Gorky's *The Lower Depths*; from the swish of silk dresses at a ball in Tolstoy's novels to the madness of Satan's flight over the city in Bulgakov's *The Master and Margarita*; from the foibles of the merchant class in Ostrovsky's plays to the bewitching romance of the Arbat lanes in the songs of Okudzhava; from the red flags of the 1905 uprising in Bryusov's verse to the crooked lanes and little houses of the old Moscow Tsvetaeva knew and loved.

guage, a language that is powerful and sonorous, sacred and prayerful.

Although the poet Anna Akhmatova was most closely associated with St Petersburg, she visited Moscow frequently (staying with friends in Zamoskvoreche) and wrote in 1963:

Everything in Moscow is saturated with verse,
Riddled with rhyme through and through…

Moscow – in Russian *Moskva*, a feminine noun – is always "she", and is often personified by Russian writers. When Moscow was captured by the French in 1812, the poet Dolgorukov wrote:

Mother-Moscow has scores of sons…
Russia, you are enslaved when Moscow is held captive!

And Lermontov wrote:

Moscow! Moscow! I love you like a son,
As only a Russian can love – powerfully, passionately and tenderly!

LEFT: Chekhov and Tolstoy exchange ideas.
ABOVE: the Russians' love of books is immediately obvious from the amount of shops and street traders selling books at very low prices.

*I love the sacred shimmer of your
grey strands,
And the Kremlin: crenellated and
imperturbable.*

Of course, writers were not always so high-flown when they wrote about Moscow. Nikolay Gogol wrote:

Moscow is a woman and Petersburg a man… Petersburg is a tidy man, a typical German who regards everything with a calculating eye. If he should decide to give a party, he'll look in his wallet first. Moscow is Russian nobility, and if the nobility decide to party, they will party until they drop and

won't worry if it costs more than they have in their pockets. Moscow doesn't like to do anything halfway.

Unchanged vision

You have only to look at Moscow's nouveaux riches today to see how little the city has changed over the centuries: there is nothing halfway about their luxury cars or haute couture.

Or read this passage from Alexander Pushkin's novel in verse, *Evgeny Onegin*, when the hero rides along Tverskaya ulitsa:

Watch booths flash past, and old women,

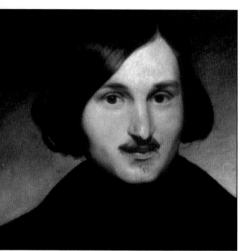

MOSCOW'S TOP FIVE FICTION

To get into a Moscow mood, dip into a classic of Russian literature. If possible, curl up on a snowy winter's night, in front of a roaring fire with a glass of tea.

● *Evgeny Onegin* by Alexander Pushkin. A novel in verse written in the early 19th century that follows its cynical hero from the glitter of high society to the comfort of village life, from a fatal duel to love found and lost.

● *War and Peace* by Leo Tolstoy. Immerse yourself in Tolstoy's complex, compelling world of Moscow families before, during and after Napoleon's invasion of 1812: a profound examination of individuals' role in the making of history, and the quest for love and happiness.

● *Woe from Wit* by Alexander Griboedov. A comic play about a homesick Russian nobleman who returns to Moscow after touring Europe to find the pettiness and hypocrisy of Russian high society and a yearning for freedom.

● *Master and Margarita* by Mikhail Bulgakov. The devil and his band descend upon Moscow in the 1930s, as the Master writes his story of Christ and Pontius Pilate.

● *The Elagin Affair and Other Stories* by Ivan Bunin. Moscow at the turn of the 20th century by the first Russian to win the Nobel Prize for literature: love, loss, aspiration and skepticism, against the bewitching landscape of Moscow and the provinces.

Street urchins, shops and lamp-
*   posts,*
Palaces, flower beds, monasteries,
Asians, sleighs, kitchen gardens,
Merchants, hovels, peasant men,
Towers, boulevards, Cossacks,
Chemists and fashion shops,
Balconies and lions on the gates,
And flocks of jackdaws atop church
*   crosses.*

If you changed "watch booths" to "traffic-police booths" and "street urchins" to "punk kids", you'd have Tverskaya ulitsa today in all its bright confusion. Only the sleighs, hovels and kitchen gardens have disappeared into the past.

Of course, some fictional depictions of Moscow were never confused with reality. A favourite pastime of Muscovites is finding all the places mentioned in Bulgakov's novel *The Master and Margarita*, when Satan and his devils descend upon the city (a chillingly apt description of Moscow during the political purges and repressions of the 1930s). Many are certain that Satan's Ball is really a description of a party held by the US Ambassador in Spaso House:

In the next hall, there were no
columns, but instead walls of red,
pink, and milk-white roses on one
side and a wall of Japanese double
camellias on the other. Between the
two walls, fountains were already
shooting up fizz, and champagne
pooled and bubbled in three basins...

Satan might not have been there, but the description matches the Ambassador's residence perfectly.

In the poems about their city Muscovites love best, Moscow is "white stone and gold crowned" by thousands of cupolas glittering in the sunlight against blue skies. Sometimes in Marina Tsvetaeva's poetry, the city is violently, vividly alive:

In my Moscow cupolas are blazing,
In my Moscow bells are pealing...

LEFT: Gogol and Marina Tsvetaeva are both associated with Moscow.
RIGHT: graffiti marks the entrance to Café Margarita – a place of pilgrimage for lovers of Bulgakov.

But for other poets – and in other times – it was a quiet city, where narrow little streets were meant for dreamy contemplation. Andrey Bely wrote of the tangle of streets around Arbat:

Such unforgettable strolls,
Such unforgettable dreams,
Along the crooked lanes of
*   Moscow...*

A half-century later Bulat Okudzhava wrote his "Song About Arbat", a haunting tune that virtually everyone in the country can sing by heart. Okudzhava's Arbat is a homeland, a destiny, a religion:

You flow like a river. Such a
strange name!

Your asphalt is clear like water.
Oh, Arbat, my Arbat,
*   You are my destiny.*
You are my joy, you are my sorrow.

All of Moscow's joys and its many sorrows, its extravagance and piety, its grandeur and folly have been reflected through the ages on the pages of novels and in volumes of poetry. These books make excellent travel companions, providing intimate insights into the city. And as you explore the city, every once in a while step off today's streets and slip into the courtyards of the imagination, where Moscow's poets and writers dreamed other cities and other times. ❑

FAIRY TALES AND MAGIC

Advertisements for magicians and fortune-tellers fill the classified section of Moscow's most popular newspapers. This may seem mere superstition to most visitors, but it stems from a long tradition of fantasy and wizardry

Move over, Harry Potter. Long before small British wizards were donning invisibility capes and casting spells, Russian magicians were putting on "invisibility caps" or holding "invisibility bones" to move about their villages unseen, or using their "set tablecloth" to bring food and drink whenever they needed it. Not to mention using their magic wands to open doors and transform the village gossip into the form of a cat.

Spirits and sprites

Russia has a rich tradition of folk magic and fairy tales. Even today, everyone from lovelorn schoolgirls to Cabinet ministers consults respected practitioners of the white (benevolent) and black (evil) magical arts.

When something goes awry in your hotel room, the staff might mutter that it's a *domovoy* (house sprite) making mischief. The solution? A glass of vodka and chunk of bread in the corner of the room usually placates them. In the woods, always the setting for supernatural goings-on, the troublemakers are usually the *leshie* (wood spirits) or the *vodyanie* (water spirits) ready to lure the unsuspecting into their underwater world. The most dangerous spirits of the woods are the *rusalki*: beautiful women whose songs lure men below the waters.

Helping hands

If you need help with a nasty spirit or the evil eye, you can call in *volshebniki* (wizards), *vedmy* (witches), *kudesniki* (warlocks who cast spells), *kolduny* (wizards of a dark nature), *magy* (magicians) or even *chernoknizhniki*

("men of the black book", who practice the Black Arts). If you need help with an incantation (to rekindle your spouse's passion or cure an ingrown toenail), you can call on a *sheptun* (a whisperer of spells). If you can't find your car keys, call an *otgadnik* (someone who specialises in finding lost or stolen possessions). If you want to see what's really going on in your life, ask a *gadalka* (fortune-teller) or someone who calls herself "the all-seeing".

During the Christmas holidays young women put a gold ring in a glass of water and move a candle around it to create images within the circle, or let a candle drip in the water and divine the future in the shape of the wax. For centuries unmarried women have done this to see if the new year will bring them a husband. You can read about Tatiana and Olga conjuring in similar fashion in *Evgeny Onegin*, the verse novel by Alexander Pushkin.

Fairy tales

Russian children grow up on fairy tales in which fearful creatures roam the earth, but good almost always prevails in the end. They are terrified of Baba Yaga, a nasty old witch who lives in a house on chicken legs that turns around to lure children to their deaths. This is the same Hut on Chicken Legs the artists built at Abramtsevo for their children, although no witch cackled from the carved windows in the artists' colony *(see page 203)*.

Equally terrifying to small people is Gorynych the Dragon, a winged beast with three fire-breathing heads. Or Koshey the Immortal, a skinny old dark wizard who can only be defeated when the hero finds his death on the tip of a pin, which is hidden in an egg, in a duck, in a hare, in a trunk hanging from an enormous oak tree. Another nasty fellow is Karabas-Barabas, the cruel director of a puppet theatre in *The Golden Key* by Aleksey Tolstoy. The Golden Key is worth finding: it opens the door to the Land of Happiness.

A benevolent magical being is the Firebird, whose feathers are flame red. She brings happiness to anyone who catches her – the Firebird has become the national symbol of rarely attainable joy. One of the heroes who searched for and found her is Ivan the Fool. In *The Little Hunchbacked Horse*, Ivan, the youngest brother of a large family, is inept but kind, and ultimately succeeds in carrying out the impossible tasks set before him. Transformed into a handsome lad, he marries the beautiful maiden and – of course – lives happily ever after.

In the tale of *Sadko*, a poor musician plays his *gusli* (dulcimer) by the banks of a lake, and a water sprite rewards him by telling him the story of a golden fish, who restores youth to anyone who can catch and eat it. Sadko succeeds in doing this and is rewarded by gifts from the local merchants. In another tale, the wicked stepmother sends her stepdaughter to her death in the woods on a cold winter night, but when Morozko (Old Man Winter) asks if she is cold, she is too polite to complain. He makes a fire to keep her warm and sends her home with riches. Most satisfyingly, the wicked stepmother sends her own nasty daughter back into the woods at night to gain her mother riches but the girl complains to Morozko and is punished by freezing to death.

Some tales tell of fleeting happiness. In *Snegurochka* (*The Snow Maiden*), an old couple long for a child, so they make a maiden out of snow. She comes to life and is joyful in the winter but becomes sad as the

days grow longer and the sun shines more brightly. One evening she goes into the woods to pick flowers with the village girls who make a bonfire to jump through. When the Snow Maiden jumps through the flames she melts and disappears in a cloud of white mist.

Today you can find beautifully illustrated books of Russian fairy tales (look for reproductions with illustrations by *style moderne* artist Ivan Bilibin). Or choose your favourite tale and find a scene from it decorating a lacquer box made in the towns of Palekh, Mstera, Fedoskino and Kholui. And if you need a wizard or a fortune-teller, advertisements can be found in every Russian newspaper. ❏

LEFT: Baba Yaga – one of Russia's most feared fairy-tale characters. **RIGHT:** lacquered boxes that portray scenes from famous fairy tales are popular souvenirs.

MOSCOW ON STAGE

The performing arts have a long tradition of excellence, fostered in the Soviet period when innovation was frowned on. Now, creative talent is breaking out, but it is still the established works that musicians, actors, dancers and singers perform best

Moscow's performing arts are among the finest in the world. Every evening you can choose between dozens of operas, ballets, concerts and plays with some of the world's best performers. Entrance is always at reasonable prices, and some performances are worth seeking out just to see the wonderful venues in which they are performed.

Ballet and dance

Performed in the capital since the 1730s, Russian classical ballet emerged in its full glory at the end of the 19th century. Its inspiration was Marius Petipa (1818–1910), a French choreographer considered to be "the father of classical ballet", who lived and worked in Russia as choreographer-in-chief of the Imperial Theatre for more than 50 years, staging ballets that are now part of repertories throughout the world. After Petipa came Mikhail Fokin (1880–1942), who scandalised audiences with his daring costumes and productions, and Sergey Diaghelev (1872–1929), whose *Russian Seasons* with Nijinsky debuted in Paris in 1909 and changed dance for ever.

A period of experimentation continued for a few years after the Revolution, until, like the other arts, dance fell prey to the dictates of Socialist Realism, and some of the country's finest dancers defected to the West. However, dance training remained at an extraordinarily high level, and balletomanes say there is still nothing in the world like the delicacy and technical perfection of Russian dancers.

The best troupes in Moscow are the Bolshoy Ballet at the Bolshoy Theatre, founded in 1776, and the Kremlin Ballet Company at the Kremlin Palace of Congresses, though their prima ballerinas are often on loan to touring companies and other world theatres. The Moskva Russian Chamber Ballet has two troupes that perform both traditional and modern ballets on several stages throughout the city, and the New Ballet has a small permanent stage where they perform dance pieces that include ballet, pantomime and drama.

The Kinetic Theatre, a modern dance troupe led by Alexander Pepelyaev, is often on tour, but worth seeing at various venues around the city when they are in town. And don't forget folk dance: the Moiseyev troupe is the best and often performs in the capital. Visiting folk-dance troupes from the former Soviet republics also come to Moscow on tour; check local listings and theatre kiosks.

Opera

Russians' love of opera is deeply rooted. By the late 18th century the Medoks Theatre in Moscow was performing a repertory of more that 400 operas, ballets and dramas, including many Russian operas by composers such as Mikhail Sokolovsky and Vasily Pashkevich. The greatest period in Russian opera was the late 19th century, when Tchaikovsky taught at the Conservatory, and his operas,

tic evening out, and there is nothing like Moscow for lavish sets, often including live animals, top-notch choruses and great booming Russian basses – they are trained to sing several notes lower than in the West.

The Bolshoy performs a repertory heavy on traditional opera, and their foray into modern opera in 2005 in a performance of *Rosenthal's Children* with a libretto by the controversial author Vladimir Sorokin resulted in demonstrations and even a parliamentary inquiry, which may further inhibit experimentation. The Gelikon Opera House has two small stages where their troupes perform traditional operas in unusual productions and a variety of lesser-

ballets and symphonic music premiered on Moscow's stages. Once the imperial monopoly on opera troupes was lifted in 1882, several private opera houses opened that rivalled the Bolshoy in artistry.

Today you can see both traditional productions and original stagings. While European opera is performed frequently, the great Russian operas by Glinka, Mussorgsky, Borodin and Tchaikovsky provide an authen-

LEFT: just to see the interior of the Bolshoy Theatre is worth the price of admission.
ABOVE: Russian ballerinas are still considered to be the best technical dancers in the world.

known Russian and foreign operas. The New *(Novaya)* Opera performs a mixed repertory in a beautifully renovated hall. The Moscow Chamber Musical Theatre, led by Boris Pokrovsky, puts on interesting, albeit rather obscure chamber pieces, such as Dmitry Shostakovich's first opera, *The Nose*. The Moscow Operetta Theatre stages light opera and musicals, such as *My Fair Lady*, in Russian.

Impresarios have attempted to break out of the repertory tradition with stage musicals that perform every night, usually on the stage of one of the city's Soviet-era Houses of Culture. The experiment, which brought *Cats* to the Moscow stage, has had mixed results.

Classical music venues

Until the late 18th century, Moscow's musical culture lagged behind the court-supported theatres and troupes in St Petersburg. It wasn't until music began to be printed at the University Printing House in 1772 that it became more accessible; and by the end of the century it had become vibrant. In the early 19th century, one of the most popular concert instruments was the guitar, and music was played as frequently in the city's literary salons as in its concert halls. With the founding of the Conservatory in 1866, performance and training were established on the highest level of professionalism, so that by

the end of the 19th century there were dozens of concert halls and schools, including a school for women and academies for liturgical music and bell-ringing.

Musical life changed radically after the Revolution. Although Moscow grew as the centre of musical culture in the 1920s, in 1932 the Composers' Union was founded to apply the strictures of Socialist Realism. In a famous article denouncing Dmitry Shostakovich called "Muddle Instead of Music", the state made clear that "formalism", which meant any kind of innovative music, was not to be tolerated. It was only after Stalin's death that composers breathed more freely, and only after the 1980s that innovation was once again celebrated.

The finest auditorium for classical music is the Great Hall of the Moscow Conservatory; the acoustics are sublime, and the performances are usually the best in the city. The Conservatory has two other spaces, the Small Hall and the Rakhmaninov Hall, that offer chamber concerts and performances by soloists, often young performers just starting out. The Tchaikovsky Concert Hall is home to the Moscow State Academic Philharmonic, and the venue of the Moscow Symphony Orchestra and a variety of musical and dance performances. The newest music hall is the Moscow International House of Music, which hosts a variety of festivals and performers; it is worth getting tickets to any performance that includes the hall's magnificent new organ.

Some of the best of Moscow's concerts are held in unexpected places. During the summer

---

THEATRE IN MOSCOW

Theatre has thrived in the city since the late 18th century. After a little over a century of academic and mannered performances, Stanislavsky and Nemirovich-Danchenko changed the world of Russian drama with their Moscow Art Theatre (MKhAT), and avant-garde writers, directors and actors changed it once again in the first decades of the 20th century. Throughout the Soviet period the training of actors was one of the finest in the world, producing several generations of brilliant actors – even if Soviet political and artistic conservatism severely limited the theatres' repertories. After a dip in the early post-Soviet period, when funding was hard to find, theatre life has

perked up, with fine productions in the classical repertory theatres like the Sovremennik, Lenkom, Theatre on Malaya Bronnaya, and the Moscow Art Theatre. The Taganka Theatre is no longer the cutting edge of drama that it was during the 1980s, but it still puts on interesting productions. The Maly Theatre is the most conservative theatre, and the place to see Ostrovsky's plays; for innovation, try the Fomenko Studio Theatre. If you don't know Russian, try seeing a play you know well, by Chekhov or Shakespeare, for example. Seeing the seagull-decorated curtain at the old Moscow Art Theatre is worth the price of admission alone.

the Arkhangelskoye, Tsaritsyno and Ostankino estates *(see pages 208, 195 and 166 respectively)* host chamber concerts in their elegant halls. When you visit small "house museums", enquire about concerts: the apartments where Chaliapin, Aleksey Tolstoy, Chekhov, Skriabin and other notables lived are now the venue of chamber concerts throughout the year. Sometimes the performers are young or not top-caliber, but you can hear excellent performances of little-played works, such as 20th-century or baroque music, that don't draw large audiences, and the ambience in small halls a few steps from where Chekhov wrote his short stories or Skriabin composed his music is divine. Larger

jazz regularly. One of the best is the Sinaya Ptitsa (Blue Bird), which has been in the same location for more than 40 years and is packed to the rafters every night. Forte, Le Club and the Jazz Art Club can also be counted on to provide high-quality music.

For an evening of "urban folk songs" try one of the clubs specialising in bards, singer-songwriters who usually accompany themselves on guitar. The best of the cafés is the Nest of Wood Grouse across from the Conservatory.

For children of every age

If you have bad childhood associations with sad elephants and frightening sideshows, the

museums, such as the Tretyakov Gallery, the Pushkin Museum of Fine Arts and the Pushkin Literary Museum, also hold concerts in their halls, where you can listen to music surrounded by the world's finest works of art.

Popular music

The first jazz bands appeared in Moscow in 1922 and were hugely popular throughout Soviet times. They still enjoy a fanatical following, and more than a dozen clubs perform

Moscow Circus may help change your view of the Big Top. Either on the old stage on Tsvetnoy bulvar or the new stage on prospekt Vernadskovo, the shows are filled with dozens of exuberant short acts, from trapeze artists to trained yaks, at a level of artistry that makes it seem like another art form. If you don't object to performing animals, try the circus at Durov's Circle, where performers range from rats to a hippo, or the odd House of Cats, where the trainers have convinced felines to perform tricks and routines without blinking at the shouts and applause of the audience. The Obraztsov Puppet Theatre is another delight that requires little knowledge of Russian. ❑

LEFT: more Broadway-style performances are making it onto Moscow's elite stages.
ABOVE: the Great Hall of the Moscow Conservatory.

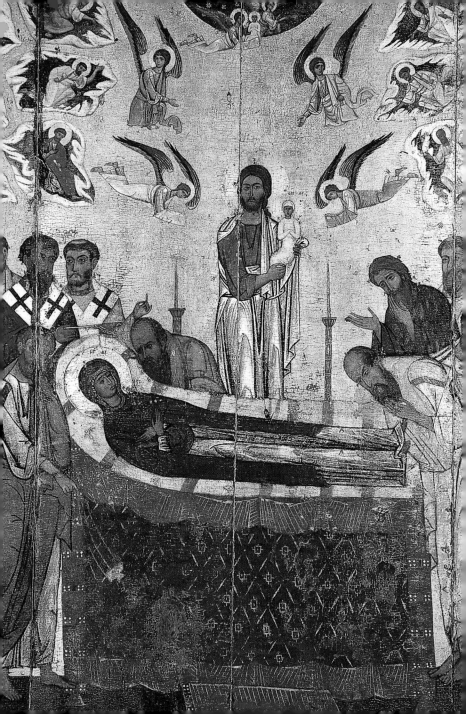

UNRAVELLING THE RUSSIAN ORTHODOX CHURCH

At the heart of Moscow's culture is its historic role as the seat of the Russian Orthodox Church. The religious past and the significance of its contemporary symbols are explored here by William Craft Brumfield, a leading scholar of the Russian Church and its architecture

The art of the Russian Orthodox Church is one of the great achievements of Russian culture. Any visit to Moscow can be enhanced by a perception of this art. Most churches are open throughout the day and may be entered for contemplation of Russia's cultural and spiritual legacy in sacred art.

Moscow has many religions and faiths, and all have their places of worship. Catholic and Protestant churches, synagogues, mosques and other prayer houses coexist and contribute to the city's vibrant urban mix. By far the major religious presence, however, is the Russian Orthodox Church, headed by Patriarch Aleksey II. From the time of the acceptance of Orthodox Christianity by Prince Vladimir of Kiev in 988, the Orthodox Church has remained the leading religious presence among the eastern Slavs and has had a profound impact not only on Russian religious life, but also on the arts, on society – indeed, on virtually every aspect of Muscovite and Russian culture. Although relations between Moscow and the Orthodox Church have at times been troubled (to say the least), the extent of Moscow's power has rested in no small measure on the Church.

Following the fragmentation of Kievan Rus and the invasion by Mongol Tatars in 1237, Moscow began its gradual, methodical rise to power among the ruins left by the Mongols. In 1325 the leading Church prelate, Metro-

LEFT: the "dormition" or "sleeping" of the Virgin Mary (12th–13th century).
RIGHT: a worshipper places a votive candle before an icon in the church.

politan Peter of Vladimir, made the Moscow Kremlin his de facto residence, and, the following year, under Ivan Kalita, or "Moneybags", the foundation was laid for the Kremlin's first stone cathedral, dedicated to the Dormition of the Mother of God.

With the patriarchate established in the Kremlin, the increasingly militant Orthodox Church, which had long accepted the authority of the Mongol Horde, played a major part in rallying Russian forces around the banner of Moscow in a crusade against the Tatars.

In Constantinople, it was not just the Turks who threatened the independence of the Byzantine Church. In 1439 it finally agreed to unite with the Roman Catholic Church (the Union of Florence) on terms that reflected doctrinal concessions and an acceptance of the authority of the Pope. Isidore, the Metropolitan of Russia and an appointee of Constantinople, supported the union, but a number of the accompanying Russian delegates in Florence refused. This faction succeeded in rejecting the union and in expelling Isidore from Russia. By repudiation of the authority of the Patriarch in Constantinople, the Russian Church had become autocephalous. The fall of Constantinople to the Turks in 1453 further increased the isolation of Russian Orthodoxy, and reinforced the mission of Muscovy as defender of the Orthodox faith.

This sense of Moscow as the sole independent Orthodox power was consolidated during the reign of Ivan III (1462–1505), who supported a major rebuilding of the Kremlin cathedrals and walls, hiring a number of Italian architects, among whom the most notable was Alberti Fioravanti, who undertook the rebuilding of the the Cathedral of the Dormition in the Kremlin.

Structure and meaning

Although Fioravanti fundamentally reconstructed the Dormition Cathedral from the foundation trenches to the cupolas, its general form follows a pattern inherited from Byzan-

---

AN IMPORTANT DISTINCTION

Western publications often refer to the Kremlin's Cathedral of the Dormition of the Mother of God in the Catholic manner as the Assumption of the Virgin. But the dormition or "falling asleep" of the Virgin describes her death, three days before her "assumption" into heaven. Catholics only celebrate the Assumption of Mary, Orthodox icons and churches are dedicated to her passing.

---

tine culture and indicative of the relation between structure and meaning in the design of the church. The Dormition Cathedral has five cupolas, but whether a church has one or many, the main cupola is always placed above a cylinder – also known as a drum – at the centre of the church. The holy of holies is the apse sanctuary with the altar, which is situated at the east end of the structure.

The main altar of a church is dedicated to a sacred figure or event in the calendar, such as the Dormition of the Mother of God. It is this consecration that gives a church its name. Thus every church dedication has its date in the religious calendar, and the day allotted to this dedication is also that church's main festival day.

The Dormition Cathedral displays in grand form the Russian Orthodox practice of painting the walls and ceiling vaults with scenes from the Bible and the lives of the saints. The interior of the main dome traditionally has an image of Christ Pantocrator (Ruler of All), while above the altar the apse is devoted to an image of Mary Mother of God standing in a pose that indicates a blessing extended to the worshippers. The altar is screened from the laity by an icon stand, or iconostasis. This is the general pattern of meaning that integrates building and sacred image in Russian Orthodox churches.

The design of most parish churches in Moscow is a modification of the earlier, rectangular structures exemplified by the Kremlin cathedrals. During the expansion of church construction for Moscow's parishes in the 17th century, there evolved a new form known as the "ship". In this plan the church consists of a cuboid main structure with an extension (the apse) for the altar at the east end, a low vestibule *(trapeza)* attached to the west, and, attached to the vestibule, a bell tower culminating in a "tent" (conical) tower. The bell tower in the west can be seen as the "prow" of the ship, providing a counterpoint to the "sails", represented by the usual five cupolas, which are often gilded or decorated with bright metal stars. From the 17th century, hundreds of such churches were built throughout Russia.

Entering the church

Despite the apparently endless variety of artistic detail, the plan underlying each church is readily comprehensible. The entrance is in most cases from the west, usually through a passage on the ground floor of the bell tower. (In some churches the bell tower

contains its subsidiary altars, where baptisms and memorial services are held. Each of these altars has its own dedication to a sacred figure or church holiday, and each has its own icon screen. In addition to the altars, the vestibule can have separate icons placed against the wall or pillars, with a stand for votive candles.

In most churches the passage from the vestibule, with relatively low ceiling vaults, to the main space of the church produces a dramatic impression. Once again, structure provides insight into sacred meaning in the central part of the temple, with its brighter illumination, its rows of wall-paintings and the high vaults that rise above the richly carved

itself will have an altar, or chapel, above the entrance.) Proper attire and behavior are expected from anyone entering an active church, and this includes acceptable head covering for women and modest dress.

Passing through the main portal, you will enter the space of the vestibule, which typically is dimly lit and aglow with the light of votive candles. To the side of the entrance is a counter where devotional literature and votive candles are sold. The vestibule also usually

and painted icon screen. It is with the icon screen that the visual message of the church achieves its greatest concentration. The icons serve as a conduit of spiritual power and meaning from the realm of the divine.

Reading the icons

In the early medieval period the icons in front of the altar presumably stood in a single row or a low configuration, thus allowing worshippers to see the image of Mary Mother of God (Theotokos) rising from the apse. But probably by the 15th century the Russian Church had developed a complex ranking of icons that placed the world of faith in an

LEFT: inside St Nicholas of the Weavers.
ABOVE: painted pillars and iconastasis of the Cathedral of the Dormition.

immediately visible hierarchy. And while the multitude of images may overwhelm the first-time visitor, the system underlying the iconostasis is readily accessible.

At the centre of the **first row** (known as the **Local Row**) are the Royal Gates, the passage used by the priests between the main part of the church and the altar. The top of the Royal Gates contains a depiction of the Annunciation (the Archangel Gabriel announcing to Mary the conception of Christ), beneath which are four panels – one for each of the Evangelists, Matthew, Mark, Luke and John. The space above the Royal Gates will often have a representation of the Last Supper.

The images of the Local Row are among the largest in the iconostasis. The central Royal Gates are flanked by icons of Christ the Saviour (on the viewer's right) and Mary Mother of God. The Local Row also contains the icon of the saint or holiday to which the church is dedicated. This dedicatory icon is located to the right of the Royal Gates.

In some cases the church is dedicated to a miraculous icon, such as the Kazan Icon of the Mother of God, which is a particularly revered image of Mary and the Christ child. Visitors are often confused by the presence of a "Kazan Church" on Red Square. Kazan, after all, is a distant city on the Volga River. In fact, this is

OLD BELIEVERS

In the 17th century, Patriarch Nikon approved changes to Russian Orthodox liturgical texts and practices. Today the changes seem minor: a different way of spelling Jesus and making the sign of the cross with three fingers, not two. But millions of Russian Christians rejected the changes as a break with sacred tradition, and the church split, with the Old Believers persecuted by Church and state. The Old Believers also divided; some lived outside society, much like the Amish in the US; others, like the Ryabunshinsky banking family and Morozov textile magnates, lived within society, but with a tradition of industriousness that made them immensely rich.

the shortened, popular Russian name for churches dedicated to the Theotokos of Kazan, or Kazan Icon of the Mother of God.

The Local Row is completed with other icons that are of special importance to the local parish. Each side of the Local Row has an additional door. The one on the north side (to the viewer's left) leads to the *prothesis*, which is used for the preparation of the sacraments. The one on the south side leads to the *diakonikon*, used by the deacons for the preparation of vestments.

The **second row** of the icon screen is known as the **Deesis** ("prayer" or "supplication") **Row**, which is the most significant part of the icon screen in theological terms. At its centre is an image of Christ enthroned, with Mary Mother of God at his right hand (the viewer's left) and John the Baptist on his left. Beyond Mary stand Archangel Michael and Apostle Peter, while Archangel Gabriel and Apostle Paul are at the side of John the Baptist. The Deesis Row concludes on either side with figures of prelates and Church fathers, whose number can vary with the size of the iconostasis. The heads of all the figures in this row are bowed towards Christ in a posture of reverence and supplication (hence the name "Deesis"). The icons are particularly elongated, thus increasing the height and the number of figures portrayed in prayer to the central figure of Christ.

In most churches the **third row** of the icon screen is the **Festival Row**, although in a few cases the position of the Deesis and Festival rows is switched. The Festival Row is distinguished by the fact that all of the icons within it are of square format, in contrast to the elongated, rectangular icons in the other rows. This row contains depictions of the 12 major festivals of the Russian Orthodox Church (*see page 223*). Most of these are celebrated on fixed days in the Church calendar and are known as Immovable Feasts. Those related to Easter, however, do not have fixed dates and are known as Movable Feasts. It should be noted that the Russian Orthodox Church adheres to the Julian calendar, which is 13 days behind the Gregorian calendar generally in use throughout the world.

The **fourth row** is dedicated to the Old Testament Prophets, such as Isaiah, Jeremiah, Ezekiel and Daniel. The centre of **Prophets' Row** is usually occupied by an image of Mary Mother of God holding the Christ Child in the form known as "the Sign" (*znamenie*). In the Russian Orthodox Church this central figure is interpreted as the ultimate goal of Old Testament prophecy.

The **fifth row** (sometimes absent in smaller churches) contains icons of the Old Testament Patriarchs from the Book of Genesis, and usually includes Adam, Seth, Noah, Abraham, Isaac and Jacob. The centre of this row can be occupied by an image of God the Father, or

by a depiction of the Old Testament Trinity, the three angels that visited Abraham on the Plains of Mamre. This icon is particularly revered as a prophecy of the miraculous birth of Christ. If the church is dedicated to the Trinity, this icon will also be found in the Local Row.

The culminating point of the icon screen is a painted crucifix with an image of Christ. (In some churches the figure of Christ above the iconostasis is carved, although the Orthodox Church frowns upon sculpted images.) A similar, free-standing crucifix can often be found in the church, to the left of the iconostasis.

Wall and ceiling frescoes

The interior walls of most Russian Orthodox churches are covered with wall-paintings, usually in the fresco technique, that amplify the depictions of the sacred world. These are arranged in rows of scenes rising to the ceiling vaults. Although certain important scenes from the life of Christ are virtually mandatory, the choice of scenes will depend on the dedication of the church itself. In large churches with piers or columns these structural elements will also be painted with images of saints and archangels.

The west wall of the main space of the church is reserved for a depiction of the Last Judgement. ❑

LEFT: St George, by Andrei Rublev (c.1360–1430).
RIGHT: St Nicholas of Zaraisk, also by Rublev.

BOOM TIME FOR THE CITY BUILDERS

Mayor Luzhkov's drive tries to reconcile God and Mammon

Moscow is in the midst of an unprecedented building boom that is doing more to alter the face of the city than either the post-1812 rebuild or the sweeping Stalin plans of the 1930s that poduced monster boulevards and squares. The process has been accelerating ever since private businesses starting operating in the capital in 1991. Behind all the massive construction works is Yuri Luzhkov *(pictured above with the Patriarch of Moscow and all Russia, Aleksey II)*. Elected mayor in 1992 and involved in many of the schemes that are said to have helped his own personal fortune, Luzhkov is known as the city's "mayor-builder" and is renowned for his endless energy. Under his watchful eye, street signs have been installed, roads built, churches that had been demolished under Stalin rebuilt, and the forest of temporary "train wagon" kiosks set up by the initial entrepreneurs replaced by stores.

Conservationists complain that rare pre-Revolutionary buildings have been knocked down to make way for faceless office buildings and elite apartment houses. Some 500 buildings from the 17th to 19th centuries have been identified as being lost. Building contracts have also raised a few eyebrows. Companies owned by the mayor's wife have an estimated 20 percent of the city construction market, and according to *Forbes* magazine, she herself is one of Moscow's 30-plus resident billionaires. Insiders claim that building regulations can be ignored for the right price.

But allegations of corruption bother few Muscovites, who are proud of the modern new mien of their city.

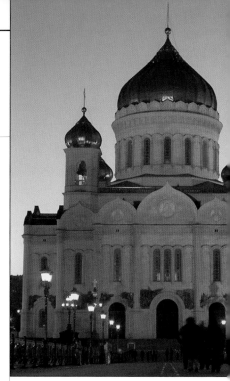

ABOVE: on Stalin's orders, the Cathedral of Christ the Saviour was dynamited in 1931 and the desolated site eventually became a swimming pool. In 1992 rebuilding began, and within eight years the largest Orthodox church in the world was reconsecrated.

ABOVE: making repairs on Arbat shopping street. Lacking quaint shopping quarters or lanes, retail action in Moscow is on the main streets. At first, private businesses built stands in the cavernous lobbies of Soviet-era buildings, put up retail "train wagons" by metro stations and built flimsy structures on empty squares. Today it is profitable to turn ground-floor housing space into shops and cafés.

MASTER OF MONUMENTAL ART

One of the most visible artists working in Moscow today is Zurab Tsereteli, president of the Moscow Academy of Arts. His favoured line of work is monumental sculptures, and his designs include the ostentatious monument to Peter the Great *(left)*, which is not much liked by Muscovites, who find it overpowers the narrow stretch of the Moscow River.

Born in Georgia in 1934, Tsereteli has his own gallery in Moscow and has made a number of scupltures commemorating World War II leaders *(see below)*. His work extends beyond Russia, and he has been appointed a Goodwill Ambassador for Unesco. *Good Defeats Evil*, his large bronze peace statue, was unveiled outside the United Nations building in New York in 1990. In 2006 his memorial to the victims of the September 11 attack on New York's Twin Towers will be erected on the peninsula of Bayonne harbour, New Jersey. The 30-metre (99-ft) bronze contains a single stainless-steel tear.

BELOW: since 1991 scaffolding has been a common site in Red Square. Kazan Cathedral and the 16th-century Resurrection Gates to the square were both torn down by Stalin in the 1930s but have now been fully restored under Mayor Luzhkov. Stalin also had the bright idea to blow up the inimitable St Basil's Cathedral "because it hindered automobile movement across the square", but his plan came to nothing.

BELOW: Zurab Tsereteli with his sculpture of World War II allies Churchill, Roosevelt and Stalin at the 1945 Yalta Conference, where it was agreed to divide Europe between the Soviet and Western spheres of influence. The statue was made in 2005 to mark the 60th anniversary of the Soviet victory in the terrible battle of Stalingrad, now Volgograd, and is pictured at the artist's personal museum in Moscow. At the same time a statue of another allied leader, Charles de Gaulle, was erected outside the Kosmos Hotel.

ARCHITECTURE

The glistening onion domes of Moscow's skyline symbolise
the city, but they are just part of a monumental heritage.
Walking the streets, you will find a vibrant mix of styles –
from neoclassical to the fabulous examples of
style moderne, Russian Revival and Constructivism

The architecture of Moscow has its origins
in the architectural traditions of the
medieval state of Kievan Rus. These traditions were themselves derived from the
Byzantine Empire and, in particular, the Eastern Orthodox Church, which became the
accepted religion in 988.

Little more than a log fort and trading settlement on the site of the Kremlin, Moscow
was quickly rebuilt after being burned during
the Mongol invasion in 1237, and gradually
increased its territory. But enduring stone
buildings were not constructed until the 15th
century. The earliest surviving architectural
monument is the Cathedral of the Icon of the
Saviour Not Made by Hands, located within
the Saviour-Andronikov Monastery. Built at
some point between 1410 and 1427, the church
was endowed by a Moscow merchant family,
the Yermolins, and was the most ornamental to
be found throughout Muscovy at that time.

Italian masters

Although this and other limestone churches
indicate a modest architectural revival during
the first half of the 15th century, it was not
until the latter part of the century that major
monuments began to appear in the Kremlin
under the direction of Italian masters imported
during the long and successful reign of Ivan
III (the Great). The first was the Dormition
Cathedral (1475–9) by Alberti Fioravanti, who
introduced both a rigorously geometric plan
and technical improvements such as deep
foundation trenches with oak pilings, strong
brick for the vaulting and iron tie-rods. The

interior, devoid of a choir gallery and with
round columns, is spacious and well lit.

Brick soon displaced limestone for most
masonry construction. Aleviz Novy used it in
his Cathedral of the Archangel Michael
(1505–9), which had a number of Italianate
elements. Italian influence also appeared in
Bon Fryazin and Pietro Antonio Solari's
design of the Facated Palace (1487–91), and
in the Kremlin walls and towers (1485–1516)
built by Antonio Fryazin, Marco Ryazin,
Solari and others. (The distinctive Kremlin
tower spires were added by Russian builders
in the 17th century.) The dominant element of
the Kremlin, the Bell Tower of Ivan the Great,

was constructed in two stages, the lower two tiers in 1505–8 by Bon Fryazin and the upper tier with cupola in 1599–1600, during the reign of Boris Godunov.

During the 16th century, Moscow's brick-tower churches, designed as votive offerings, displayed boldly inventive designs and a continued Italian influence. The first of these great monuments is the Church of the Ascension at Kolomenskoye, commissioned by Vasily III in 1529 as a votive offering for the birth of his heir, Ivan IV. The church is of unprecedented height, culminating in an elongated brick conical roof (the *shatyor*, or "tent" roof) rather than the traditional cupolas.

The distinctive impression of the Church of the Ascension was intensified by its site on a steep bank above the Moscow River with a dramatic view of the princely domains. Its location in the middle of a compound of wooden structures, including a large palace of haphazard form (burned in 1571 and twice rebuilt), created an ensemble whose silhouette was richer than today's surviving masonry monuments that stand in isolation.

The walls of the Church of the Ascension, which rest on massive brick vaults reinforced with iron tie-rods, are between 2.5 and 3 metres (8–10 ft) thick, and are further supported by the buttressing effect of the cruciform plan. The raised terrace, originally without a roof, girding the lower part of the church is reached by three staircases, each with a perpendicular turn that would have increased the visual drama of ritual processions. The main block of the tower, edged with massive pilasters, leads upward to three tiers of pointed *kokoshniki* (decorated arches) whose design is echoed in the cornice of the octagon. From this point the "tent" ascends, with eight facets delineated by limestone ribs. The tower concludes with an octagonal lantern, a cupola and, at 58 metres (190 ft), a cross.

The chapel-churches

Within two decades of the completion of the Church of the Ascension at Kolomenskoye, Vasily III's heir, Ivan IV (r.1533–84), had commissioned another dynastic votive structure, the Church of the Decapitation of John the Baptist, at the nearby village of Dyakovo. The symmetrical arrangement of small churches around the central tower here – all resting on the same base – is the most intriguing feature of the church. Following the example of his father, Ivan and his clerics dedicated the separate altars as an affirmation of the personal relation between the tsar and the deity. These ancillary chapel-churches are part of a highly integrated design that reproduces the central tower form at the four corners of a square base. This concept would soon be elaborated at the greatest of Russian

churches, the Cathedral of the Intercession on the Moat, known as St Basil's.

Located on Red Square, the Cathedral of the Intercession (1555–61) has come to epitomise the extravagance of the Moscow imagination. The notorious character of Ivan IV (the Terrible), who built the Cathedral to commemorate his taking of the Tatar city of Kazan in 1552, and the savagery of the latter part of his reign have fostered the notion of a structure devoid of restraint or reason. Yet the builders, traditionally identified as Barma and Postnik Yakovlev (the latter from the city of Pskov), created a coherent, logical plan. The Cathedral of the Intercession consists of

LEFT: the reconstruction of the Cathedral of Christ the Saviour in the 1990s.

RIGHT: Church of the Decapitation of John the Baptist.

a central tower dedicated to the Intercession of the Mother of God and flanked by ancillary, free-standing churches – each with its own dedication – in an alternating pattern of major and minor forms: major at the compass points and minor on the diagonal. The four octagonal churches at the compass points repeat the octagonal motif at the base of the plan and in the drum and "tent" roof of the central tower. The four smaller churches are cuboid, surmounted by a cupola and round drum raised on three tiers of *kokoshniki*. The height of their onion domes is measured to complement those of the alternating, larger churches. Within this interplay of tower

Romanov revival

Although the end of the 16th century witnessed the expansion of Moscow's monasteries and fortresses, other construction declined, as an exhausted country tried to recover from the depredations of Ivan's reign, only to be followed in 1604 with an interregnum known as the "Time of Troubles", which led to chaos throughout the realm. With the establishment of the Romanov dynasty in 1613, the country began a recovery that was reflected in a marked increase in church construction during the long reign of Aleksey Mikhailovich (1645–76).

Of the many Moscow parish churches that date from this period, the most notable is the

forms, the silhouette of the Cathedral gives remarkably different impressions of its shape, depending on the approach and perspective of the viewer. Like much great architecture, the Cathedral includes a calculated distortion: the central tower is not in the geometric centre of the plan but is shifted substantially westward to allow the addition of an apse with the main altar. To accommodate this shift, the small churches on the west side are reduced to a size only large enough to contain a few worshippers. Thus, seen from the north or south, the Cathedral has a dual centre: that of the tower itself and that of the structure as a whole.

Church of the Trinity in Nikitniki, located in the commercial district known as Kitai-gorod. Endowed by the wealthy merchant Grigory Nikitnikov, the Trinity Church exemplifies the elaborate exterior decoration favoured by merchant patrons. Relatively modest in size, the church consists of a central cube decorated with carved limestone window surrounds (*nalichnik*), rows of *kokoshniki*, and five cupolas, four of which are purely decorative; they admit no light. After its completion in 1634, over the next two decades the original structure acquired two chapels, attached at the northeast and southeast and an enclosed gallery leading to a bell tower with a "tent" roof on the northwest corner. This is the earliest example of the placement of a bell tower within the church ensemble – a practice that would become generally accepted in parish architecture during the 17th century.

Indeed, despite its decorative effusions, 17th-century church architecture achieved a measure of stability through the evolution of a basic plan known as the "ship", consisting of a cuboid main structure with a low spacious apse for the altar at the east end, a low vestibule *(trapeza)* attached to the west, and, attached to the vestibule, a bell tower culminating in a "tent" tower. This tower provided a counterpoint to the "sails" of the ship – its

Naryshkin and Sheremetev families on estates in and around Moscow. Notable examples of the "Naryshkin baroque" style, such as the Church of the Intercession at Fili (1690–9) and the Church of the Trinity at Troitskoye-Lykovo (1698–1703), show a revival of the tower form,

five cupolas, usually gilded or decorated with bright metal stars. An excellent example of this design is the Church of St Nicholas the Wonderworker in Khamovniki but this is only one of dozens of such churches throughout Moscow.

As Russia experienced increased contact with the West during the latter half of the 17th century, the influence of Ukrainian, Polish and Central European architecture appeared in churches commissioned primarily by the

often elevated above a quatrefoil terrace. The 17th century also witnessed the use of brick for residences *(palaty)*, a number of which are still preserved in areas of central Moscow such as Kitai-gorod and the Kremlin itself.

The assimilation of Western architectural styles increased dramatically with the reign of Peter the Great. Of course the founding of St Petersburg in 1703 meant that most construction activity was shifted to what would soon become the new Russian capital, but new approaches to architecture also reached Moscow. A curious example is the Church of the Archangel Gabriel (1701–7), also known as the Menshikov Tower.

LEFT: detail of Menshikov Tower and the restoration of a fresco.
ABOVE: the Church of St Nicholas in Khamovniki.

Neoclassical estates

During the reign of Catherine the Great, neoclassicism appeared in the design not only of numerous churches but also of houses and other institutions built by the nobility and wealthy merchants. Talented serf builders erected many of the grand estate houses, and the most prominent neoclassical architects in Moscow were Matvey Kazakov, Rodion Kazakov and Vasily Bazhenov. During Catherine's reign, period styles such as Gothic Revival entered the work of Bazhenov and Matvey Kazakov.

In the 1770s–80s Bazhenov and Kazakov were also involved in the building of a "Moor-

ish" Gothic Revival imperial estate at Tsaritsyno, but Catherine abandoned the project.

After the fire of 1812, damaged landmarks such as Bazhenov's Pashkov House and Kazakov's Moscow University – both facing the west wall of the Kremlin – were rebuilt, while new houses appeared in the Empire style as interpreted by Dominco Gilardi, Osip Bove and Afanasy Grigoriev. Many of these neoclassical buildings still grace sections of central Moscow.

During the 1830s the waning influence of neoclassicism made way for various historicist styles, such as Konstantin Ton's Great Kremlin Palace (1838–49) and his Cathedral of

Christ the Saviour (1818–58; destroyed in 1931; rebuilt in the 1990s). Secular architecture in the latter half of the 19th century was largely an eclectic combination of various periods in Western architecture. Eclectic decorative styles were applied profusely to the façades of apartment houses and commercial buildings.

Russian Revival and *style moderne*

By the 1870s there arose a new national style based on decorative elements from 16th- and 17th-century Muscovy, as well as on motifs from folk art and traditional wooden architecture. Major examples of this Russian Revival style in Moscow include the Historical Museum (1874–83), built on the north side of Red Square to a design by Vladimir Shervud, the adjacent Moscow City Hall (Duma, 1890–2), built by Dmitry Chichagov, and the Upper Trading Rows (now known as GUM, 1889–93), by Alexander Pomerantsev.

The Russian Revival style also characterised many mansions and apartment buildings, and its influence continued through the early 1900s in the "neo-Russian" component of *style moderne*, Russia's art nouveau. Painters such as Viktor Vasnetsov, who created the entrance building at the Tretyakov Gallery (*c.*1905) and Sergey Malyutin, who designed the Pertsov apartment house (1905–7) opposite the Cathedral of Christ the Saviour, were particularly active in using traditional Russian decorative arts as part of a new architectural aesthetic.

Style moderne displayed a number of stylistic tendencies in Russian architecture at the turn of the 20th century. Its primary emphasis was on the innovative use of materials such as glass, iron, and glazed brick in designs that were both functional and receptive to the applied arts. The style flourished above all in Moscow, where its main patrons came from the merchant elite. Its leading practitioner, Fyodor Shekhtel, is known for such landmarks as Yaroslavl station (1902), the house for Stepan Pavlovich Ryabushinsky (1900–2; now the Gorky Museum) and his modernist design for the mansion of Alexandra Derozhinskaya (1901; now the Australian Embassy residence). Other leading modernist architects of the period include Lev Kekushev, Adolf Erikhson and William Walcot. All three were involved in the prolonged construction of one of the largest and most significant *style moderne* buildings in Moscow: the Hotel Metropol (1899–1905). Like Shekhtel, both Kekushev and Walcot designed houses in the modern style for wealthy clients. These houses still grace the central part of Moscow, and many of them are now used as embassies.

By the end of the 1900s, *style moderne* had yielded to or merged with a modernised form of neoclassicism. In Moscow this neoclassical revival is best represented by the work of Roman Klein, who designed the Museum of Fine Arts (1897–1912; now the Pushkin Museum) and the Muir and Mirrielees emporium (1906–8; now known as TsUM). The latter was the first modern department store in Moscow and its functional frame was clad in gothic revival elements. Although less prolific than Klein, other architects designed in a more austere variant of the neoclassical revival for major office buildings that still function in Moscow's traditional commercial centre.

Utopia and the Constructivists

The economic chaos engendered in Russia by World War I, the 1917 Revolution and the ensuing Civil War proved catastrophic for building activity. However, with the limited recovery of the economy in the 1920s, bold new designs, often utopian in concept, brought Russia to the attention of modern architects throughout the world. Constructivism, the most productive modernist movement, included architects such as Moysey Ginzburg, Ilya Golosov, Grigory Barkhin, Aleksey Shchusev and the Vesnin brothers Leonid, Viktor and Alexander. Their work set a standard for streamlined, functional design in Moscow's administrative and apartment buildings, as well as in social institutions such as workers' clubs. Unfortunately, many of these buildings stand in a state of disrepair that belie their importance to the international modern movement. Another modernist architect active during the same period, but not a part of Constructivism, was Konstantin Melnikov, creator of designs for workers' clubs, transport structures and exposition pavilions.

During the 1930s more conservative trends asserted themselves, as designs inspired by neoclassical, Renaissance and historicist models received the approval of the Communist leadership. Moscow's most prominent architectural traditionalists during the 1930s were Ivan Zholtovsky and the versatile Aleksey Shchusev.

After World War II, architectural design became still more firmly locked in traditional, often highly ornate eclectic styles epitomised by the post-war skyscrapers that still define the cityscape, from Moscow State University to the apartment building on Kotelnicheskaya Embankment.

After the death of Stalin in 1953, pressing social needs – above all in housing – led to the development of "micro-regions" composed of standardised apartment blocks with prefabricated components. Most Muscovites live in such regions, served by an extensive transport system linked by the unparalleled Moscow metro. Many underground stations are significant works of architectural design.

With the demise of Communism, entrepreneurial developers and the revival of private practices are changing the face of Moscow. Whether design excellence will appear in the proliferation of office and residential towers is a question yet to be answered. ❑

LEFT: the Historical Museum, in Russian Revival style.
RIGHT: *style moderne* buildings have a wealth of fine details – such as these doors at the Moscow Art Theatre.

PLACES

A detailed guide to the entire city with the
principal sites clearly cross-referenced
by number to the maps

The riches of Moscow's city centre are haphazardly scattered. Regardless of which part of the city you choose to explore, you are sure to find art museums; "house-museums" that preserve the lives of legendary writers, actors and theatre directors; historic churches and monasteries; first-rate theatres; and shops filled with everything from rye bread to the latest fashions.

This wide dispersion of attractions bears out the base vision of Soviet planners. Pre-Revolutionary neighbourhoods, with their winding medieval streets and historic buildings, were bisected or destroyed by the authorities who craved broad, straight boulevards built to accommodate tanks more than comrades, and believed society functioned better in communal apartments than along café-lined streets.

Only the heart of the city still falls into self-contained sections: the Kremlin – with breathtaking cathedrals and imperial treasures in its museums; Red Square and Kitai-gorod – the most ancient trading area of the city with magnificent trading houses; and Theatre and Manege Squares that include some of the city's finest theatres, hotels, shops and exhibition spaces.

The area to the southeast of the Kremlin, described in the chapter Classic Art and Old Arbat, is a must-see for lovers of art, with four major museums – including the Pushkin Museum of Fine Art with its extraordinary collection of European masterpieces – and Moscow's best little street, Old Arbat. Two more world-class museums, the Old and New Tretyakov Galleries, which have brilliant collections of Russian art, lie beyond the Moscow River.

Be sure to stroll up Tverskaya ulitsa, Moscow's main drag, and slip into courtyards to see what treasures have remained from centuries past or what flashy nightclub has just opened. To the north, revisit the Soviet past at the Museum of Cosmonauts.

Wherever you go you'll see that Moscow is redesigning itself. New neighbourhoods may have yet to take hold, but since communal flats have become individually owned, society has returned to its natural, European home – the café-lined street.   ❏

PRECEDING PAGES: Moscow State University's campus in Sparrow Hills.
The Cathedral of Christ the Saviour. LEFT: ice begins to float down the
Moscow River as Russia's harsh winter sets in.

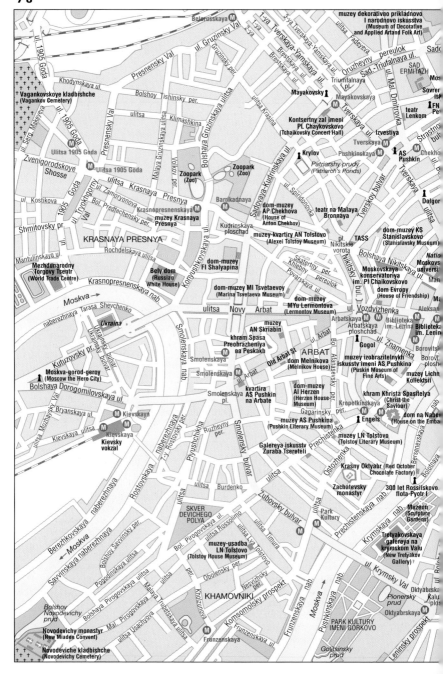

7 8

muzey dekorativno prikladnovo
I narodnovo iskusstva
(Museum of Decorative
and Applied Artand Folk Art)

Belorusskaya

ul. Gruzinsky Val
ul. Gruzinsky per.
Presnensky Val

1-ya Tverskaya-Yamskaya ul.
1-ya Tverskaya-Yamskaya ul.
2-ya
Brestskaya per.
Bol. Bresteskaya ul.

Oruzheyny pereulok
Sad.-Triufalnaya ul.
ulitsa Fadeyeva

SAD
ERMITAZH

Khodynskaya ul.
Vagankovskoye kladbishche
(Vagankov Cemetery)
ul. Sergia Makeeva

Bolshoy Tishinsky per.

Triumfalnaya
pl.

Mayakovsky

Mayakovskaya

teatr
Lenkom

Sovrem
isk

ul. 1905 Goda

ulitsa Klimashkina

Bolshaya Gruzinskaya ulitsa

ulitsa Krasina

Kontsertny zal imeni
PI. Chaykovskovo
(Tchaikovsky Concert Hall)

Tverskaya ul.

Izvestiya

Tverskaya

FN
Pe

Zvenigorodskoye
Shosse
Ulitsa 1905 Goda
Ulitsa 1905 Goda

ul. 1905 Goda
Malaya gruzinsky per.
Volkov per.

Krylov

Pushkinskaya

AS
Pushkin

Chekho

ul. Kostikova
ulitsa Krasnaya Presnya
ul. Zamoryonova
Bol. Trryokhgorny
ul. Zamoryonova

Zoopark
(Zoo)

Zoopark
(Zoo)

Sadovaya-Kudrinskaya ul.
ul. Spiridonovka

Patriarshy prudy
(Patriarch's Ponds)

Strastno
bul

Tverskoy bulvar

Dolgor

Shmitovsky pr.
1905 Goda

Krasnopresnenskaya

muzey Krasnaya
Presnya

Barrikadnaya

dom-muzey
AP Chekhova
(House of
Anton Chekhov)

Kudrinskaya
ploschad

teatr na Malaya
Bronnaya

pl.
Nikitskie
vorota

TASS

dom-muzey KS
Stanislavskovo
(Stanislavsky Museum)

KRASNAYA PRESNYA

Rochdelskaya ulitsa

Mantulinskaya ul.

Mezhdunarodny
Torgovy Tsentr
(World Trade Centre)

muzey-kvartira AN Tolstovo
(Alexei Tolstoy Museum)

dom-muzey
FI Shalyapina

Bely dom
(Russian
White House)

Konyushkovskaya ul.

Skatertny per.
Khlebny pereulok
Povarskaya ul.

Bolshaya Nikitskaya ul.

Moskovskaya
konservatoriya
im. PI Chaikovskovo

Natio
Moskvs
universi

Man

Krasnopresnenskaya nab.

Moskva

naberezhnaya Tarasa Shevchenko

Ukraina

dom-muzey
MI Tsvetaevoy
(Marina Tsvetaeva Museum)

ulitsa Novy Arbat

dom-muzey
MYu Lermontova
(Lermontov Museum)

ul. Vozdvizhenka

dom-muzey
(House of Friendship)

Ma
Aleksan

muzey
AN Skriabin

Arbatskaya

Biblioteka
im. Lenina

Biblioteka
im. Lenin

Kutuzovsky pr.
Ukrainsky bulvar
Ukrainsky bulvar

khram Spasa
Preobrazheniya
na Peskakh

Old Arbat St

ul. Arbat

Arbatskaya
ploschad

Gogol

Znamenka

Borovits

Moskva-gorod-geroy
(Moscow the Hero City)

Smolenskaya

Smolenskaya

ARBAT

Bol. Afanasyevsky per.

muzey izobrazitelnykh
iskusstv imeni AS Pushkina
(Puskin Museum of
Fine Arts)

Borovi
plosh

Bolshaya Dorogomilovskaya ul.

Smolenskaya

dom Melnikova
(Melnikov House)

muzey Lichn
Kollektsii

Bryanskaya ul.

Kievskaya ulitsa

Kievskaya

Kievsky
vokzal

Smolenskaya
pl.

Smolenskaya nab.

kvartira
AS Pushkin
na Arbate

dom-muzey
AI Herzen
(Herzen House
Museum)

Gagarinsky per.

Kropotkinskaya

Engels

khram Khrista Spasitelya
(Christ the
Saviour)

dom na Naber
(House on the Emba

Rostovskaya naberezhnaya
3-y Rostovsky per.

Plyuschikha

Ruzheyny
per.

muzey AS Pushkina
(Pushkin Literary Museum)

Prechistenka

muzey LN Tolstovo
(Tolstoy Literary Museum)

Smolensky bulvar

Galereya iskusstv
Zuraba Tsereteli

Ostozhenka

Krasny Oktyabr (Red October
Chocolate Factory)

Berezhkovskaya naberezhnaya

Savvinskaya naberezhnaya

ulitsa Burdenko

Zubovsky bulvar

ulitsa

Park
Kultury

Zachatevsky
monastyr

Prechistenskaya nab.

Krymskaya nab.

300 let Rossiiskovo
flota-Pyotr I

Muzeon
(Sculpture
Gardens)

Moskva

Bolshaya Savvinskaya ulitsa

Pogodinskaya ulitsa

SKVER
DEVICHEGO
POLYA

ul. Pirogovskaya ul.
ulitsa Rossolimo

ulitsa Timura

Tretyakovskaya
galereya na
krymskom Valu
(New Tretyakov
Gallery)

Bolshoy
Novodevichy
prud

Novodevichy monastyr
(New Miaden Convent)

Novodeviche kladbishche
(Novodevichy Cemetery)

Bol. Pirogovskaya ulitsa
Mal. Pirogovskaya ulitsa
ulitsa Usachova

Malaya Trubetskaya ulitsa

muzey-usadba
LN Tolstovo
(Tolstoy House Museum)

Obolensky per.

KHAMOVNIKI

Kholzunova

Nesvizhsky
per.

Komsomolsky prospekt

Frunzenskaya

Frunzenskaya

Pushkinskaya nab.

Moskva

PARK KULTURY
IMENI GORKOVO

Golitsinsky
prud

ul. Krymsky Val

Oktyabrska

Pionersky
prud

Oktyabrskaya

Kalu
plos

Leninsky prospekt

Bol.

rstvenny akademichesky
lny teatr kukol
lov Puppet Theatre)

Kalanchyovskaya
ulitsa
Komsomolskaya
ploshchad

Komsomolskaya

Yaroslavsky
vokzal

Kazansky
vokzal

Bogoyavlensky Kafedralny
Sobor v Yelokhove
(Epiphany in Yelokhove)

vochnaya ul.
Sad. Sukharevskaya ul.

tnoy
ulvar
Tsvetnoy

Pr. Mira

1-y Kopyelsky per.

Bol. Spasskaya-Dukhovaya per.

ul. Mashy Poryvaevoy

Novoryazanskaya ulitsa

Sukharevskaya

Sukharevsky per.

Sadovaya-Spasskaya ul.

Krasne
Vorota

MYu
Lermontovu

Basmannaya

ulitsa

Spartakovskaya

kovsky tsirk
. Nikulina
cow Circus)

Daev

ul.

per.

Sretenka

Kalanchyovskaya ul.

Novaya

Sad.-Chernogryazskaya

Staraya Basmannaya ulitsa

Yokhakov

Denisovsky per.

Trubnaya

Uiansky per.

Pr. Akad. Sakharova

Krasnye
Vorota

Zemlyanoy per.

Gorokhovsky per.

ulitsa Radio

r Trubnaya
ploshchad

Krupskaya

Myasnitskaya ulitsa

Furmanny per.

ul. Kazakova

akademika Tupoleva

Bogoroditse-
Rozhdestveny
monastyr

Turgenevskaya

Chistye Prudy

Kharitonevsky per.

muzey-kvartira
AM Vasnetsova
(Apollari Vasnetsov
Museum)

Velizavetinsky per.

Sandunovsky bani
(Sanduny Bath House)

Glavpochshtamp
(Main Post Office)

Griboedov

Staraya

Bol. Lubyanka

Menshikova bashnya
(Menshikov's Tower)

muzey istorii gorodskovo
osveshcheniya

Chistye prudy
(Clean Ponds)

nab. akademika Tupoleva

Petrovsky
Passazh

Kuznetsky
Most

Isforiko-
Demonstratsionny
Zal FSB Rossii

Ogni Moskvy
(Fires of Moscow)

Pokrovka

Kurskaya

TsUM

Detsky
Mir

Lubyanka

Armyansky per.

Figurny dom
("Figured House")

ulitsa

Pokrovsky bul.

Kursky
vokzal

PARK IM.
1 MAY

Maly teatr

Lubyanka

Novaya pl.

Politekhnichesky muzey
(Polytechnic Museum)

Podsosensky

Lyalin per.

Zemlyanoy Val

Chkafovskaya

Metropol
Teatralnaya
pl.
Ploshchad
Revolutsii
sky

Kitai-gorod

Staraya pl.

Khoralnaya
sinagoga

Kolpachny per.

Kazansky sobor
(Kazan Cathedral)

naya
chad

GUM

Gostiny
dvor

Kitai-
gorod

Kiril e Metody

osobnyak
Morozovikh

Voronstovo Pole

muzey i obshchestvenny
tsentr Andreya Sakharova
(Sakharov Museum and
Public Centre)

Syromyanichesky

Zolotorozhsky

mavzoley
Vl Lenina

ul. Varvarka

khram Troitsy
Zhivonachalnoy
v Khokhkakh

Yaursky bulvar

Zemlyanoy Val

Spaso-Andronikov
monastyr
(Andronikov Monastery)

sobor Vasiliya
Blazhennovo
(St Basil's)
n)

muzey Palaty
v Zaryade

Sobyanka

tserkov Zachatiya Anny
(Conception of St Anne)

Serebryanicheskaya nab.

Yauza

Nikoloyamskaya

skaya nab.

Moskvoretskaya nab.

Bernikovskaya nab.

Nikoloyamskaya ul.

ay ostrov

na nab.

Raushskaya naberezhnaya

Balchug-
Kempinski

Sadovnicheskaya nab.

dom na
Kotelnicheskoy

Kotelnicheskaya nab.

Gonchalnaya

Nikoloyamskaya ul.

Bol. Androniovsky per.

Shkolnaya ul.

Bibliotechnaya ul.

.skaya nab.
nd

muzey russkovo pitiya
(Museum of Drinking Traditions)

Kosmodamianskaya nab.

Moskva

Tsentr-muzey
VM Vysotskovo
(Museum to Vysotsky)

teatr
na Taganke

Tovarishcheskaya pereiok.

muzey mebeli
(Furniture Museum)

Dobrovolcheskaya ul.

ulitsa Rogozhsky Val

yakovskaya
ereya
tyakov Gallery)

Novokuznetskaya

Bol.

Tretyakovskaya

Sadovnicheskaya naberezhnaya

Taganskaya

Taganskaya
ploshchad

Marksistskaya

Taganskaya

Bol. Kommunisticheskaya

Taganskaya

Bol. Kamenshchiki

Marksistskaya ulitsa

Abelmanovskaya ulitsa

v

khram sv. Nikolaya v Pyzhakh
(St Nicholas in Pyzhakh)

tserkov Grigoriya
Neokessariyskovo
(St Gregory of Neocaesarea)

Bol. Ordynka

ZAMOSKVORECHE

ul. Mal. Ordynka

Pyatnitskaya

ulitsa Bakhrushina

Ozerkovskaya naberezhnaya

Tatarsky ul.

Taganskaya

Mal. Kamenshchiki

Vorontsovskaya ulitsa

Novospassky proezd

Novospassky monastyr
(Novospassky monastery)

Krestyanskaya
Zastava

Proletarskaya

Volgogradsky pr.

Stroykovskaya ul.

Kachalinskaya ul.

Talalikhina

ul.

Val
ul.

Serpukhovskaya per.

Lyusihovskaya

Stremyanny per.

Zatsepa

ulitsa

Valovaya ul.

Paveletskaya

Paveletskaya
naberezhnaya

Kozhevnicheskaya ul.

Dubiminskaya

Paveletsky
vokzal

Shlyuzovaya nab.

Krasnokholmskaya

nab.

Kozhevnicheskaya ul.

Letnikovskaya ul.

Krutitskaya nab.

Moscow

0   800 m

0   800 yds

N

THE KREMLIN

As the symbol of Russia's religious heritage and the seat of the country's political power, the Kremlin is Moscow in a nutshell. Flash, presidential limos drive past ancient cathedrals full of sacred icons, leaving tourists to gasp at tales of bygone intrigue and to gawp at extravagant displays of wealth

The Russian poet Konstantin Batyushkov described Moscow as "a gargantuan city built by giants; tower upon tower, wall upon wall, palace next to palace. A strange mixture of ancient and modern architecture, of poverty and wealth, the morals of Europeans and the morals and customs of Easterners. A divine, incomprehensible synthesis of vanity, conceit and true glory, of ignorance and enlightenment, of humanity and barbarism." That was in 1811, but the sentiments still ring true today. And at the core of this megalopolis, a city within a city, is the Kremlin, the original fortress around which it first grew. A must-see on any itinerary, an intoxicating mixture of old Muscovy, imperial elegance and remnants of the Soviet era awaits within its mighty walls.

The Kremlin fortress

The original citadel, the **Kremlin ❶**, was built by Yuri Dolgoruky (see page 17) in the 12th century as a humble, wooden stockade fortress. The site was chosen for its well-protected location on a thickly wooded hill surrounded by rivers. The waterways later proved conducive to transport and trade, which, together with rich mineral deposits in the area, encouraged rapid growth. Originally, the fortress was a city

unto itself, with dwellings, churches and monasteries, traders and craftsmen. It was repeatedly devastated by fires and Tatar raids until 1340, when Tsar Ivan Kalita ("Moneybags") built a new oak fortress reinforced with stucco, which lasted an unprecedented 26 years. When this, too, burned to the ground in 1366, Dmitry Donskoy (see page 18) decided to build walls made of white stone quarried from the nearby town of Myachkovo. Construction went on for 15 years, and the resulting fortress

Maps:
Area 92
Plan 82

LEFT: the Ivan the Great Bell Tower, though not the tallest building in the city, still dominates the Kremlin's skyline.
BELOW: choral singers in the Cathedral of the Annunciation.

In 1937 the two-headed eagles – the tsarist symbol – were removed from the Kremlin walls and replaced by Communist red stars. Kremlin guards report that two of the stars are made not of glass, but of rubies, and can be identified by their slightly darker hue.

with eight towers became the symbol of Moscow (to this day, the city is still referred to in literature as "white-stone Moscow"). By the end of the 15th century, the famous white stone walls were crumbling. Tsar Ivan III asked the Italian builders who were assisting Russian architects construct churches in the Kremlin to re-fortify the walls. Between 1485 and 1495, the white stone walls were bricked over, and sturdy replacements erected to extend the fortress to its present size. To improve security, the new walls were made taller and thicker, topped by entry and defence towers and lined with swallow-tailed crenellations.

Despite periodic repairs and modifications, the walls we see today are essentially those commissioned by Ivan III. Napoleon and his armies blew up certain sections and destroyed several towers, but these were rebuilt to the original design by the architect Osip Bove in 1817.

Protective towers

Overall, the Kremlin wall has 20 towers, which vary in shape, height and design. The tallest is the **Trinity Tower A** (*Troitskaya*, 80 metres/260 ft), originally connected by a drawbridge stretching over the Neglinnaya River to the **Kutafya Tower**, but replaced by one of the city's first stone bridges in 1516. The Trinity Tower is now the main entrance for visiting tourists. Russian leaders and delegations (and some tour groups) usually enter through the **Borovitsky Gates** on the southwest corner.

The **Saviour Gates B**, on the other side of the Kremlin opposite St Basil's Cathedral, take their name from an icon of the Saviour that graced the archway. Once fortified by two bastions and reached by a drawbridge over a moat that ran along the wall, this was the grandest tower of the fortress, through which tsars and foreign dignitaries entered. Today it is used by official visitors.

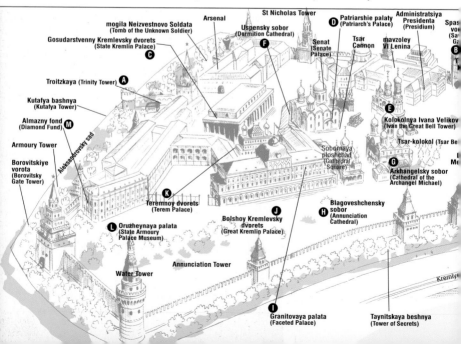

The Saviour Gates also house the famous clock that overlooks Red Square. The first clock was placed in the tower in the 16th century. In 1625 the tower was modified by English architect Christopher Halloway to its present Gothic appearance, and a new clock was installed. It was later replaced, but the Halloway clock was discovered in 1850, found to be functioning, and reinstated. It sustained damage in the Revolutionary fighting of 1917, and during repairs, the old melody that rang out on the hour (the *Preobrazhensky March*) was replaced with the opening tones of "The Internationale", which the Kremlin Chimes play to this day.

Other towers along the walls have their own stories and secrets. The **Sobakina Tower** (at the corner of the Aleksandrovsky sad) and the **Taynit-sky Tower** (Tower of Secrets; the third tower from the left when facing the Kremlin from the Moscow River) reportedly have tunnels for escaping by boat – the Sobakina Tower's tunnel once led to the Neglinnaya River, now in the Aleksandrovsky sad *(see page 110)*. The small **Tsar's Tower** (to the left of the Saviour Tower when viewed from Red Square) was added in 1680 in the place where Ivan the Terrible once watched ceremonies on Red Square.

The seat of power

When Ivan III moved the tradesmen outside the Kremlin walls and onto Red Square in the late 15th century, the Kremlin was no longer a small fortified town; it was now the seat of power for both state and Church, and was to become filled with palaces, administrative buildings, monasteries and churches. Over the centuries these buildings have been destroyed by fire, damaged by war or rebuilt to the taste of the current rulers.

Though visitors come to see the Kremlin's historic churches and museums, there is no escaping the

Map below left

The word kreml *in Russian means "fortress" and is often used to describe citadels in other historic Russian cities. The origins of the word are obscure, but it may have been derived from the Greek* kremn *or* krimnos, *meaning a hill over a ravine.*

BELOW: the Saviour Gates of the Kremlin on Red Square.

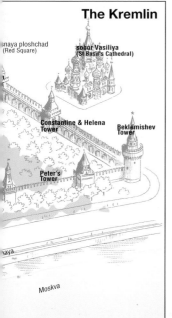

The Kremlin

snaya ploshchad (Red Square)

sobor Vasiliya (St Basil's Cathedral)

Constantine & Helena Tower

Beklemishev Tower

Peter's Tower

naya

Moskva

BELOW: elaborate frescos in the Cathedral of the Archangel Michael.

fact that this is the centre of Russian power. After passing through the Trinity Tower, all buildings to the left belong to Putin's administration and are strictly off limits to tourists. The first building on the left is the **Arsenal**, built in 1736. In front are more than 800 cannons, some captured from Napoleon's armies, others Russian-made.

Straight ahead and across a small garden is the former **Senate Palace**, commissioned by Catherine the Great to convene the Moscow senators. It was built by the Russian architect Matvey Kazakov between 1776–87 in the classical style and shaped as a triangle to fit the space. Today it is the President's official residence, and guards will move dallying tourists on their way. The Senate and Great Kremlin Palace *(see page 87)* were refurbished and renovated at massive expense in the 1990s; a later investigation revealed the so-called Mabetex scandal – a case of suspected misappropriation of funds by officials. To the right of the Senate is the **Presidential Administration**, another administration building,

erected on the site of the Miracles and Ascension monasteries, which were torn down in the 1930s.

To the right of the Trinity Gates is the **State Kremlin Palace** , built in 1959–61 to house Communist Party Congresses. The large, deep stage has been used for opera and ballet, and the 6,000-seat auditorium is a venue for state festivities and pop concerts, as well as a temporary home for the Bolshoy Theatre *(see page 107)*.

Patriarch's Palace

Just past the State Kremlin Palace on the right is the **Patriarch's Palace and Church of the Twelve Apostles** *(Patriarshie palaty i Tserkov Dvenadtsati apolstolov)*. The main entrance is behind the Dormition Cathedral. Completed in 1656 at the behest of the new Patriarch Nikon, it replaced the Metropolitan's modest apartments and the small private church used by the higher clergy, the Church of the Disposition of the Robe. It is now the **Museum of 17th-Century Life and Applied Art** and contains exhibitions of religious vestments and vessels, as well as rooms reconstructed to look as they would have been when used by a boyar. Of particular interest is the Cross Chamber, which was the largest room without supporting columns built at the time.

Ivan the Great Bell Tower

Still visible for miles around, though no longer Moscow's tallest building, the **Ivan the Great Bell Tower** *(Kolokolnya Ivana Velikovo)* dominates the Kremlin's skyline. Named after the Church of St Ivan Climacus that once stood on this spot, it was built in two tiers: in 1505–8 Italian master architect Bon Friazin constructed the main bell tower; in 1599 Tsar Boris Gudonov commissioned its final tier to make it, at 81 metres (265 ft), the tallest building in Moscow. The adjacent Assump-

tion Belfry was added in 1543, and the annexe was commissioned by Patriarch Filaret in 1642. The 21 bells, including the 64-ton Resurrection or Festival bell, are rung on special occasions.

The huge **Tsar Bell** was cast from the pieces of one that shattered during attempts to raise it into the belfry; the 200-ton bell was still in its casting pit when fire swept the Kremlin. To protect it, cold water was thrown into the pit, causing the surface to crack. It was then left in its pit for almost a century; when it was finally excavated, an 11-ton chunk broke off.

Cathedral Square

At the heart of the Kremlin lies **Cathedral Square**. This has been a ceremonial centre since the 14th century. Instead of a single state church, the tsars used several, and each of the four lining the square played a unique role in the life of the imperial family.

The oldest, grandest and most important is the **Dormition Cathedral ❻** *(Uspensky sobor)*, which symbolises Moscow's claim to be the protector of Russian Orthodoxy.

It is the only one of the four churches used for services – just once a year, on the Feast of the Dormition (15 August). The current church was built between 1475 and 1479 by Aristotele Fioravanti. Its exterior is simple to the point of plainness, with only a decorative arcade band around the bays and helmet-like cupolas. Nevertheless, it has been the country's premier church since its inception, and has hosted coronations of the tsars and granted them intercession during times of trouble. Every grand prince and tsar was crowned here from 1498.

In contrast to its plain exterior, the interior of the church is richly decorated with a five-tiered iconostasis and frescos on every surface of the walls, domes and pillars. The iconostasis dates from 1652, but some of its icons were made in the 14th century. Tombs of Church leaders, metropolitans and patriarchs line the walls. The Monomakh Throne, in the Cathedral's back right-hand corner, was installed for Ivan the Terrible in 1551; its carvings show scenes from the life of Vladimir Monomakh

Map on pages 82–3

The Tsar Cannon is the world's largest. Weighing 40 ton, it was designed to defend the Saviour Gates but it was only fired once, to blast the false Dmitry's remains towards Poland (see page 20).

BELOW: a collection of vintage artillery stands outside the Arsenal.

The Changing of the Guard takes place at midday every Saturday in the Kremlin's Cathedral Square.

BELOW: the splendid domes above Cathedral Square.

(see page 17). During the Napoleonic invasion of the Kremlin, the French armies used this cathedral as a stable and gutted it of gold and silver. Later, Cossack armies recovered much of the looted metal and used it to create the 46-branch Harvest Chandelier that lights the interior.

Across from the main entrance of the Dormition Cathedral is the small **Church of the Deposition of the Robe** *(Tserkov Rizopolozheniya)*, built by Pskov architects in 1486. Once the private chapel of patriarchs and metropolitans, it now houses a small collection of wooden religious sculpture.

The **Cathedral of the Archangel Michael ** *(Arkhangelsky sobor)*, opposite the Cathedral of the Dormition, is the most unusual church on the square and the final resting place for the early tsars. Commissioned in 1505 by Ivan III to replace an older church, it was built by Alevisio Novo and incorporates much Western ornamentation, such as the scalloping on the gables and Corinthian capitals, decoration unknown in Russia at the time. However, the structure of the church is the traditional Russian cross

plan. The frescos were painted by Simon Ushakov and his co-operative between 1652 and 1660. The original iconostasis was destroyed by the French in 1812, and the present one was installed the following year. The tsars were interred in this church from 1340 until 1712, when the capital was moved to St Petersburg. The first tsar in the Romanov dynasty, Mikhail Romanov and his family, are interred here, as is Ivan the Terrible, whose tomb is hidden behind the iconostasis.

The **Annunciation Cathedral** *(Blagoveshchensky sobor)*, opposite, was built on the basis of a church thought to have been constructed in the 1360s. The iconostasis from the original church was preserved, and it is considered the finest in all Russia. Its icons and frescos were painted by three of the finest icon-painters: Theophanes the Greek, Prokhor of Gorodets and Andrey Rublyov, who painted two icons in the upper, Feast Day or Festival Tier, the *Annunciation* and the *Nativity*. The church was constructed by builders from Pskov between 1484 and 1489, but rebuilt so many times that the sense of the

original structure has been lost.

The Cathedral served as the private church of the tsars and grand princes. The extended porch, called the Ivan the Terrible Steps, was built after the Metropolitan banned him from entering the church, in punishment for his seven marriages and countless concubines. Here Tsar Ivan listened to the service from a space just outside the church walls.

The Kremlin palaces

Between Cathedral Square and the Borovitsky Gate are three palaces that combined the imperial family's living and reception quarters and are now connected under one roof. (The three palaces can be seen by tour only, arranged through Patriarshy Dom; approximately twice a month; admission charge, *see page 227*).

The most striking of the three palaces is the **Faceted Palace ❶** *(Granitovaya palata)*, named after the unusual diamond-patterned facets decorating the façade and entered through Cathedral Square. It was built in 1487–91 by Marco Ruffo and Pietro Solario as one of the main administrative buildings for the tsar. The lower floor consists of chambers, and the upper floor is one enormous hall supported by a central pillar and lavishly painted with historical and Biblical scenes. Here the tsar held audiences, banquets and received foreign ambassadors. Later the Zemsky sobor (a proto-parliament) convened here. A small window allowed the tsarina and women family members to eavesdrop on the proceedings.

Leading down to Cathedral Square is the Red (or, more properly translated, "Beautiful") Staircase by which the tsars entered Cathedral Square. It was from here that in 1682 the young Peter the Great saw his relatives murdered in a rebellion. an experience so horrible it may have led him to found another capital – St Petersburg. The staircase was demolished by Stalin, but under Boris Yeltsin it was rebuilt according to the original plans.

Attached to the Faceted Palace and stretching westwards for 125 metres (410 ft) along the Kremlin Wall overlooking the Moscow River is the **Great Kremlin Palace ❷** *(Bolshoy Kremlevsky dvorets)*. Built under Nicholas I by the Russian architect Konstantin Ton, it served as the residence of the imperial family. Two rows of windows on the second floor give the illusion of three stories, but there are only two, the family occupying the ground floor, and the second floor given over to lavishly decorated reception and meeting halls named after Russia's most honoured saints. During the Soviet period two grand halls were turned into one room to house meetings of the Supreme Soviet. Boris Yeltsin made a point of restoring them both. Now the St Alexander and St Andrew halls serve vital functions in the ceremonies of the Russian Federation; the former as a backdrop to conclaves of the Federation Council, the latter for swearing in Russian presidents.

Map on pages 82–3

The elaborate decoration of church interiors can be overwhelming for first time visitors. For an explanation of the significance of the various rooms and icons, see pages 61–3.

The Armoury collection has twice left the Kremlin: when Ivan the Terrible feared a raid by the Tatars, it was moved on 450 sleighs to Novgorod the Great; and when Napoleon threatened, it was moved to Nizhni Novgorod. After the Revolution, the Bolsheviks kept the Armoury's treasures secure, as they needed money. A committee was set up, with Trotsky at its head, to manage the sale of these imperial artefacts.

BELOW: crowns of state at the Armoury Palace Museum.

The third palace is the **Terem Palace ⓚ** *(Teremnoy dvorets)*, built in 1635 by a group of Russian architects. Much of the palace fell into disuse in the 18th century, but was restored in the original style in 1837. Under the low-vaulted and profusely decorated ceilings the early tsars had their residence and reception rooms – an antechamber, the Cross Chamber, where the tsar met with his boyars and noblemen, and the Throne Room. From the small petition window in the Throne Room, a box would be lowered to the square. Anyone – from peasant to prince – could put a written petition in the box for the tsar's consideration. Since these rarely brought a swift response, it was called the "long box"; hence the Russian expression "to put something in a long box" for future consideration.

Armoury Palace Museum

In the southwest corner of the Kremlin, between the Great Kremlin Palace and the Borovitsky Gates, is the highlight of any visit – the **State Armoury Palace Museum ⓛ** *(Oruzheynaya palata)*, believed to have been established as a workshop by Tsar Basil III in 1511. The current building, completed in 1851 by Konstantin Ton, houses an amazing collection of treasures that celebrate Russia's imperial heritage. Many items were created by master craftsmen of the Kremlin and Russian workshops; others were given as ambassadorial and state gifts.

The first, small room on the upper floor contains a collection of Russian gold and silver tableware from the 12th to 16th centuries, and includes a 12th-century chalice given by the founder of Moscow, Yuri Dolgoruky *(see page 17)*, to a cathedral in the town of Pereslavl-Zalessky. There are also a number of traditional drinking vessels encrusted with enamel and precious stones.

The dark-green hall beyond holds the famous Fabergé eggs, with their extraordinarily fine craftsmanship. Nicholas II, the last tsar, commissioned two eggs each Easter from the German jeweller Carl Fabergé from 1884 until 1917. Among the 14

eggs in the original Kremlin collection are the Clock Egg (nestled in a bouquet of diamond lilies) and the Trans-Siberian Railway Egg, which has a gold model train that could be wound up. The second-largest collection of Fabergé eggs in the world was recently bought for $120 million by a Russian businessman, and has been exhibited here. Elsewhere in the green room are gold and silver items and a diamond-studded Bible.

The red room beyond is filled with European silver and gold items, mostly dinner sets, state gifts for imperial families. Weaponry and armour from Russia, Persia and Turkey fill the side rooms.

The first room on the lower floor displays imperial clothing, from the enormous boots worn by Peter the Great while working in Amsterdam shipyards, to the ermine-lined cape worn by the last tsarina, Alexandra.

State regalia in the next room include Ivan the Terrible's ivory throne, the Diamond Throne of Tsar Aleksey (with over 800 diamonds) and the double throne made for young Peter the Great and his brother Ivan – with a small window through which their elder sister Sophia could whisper instructions. Among crowns on display is one believed to have been given to Grand Prince Vladimir of Kiev by Constantine XI of Constantinople. The octagonal room to the side houses a fine collection of equestrian regalia, while ahead is a room of grand carriages and coaches.

Diamond Fund

A short tour of the **Diamond Fund** Ⓜ (*Almazny fond*; Fri–Wed 10am–6.30pm, tours every 20 minutes from 10am; tel: 629-2036; ticket booths within the Kremlin at the top of the hill leading to the Armoury Palace Museum or inside where the Armoury Palace tour begins), for those with the stamina after the Armoury Palace Museum, reveals an even more impressive collection of imperial jewels. Most noteworthy is Catherine the Great's coronation crown. There is a breathtaking array of imperial baubles, as well as diamond-encrusted victory orders awarded to Stalin's marshals. ❑

Map on pages 82–3

TIP

Arrive at the Armoury at least 15 minutes before your designated tour time. Doors open 10 minutes before the tour begins, and this will give you time to check your coat in before beginning your visit.

LEFT: an intricately designed Fabergé egg.
BELOW: an ornately decorated Bible cover.

RED SQUARE AND KITAI-GOROD

Red Square is the ceremonial heart of Moscow, the familiar scene of parades and proclamations. Steeped in history, it is home to the State Historical Museum, Lenin's Mausoleum and the magnificent St Basil's Cathedral. Close by are relics of tsarist-era trade – the Old English Court, Old Merchants' Quarters and the Stock Exchange

The Old Russian word *krasny* translates as both "beautiful" and "red", and Russia's main public space was meant to be called "Beautiful Square". Whatever its name, for centuries **Red Square ❷** *(Krasnaya ploshchad)* has been the heart of Russia: a place of celebration and public execution, a stage for leaders' public appearances and the main hub for trade, news and gossip. The vast expanse (700 metres/yds long and 130 metres/yds wide) is enclosed by the Kremlin walls, the birthday-cake façades of GUM (State Department Store) and the State Historical Museum, with the riotous colours and forms of the Church of the Intercession on the Moat (St Basil's) rising on the fourth side.

Since Tsar Ivan III cleared the area of houses and moved the trading booths from inside the Kremlin in the 16th century, it had been filled with traders, shoppers and businessmen, or crowded with throngs of peasants and noblemen attending the nation's most important religious and state ceremonies.

The square was originally called Trinity Square, after the Church of the Trinity that stood where St Basil's is now. It was then called *Torg* (Market), until one of the fires that devastated the timber-built city gave it the name of The Fire. "What news did you hear at The Fire today?" traders would ask each other at one of the taverns in the side streets. Only in the 17th century did the square become "Red". Today, however, Red Square is mostly empty but for tourists and the occasional limousine zipping through the Saviour Gates of the Kremlin.

Entering the square

Red Square is most impressive when entered through the **Resurrection or Iberian Gates ❸** *(Iversky vorota)* from **Manege Square** *(Manezhnaya*

Map
on pages
92–3

LEFT: waiting for the tourist dollar.
BELOW: the GUM department store is Moscow's main shopping mall.

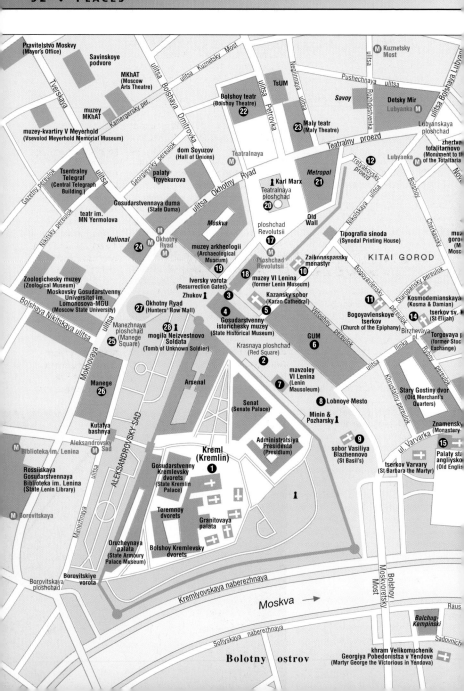

emonstratsionny Zal FSB Rossii
eum)

muzey istorii gorodskovo
osveshcheniya
Ogni Moskvy
(Fires of Moscow)

muzey
ayakovskovo
vsky Museum)

nichesky muzey
chnic Museum)

Ⓜ Kitai-gorod

Maraseyka-
Pokrovka

ILINSKY
GARDENS

tserkov Troitsy
v Nikitnikakh
(Trinity in Nikitniki)

Kiril e Metody

Kitai-gorod Ⓜ

m sv. Nikolaya Krasny Zvon
icholas of
eautiful Sound)

khram Vsekh Svyatykh
na Kulishkakh
(All Saints in Kulishkakh)

alaty v Zaryade
s in Zaryade)

tserkov Georgina
na Pskovskoy Gorke
(St George)

aksima
o
Blessed)

achatiya Anny
on of St Anne)

Moskvoretskaya naberezhnaya

naya

ulitsa Maroseyka

Boshoy Spasoglinischevsky pereulok

Khoralnaya
sinagoga

ploshchad

ul. Varvarka

Solyansky proezd

Solyansky tupik

proezd

Kitaygorodsky

Central Moscow

0 ——————— 200 m
0 ——————— 200 yds

ploshchad, see page 109). The gate was part of the wall (built 1535–8) that surrounded the area to the east of the Kremlin. In the 17th century an icon of the Iberian Mother of God (or the Iberian Virgin), from the Iberian Monastery on Mount Athos, was placed here, and in 1782 the gate was rebuilt outside the walls. Before entering the Kremlin, tsars and emperors would stop at the gate's tiny chapel to pay homage to this miracle-working icon.

Stalin had the gates torn down in 1931, but the structure was rebuilt according to the original plans and dedicated in 1996. Note the icon of St George and the dragon – the symbol of Moscow – above the left gate, and St Sergius – patron saint of Russia – above the right, as well as the marker on the pavement just outside the gate for "kilometre zero", from which all distances in Russia are measured, a popular photo spot for tourists.

State Historical Museum

Immediately on the right through the gates is the **State Historical Museum ❹** (*Gosudarstvenny isto-*

Map
Left

TIP

Red Square is closed to pedestrians 10am–1pm on Wed, Thur, Sat and Sun, when viewing of V.I. Lenin is permitted in the Mausoleum. You can cross the square on the pavement next to GUM.

BELOW: a doorman dressed as a Russian boyar outside the 1 Red Square Restaurant.

Since the break-up of the Soviet Union, there have been frequent public debates about the burial of Lenin. His fate remains undecided, however.

BELOW: eye-catching images at GUM.

richesky muzey; 1/2 Krasnaya ploshchad; tel: 921-4311; Wed–Mon 11am–6pm; closed first Mon of the month; admission charge; foreign-language audio tours available in the excursion bureau off the first exhibition hall).

The museum was founded in 1872 as the Imperial Russian Historical Museum and is itself an important monument to Russian culture. Built by the architect Vladimir Shervud (of English descent, his surname was probably Sherwood) in 1874–83 in the Russian Revival style, its turrets, *kokoshniki*, gables and towers celebrate pre-Petrine architecture. Selections from the enormous collection narrate the country's history from the Stone Age to the 19th century, in halls decorated in old Russia styles and filled with paintings and murals of historical scenes.

The museum also has an interesting restaurant (1 Red Square, *see page 103*) that serves traditional Russian recipes, and a shop with a range of quality souvenirs, including museum jewellery reproductions.

Icons and idols

On the other side of the lane leading from the Resurrection Gates to Red Square is the diminutive, pink **Kazan Cathedral ❺** (*Kazansky sobor*; daily 8am–8pm). The church was built in 1636 to celebrate Tsar Mikhail Romanov's victory over the Poles, and dedicated to the icon of the Virgin of Kazan, which was carried into battle by Prince Pozharsky *(see page 20)*. It was torn down in 1936 but rebuilt under the indefatigable "mayor-builder" of Moscow, Yuri Luzhkov *(see pages 64–5)*, in 1993. The interior has been fully restored, with remarkable frescos and iconostasis.

Across Nikolskaya ulitsa is the entrance to **GUM ❻** (pronounced "goom"), the State Department Store (3 Krasnaya ploshchad; tel: 921-5763; Mon–Sat 10am–8pm, Sun 11am–7pm). The marketplace was called the Upper Trading Rows when built in 1889–93, but the bland name GUM, given when it was nationalised in 1921, has remained. During the Soviet years, it was one of the few department

stores with a constant and relatively high-quality selection of goods. It has been extensively renovated and is now filled largely with foreign shops and snack bars, although the fountains, wrought-iron balconies and glass roof still give a sense of the pre-Revolutionary shopping experience.

Lenin's mausoleum

Opposite GUM in front of the Kremlin wall is the **Mausoleum of V.I. Lenin ❼** (*Mavzoley V.I. Lenina*; Wed, Thur, Sat and Sun 10am–1pm; tel: 623-5527). Please note that the mausoleum is closed for long periods for the treatment of Lenin's body, and the entrance line forms by the Kremlin wall in the Aleksandrovsky sad; as it begins to move, visitors are required to leave all bags and cameras in a room in the State Historical Museum.

When the leader of the October Revolution and Soviet state died on 21 January 1924, Party leaders overruled the objections of his wife, Nadezhda Krupskaya, and had a wooden mausoleum quickly built so the devoted could pay their last respects. Lenin's body was then embalmed according to a unique process that involves submerging the body in a special solution every 18 months or so. When the embalming process proved successful, the wooden mausoleum was replaced by the Constructivist pyramid of red granite and black labradorite, designed by Aleksey Shchusev, in 1930. From 1953 to 1961, Stalin was also preserved and placed on view.

Visitors file through the mausoleum in silence, hands at their sides (not in their pockets) and all hats removed. Steps and corridors lead down to the sombre viewing room, where Lenin lies in state under a glass dome. A few minutes later the line emerges by the Kremlin wall, where over 400 luminaries of the Soviet state have their final resting place. Here are the graves of Stalin, cosmonaut Yuri Gagarin *(see page 165)* and American journalist John Reed, whose eyewitness account of the Revolution, *Ten Days That Shook the World,* was revered in the USSR.

Map on pages 92–3

TIP

On the ground and first floors of GUM you can buy traditional Russian scarves, delftware (called *Gzhel*), fur hats and other souvenirs. There are pay toilets on the basement level at either end.

BELOW: Communists at a demonstration in front of Lenin's Mausoleum.

In front of St Basil's is a statue to Pozharsky and Minin. In 1612 they led the Russian forces that drove out the Polish invaders and the "false Dmitry" the Poles tried to pass off as the heir to the Russian throne (see page 20).

RIGHT: St Basil's remains lie inside this tent-spired chapel.

Close to St Basil's is a round white stone platform called **Lobnoye mesto** ❽ ("a high, protruding place") dating from 1534. It was made of brick, with pillars, a roof and a wooden fence surrounding it. The current podium, faced with white stone, was constructed in 1786. On this spot Ivan the Terrible confessed his sins after the devastating fire of 1547; also from here state proclamations were read, religious ceremonies, held and, once a year, the tsar appeared before the people. It was also the custom to show the heir apparent when he reached the age of 16, so no usurper could later deceive the population.

St Basil's

Red Square is dominated by the Cathedral of the Intercession on the Moat, known as **St Basil's** ❾ (*Khram Vasiliya Blazhennovo*; 2 Krasnaya ploshchad; tel: 267-7591; Wed– Mon 11am–6pm; closed first Mon of the month; admission charge). Ivan the Terrible commissioned the Cathedral to commemorate the Russian victory over the "Tatar infidels" in Kazan on the Volga River in 1552. When the Tsar succeeded in subduing the khanate in Astrakhan in 1556, the Cathedral became a symbol of the victory of the Russian state and Orthodoxy. Since the battle that led to victory in Kazan took place on the day of the Feast of Intercession of the Virgin, the full name of the church is the Cathedral of the Intercession by the Moat, referring to the moat that once flowed along the wall of the Kremlin by Red Square. Later it became known as St Basil's in honour of St Basil the Blessed (1468–1552), a popular and prophetic "holy fool in Christ" who on occasion went around naked and in chains. His remains were later interred in a separate chapel added to the Cathedral.

Historians attribute the Cathedral to two architects from Pskov, Barma and Postnik Yakovlev; however, recent research indicates that this might have been one architect, who had the nickname of Barma ("the Mumbler"). The story that Ivan the Terrible had the builders blinded so they could never build anything

A City of Churches

Moscow was once called the city of "40 times 40" churches. Spires filled the skies with gold, and bells rang out across the city. In the Soviet period and during the campaign against religion in the 1930s, most churches were emptied of their religious treasures, destroyed or turned into offices, warehouses or apartments. A few remained functioning; others were stripped of religious meaning and called "monuments of Russian architecture". Today, nearly all of Moscow's churches and cathedrals have been returned to the patriarchy. However, many churches are closed for refurbishment, while others are only open for services (usually at 8am and 5pm). While many churches have had their exteriors repaired, the interiors can often be disappointing: bare walls and a few modern icons where once there were frescos, a gleaming multi-tiered iconostasis and shelves of golden vessels. Women should cover their heads with scarves when visiting a church. Photography, talking and turning one's back to the altar are considered highly disrespectful. It is acceptable for anyone to buy a candle and place it in front of an icon, and there is usually a box by the door for donations.

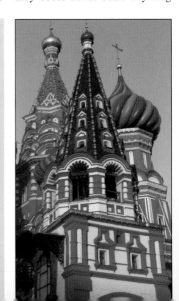

more beautiful is apocryphal. Napoleon ordered it blown up in 1812 (it was saved from destruction, but pillaged by his army) and in 1936 Stalin planned to blow it up "because it hindered automobile movement across the square".

The present Cathedral is built on the site of the Church of the Trinity, which has been retained as an interior chapel. Until the final tier of the Ivan the Great Bell Tower in the Kremlin was erected in 1600, the Cathedral's spire was the highest in Moscow.

At first glance St Basil's seems exotically asymmetrical, but this is an optical illusion caused by additions that conceal the original design. It is in fact utterly symmetrical, an octagon with a central tent spire surrounded by eight cupolas. The cupolas at the four compass points are taller than the four at the diagonal points. The Cathedral is structured architecturally by the Trinity: there are three towers on each compass axis, diagonal and side; each tower has three sections: the main octagon or cube, the tiers

of *kokoshniki* and then a culminating octagon topped by a cupola. In 1588 Tsar Fyodor added a small chapel for the remains of St Basil. Some later additions, such as the covered terrace and bell tower (1630), have remained; others (such as 13 small chapels built around the structure) were dismantled in a large-scale reconstruction in the 1780s.

Inside, the Cathedral is not one large space, but nine small chapels linked by passageways painted dark red with white lines to look like brick, or decorated in profuse and brightly coloured geometric and floral designs. Entry is through the **Church of St Basil the Blessed**, where his relics are kept in an elaborate gold-and-silver shrine, then up a very steep winding staircase into the **Church of the Intercession** under the tent steeple. This is surrounded by eight motley chapels. Some are gift shops, some are empty, but some are well preserved.

The exit is through the **Church of the Entrance of Christ into Jerusalem**. On Palm Sunday (called

Map on pages 92–3

Historians do not know what St Basil's original cupolas looked like; after a fire in 1583, they were rebuilt in the onion-dome shape and lavishly decorated.

BELOW:
Red Square looks most impressive at night.

Pussy Willow Sunday in Russia), the tsar would ride on a horse from the Kremlin to this church.

St Basil's is maintained by the State Historical Museum but it has been reconsecrated, and services are held occasionally.

Kitai-gorod

The area to the east of Red Square that stretches from GUM to New and Old squares (Novaya and Staraya ploshchad respectively) was called **Kitai-gorod**. The name is either derived from the Russian word *kita* (wattle) used in its original fences, or a Mongol word that meant "central fortress". In 1535–8, the area was enclosed by a thick (6-metre/20-ft) wall with 14 towers. To prevent attacks through tunnels, the wall extended 12 metres (40 ft) underground and contained listening chambers with hanging copper sheets that jangled at the slightest disturbance.

This was the main trading district of old Moscow: streets were full of shops, outdoor markets, tenements, taverns and trading houses – as well

as four monasteries and 18 churches. Armenians, Persians, Jews and countless other nationalities mingled and haggled over prices at rowdy outdoor markets on Red, Old and New squares. In the late 19th and early 20th centuries, elegant shopping centres, banks, insurance companies and the Stock Exchange were built on the narrow streets.

During Soviet times much of the area was taken over by government buildings; Old Square was occupied by the Central Committee of the Communist Party, the USSR's ruling body. Today, the narrow streets are taken up by various ministries and higher courts, the ground-floor windows often discreetly curtained. Only the streets closest to Red Square are emerging as up-scale shopping areas.

Three main streets cross the district from Red Square to Old and New squares: Nikolskaya ulitsa (closest to the Resurrection Gates), ulitsa Ilinka and ulitsa Varvarka (leading from St Basil's), the latter is the main street of the old Zaryade neighbourhood.

So much of Moscow makes every effort to appeal to modern sensibilities, but "Old Russia" is still a popular marketing theme around Red Square.

BELOW: the enchanting façade of the Synodal Printing House on Nikolskaya ulitsa.

Nikolskaya ulitsa

Taking its name from the Nikol-skaya (St Nicholas) Tower of the Kremlin, **Nikolskaya ulitsa** runs from the Historical Museum in Red Square to New Square. It is lined with low- to medium-end stores, cafés and dense crowds of shop-pers, dodging scaffolding that has draped entire blocks for reconstruc-tion and renovation in recent years. On the left when walking from Red Square are tightly packed buildings with archways leading to court-yards. The arch at No. 9. leads to the **Zaikonospassky Monastery** ❿ (*Zaikonospassky monastyr*). The name translates as "The Saviour Monastery behind the Icon", which identified it as "the monastery behind the icon-seller's stand". In 1687 the monastery was converted into Russia's first institution of higher learning, called the Russian-Greek-Latin Academy. Mikhail Lomonosov, founder of the Moscow State University *(see page 128)*, studied here. The monastery has now been returned to the patriarchy and is under restoration. Only the church, which is renowned for its choir, is open for services.

Further down Nikolskaya at No. 15, and rather out of kilter with the downbeat shops and cafés, is the for-mer **Synodal Printing House**, a magnificent pale-blue Gothic edifice with white floral carvings and a whimsical lion and unicorn dating from 1815. Tradition has it that Russia's first printed book, *The Apos-tles*, was produced on this site in 1563. Later it housed the Russian newspaper *Vedomosti*. It is currently under reconstruction.

Next to it, and now part of the Humanities University, is the for-mer **Slavyansky Bazar Hotel and Restaurant**. Here the theatre direc-tors Stanislavsky and Nemerovich-Danchenko spent an evening enjoy-ing food, drink and conversation that culminated in their decision to found the Moscow Art Theatre *(see page 146)*. It is now home to the Pokrovsky Theatre

Though close to shops and gov-ernment blocks, the narrow streets intersecting the main thoroughfares of Kitai-gorod are little-used, as many

Map on pages 92–3

Muscovites take great pride in the cleanliness of the city centre.

BELOW: souvenirs near Red Square are, unsurprisingly, overpriced compared to other outlets.

buildings are awaiting refurbishment. It is, however, worth a walk down **Bogoyavlensky** (Epiphany) **pereulok** from Nikolskaya towards Stock Exchange Square. On the right is the renovated baroque **Church of the Epiphany**  (*Bogoyavlenskaya tserkov*, 2 Bogoyavlensky pereulok), with rows of mosaic saints on the drum of the cupola and an impressive gold dome. The church is on the grounds of a monastery founded in 1296; it now houses a liturgical music school, and is worth a visit for the chance of catching the talented students rehearsing inside the church.

On the left just before Stock Exchange Square is a narrow street, **Staropansky pereulok**, originally settled by traders from Lithuania. Halfway down the street on the right is the tiny **Church of Kosma and Damian**, a bright patch of pink and gold nearly hidden by the tall buildings around it. Across the street at No. 5 is the former **Arshinov Trading House**, built in 1899 in the Russian *style moderne* by Fyodor Shekhtel.

Back on Nikolskaya ulitsa and heading west, you'll come to one of

Tucked in around the construction site of the Rossiya Hotel are some of central Moscow's most charming little churches.

BELOW: the Old English Court is one of the oldest buildings in the city.

Moscow's most exclusive shopping streets. **Tretyakov Passage**  *(Tretyakovsky proezd)*, painted gleaming white, was built by the Tretyakov brothers in 1872. It is now packed with luxury cars, stylish women and super-rich oligarchs buying baubles at Gucci, Tiffany & Co. and other exclusive boutiques.

At the eastern end of Nikolskaya ulitsa is the Lubyanka *(see page 159)*. Turn right onto **Novaya ploshchad** to visit the **Museum of Moscow History**  (*Muzey istorii goroda Moskvy*; 12 Novaya ploshchad; tel: 924-8058; Tues, Thur, Sat and Sun 10am–5.30pm; Wed and Fri 11am–6.30pm; closed Mon and last Fri of the month; admission charge), which occupies the former Church of St John the Apostle under the Elm. The extensive collection includes many reconstructions of daily life in medieval Moscow and a scale model of the Kremlin when it was surrounded by water.

Ulitsa Ilinka

Bisecting Kitai-gorod from the centre of Red Square, **ulitsa Ilinka** (from Ilya, the Russian translation of Elijah), was once the centre of the Russian business world. The street takes its name from the Monastery of Elijah that once stood here. The small 16th-century **Church of St Elijah**  is being restored at No. 3.

The biggest attraction on ulitsa Ilinka is the architecture on **Stock Exchange Square**, where it meets Rybny pereulok. It is dominated by the orange **Chamber of Commerce** (formerly the Stock Exchange). Built in classical style between 1873 and 1875, it stands in contrast to the more highly decorated pale-green structures surrounding it. Across the square is the former **Ryabushinsky Bank**, another *style moderne* building by Shekhtel. Ryabushinksy, the head of the Stock Exchange and an ardent art collector, later commis-

Maps on page 92–3

sioned Shekhtel to build his home. On the left side of the street as you walk towards Red Square is the northern end of the **Old Merchants' Quarters** *(Stary Gostiny dvor)* that covers the large square stretching to ulitsa Varvarka. It once housed trading booths of visiting merchants, but has been rebuilt many times. The current structure was built by Catherine the Great's favourite architect, Giacomo Quarenghi, in the late 18th century, and recently restored. At present there are only a few stores and restaurants within. The vast central hall is used for trade fairs and temporary exhibitions. It's still worth stopping in the shops along ulitsa Ilinka selling *Vologda* linen and traditional Russian crystal. The rest of ulitsa Ilinka is mostly filled with ministries, higher courts and state offices.

Zaryade and ulitsa Varvarka

The area from St Basil's to the river (called *Vasilevsky spusk*) and to the east where the Rossiya Hotel once stood, bounded by **ulitsa Varvarka**, was originally called **Zaryade**,

which meant "beyond the rows" of traders' booths on Red Square. It was settled in the 14th century by builders brought in to put up the Kremlin walls, then occupied by foreign traders, boyars and princes. By the 17th century it was a teeming slum of crooked streets and emitted a stench so bad that, as one writer noted, "Once you broke out of there, you joyfully gulped the fresh air."

Virtually nothing but the churches and buildings on ulitsa Varvarka remain, but they are still lovely, despite the construction site at the former **Rossiya Hotel** below. The Rossiya was built in 1964–7, touted as the world's largest hotel (with 6,000 rooms) and bemoaned as the world's greatest eyesore before being demolished in 2006. A new complex of office and shopping buildings is planned to fill the area.

At the corner closest to Red Square is the **Church of St Barbara the Martyr** *(Tserkov Varvary)*, built in 1796–84 to replace an earlier structure. Next to this church is the white, wooden-eaved **Old English Court** ⑮ *(Palaty starovo*

Historic Kitai-gorod, the city's trading quarter.

BELOW: pricey shops line Tretyakov Passage.

The English visitors at the Old English Court were not used to Moscow's brutal winters; doubting the superior heating capacity of closed stoves (like the one above), *they insisted on modifying the room by adding an open fireplace.*

BELOW: the Chambers in Zaryade carefully recreate life in medieval Russia.

angliyskovo dvora; 4 ulitsa Varvarka; tel: 298-3961; Mon, Tues, Thur, Sat and Sun 10am–6pm, Wed and Fri 11am–7pm; closed Mon and last Fri of the month; admission and photo charges; accessed from the old Rossiya car park).

Built as a merchant's palace and one of the oldest secular buildings in the city, it was given to the Muscovy Company by Ivan the Terrible after the visit of Richard Chancellor, and became the house of visiting merchants and dignitaries from England. After the expulsion of the British Trade Company in 1649 following the execution of King Charles I, the building was bought for 500 roubles by a local boyar; it later passed through many hands before being so completely hidden by an apartment house that 19th-century guidebooks listed the Court as "not preserved". It was restored for the 1994 state visit of Queen Elizabeth II, and is a fine concert venue. An exhibition (with explanations in Russian and English) narrates the history of relations between England and Russia. Of note is the **Official Hall** upstairs, with its Russian-style ceramic corner stove decorated with fantastical animal figures *(see margin left)*.

Three other churches line ulitsa Varvarka: the **Church of Maxim the Blessed** (*Tserkov Maksima Blazhenovo*; 4 ulitsa Varvarka), built in 1698–9 by Novgorod merchants; the **Cathedral of the Monastery of the Sign** (*Znamensky monastyr*; 8a ulitsa Varvarka), founded in 1634; and the **Church of St George** (*Tserkov Georgiya na Pskovskoy Gorke*; 12 ulitsa Varvarka). All have been returned to the patriarchy; only the Church of St George and the Cathedral of the Monastery of the Sign are open for services. There is a small store selling books, icons and other religious items at the Monastery.

Just before you reach the Church of St George is the small museum called the **Chambers in Zaryade** ⓰ (*Muzey Palaty v Zaryade*; 10 ulitsa Varvarka; tel: 298-3706; Thur–Mon 10am–6pm, Wed 11am–7pm; closed Tues; admission and photo charges, last ticket one hour from closing), where the first of the Romanov

Map on pages 92–3

tsars, Mikhail, was born. Entered from a courtyard adjacent to the old Rossiya car park, it is a beautifully reconstructed medieval Russian dwelling, with low-vaulted ceilings, deep-set mica windows, chased-leather "wallpaper" and a *terem* – a section at the top floor of the house where women were secluded. The practice of secluding women in a *terem* (not a corruption of the word *harem*, but derived from the Greek *teremnon*, meaning "special quarters") was instituted in Russia in the 15th century. One of the rooms, the "Bright Room", was well lit by natural light and used for embroidery and other handicrafts.

On the other side of the street, opposite the Church of Maxim the Blessed is the southern façade of the **Old Merchants' Quarters** (*Stary Gostiny dvor, see page 101*).

Ancient remains

Three ancient churches worth noting are tucked away on nearby side streets. On Nikolsky pereulok is the tiny **Church of St Nicholas of the "Beautiful Sound"** (*Khram Svy-atitelya Nikolaya "Krasny Zvon"*), built in 1561 and named for the sweet tones of its bells. Further down ulitsa Varvarka towards Old Square, turn left on Ipatyevksy pereulok to see the **Church of the Trinity in Nikitniki** (*see page 68*). Built in 1634 and modified over the centuries, it is a spectacularly ornamented small gem. The belltower was the first to be built into the structure of a church in Moscow. Frescos from 1652–8 by the school of Simon Ushakov fill the walls.

At the end of ulitsa Varvarka, on the street to the right leading down to the river, are remains of the **Kitai-gorod wall**. Several sections of the wall are preserved behind glass in the pedestrian underpass.

On the Moscow River in front of the old Rossiya Hotel site is the small white **Church of the Conception of St Anne** (*Tserkov Zachatiya Anny*), built in the 1530s. It was once a wealthy church, at an important intersection in Zaryade, where tsars and their families attended services. It is now been returned to the patriarchy and is currently under reconstruction. ❏

Moscow's historic role as an international trading city is well illustrated at the Chambers in Zaryade museum.

RESTAURANTS & BARS

1 Red Square
1 Krasnaya ploshchad. Metro: Ploshchad Revolut-sii. Tel: 925-3600. Open: L & D daily. $$$
Not the tourist trap you might expect, given its location on Red Square within the historical museum. The menu has lavish, centuries-old recipes from tsars' coronation menus and interesting anecdotes. Expect cream-laden food, meat dishes with sticky fruit-based sauces and live folk music.

Bosco
3 Krasnaya ploshchad. Metro: Ploshchad Revolut-sii. Tel: 929-3182. Open: B, L & D daily. $$$
A stylish Italian café and restaurant on the ground floor of GUM department store. '70s retro-chic décor with pricey modern European cuisine.

Pirogi Na Nikolskoi
19/21 Nikolskaya ulitsa. Metro: Lubyanka. Tel: 921-5827. Open: 24 hrs, daily. $$
A basement café, bar and bookshop favoured by students and intellectual types. Passable food and an extensive list of reasonably priced drinks, including cheap carafes of vodka.

Porto Maltese
3 ulitsa Varvarka. Metro: Kitai-Gorod. Tel: 298-0755. Open: L & D daily. $$$
Considered by many to have the freshest seafood in Moscow, it serves an extensive range, flown in four times a week. Choose from the iced display and tell them how you would like it prepared. Pastas, risottos and other Italian dishes are also served.

Tretyakov Lounge
1 Tretyakovsky proezd. Metro: Lubyanka. Tel: 771-7295. Open: L & D daily. $$$$
The expensive, plush interior has elite clientele and prices to match. The primarily modern French cuisine is well executed, although this is not a place to feel relaxed.

● ● ● ● ● ● ● ● ● ● ● ●

Price includes a three-course dinner for one and a glass of house wine. **$$$$** *$60 and up,* **$$$** *under $60,* **$$** *under $40,* **$** *under $25*

THEATRE AND MANEGE SQUARES

Remnants of the Revolution are fading, world-famous
theatres are being refurbished, and a multi-million-dollar
development has brought even more shopping to the
heart of old Moscow. Theatre and Manege squares
are in the vanguard of Moscow's evolution from
cloak-and-dagger capital to modern metropolis

The centre of Moscow's street life has shifted. No longer is it set amidst the traditional architecture of Red Square. It now focuses on the three redeveloped open spaces to the north that separate the Kremlin from Tverskaya ulitsa: Revolution, Theatre and Manege squares. This vast expanse of construction sites and building refurbishments reveals the vision of current city planners. Soviet relics such as the Moskva Hotel have been destroyed. Elite shopping centres have become a priority, while reminders of Russia's great, tsarist past – such as the Bolshoy Theatre – are being comprehensively spruced up. Even the long-forgotten Neglinnaya River, which once ran beside the walls of the Kremlin, has been allowed to return to the surface, if only to water a parade of traditional Russian fairytale characters.

In a country where history is constantly being rewritten, this is where the full story of "New Russia" is emerging, from the pageantry of its history to some of the most expensive shopping centres in Europe.

The three squares covered in this chapter are well served by the metro and can be visited in any order. We start in the middle, at ploshchad Revolutsii, head north to Teatralnaya ploshchad and then on to Manezhnaya ploshchad to the southwest.

Revolution Square

Despite its name, the most revolutionary sight today on **Revolution Square** *(ploshchad Revolutsii)* is of old people hawking Communist papers and memorabilia by the steps of the former **Lenin Museum** ⓲ *(Muzey V.I. Lenina*; 1/2 Krasnaya ploshchad). The largest collection of Lenin memorabilia in the world was once housed in this red-brick building, just west of ploshchad Revolutsii metro station. But it has been transferred to the State Historical

Maps
on page
92–3

LEFT: Lenin, Marx and Putin lookalikes pose for photos with tourists. **BELOW:** the Bolshoy Theatre.

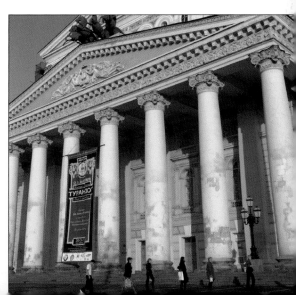

Karl Marx was considered Lenin's "teacher". His statues can still be found in most Russian cities.

Museum, and the space is now used as a gallery. The first Moscow Biennale of contemporary art was held here in January 2006.

Lenin's museum may have gone, but Soviet heritage remains underground. Filled with bronze statues celebrating ordinary, socialist citizens, Ploshchad Revolutsii is one of the finest metro stations in Moscow.

Amid the kiosks to the east of the station are steps up to a passage lined with tiny clothing and electronics stores that leads onto Nikolskaya ulitsa *(see page 99)*. There is also a bit of reconstructed Kitaigorod wall here, with a kitschy restaurant in a faux tower. During the summer, outdoor café-bars and snack stands fill the square. For an original section of the Kitai-gorod wall, look a little further to the east behind the Metropol Hotel.

Archaeological Museum

At the rear of the State Historical Museum is an equestrian statue of **Marshal Zhukov**, erected in 1995 to commemorate the 50th anniversary of the end of World War II. Just before the statue, on the northern side of the square, a marble pavilion covers the entrance to the underground **Archaeological Museum** ⓳ (*Muzey arkheologii*; 1a Manezhnaya ploshchad; tel: 692-4171; Tues, Thur, Sat and Sun 10am–6pm; Wed and Fri 11am–7pm; closed Mon and last Fri of the month; admission charge; some English captioning). Opened in 1997 the museum includes a large collection of artefacts found during excavations of Manege Square. Some of the items date from the 12th century and include a pile of Spanish doubloons. The highlight is a portion of the Voskresensky Bridge (16th–17th century) that once spanned the Neglinnaya River and connected the White City *(Bely Gorod, see page 131)* to Red Square.

The area between the Archaeological Museum and ulitsa Okhotny Ryad is an enormous construction pit surrounded by giant billboards. The **Hotel Moskva** was dismantled and is to be rebuilt to the original plans using modern construction techniques to protect it from water seepage and the effects of the metro.

Theatre Square

On the other side of the construction site is a monument to Karl Marx in the centre of the southern section of **Theatre Square ⑳** *(Teatralnaya ploshchad)*, incongruous among its elegant neighbours, the Metropol Hotel and the Bolshoy and Maly theatres across the street.

Theatre Square has certainly seen better days. During the 19th century, when it wasn't coarsely bisected by the eight lanes of ulitsa Okhotny Ryad, it made a grand impression. In the evenings it was filled with carriages awaiting elegant theatregoers, and in December an enormous Christmas-tree market made it look like a forest of trees in the snow, with bonfires to warm the patrons and vendors of hot drinks and rolls strolling the paths.

Now much of this once lively square is taken up by car parks. On the square's eastern side is the elegantly renovated **Metropol Hotel ㉑** (1/4 Teatralny proezd; tel: 927-6000). An Englishman named William Walcot, who was born in Odessa and educated in Russia, finished this *style moderne* masterpiece in1901. Its north wall is decorated with *The Princess of Dreams*, a mosaic panel designed by Mikhail Vrubel. It's worth a pause to examine it; it's also worth a short stop in the hotel to see the fountain with its statue *Cupids at Play* in the glass-domed main dining room. On the eastern side of the Metropol Hotel is one of the original Kitai-gorod towers.

Home of the arts

Until the 19th century Theatre Square was called St Peter's Square, then it briefly became Flower Square as it was the main outdoor market for flowers. It was renamed Theatre Square in the 1820s, when the main venues for the performing arts, the Bolshoy (Great) and Maly (Small) theatres, were built.

The **Bolshoy Theatre ㉒** company started life in 1776 when Prince Urusov, backed by the English entrepreneur Michael Maddox, received imperial permission to found a permanent performing-arts troupe. Performers were drawn from serf troupes, private and university theatres. After the first building burned down, the theatre was given the status of Great Imperial Theatre in 1805, and its original architect, Osip Bove, was entrusted with redesigning the square and its two theatres. The Bolshoy was again destroyed by fire in 1853, after which the architect Albert Kavos rebuilt the theatre as it is today. Its clean, classical lines, eight enormous columns and figure of Apollo riding his chariot along the top (by Pyotr Klodt) are emblems of Russian brilliance in opera and ballet. Inside, the gold-and-red velvet décor, elegant cafés, shimmering chandeliers and sconces have delighted ballet- and opera-lovers for generations.

Today it is not fire, but water that threatens the building. The motion of the metro exacerbates the seeping waters from the buried Neglinnaya

Map on pages 92–3

A rather incongruous inscription around the façade of the five-star Metropol Hotel – a favourite place for travelling businessmen – reads: "Only the dictatorship of the proletariat can free the world of the oppression of capitalism".

BELOW: old Communists protest against New Russia.

The National Hotel and foibles of tourism during the Soviet era were immortalised in Eloise in Moscow, *written by Kay Thompson and illustrated by Hilary Knight. "And here's the thing of it: when you go out of your room you can lock your door and leave your key with these ladies if you want to, but actually you do not need to bother because the minute you go out somebody else goes right in…"*

BELOW: huge advertising signs conceal construction work on Manege Square.

River, creating a serious subsidence problem. In 2005 the theatre was closed for a complete renovation and is not scheduled to reopen until March 2008. The troupes will still perform in the smaller New Stage (to the west of the theatre) and the State Kremlin Palace *(see page 84).*

The **Maly Theatre** ㉓ *(Maly teatr,* 1/6 Teatralnaya ploshchad), immediately to the east of the Bolshoy, was redesigned from a mansion and once called the "Small Imperial Theatre".

West of the Bolshoy along ulitsa Okhotny Ryad is an unimposing, but graceful pale-green classical building with white columns. Built for the Club of the Russian Nobility by Matvey Kazakov in the 1770s, it was nationalised in 1919 and renamed the **Hall of Unions** *(dom Soyuzov;* 1 ulitsa Bolshaya Dmitrovka). Both Lenin and Stalin were laid in state here before being moved to the mausoleum on Red Square *(see page 95).* Several thousand mourners are said to have been trampled to death trying to see Stalin's body. Many other Bolsheviks met their fate here when it was used for the show trials of the late

1930s. Today it is used for state functions, concerts and special events.

Towards Manege Square

The stretch of ulitsa Okhotny Ryad between ulitsa Bolshaya Dmitrovka and Tverskaya ulitsa was once a boggy warren of small lanes, shacks and booths where trappers sold their catches. Cleared in the 1930s, they were replaced by the Hotel Moskva – now destroyed – and the grey and imposing edifice on the corner of Tverskaya ulitsa, which is now the **State Duma** *(Gosudarstvennaya Duma)* the lower house of parliament *(see page 33).*

On the other side of Tverskaya is the elegant **National Hotel** ㉔ *(Hotel National;* 15/1 Mokhovaya ulitsa, str. 1; tel: 258-7000), built in 1903. From 1918 until the late 1920s it housed state officials moved from St Petersburg (then Petrograd) and was called the "First House of Soviets". Since its renovation in the 1990s, it has competed with the Metropol and Balchug-Kampinski for the reputation of Moscow's finest hotel. Its rooms and restaurants have good views of the

Kremlin. Next to the National (and under reconstruction) is a building erected in 1934 in 16th-century Italian style. It once housed the **American Embassy**, and on 9 May 1945, when word came that World War II in Europe was over, crowds gathered and cheered. George Kennan, then chargé d'affaires, described in his memoirs the thousands of people who stood in front of the Embassy all day and into the evening. When anyone ventured into the street, he was, in Russian fashion, kissed soundly, tossed in the air and carried off for more merriment, presumably involving jubilant toasts to victory.

Further down Mokhovaya ulitsa is **Moscow State University**, considered one of Russia's finest neoclassical buildings. It was built by Matvey Kazakov in 1793 and rebuilt after the fire of 1812. On the other side of Bolshaya Nikitskaya ulitsa is the "new building" of the university, built in 1836 with a statue to its founder, Mikhail Lomonosov *(see page 128)*, in the courtyard. Both buildings are still part of the university, though the main campus is now

in Sparrow Hills *(see page 128)*. A church dedicated to St Tatyana, patron saint of students, is in the corner of the new building – a refuge during the rigorous exam season.

Manege Square

The broad square on the other side of Mokhovaya ulitsa is **Manege Square** ㉕ *(Manezhnaya ploshchad)*. Once the site of rag and food markets, it is the city's latest redevelopment. During Soviet times, the area would often be filled with crowds or tanks waiting to enter Red Square for parades, celebrations or protests. Crowds of almost a million demonstrated here against the Soviet authorities and, in 2002, it was the scene of a riot of soccer fans watching large outdoor screens.

At the southern end of the square is the **Manege** ㉖, a neoclassical yellow structure with white columns. Built as a riding school under Alexander I in 1817, it had an uninterrupted roof-span of 45 metres (148 ft). After serving as a garage in the early Soviet years, it was turned into the Central Exhibition Hall. In 1962 Nikita Khrushchev attended an exhibition

Map on pages 92–3

The Maly Theatre was the premier classical drama theatre in the capital for much of the 19th and early 20th centuries.

BELOW: the Manege building.

Mokhovaya ulitsa gets its name from the many stands that once stood here and sold moss (mokh in Russian), which was used as insulation in log houses.

BELOW: the changing of the Guard near the Tomb of the Unknown Soldier.

of modern art here and started a shouting match with the artists by calling one work "dogshit". In March 2004, on the eve of the presidential elections, it was burned almost to the ground. It was quickly restored, reopened the following summer and now holds exhibitions.

The centrepiece of the Manege Square redevelopment is the de luxe underground mall known as **Okhotny Ryad ㉗** or Hunters' Row (daily 11am–10pm; tel: 737-8449). This was the name once given to the former meat market near by that was famous in the 19th century for its taverns and nightlife. The mall today has a much more contrived nature. It was funded under Mayor Luzhkov, who gave free reign to his favourite artist, Zurab Tsereteli *(see page 65)*, to decorate the building – to mixed effect. From above ground all that is visible is the mall's glass cupola – a dome-map of the northern hemisphere. Tsereteli also designed a modern garden to lead to **Aleksandrovsky sad** (gardens), which was laid in 1819–22 when the Neglinnaya River was forced into underground pipes.

Today these gardens are enlivened by a trickle of the Neglinnaya River that has been released above ground to flow amid sculptures of fairy-tale characters. Across from the fountain is a **Grotto**, or "Ruins", designed by Bove as a romantic nook for poetic thoughts. The nearby obelisk was dedicated in 1913 to the 300th anniversary of the Romanov dynasty, but soon converted into a Monument to Revolutionary Thinkers.

At the gardens' north end is the **Tomb of the Unknown Soldier ㉘**, *(Mogila Neizvestnovo Soldata)*, which was dedicated in 1967, on the 25th anniversary of the battle of Moscow. Under an eternal flame is a tomb decorated with a helmet and banner inscribed: "Your name is unknown, your deed is immortal." Wreaths are laid here for the war dead on Victory Day (9 May), and newlyweds come to pay their respects in between the registry office ceremony and the wedding party. The guard changes every hour with great ceremony. In winter they change every 30 minutes. The nearby gates open onto the rear of the Historical Museum. ❑

RESTAURANTS & BARS

Restaurants

Café Maner
5 ulitsa Petrovka. Metro: Teatralnaya. Tel: 775-1969. Open: B, L & D daily. $$$
A classy, upscale café located in the sleek Berlin. The menu is modern European, and portions are small – the best option is a sandwich if you're hungry. Or, come to sample the excellent range of pastries while watching Moscow's elite.

Godunov
5/1 Teatralnaya ploshchad. Metro: Teatralnaya. Tel: 298-5609. Open: L & D daily. $$$
Located in a monastery built during the rule of Boris Godunov. Riotous colours decorate the walls and staff, and there is an atmosphere to match in the evenings courtesy of the live band. Try the home-made almond vodka or *medovukha* (honey mead).

O'Mar
5 Teatralnaya ploshchad, building 3. Metro: Teatralnaya. Tel: 298-3254. Open: L & D daily. $$$
A pricey but good Mediterranean-style restaurant with a range of Italian dishes. Seafood, particularly lobster, is the speciality. The excellent summer veranda has a view of the Bolshoy Theatre.

Staraya Bashnya
5/1 Teatralnaya ploshchad. Metro: Teatralnaya. Tel: 298-4008. Open: L & D daily. $$$
Five floors of dining – choose from two floors of traditional Russian food, three of European. Cosy and intimate, but conversation can be difficult when the live folk ensembles kick in at night. Russian cuisine is the best bet – try the reindeer. Set lunch is a good option for a quick bite if you're in the area.

Teatro
1/4 Teatralny proezd. Metro: Lubyanka. Tel: 927-6067. Open: L & D daily. $$$$
Located in the Metropol Hotel, this elegant Italian restaurant has dishes that are inventive but simple, with an emphasis on using seasonal ingredients. Mouth-watering dessert menu.

Temple Bar
Okhotny Ryad Mall, upper level. Metro: Okhotny Ryad. Tel: 737-8476. Open 24 hrs daily. $
One of the many restaurants on the terrace of the Okhotny Ryad mall that overlooks the fountains of Aleksandrovsky sad. The informal atmosphere makes it a good place to relax after trekking around the Kremlin, and despite its central location prices are very reasonable. You might want to note that they do a Full English Breakfast from 5am if you fancy a taste of home, or just some sustenance after a late night.

Bars

Conservatory Lounge and Bar
4 Neglinnaya ulitsa. Metro: Teatralnaya. Tel: 783-1234. Open: 10am–2am daily. $$$$
Excellent views of Theatre Square and the Kremlin from the terrace of the Ararat Park Hyatt's bar. Friendly, professional staff who'll provide you with a blanket if you're outdoors and feeling chilly. Even a glass of wine will cost plenty, so come here for a pre- or post-dinner drink.

Phlegmatic Dog
Okhotny Ryad Mall, upper level. Metro: Okhotny Ryad. Tel: 995-9554. Open: noon–1am daily. $
This is a relaxed bar overlooking the fountains of the Aleksandrovsky sad. The food is mostly pub grub, but done to a very high level. Uniquely, the bar is fully wired, allowing guests to chat to other guests via computers at each table.

PRICE CATEGORIES
Prices for three-course dinner per person with a glass of house wine:
$ = under $25
$$ = $25–40
$$$ = $40–60
$$$$ = more than $60

RIGHT: the Metropol's grand dining room.

PALACES BENEATH THE STREETS

Muscovites are extremely proud of their metro system, and rightfully so – it is clean, fast, efficient, cheap, and spectacular to look at

Public transport in Moscow seems more like entertainment than a daily grind to visitors. You leave street reality, step on a fast-moving escalator that plunges you under the earth, and step off into a palace of marble and coloured stone lit by chandeliers and decorated with sculpture and mosaics.

The Moscow metro is not only one of the world's most beautiful forms of public transport, it's one of the world's most efficient. It handles more than 9 million passengers every day, ferrying them at about 42 kph (26 mph) to 171 stations over 600 km (373 miles) of track, with a wait of about two minutes between trains. And the stations – particularly the older ones on the Circle Line and in the city centre – are elegant and majestic, even if the mosaics of farm workers or bas-reliefs of hearty athletes seem anachronistic in today's booming post-Soviet capitalism.

But the sleek, stainless-steel-arched Mayakovskaya station that won the Grand Prix at the New York World's Fair in 1938 fits right into postmodernist Moscow. In the newly restored station, be sure to glance up at the ceiling mosaic designed by the artist Alexander Deneyka. This station served as a bomb shelter during World War II and was the venue of the Moscow City Council's celebration of the 24th anniversary of the October Revolution in 1941.

ABOVE: the grand décor of Komsomolskaya metro station would not be out of place in the Bolshoy Theatre.

ABOVE: Khrushchev (third from left) began his career organising the building of the metro.

LEFT: the metro stations are marked with a red-neon M, but are sometimes hidden behind the trading booths that now crowd around the stations.

DIGGING TUNNELS FOR SOCIALISM

Although the Moscow City Council had discussed building a metro as early as 1902, the first tunnels were not dug until 1931. Designed to be the showcase of the Soviet Union's first Five-Year Plan to modernise industry, the metro combined technical innovation with artistic celebration of the working class. Like many of the industrial undertakings of the 1930s, it was a symbolic project, intended to show that Socialism could achieve anything capitalism could.

The luxury of the first line (the Red Line) was opened with much pomp in 1935. Kropotkinskaya is one of the most beautiful and restrained stations. It is lined with marble taken from the façade of the demolished Cathedral of Christ the Saviour, now reconstructed near by *(see page 120)*.

Newer stations in the outer districts are not as elegant or as deep as those in the centre. The exception to the rule is the station at Park Pobedy, completed in 2003. It is the deepest station in the city with the world's longest escalator: an ear-popping 126 metres/yds.

BELOW: the tunnels of the metro are a world of their own, filled with fast-food stands, news-stands and people selling everything from books to puppies. In the winter they are a welcome shelter from the cold, but during the summer they resemble a Russian bathhouse. Still, despite the noise of the trains coming and going nearly every minute, they make a very popular place to meet friends or dates.

ABOVE: thanks to its engineering and optimism, the metro symbolises how much the Soviet regime could accomplish. Not only is it an extremely efficient form of public transport, but intricate mosaics such as the one above remind visitors of the ideology that powered its construction. Newer stations are mostly utilitarian, with simple wipe-clean tiles.

CLASSIC ART AND OLD ARBAT

Celebrated in song and verse, the Arbat was once the Bohemian centre of the capital, and it is still vibrant today, even if it has lost some of its edge. Along with a visit to the best little street in Moscow, there's a chance to see two world-class museums, Russia's largest church and a host of homes of Russian literary heroes

The part of the city southwest of the Kremlin is filled with museums and good shopping. Further afield, two visual feasts await: the surreal beauty of Novodevichy Convent and the view over the city from the Sparrow Hills.

Opposite the Kremlin's southwest tip stands the magnificent **Pashkov House** (*Dom Pashkova*; metro Borovitskaya), designed by Bazhenov for Pytor Pashkov, a captain in the Semyonovsky regiment, who was granted the land by Peter the Great. Today, obscured by an enormous billboard, it is difficult to appreciate its graceful proportions and grandeur, which earned it the name of "the enchanted castle". In 1861, the Rumyantsev library and art collection was brought here from St Petersburg. In 1924 it was turned into the Lenin Library, and the non-book collections were distributed among other Moscow museums. It is still part of the State Library, but has been under reconstruction for nearly a decade.

The street that begins at Borovitskaya ploshchad, a massive roadway in front of the Kremlin's Borovitsky Gates, is ulitsa Znamenka, named after a church that once stood here: the Mother of God of the Sign (*znamenie*). At No. 5 is the **Shilov Art Gallery ❶** (*Kartinnaya galereya A. Shilova*; 5 ulitsa Znamenka; tel: 203-4450 or 203-4208; Tues–Sun 11am–6pm; admission charge). Alexander Shilov's (b. 1943) portraits of famous Russians, still lifes and landscapes are hugely popular. In 1997 he donated more than 300 canvases to the state, which provided this 19th-century manor house to house them.

Street of the arts

Ulitsa Volkhonka starts at Borovitskaya ploshchad and goes to the southwest. This area leading down to the Moscow River was called

Map on page 116

LEFT: walking the Arbat is one of Moscow's simple pleasures.
BELOW: the Wall of Peace, created by hopeful children of the 1980s.

Behind Pashkov House on Starovaganovsky pereulok is the lovely Church of St Nicholas on Old Vagankov (Khram Svyatovo Nikolaya na Starom Vagankove), built in 1531, but rebuilt in the 19th century. The writer Nikolay Gogol attended this church.

Chertole ("The Devil's Land") from Chertornaya, a tributary of the Moscow River. Another tributary, the Volkhonka, gave the street its name. The area was once settled by Ivan the Terrible's *oprichniki (see page 19)*, but by the 19th century it was lined by noble mansions. Today this short street has four major museums and the country's main church, the Cathedral of Christ the Saviour.

The **Pushkin Museum of Fine Arts ②** (*Muzey izobrazitelnykh iskusstv imeni A.S. Pushkina*; 12 ulitsa Volkhonka; tel: 203-7998/203-9578; admission charge; open 10am–7pm,

last ticket at 6pm; English audio players; maps of the museum and Moscow are available in the basement) is a handsome classical building set back among tall pines. It was the "child" of Ivan Tsvetaev (1847–1913), a professor of art history and father of the poet Marina Tsvetaeva, who was possessed with the idea of creating a museum that would present the finest examples of Western art to the public. The museum was finally opened by Tsar Nicholas II and his family. Under Soviet power the museum collection grew to include expropriated private collections from

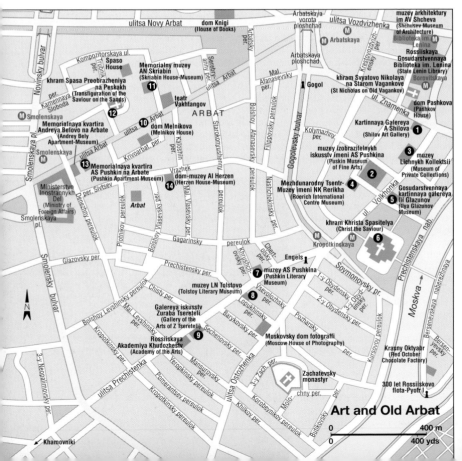

Art and Old Arbat

0 — 400 m
0 — 400 yds

Sergey Shchukin, Ivan Morozov, Sergey Tretyakov, the Yusupov and Shuvalov families and other Soviet museums. The bulk of the collection was fortuitously evacuated to the east during World War II. In 1953 the museum resumed displays of its main collection and began to exhibit art "saved" from Nazi Germany.

Today the museum has more than half a million works of art retaining the founders' concept of an educational institution with many copies of antique and European statuary.

Highlights of the Pushkin

Our tour begins at the top of the stairwell accessed from the cloakroom; note the buffet and café on the right for later refreshment. Stop in Hall 7, straight ahead at the top of the stairs, where the **Schliemann Gold** is usually on display, while the debate as to which country the collection truly belongs continues. Heinrich Schliemann discovered the huge cache of gold jewellery and objects, dated to 2500 BC, in Turkey in 1873. The hall also showcases antiquities and special exhibits.

To see the Pushkin's collection chronologically, turn left at the top of the stairs and go through Halls 3 and 4, where you turn left again into Hall 2 and then into Hall 1, which holds the museum's small, but truly excellent, collection of **Egyptian art**.

Hall 2 showcases the art of Ancient civilisations: bas-reliefs from Persepolis and Babylon, pottery and statues from India and pre-Columbian America. Before visiting 13th- and 14th-century Italy (Hall 4), look at the eerily lifelike Faiyum funeral masks (1st century AD) in Hall 3, as well as the still bright and festive Coptic textiles.

The museum's collection of early Italian art in Hall 4 (13th–15th centuries) is not extensive, but the *Virgin and Child Enthroned,* by an anonymous Florentine artist, and the icon *The*

Twelve Apostles (Hall 3), both from the 1330s, are exquisite. Halls 5 and 6 highlight the museum's collection of art from the medieval to Renaissance periods in Italy, Germany and the Netherlands. In Hall 5 the masterpiece is the *Annunciation*, part of an altarpiece painted by Sandro Botticelli in the 1490s. It overpowers the delicate *Madonna and Child* by Lucas Cranach the Elder (1525) and several lovely landscapes, including Pieter Brueghel the Younger's *Winter Landscape with a Bird Trap.*

El Greco's *St John the Baptist*, thought to have been lost in World War II, appeared not long ago in Hall 6, which is otherwise devoted to the **Renaissance art of Venice**. Note Tintoretto's *Portrait of a Man* and Paolo Veronese's *Minerva*. Hall 6 is a dead end, so backtrack to the central lobby. Off the lobby on either side in Halls 14 and 15 are the Greek and Italian courtyards, brightly lit from skylights, beautifully appointed and filled with plaster casts and copies of statuary.

Directly opposite Hall 3 is Hall 11, which contains Flemish art of the 17th century, with some Spanish art

Maps:
Area 116
Plan 118

Botticelli's Annunciation *is one of the museum's many masterpieces from the Italian Renaissance.*

BELOW: beginning a tour of the Pushkin museum.

During Soviet times collectors saved works of art that were due to be burned and traded art that had been hidden since the Revolution. In 1972 Ilya Zilbershtein, a collector and art historian, proposed a Museum of Private Collections. It was approved by Mikhail Gorbachev in 1983.

from the same period. The museum's collection of Spanish art is not representative, but Bartolomé Murillo's *The Fruit Seller* and *Archangel Raphael and Bishop Domonte* are excellent. The Flemish school is well represented by Peter Paul Rubens's *Bacchanalia*, several canvases by Van Dyke and Snyders, and the lush Jacob Jordeans paintings of *Ulysses in the Cave of Polyphemus* and *The Flight into Egypt.*

To the left in Hall 10 is one of the museum's finest collections: 17th-century Dutch art. The highlight is **Rembrandt.** Canvases include the luminous *Ahasuerus, Haman and Esther* and three portraits of Rembrandt's family: *An Old Woman, An Old Man* and *An Elderly Woman.* From the dead-end Hall 10 backtrack through Hall 11 to Hall 12, Italian art of the 17th and 18th centuries. This collection is also excellent, containing works from all the main centres: Rome, Florence,

Bologna, Naples, Genoa and Venice. The museum's collection of **French art** begins in Hall 13. The Pushkin Museum is second only to the Louvre in the scope and size of its French collection, mostly expropriated from Moscow's great arts patrons, Shchukin, Morozov and Tretyakov. Hall 13 displays the 17th and 18th centuries, with splendid works by Greuze, Fragonard, Watteau, Boucher and Poussin.

From Hall 13 you can enter the Italian Courtyard (through a copy of the Golden Arch of the Cathedral in Frieburg) and take the stairs to the second floor. The halls in the back half of the museum (24–9) and the first halls at the top of the stairs (16 and 16a) are taken up by plaster casts and copies. The central halls (19, 20 and 30) are used for temporary exhibits, but the five halls on this floor devoted to painting are the museum's Holy Grail: the magnificent collection of **pre-Impressionist,**

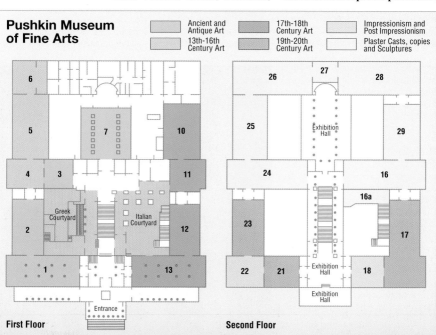

Pushkin Museum of Fine Arts

- Ancient and Antique Art
- 13th-16th Century Art
- 17th-18th Century Art
- 19th-20th Century Art
- Impressionism and Post Impressionism
- Plaster Casts, copies and Sculptures

First Floor

6, 5, 7, 10, 4, 3, 11, Greek Courtyard, Italian Courtyard, 2, 12, 1, 13, Entrance

Second Floor

26, 27, 28, 25, Exhibition Hall, 29, 24, 16, 16a, 23, 17, 22, 21, Exhibition Hall, 18, Exhibition Hall

Impressionist and **European art** of the late 19th and early 20th centuries.

To continue chronologically, walk past the main staircase and through Hall 24 (Greek art) to Hall 23 and 22 on the left. These exhibit European art of the first half of the 19th century. Wonderful canvases of the Barbizon school include fine works by Courbet, Corot and Millet. The museum has several landscapes by John Constable and an excellent landscape by the German Romantic painter Caspar David Friedrich. Delacroix's *After the Shipwreck* is one of the the collection's treasures, as is the study for Rodin's *The Kiss*.

Hall 21 has a changing exhibition of **French Impressionists**. Renoir's *Portrait of Jeanne Samary* and his luscious *Nude* are usually on display, as are Monet's *Luncheon on the Grass* and one of his series of the Cathedral in Rouen. Across the staircase landing and past the halls for temporary exhibits, the collection continues in Hall 18 with the **post-Impressionists**: primarily Van Gogh, Cézanne and Gaugin, whose *Red Vineyards in Arles* and *The Prisoner's Walk* are breathtaking. The last large hall, No. 17, displays works of the late 19th and early 20th century.

Collectors Shchukin and Morozov each bought nearly 50 paintings by **Picasso** and **Matisse**; three or four are on display. Picasso's *Girl on a Ball* and the *Portrait of Ambroise Vollard* are usually exhibited, as are Matisse's bright *Goldfish* and one of the smaller versions of *The Dance*. The hall only displays two canvases by Marc Chagall, but there are excellent works by Kandinsky, Léger and Miró, and the Maillol sculpture *Pomona*.

The Private Collections

Across Kolymazhny pereulok, just opposite the exit of the Pushkin Museum, is another branch of the institution – the **Museum of Private Collections** ❸ (*Muzey lichnykh kollektsii*; 8/10 ulitsaVolkhonka; tel: 203-1546; Wed–Sun 12–7pm; admission charge; English guide on sale in kiosk, English room descriptions and exhibit notes), opened in 1994. The museum makes no pretense of being comprehensive, but there is a bit of everything. The focus is on Russian

Maps:
Area 116
Plan 118

Many of the works mentioned in the text may not be on view when you visit. If there is something specific you want to see – or even draw – phone before visiting.

BELOW: private group tours are available.

When Christ the Saviour (cupola above) *was built on the site of a convent, the abbess cursed: "Nothing but a fetid and filthy pond shall ever be on this land!" In 1958, after the site had remained empty for over 25 years, the Moskva outdoor swimming pool was finally put in – confirming the abbess's curse.*

BELOW: the Cathedral of Christ the Saviour.

art, including icons, 18th- and 19th-century folk art, paintings by such masters as Polenov and Repin, as well as the world's largest collection of art by **Alexander Rodchenko** and **Varvara Stepanova**.

This is Russia's first truly international-standard museum, and it is a delight to view the art in the airy, well-lit and comfortable building.

Roerich and Glazunov

To the left of the Pushkin Museum, at the end of a small side street, is the **Nikolay Roerich International Centre Museum ❹** (*Mezhdunarodny tsentr-muzey imeni N.K. Rerikha*; 3/5 Maly Znamensky pereulok; tel: 975-0745; Tues–Sun 11am–7pm; admission charge; English descriptions). The museum displays every aspect and period of Roerich's life: from his work as a set designer for Diaghilev, and his ethnographic and artistic travels through Asia, to his paintings and his philosophical and political activities to promote the Banner of Peace *(see margin note opposite)*. The museum is well annotated in Russian and English.

On the other side of ulitsa Volkhonka is a turquoise neoclassical mansion that houses paintings by Roerich's artistic and philosophical opposite: the **Ilya Glazunov Museum ❺** (*Gosudarstvennaya kartinnaya galereya Ili Glazunov*; 13 ulitsa Volkhonka; tel: 291-6949; Tues–Sun 11am–7pm; admission charge). Glazunov (born 1930) is one of Russia's most controversial figures, whose nationalistic views and kitschy canvases have earned the scorn of the intelligentsia and the love of the masses. If you want to see what the fuss is about, stop in to see his wall-sized canvases filled with state leaders, historical figures, sad-eyed old women, poor people holding signs "selling Russian children", nuclear explosions, vulgar Bolsheviks, Bill Clinton and Monica Lewinsky.

Christ the Saviour

Once again dominating ulitsa Volkhonka is the spectacular **Cathedral of Christ the Saviour ❻** (*Khram Khrista Spasitelya*; 15 ulitsa Volkhonka; tel: 201-2847; daily 8am–8pm; Russian-language tours, includ-

ing a trip to the observation deck, can be arranged at the booths on the south side or in English through Patriarshy Dom, *see page 227*). The Cathedral was built over the course of 44 years (1839–83) to commemorate the Russian victory over Napoleon in 1812. It was meant to be built in the Sparrow Hills overlooking the city, but Nicholas I decided on a site by the Moscow River occupied by a convent *(see margin note opposite)*. In 1931 Stalin ordered its destruction and the construction of an enormous Palace of the Soviets, topped with a giant statue of Lenin, but engineers determined that the boggy land would not support it. The cathedral was reconsecrated on 31 December 1999.

Measuring over 103 metres (338 ft) high with an interior of 8,000 sq. metres (86,111 sq. ft) and large enough to hold 10,000 worshippers, this is the largest church in Russia. The cupola, gilded with 53 kg (117 lb) of a titanium and gold alloy, is nearly 30 metres (98ft) in diameter. The galleries are inscribed with manifestos of war and victory, as well as descriptions of battles. The icons and frescos in the huge main nave continue the religious-patriotic theme of the Cathedral.

On the lower floor of the Cathedral, kiosks sell a variety of books, and religious objects; there is also a chapel and a small museum of the history of the Cathedral and the Church in Russia. Outside, note the lovely *style moderne* apartment building opposite on Soymonovsky pereulok. Called the House of Pertsov, after the engineer who commissioned it in 1907, it is lavishly decorated with tile friezes, with a dragon or two under the drain pipes.

Literary heritage

Ulitsa Volkhonka splits into two formerly aristocratic streets as it heads southwest: Ostozhenka (closer to the Moscow River) and Prechistenka, with a statue to **Friedrich Engels** standing between them. Most buildings on Prechistenka are graceful 19th-century classical and Empire-style mansions. The former Khrushchev mansion at No. 12/2 houses the **Pushkin Literary Museum** ❼ (*Muzey A.S. Pushkina*; tel: 201-5674; Tues–Sun 10am–5.30pm, closed last Fri of the month; admission charge; entrance in Khrushchovsky pereulok). The biggest museum devoted to Alexander Pushkin outside St Petersburg is filled with manuscripts, possessions and extensive collections of applied and fine arts that recreate the life and times of Russia's premier poet.

The **Tolstoy Literary Museum** ❽ (*Muzey L.N. Tolstovo*; 11 ulitsa Prechistenka; tel: 202-2190/201-3811; Tues–Sun 10am–5.30pm, closed last Fri of the month; admission charge) is in the former Lopukhin mansion. The focus is on Tolstoy's legacy, with books, manuscripts and memorabilia. Further down is the **Academy of the Arts** (at No. 21) and the gallery dedicated to

Map on page 116

Nikolay Roerich (1874–1947), painter, set designer, teacher and philosopher, spent many years in Asia. To protect the world's cultural treasures, he developed the Banner of Peace to be flown by cultural monuments to protect them during times of hostilities. The Roerich Pact to protect cultural treasures in war and peace was signed in 1935 by members of the Pan-American Union, including the US. It is still in force today.

BELOW: the controversial Ilya Glazunov Museum.

BELOW: some
Russian dolls with
some foreign faces.

its president, Zurab Tsereteli (at No. 19). The Academy's building is considered one of Moscow's finest examples of classicism. Before the Revolution it belonged to the Morozovs and housed the family's art collection. It was reconstructed in 2000.

The **Gallery of the Arts of Zurab Tsereteli** ❾ (*Galereya iskusstv Zuraba Tsereteli*; 19 ulitsa Prechistenka; tel: 201-2569/201-4150; Tues–Sat 12–8pm, Sun 12–7pm; admission charge) showcases this flamboyant artist *(see page 65)*.

Most of the buildings on Prechistenka's sister street of Ostozhenka are occupied by businesses and restaurants. Security cameras are all over the apartment blocks on the lovely streets in between, which have been remodelled for wealthy foreign and Russian tenants.

Boulevard Ring to Old Arbat

The first long leg of the Boulevard Ring is called Gogolevsky, in honour of the writer Nikolay Gogol, who lived near here. It stretches up a gentle slope to the north past a few urban mansions on the east side (note the

pink-and-white mansion at No. 10 – now the Russian Cultural Foundation) and apartment houses-turned-offices on the west side, to Arbatskie vorota ploshchad. In 1951 Stalin drove past the original 1909 statue of Gogol at the top of the boulevard and said that it "did not fit in with postwar optimism". Gloomy Gogol was removed – he's tucked in the courtyard of 7 Nikitsky bulvar – and a newly commissioned "Happy Gogol" (by Nikolay Tomsky) put in place.

Old Arbat

The labyrinth of lanes between Prechistenka and Povarskaya ulitsas on the far side of ulitsa Novy Arbat *(see page 137)* are still celebrated in songs and poetry as the charming "Arbat lanes", even though much of the neighbourhood's charms have been destroyed by successive building booms. Ulitsa Prechistenka was originally called Chertolskaya, after the small river here, and known as the road that led to the Novodevichy Convent. But in 1658 Tsar Aleksey renamed it in honour of the church of the "Most Pure *(prechistaya)* Mother of God of Smolensk" in the convent.

The heart of the neighbourhood is **ulitsa Arbat** ❿, which stretches from the southwest from Arbatskie vorota ploshchad. The street's name is believed to come from the Turkic word *rabat*, meaning "caravan", and was settled by traders from the south.

Over the centuries it remained a trading street, the lanes around it slowly filling with the middle and upper-middle classes, and, by the turn of the 20th century, Moscow's poets, writers and artists. In the early 1980s the Arbat was pedestrianised and immediately overtaken by artists, street vendors and bearded singers doing their best imitations of the Russian bard Vladimir Vysotsky *(see page 170)*.

The Arbat is graced at one end by the elegant Praga restaurant at Arbatskie vorota ploshchad and overshadowed at the other by the Stalinist giant of the **Ministry of Foreign Affairs** at Smolenskaya ploshchad on the Garden Ring Road. As you walk from Arbatskie vorota ploshchad, just past Arbatsky pereulok you'll see a confused mass of colour on a wall. This is the **Wall of Peace** – tiles decorated by Soviet schoolchildren in the 1980s, now covered with post-Soviet graffiti *(see picture, page 115)*. Among the dozens of souvenir shops, the one at No. 27 has a large selection of high-quality crafts of every kind, from glassware to *Palekh* boxes. Past it is the **Vakhtangov Theatre**, a grey Stalinist structure on the right, enlivened by a delicate statue of Turandot (now a teenage hang-out).

After the Vakhtangov Theatre, make a short detour to the **Skriabin House-Museum** ⓫ *(Memorialny muzey A.N. Skriabina*; 11 Bolshoy Nikolopeskovsky pereulok; tel: 241-1901/241-5156; Wed and Fri 12–6.30pm; Thur, Sat and Sun 10am–4.30pm; closed last Fri of the month; admission charge; English room description and brochures; tours in English by appointment; concerts and other events). The composer and pianist Alexander Skriabin lived in this second-floor apartment for the last three years of his life, from 1912 to 1915. You can see the simple but elegant *style moderne* furniture and personal possessions in several modest rooms, but the highlight of the museum is the "light keyboard". Here, as he played the *Prometheus* symphonic poem on the piano, his wife would "play" the colours that Skriabin "saw" as the notes. The museum staff play the light keyboard to a recording of *Prometheus*.

On the other side of the Arbat is the small Krivoarbatsky pereulok ("Bent Arbat"), notable for the wall near the Arbat plastered with graffiti in honour of the rock musician Viktor Tsoy, who died in a car acci-

dent in 1990. Teenagers pose and chat by the wall.

As you follow the crooked lane, you come across one of Moscow's most famous architectural landmarks, tucked behind a wall amid renovated apartment buildings. The Constructivist masterpiece of the **Melnikov House** *(Dom Melnikova)* at No. 10 is easy to miss behind the ramshackle fence; if you peer between the posts, you can see the two cylinders decorated by rhomboid windows of the only private residence Konstantin Melnikov built in the Soviet period (1927–9). He fell out of favour at the end of the 1930s, but continued to live in the house until his death in 1974. The architect's family, who inherited the house, are quarrelling in court, and conservationists say its preservation is not guaranteed.

You can continue on Krivoarbatsky pereulok and then turn right on Plotnikov pereulok to return to the Arbat – passing on the way the statue of the Arbat's most famous poet, Bulat Okudzhava *(see page 51)*. Across the street and a few paces

Map on page 116

Personal pavement greetings outside the Vakhtangov Theatre are sold by the city.

BELOW: A typical Russian bard on Old Arbat.

A detail from the Stalinist Ministry of Foreign Affairs building still carries the familiar mark of the old regime.

BELOW: Lev Tolstoy.

back to the north, you can take another detour along Spasopeskovsky pereulok to see the charming white stone **Church of the Transfiguration of the Saviour on the Sands** *(Khram Spasa Preobrazheniya na Peskakh)*, named because the land here under the high-rises is sandy. The five-domed church was first built in stone in 1689, with a lovely tent spire over the belfry. The church has been immortalised in the Polenov canvas *Moscow Courtyard* (1878) now in the Tretyakov Gallery: it is strange to see the delicate church, now dwarfed by modern buildings and blocked by cars, standing amid farmland and small wooden houses just a little over 100 years ago.

On the far side of the square is **Spaso House**, the residence of the US Ambassador, a beautiful neoclassical mansion built in 1913 by the Vtrorov family. The US was granted the house in 1933; two years later the Ambassador held a Spring Ball, with

hundreds of animals and birds on loan from the Moscow zoo, roses and tulips filling the mansion, mountains of food and rivers of champagne. One of the guests was the writer Mikhail Bulgakov, and the lavish evening reappears as Satan's Ball in *The Master and Margarita (see page 51)*.

Back on the Arbat, further towards Smolenskaya ploshchad are two house-museums of writers: Alexander Pushkin and Andrey Bely. The **Pushkin Apartment-Museum** *(Memorialnaya kvartira A.S. Pushkina na Arbate*; 53 ulitsa Arbat; tel: 241-9295; Wed–Sun 11am–6pm, closed last Fri of the month; admission charge; English tours available by appointment) was home to Pushkin and his bride for five months immediately after their marriage. Although they only rented the second floor, the first floor has an exhibition of Moscow and Pushkin's life and friends. Much of the museum requires a guide, but on the first floor

Moscow River and Sparrow Hills

you can soak up the atmosphere of literary and aristocratic 19th-century Moscow. The second floor, where Pushkin lived, consists of a drawing room and several rooms with a few pieces of furniture and manuscript copies that serve as foils for the tour guide's discourses.

Next door is the **Andrey Bely Apartment-Museum** (*Memorialnaya kvartira Andreya Belovo na Arbate*; 55 ulitsa Arbat; tel: 241-7702; Wed–Sun 11am–6pm, closed last Fri of the month; admission charge), where Boris Bugayev (the writer's real name) was born and lived for the first 26 years of his life. Bugayev, novelist, poet and literary critic, lead the group of Symbolists that appeared on the Russian literary scene at the end of the 19th century.

At the Smolenskaya ploshchad end of the Arbat, you may chose to turn left on Denezhny pereulok, just before the massive Ministry of Foreign Affairs, and then another left on pereulok Sivtsev Vrazhek. The name means "Sivtsev Gully" and refers to a creek no longer here. Literature buffs may want to visit the **Herzen House-Museum ⓮** (*Dommuzey A.I. Herzen*; 27 pereulok Sivtsev Vrazhek; tel: 241-5859; Tues, Thur and Sat 11am–5.30pm, Wed and Fri 1–5.30pm; closed last day of the month; admission charge; English room descriptions). Alexander Herzen (1812–70) lived in this cosy home, now filled with his personal effects, manuscripts, portraits and memorabilia, with his family from 1843 to 1846, where he was visited by leading liberal thinkers and writers. In 1847 he wrote his most famous novel, *Who is to Blame?*

Khamovniki

Just beyond the Garden Ring Road at the Park Kultury metro station are two lovely sights that are well worth a visit. On the corner of Komsomol-sky prospekt and ulitsa Lva Tolstovo is the **Church of St Nicholas the Wonderworker in Khamovniki ⓯** (*Khram Svyatitelya Nikolaya Chudotvoretsa v Khamovnikakh*). Built in the late 17th century by weavers, its bright-green and orange-red domes and layers of *kokoshniki* make it one of Moscow's most striking churches. Inside the lavishly decorated church is a gold canopy over a small icon of the Mother of God, *The Helper of Sinners*, a miracle-working icon brought to the church in 1848.

Midway down ulitsa Lva Tolstovo on the left is the wonderful **Tolstoy House Museum ⓰** (*muzey-usadba L.N. Tolstovo*, 21 ulitsa Lva Tolstovo; tel: 246-9444; Tues–Sun 10am–6pm; closed last Fri of the month; admission charge; English room descriptions). In 1881, when Tolstoy's children needed to go to school, the family decided to find a house in Moscow to spend the winters. They settled on a 16-room wooden house with no running water, sewage system or electricity. The family spent 19 winters here and Tolstoy wrote some of his most famous

Maps on pages 116 & 124

Memorial plaque on the house where the newlywed Pushkin spent "the happiest time of his life".

BELOW: billboards often hide Moscow's distinctive architecture.

The headstones at Novodevichy Cemetery are nearly as interesting as the people they remember. This one for General Afonina leaves little doubt about his profession.

BELOW: Novodevichy Cemetery is graceful in its sadness.

late works: *What Do I Believe In? What is to Be Done?* and *The Kingdom of Heaven within Us.* The interior of the house is simple and comfortable. In the upstairs hall guides can play the waltz Tolstoy composed, and a recording of his voice. Down the narrow, dark hall that the family called the Catacombs is Tolstoy's modest study. Near-sighted and vain, he refused to wear reading glasses; instead he sawed down the legs of his chair to sit lower and closer to his work.

Novodevichy Convent

Not far from Khamovniki stands **Novodevichy Convent**  (*Novodevichy monastyr*; 1 Novodevichy proezd; tel: 246-8526; Wed–Mon 10am–5.15pm; closed first Mon of the month; admission and photo/ video charges; English place markers and some English exhibit notes; English tours by appointment; take the Novodevichy exit from Sportivnaya station and turn right). The convent was founded in 1524 in honour of the taking of Smolensk from the Poles and Lithuanians by Grand Prince Vasily III, and is one of the best-preserved and peaceful of Moscow's fortress cloisters,

For most of its history it was a kind of prison for unwanted princely and royal wives and relatives, including Irina Godunova, Tsar Fyodor's widow and the sister of Boris Godunov. Boris Godunov was at the convent when the people of Moscow came three times to ask him to take the crown. Peter the Great sent his first wife, Yevdokia, and his sister, Sophia, here. Because the convent had such distinguished nuns, it received lavish gifts from the tsars, and by 1700 it was one of the richest cloisters in Russia, with over 15,000 serfs working in 36 villages. Although it was plundered by the French armies in 1812, the nuns managed to disarm the fuses that were set to blow the entire convent to the heavens. It was also saved from destruction when the Bolsheviks decided to turn it into a museum in 1922. It was partially returned to the Church in 1944,when an agreement was signed for the Church and state museum to share the premises.

This peaceful and beautiful place is best seen first from the far side of the small duck-filled pond near the river. Inside the gate, with the **Transfiguration of the Saviour Church** (*Preobrazhenskaya nadvratnaya tserkov;* 1687–8) above it, there is a pleasing combination of medieval and baroque architecture, best expressed in the magnificent **bell tower** that rises 72 metres/yds above the walls. Tombs of nuns, military leaders and wealthy families are scattered about the grounds; note the beautiful family crypt of the Prokhorov textile magnates in front of Smolensk Cathedral. It was built in 1911 in the *style moderne*.

The central church in the convent is **Smolensk Cathedral** (*Smolensky sobor*), built in 1524–5 and similar to the Dormition Cathedral in the

Kremlin. Here the five domes (one gold and four lead) are shifted slightly to the east, with stone galleries running around three sides. The interior is magnificently preserved, with unusual floral fresco ornamentation in the galleries and late 16th-century frescos in the body of the church, their deep blues and reds both grand and solemn. The five-tiered gilded wooden iconostasis was installed in 1683–5.

Behind Smolensk Cathedral is the **Refectory** and **Church of the Dormition** (*Uspenskaya tserkov*), built in 1685 and considered an architectural wonder for the lack of supporting pillars in the vast hall (400 sq. metres/yds). The museum in the **Lopukhin Chambers** (to the right through the entrance gates) displays a variety of temporary exhibitions. A permanent exhibition of ecclesiastical vestments and vessels, icons and frescos is displayed in the **Irina Godunova Chambers** (behind Smolensk Cathedral to the left). Look out for the model of the convent inside the entrance gates by the ticket kiosk.

Novodevichy Cemetery

In 1898 Church and city authorities decided to expand the convent cemetery to the south. The new area opened in 1904 and became a prestigious cemetery. The **Novodevichy Cemetery** (*Novodeviche kladbishche*; 2 Luzhnetsky proezd; 9am–6pm in winter, 9am–7pm in summer; free; English language maps and brochures) is now open to visitors. The cemetery is a *Who's Who* of Russia. You can see Chekhov's modest *style moderne* gravestone; the monument to Vladimir Mayakovsky; the clown Yuri Nikulin and the ballet dancer Ulanova; the monuments to the aircraft designers Tupolev and Ilyushin. By the south wall is the grave of Raisa Gorbachev: a simple gravestone with a delicate and graceful muse standing watch. Be sure to find Nikita Khrushchev's grave: the family asked Ernst Neizvestny, with whom the Soviet leader publicly argued at the Manege in 1962 (see page 109), to design the gravestone. A bust of Khrushchev rests between white and black blocks, symbolising the two sides of this complex leader.

Map on page 124

BELOW: circus star Yuri Nikulin with his signature hat.

Mikhail Lomonosov published poetry and the first history of Russia and was a founder of Moscow State University.

BELOW: Moscow State University towers over the city from Sparrow Hills.

The Sparrow Hills

On the top of a high bluff across the Moscow River from Novodevichy Convent are the **Sparrow Hills** , once a favourite spot for Muscovites to rent dachas in the hot summer months and enjoy the view of the city. Anton Chekhov once said, "If you want to understand Russia, you must come here and look out over Moscow." Today the view is different but still breathtaking. You can easily get here from the Vorobyovye Gory metro stop (exit from the front of the train and follow the path to the right, up the hill). Next to the viewing platform is the classical **Church of the Life-Giving Trinity on Sparrow Hills** *(Khram Troitsy Zhivonachalnoy na Vorobyovykh gorakh)*, built in 1811–13. Behind the church are some former government dachas, still hidden behind tall fences.

Towering over all is the main building of **Moscow State University** *(Moskovsky gosudarstvenny universitet imena Lomonosova)*, the greatest of the Stalinist skyscrapers. The university complex consists of over 50 buildings (the number-loving Soviet authorities liked to tell you there were 160 km/ 110 miles of corridors), with 6,000 rooms for students and over 200 apartments for staff, all located in a beautiful park and botanical gardens.

The Mosfilm Studios

Film buffs may want to arrange a tour of the **Mosfilm Studios** *(Mosfilm*; 1 Mosfilmovskaya ulitsa, trolley 34 from Kiev Station; tel: 143-9599; tours arranged in Russian by appointment or through Patriarshy Dom, *see page 227)*. It's not Universal Studios, but it is a glimpse at one of the world's greatest film companies The two-hour tour looks at a small part of the enormous collection of costumes and props (the largest in Europe), an outdoor set of Moscow at the end of the 19th century, old film equipment and a wonderful display of models used in special effects.

The tour ends with Mosfilm's celebrated collection of transport: over 80 antique cars, trucks, motorcycles, carriages and carts, including a 1913 Rolls Royce. ❑

RESTAURANTS

Cantinetta Antinori
20 Denezhny pereulok.
Metro: Smolenskaya.
Tel: 241-3325. Open: L & D
daily. $$$$
In a 19th-century house, with fresh white walls and beamed ceilings, this pricey chain restaurant offers faultless Tuscan cuisine, friendly service, convivial atmosphere and a large list of Antinori wines. Reservations essential.

Casual
3, 1-y Obydensky pereulok.
Metro: Kropotkinskaya.T
el: 775-2310. Open: L & D
daily. $$$
Good Mediterranean food in a modern, comfortable setting. The interior is airy, with high ceilings and low lighting. The rooftop terrace has fantastic views.

Dolf
3/2, 1-y Smolensky
pereulok. Metro: Smolenskaya. Tel: 241-6217.
Open: L & D daily. $$$
An elegant restaurant tucked on a lane behind Smolensky Passage. The dining hall is classy and intimate. The modern European menu has a touch of Swiss – try the *roesti* – good-sized portions and a selection of Swiss wines.

Five Spice
3/18 pereulok Sivtsev
Vrazhek. Metro: Kropotkinskaya. Tel: 203-1283.

Open: L & D daily. $$
Chinese and Indian food served in boudoir-like interior. Good range of tofu and vegetarian dishes. Tell your waiter if you want spicier food. Lunches are best – generously portioned and reasonably priced.

Genatsvale
12/1 ulitsa Ostozhenka.
Metro: Kropotkinskaya.
Tel: 202-0445. Open: L & D
daily. $$$
Consistently good Georgian food. Try *khachapuri* or *ketsi* (molten cheese) for starters, then one of the *shashlyks*. Loud live music. The VIP section is similar but expensive. Reservations essential.

Moo-Moo
45/24 ulitsa Arbat. Metro: Smolenskaya. Tel: 241-1364. Open: L & D daily. $
This self-service restaurant serves cheap and good Russian food in two cosy, wood-panelled dining halls. The menu has all the classics – soups, heavily dressed salads, dumplings, *shashlyks* – and daily specials.

Parizhsk
13 Zubovsky bulvar, building 2. Metro: Park Kultury.
Tel: 247-0912.
Open: 24 hrs daily. $$
Cosy, informal café popular with students. The menu is French with a Russian influence – try escargots or duck confit.

Reasonably priced wine and a good-cocktail menu. Good-value breakfasts and lunch deals.

Seiji
5/2 Komsomolsky prospekt.
Metro: Park Kultury.
Tel: 246-7624.
Open: L & D daily. $$$$
Minimalist Japanese restaurant headed by a genuine sushi chef and favoured by discerning guests. Exquisite and faultlessly executed *sashimi*, *nigiri* and *maki*. The summer veranda has good views.

Shatush
17 Gogolevsky bulvar.
Metro: Kropotkinskaya.
Tel: 201-4071. Open: 24hrs
daily. $$$$
Fine Chinese dining at its most elegant. The chic,

minimalist dark-wood bar, restaurant and lounge areas offer discreet dining.Try the extensive fresh-fruit cocktail menu.

Tiflis
32 ulitsa Ostozhenka. Metro: Park Kultury. Tel: 290-2897.
Open: L & D daily. $$$
Charming, intimate Georgian restaurant. Expect all the usual Georgian classics, including the much-praised *khachapuri*. Lovely summer veranda.

PRICE CATEGORIES

Prices for three-course dinner per person with a glass of house wine:
$ = under $25
$$ = $25–40
$$$ = $40–60
$$$$ = more than $60

RIGHT: the unmissible sign of the Moo-Moo café.

NEW ARBAT AND THE WEST

Moving westward from the Kremlin, the city develops in distinct areas, from the old White City, dating from tsarist times, with its concert halls and the Patriarch's Ponds, to the former working-class districts where revolution was fomented. On the far side of the river, the Napoleonic and Second World wars are commemorated in Victory Park

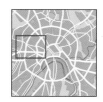

Divided into four distinct areas, Moscow's western sector has a medley of sights. Within the inner Boulevard Ring a charming assembly of tsarist-era buildings awaits exploration. This atmosphere continues out as far as the Garden Ring *(Sadovoye Koltso)* – with the exception of Novy Arbat, a street Soviet planners took enormous pride in, which is now lined with super casinos and looks more like a mini Las Vegas. Beyond the Garden Ring lies Krasnya Presnya, a former working-class district and home to the Russian White House and World Trade Centre. War monuments attract people across the river and down Kutuzovsky prospekt, the fourth area, where there is a hidden gem of a church in Fili.

White City treasures

From Manege Square west to the Boulevard Ring lies the western section of Moscow's old **White City** *(Bely gorod)* – a preserve of buildings and houses from tsarist times. The performing arts are well represented along these cosy streets, with first-rate productions at the Tchaikovsky Conservatory and the Mayakovsky and Gelikon Opera theatres. Museums are dedicated to zoology and the influential actor Konstantin Stanislavsky.

Once known as a "museum of classicism" because of its fine buildings, **Bolshaya Nikitskaya ulitsa** starts at Manege Square between the two buildings of Moscow University *(see page 109)*. It was named after a monastery that existed here from 1582 until the 1930s.

From the Manege, on the right-hand side, is the pale-blue **Zoological Museum** (*Zoologichesky muzey Moskovskovo universiteta*; 6 Bolshaya Nikitskaya ulitsa; tel: 203-8923; Tues–Sun 10am–5pm; closed

Map on page 132

LEFT: fairy-tale author Ivan Krylov still entertains the kids.
BELOW: New Arbat – Moscow's answer to Las Vegas.

Tchaikovsky conducts outside the Conservatory. To hear the music of Russian "bards" (singer-songwriters) try an evening at the café Gnezdo Glukharya (A Nest of Wood Grouse) on a narrow dead-end street called Khlynovsky tupik just past the Conservatory (tel: 291-9388).

last Tues of the month; admission charge). Nostalgically old-fashioned and smelling of formaldehyde and camphor, the ground floor has squiggly things in glass jars; on the upper floor you can see indigenous Russian creatures, such as the polar fox and the European bison, and several animals that have become endangered.

Further up the street, past sushi bars and boutiques, are a couple of hidden gems. At No. 18 is the lovely **Church of the Little Ascension** *(Tserkov Malovo Vosneseniya)*, tucked behind white stucco walls decorated with carvings. Across the street is a statue of Tchaikovsky conducting an imaginary orchestra in front of the columned portico of the **Moscow Tchaikovsky Conservatory** ➋ *(Moskovskaya gosudarstvennaya konservatoriya im. P.I. Chaikovskovo*; 13 Bolshaya Nikitskaya ulitsa; tel: 629-2060). The city's premier concert hall was

founded in 1866 by Nikolay Rubenstein and is the venue for the prestigious Tchaikovsky competition. The lobby and public spaces are in need of restoration, but the Grand Hall, decorated with medallions of composers, has an old-world elegance and impeccable acoustics.

Two more worthy performing-arts venues, the red-brick **Mayakovsky Drama Theatre** (currently closed) and the green-and-white **Gelikon Opera Theatre** *(see page 221 for booking details)*, sit further up the left-hand side of the street. If you'd rather take your art home with you, visit the friendly, cluttered **Murtuz Gallery** at No. 222. It has an eclectic assortment of contemporary art by more than 300 artists, and will arrange export (tel: 290-3139; Mon–Sat 10am–7pm).

At the top of Bolshaya Nikitskaya ulitsa, just before Nikitsky vorota, Leontevsky pereulok heads off to the right, and on its right-hand side

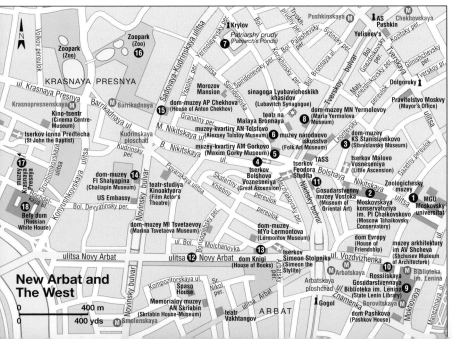

is the **Museum of Konstantin Stanislavsky** ❸ (*dom-muzey K.S. Stanislavskovo*; 6 Leontevsky pereulok; tel: 629-2855; Thur, Sat and Sun 11am–6pm, Wed and Fri 2–8pm; closed last Thur of the month; admission charge; English room descriptions). The actor, director and founder of the "method school" of acting lived in this ground-floor apartment with his wife, the actress Maria Lilina, from the late 1920s to his death in 1948. The apartment, with several rooms decorated in Stanislavsky's favourite European medieval style, is filled with memorabilia from the Moscow Art Theatre (MKhAT), including stage-set models and manuscripts.

The distinctive faux-folk Russian building across the street at No. 7 was built by Savva Morozov to house his collection of folk art. The museum was closed for renovations in 2005, but on weekdays you can visit the small Matrushka (Russian nesting doll) Museum on the second floor (free) and a folk-art store that sells quality souvenirs.

On the left side of Bolshaya Nikitskaya is Kalashny pereulok, where an antique shop, Antikvar, is filled with silver, icons, paintings and other small treasures.

Towards the Gorky Museum

The Boulevard Ring meets Bolshaya Nikitskaya ulitsa at **Nikitsky Gates** (Nikitskie vorota), the former entry gate in the walls of the White City. The square here is dominated by the ITAR-TASS building, but turn your back to the monolith of Soviet news reporting to see the majestic **Church of the Great Ascension** ❹ (*Tserkov Bolshovo Vozneseniya*). Built in the first half of the 19th century, it suffered severely during the Soviet period. Many icons were burned, and more than 50 lbs (23 kg) of gold and 27 lbs (12 kg) of silver in icons and vessels were removed before the

church was turned into offices. Now the interior is restored and once again filled with frescos, and a dazzling gold sun-ray cross crowns the sanctuary gates. In 1831 the writer Alexander Pushkin married Natalya Goncharova here, an event commemorated by bronze statues on the fountain in front of the church.

The more diminutive **Church of Theodore Studites** (*Tserkov Feodora Studita*) stands on the other side of Nikitskaya Bolshaya. Built in 1626, it is now under restoration.

On the corner of ulitsa Spiridonovka and Malaya Nikitskaya ulitsa is the Ryabunshinsky mansion, built by Fyodor Shekhtel in 1900 for the banker Ryabunshinsky and recognisable by the swirling wrought-iron fence and the frieze under the roof. Most visitors are interested only in the building, which is officially the **Maxim Gorky Museum** ❺ (*Muzey-kvartiry A.M. Gorkovo*; 6/2 Malaya Nikitskaya ulitsa, entrance in ulitsa Spiridonovka; tel: 290-5130; Wed– Sun 11am–6pm, closed last Thur of the month; free; room descriptions in

During the Soviet regime, the ITAR-TASS news agency was the only wire service in the country.

BELOW: staircase in the Maxim Gorky Museum.

*Maxim Gorky
(1868–1936) was
born into a poor
family in Nizhny
Novgorod. His works
about Russia's lower
classes garnered
him praise as a true
"writer of the prole-
tariat" and became,
in distorted form,
the credo of Soviet
literature. Although
he was portrayed as
an advocate of Soviet
power, he lived in
Italy, ostensibly for
health reasons, from
1921–8, and used his
status to help many
writers in disfavour
with the regime.*

BELOW: ice-skating is
one of the city's most
popular winter sports.

English), since the writer lived here
from 1931 to 1936.

This is one of Moscow's finest
examples of *style moderne* architecture and décor, as Shekhtel also
turned his attention to the furniture,
fixtures, wrought-iron fence, floors
and nine stained-glass windows.
The architectural centrepiece of the
house is the curved limestone staircase called "The Wave", which is
decorated with lamps that look like
jellyfish – *medusa* in Russian. It
was nearly ruined by the built-in
bookshelves Gorky installed. His
bedroom and sparsely decorated
study, with a collection of oriental
figurines, strikes a discordant note
with Shekhtel's lush ornamentation.
On the third floor is the recently
restored chapel and small bookshop.

Aleksey Tolstoy Museum

One of the service buildings of the
Gorky museum houses the museum of
another writer – **Aleksey Tolstoy** ⑥
(*Muzey-kvartiry A.N. Tolstovo*; 2/6
ulitsa Spiridonovka; tel: 290-0956;
Wed and Fri 1–7pm, Thur, Sat and
Sun 11am–6pm; closed last Wed of

the month; admission charge; room
descriptions in English). Aleksey
Tolstoy (1883–1945), related to
both writers Lev Tolstoy and Ivan
Turgenev, made a career as a popular novelist and playwright, best-
known for *Aelita* (the first science-
fiction novel written in Russia) and
his trilogy about Peter the Great.
Opposing the Revolution, he emigrated, but returned in 1922 to be
given his pick of furnishings from
Soviet warehouses filled with bourgeois booty. This apartment, where
he lived from 1941 until his death in
1945, is therefore decorated in an
eccentric assortment of styles, with
a small, but fine, collection of porcelain and paintings. Concerts and
other performances take place in the
intimate hall.

Next to the Gorky Museum is an
elegant, L-shaped house that follows the bend in Spiridonovka. It
has an excellent art gallery, the **New
Hermitage** (*Novy Ermitazh*; weekdays 12–6pm; tel: 290-4515), on
the main floor. Further down Spiridonovka, at No. 17, is another Shekhtel mansion, this one executed in

High Gothic style for the magnate Savva Morozov; it is now used for diplomatic receptions.

Patriarch's Ponds

Turn down ulitsa Malaya Bronnaya, named after the armour-makers *(bronniki)* who lived and worked here, and head north to reach one of Moscow's most picturesque, elite and expensive neighbourhoods – **Patriarch's Ponds** ❼ *(Patriarshy prudy)*. Named after the Patriarch's court that was once here, the heart of Patriarch's Ponds is a quiet stretch of water enjoyed by swans in summer and ice-skaters in winter, and surrounded by apartments, cafés, boutiques and embassies. Much of Bulgakov's *The Master and Margarita* takes place here, and there is no escaping the black cat and devil theme to the cafés. At the end of the pond are statues of the fabulist Ivan Krylov and of his fairy-tale characters.

In 2001 the Patriarch's Ponds community found the pond surrounded by fences and bulldozers; the city council had decided to face the pond in granite and erect several statues to Bulgakov and his literary characters, including a statue of Christ walking on the water. The community rebelled and won – virtually the only successful challenge to Mayor Luzhkov's projects of "urban improvement".

Returning to Nikitsky vorota from here, you pass the **Theatre of Malaya Bronnaya** (4 Malaya Bronnaya ulitsa), once the State Yiddish Theatre. Around the corner at No. 6 (building 3, Bolshaya Bronnaya ulitsa) is the **Lubavitch Synagogue.** Built in 1883, it was turned into the Moscow House for Amateur Performers in Soviet times and returned to the Jewish community in 1991. Its small museum can be viewed by appointment (tel: 202-4530).

Further down Tverskoy bulvar is the museum of the famous Russian actress **Maria Yermolova** ❽ *(Dommuzey M.N. Yermolovoy*; 11 Tverskoy bulvar; tel: 290-5416; Wed–Mon 12–7pm; closed last Mon of the month; admission charge). The premier actress at the Maly Theatre lived in this house from 1853 until her death in 1928.

Classic books and buildings

Running roughly less parallel to Bolshaya Nikitskaya ulitsa to the south is **ulitsa Vozdvizhenka**, the street of "the Exaltation of the Cross", named after a monastery that was here. The lushly ornamented building at the start of the street is the reception offices of the State Duma. On the other side is the stark-white marble **State Lenin Library** ❾. Built in 1940, and known as "Leninka", it is the main library of record and houses more than 40 million volumes. There is a small **Museum of Books** (3/5 ulitsa Vozdvizhenka through entrance 3, fourth floor; tel: 622-8672; Mon–Sat 10am– 5pm; closed last Mon of the month; free), which displays examples of printing, from ancient Egyptian papyrus to the present,

Map on page 132

Mikhail Bulgakov (1891–1940) is best known for his novel The Master and Margarita. *Set in Moscow in the 1930s – a time of brutal repressions and purges – the novel examines what would happen if the devil and his associates (including a large, talking black cat) came to town. The novel's assertion that "manuscripts don't burn" has become a credo of the power and invincibility of literature.*

BELOW: Dostoyevsky guards the entrance to the Lenin Library.

*The poet Marina
Tsvetaeva (1892–
1941), daughter of
Ivan Tsvetaev, the
founder of what is
now the Pushkin
Museum of Fine Arts,
is considered one of
Russia's best poets.
Unable to survive
under the Soviet
regime, she emigrated
in 1922, only to return
with her homesick and
now pro-Soviet
husband and family in
1939. Her son was
arrested soon after
her return and in 1941
she committed
suicide.*

BELOW: early autumn
is a mild and beautiful
time of year.

and has a rich collection of early
Russian liturgical texts.

On the right side of Vozdvizhenka,
at No. 16, is the **House of Friendship** *(dom Evropy)*, an odd, neo-
Moorish palace built in 1894–9 by
Arseny Morozov. It is rumoured
that when his mother saw the house
she exclaimed, "Before, only I knew
that you were a fool; now, all
Moscow will know." Arseny didn't
live long enough to enjoy the
house; to prove his strength of will,
he shot himself in the leg – and
died of sepsis.

Near by is the **Shchusev Museum
of Architecture ⑩** *(muzey arkhitektury im A.V. Shchuseva*; ulitsa
Vozdvizhenka 5/25; tel: 291-2109/
290-0551; Tues–Sun 12–7pm; admission charge). While the late 18th-
century building is being restored,
you can enjoy the spacious halls,
trompe l'oeil ceilings, crystal chandeliers and temporary exhibitions.
The Chambers of the Tsar's Apothe-
cary in the delightful courtyard is a
small exhibition space, built in 1670
to dry herbs for the tsar's private
pharmacy. Any of the streets off

ulitsa Vozdvizhenka to the north
lead back to Bolshaya Nikitskaya
ulitsa. Their modest classical mansions include the State Institute for
the Dramatic Arts at No. 6 Maly
Kislovsky, and the blue-and-white
skyscraper at No. 10/2 Nizhny
Kislovsky (just off the square)
designed by avant-garde artists
Alexander Rodchenko and Varvara
Stepanova. It now houses the studio
of the artist Ilya Glazunov *(see
page 120)*.

Museum of Oriental Art

Heading north from Arbat Square,
it's a pleasant stroll along **Nikitsky
bulvar**. On the right are numerous
cafés and bars, and the **Museum of
Oriental Art ⑪** *(Gosudarstvenny
muzey Vostoka*; 12a Nikitsky bulvar;
tel: 291-0341; Tues–Sun 11am–8pm;
admission charge). This has a small
but representative collection of
Eastern art, with a rare collection of
rugs from the Middle East and
Caucasus. On the first floor are
stores selling gifts, crafts and
antiques. **Bookberry** *(Bukberi*; 17
Nikitsky bulvar) on the opposite

side of the street has a small café and a good selection of art books written in English.

Novy Arbat

Ulitsa Novy Arbat ⑫ (New Arbat), a baleful mix of grey Soviet architecture and gaudy shopping centres, restaurants and casinos, runs from Arbatskie vorota ploshchad to the Moscow River. Only the lovely 17th-century **Church of Simeon the Stylite** (*Tserkov Simeon Stolpnika*) adds a note of beauty. The large **House of Books ⑬** (*Dom Knigi*; 8 Novy Arbat) by the church has a good assortment of English books, maps and posters.

Two small, but charming, literary museums nestle to the north of New Arbat. Go through the alleyway to the left of the House of Books to reach the wooden **House-Museum of Mikhail Lermontov** (*Dom-muzey M.Yu. Lermontova*; 2 ulitsa Malaya Molchanovka; tel: 291-5296; Thur, Sat and Sun 11am–5pm, Wed and Fri 2–7pm; closed last day of the month; admission charge), which has a modest exhibit of memorabilia and personal possessions. The **House-Museum of Marina Tsvetaeva** is also a cultural centre (*Dom-muzey M.I. Tsvetaevoy*; 6 Borisoglebsky pereulok; tel: 202-3543; Sun–Fri 11am–5pm; free). Tsvetaeva lived in this odd, two-storey apartment she called a "surprise box" from 1914 until she emigrated in 1922. Her small study has 11 corners, the walls of which she covered with drafts of her poems.

Arts and chocolate

Near Borisoglebsky pereulok are a number of streets where purveyors to the royal court lived and worked. The street names identify their wares: Skaterny (*Tablecloth*), Khlebny (*Bread*) and Povarskaya (*Cook*). *Style moderne* architecture abounds in the neighbourhood. At No. 44

Povarskaya is a masterpiece built by the architect Kukushev in 1903–4. It is now the **New Zealand Embassy**, and only occasionally opens for viewing. Across the street, the **Red October Sweet Shop** is worth stopping in, if only for a sample. Another culinary treat is the elegant restaurant at the nearby **Central Writers' House** (No. 50). The International Association of Writers' Unions next door at No. 52 is a classical Russian mansion said to be the model Lev Tolstoy used for Natasha Rostova's house in *War and Peace*. In the tranquil courtyard pleasant cafés cater to the local creatives. Across the street, at No. 33, is the **Film Actors' Theatre**, built in 1934 by the avant-garde Vesnin brothers.

On Garden Ring Road

Povarskaya ulitsa ends at Kudrinskaya ploshchad on the Garden Ring Road, which has two interesting museums near by – the former homes of opera star Fyodor Chaliapin and writer Anton Chekhov. The "birthday cake" building towering

Map on page 132

Mikhail Lermontov (1814–41) was one of Russia's finest Romantic poets and prose writers. His most well-known prose work is A Hero of Our Times. *Exiled for his poem about the death of Pushkin, he was killed, like Pushkin, in a duel in the Caucasus a few years later.*

BELOW: taking a break at a boulevard café.

BELOW:
the White House.

over the square, completed in 1954, was one of the seven Stalinist sky-scrapers built in Moscow.

To the left, across the 10 lanes of the Garden Ring Road (here called Novinsky bulvar), is the older part of the **US Embassy**. The new part is behind it. At No. 25 is a two-storey yellow classical mansion housing the **Fyodor Chaliapin Museum** (*Dom-muzey F.I. Shalyapina*; 25 Novinsky bulvar; tel: 205-6236; Tues 10am–6pm, Wed and Thur 11.30am–7pm, Sat and Sun 10am–4pm, closed last day of the month; admission charge; concerts and events). The house is as extravagant as one would wish of an opera star.

On the right side of Kudrinsky ploshchad, on what Muscovites call the "inner" side of the Garden Ring Road, is a narrow, pink two-storey house that looks, in the words of its owner, "like dresser drawers". This is the **House of Anton Chekhov** (*Dom-muzey A.P. Chekhova*; 6 Sadovaaya-Kudrinskaya ulitsa; tel: 291-3837; Thur, Sat and Sun 11am–5.30pm, Wed and Fri 2–7.30 pm; closed last day of the month; admis-

sion and photo charges; room descriptions in English; concerts and events), where he lived with his family from 1886 to 1890. It is filled with photographs, posters, theatre, literary and medical memorabilia.

Spirit of revolution

If there is a dark spirit of revolution in Moscow, for the last century it has been focused in the area of the city below Kudrinsky Square. It is here that Russian governments seem to meet their demise. Once called simply Presnya (probably meaning "fresh water", from the small rivers and ponds), the area consisted of villages and monasteries beyond old Moscow. In 1729 Peter the Great gave one of the villages to the Georgian king in gratitude for help in fighting the Persians, and several streets called "Georgian" (*Gruzinskaya*) testify to their presence, as does the statue on Bolshaya Gruzinskaya by Zurab Tsereteli dedicated to "Friendship For Ever" between Russia and Georgia.

This industrial and working-class neighbourhood became the site of

fierce revolutionary battles in 1905 and again in 1917. To commemorate these conflicts, in 1918 the neighbourhood was renamed Red (Krasnaya) Presnya, and a number of streets were given appropriately revolutionary names. The cobblestones on Barrikadnaya ulitsa leading down past the Stalinist tower from Kudrinsky Square – the bane of drivers in winter – were left by Soviet authorities to honour the fighting spirit of the proletariat.

Still enslaved are the residents of the **Zoopark** ⑯ (1 Bolshaya Gruzinskaya ulitsa; tel: 252-3580; daily 10am–6pm; admission charge). The main entrance is at the corner of Bolshaya Gruzinskaya and Barrikadnaya streets. Founded in 1864, it's an excellent place to watch Moscow families enjoying themselves, and the polar bears always look as if they are having fun.

At No. 2 Malaya Predtechenskaya ulitsa is the **Church of St John the Baptist** *(Tserkov Ionna Predtecha)*, which has remained open since it was completed in 1730.

For a sense of the various Russian revolutions, visit the **Museum of Krasnaya Presnya** ⑰ *(Muzey Krasnaya Presnya;* 4 Bolshoy Predtechensky pereulok; tel: 252-3035; Tues–Fri 10am–6pm, Sat and Sun 10am–5pm; closed last Fri of the month; admission charge). The highlight of the museum is an enormous, room-sized diorama of the 1905 battles, with sound effects, that shows the city in historical detail. Other exhibits portray life in the district at the turn of the 20th century, and the history of the various revolutionary movements up to 1990.

The White House

From the zoo, Konyushkovskaya ulitsa leads to the new US Embassy compound on the left and the building commonly called the **Russian White House** ⑱ *(Bely dom)* on the

right. Just before the White House there is a monument to those who died in the events of 1990 and the **Hunchbacked Bridge**, which once crossed the narrow Presnya River, now underground, when it was built in 1683. It figured prominently in the 1905 fighting and was restored as a monument to the revolution.

The White House held the Council of Ministers of the Russian Federation when Russia was just one of 16 Soviet republics. During the coup attempt in 1991, it was the rallying point for Yeltsin's supporters; in 1993, the building switched sides when it was occupied by the parliament opposed to Yeltsin. It was besieged by tanks and snipers until the occupiers surrendered. Repaired immediately afterwards, the building was enclosed by an iron fence.

Across the street is the **Mayoralty**, a building shaped like an open book, that once housed the Council on Mutual Economic Achievement that united the Eastern Bloc countries. Further down the embankment to the right is a complex of grey buildings called the **World Trade Centre** ⑲

Maps on pages 132 & 140

The popular and omnipresent Mayor of Moscow.

BELOW: a leopard will pose with you for a photo at the zoo.

The Soviet-era Hotel Ukraina has become one of the best places to stay in the city.

(Tsentr mezhdunarodnoy torgovli). They were built by the American industrialist and friend of the USSR, Armand Hammer, and opened in 1980 in time for the Olympics. During Soviet years, the Mezh, as it was called by expats (an abbreviation of the Russian for "international"), was a haven for foreigners, with decent restaurants and shops selling such unheard-of delicacies as cucumbers in winter.

Vagankov Cemetery

A short walk from the 1905 metro station is **Vagankov Cemetery ⓴** (*Vagankovskoye kladbishche*; 15 ulitsa Sergeya Makeyeva; tel: 252-2541; daily 9am–6pm in winter, 9am–7pm in summer; free). This traditional, rambling Russian cemetery is less official than the Novodevichy Cemetery (*see page 127*), though it is the final resting place for the poet Sergey Yesenin (in section 17), the singer-songwriter

Vladimir Vysotsky (*see page 170*), the TV personality Vlad Listev (immediately to the right through the gates) and many other stars of sports, literature, science, the military and the performing arts. Here, too, are buried those who died on the Khodynka field during the coronation celebrations for the last tsar, Nicholas II, when 1,389 were trampled to death racing for the free food and drink. Don't be surprised to see families enjoying vodka and a bite to eat at a graveside; it is a tradition on holidays and anniversaries.

Kutuzovsky prospekt

As traffic-filled Novy Arbat crosses the Moscow River, it becomes **Kutuzovsky prospekt ㉑**, one of the city's smartest neighbourhoods, built in the 1950s. It is still one of the most expensive, filled with top-end bars, restaurants and boutiques, but it's not good for strolling, as 10 lanes of non-stop traffic rush by.

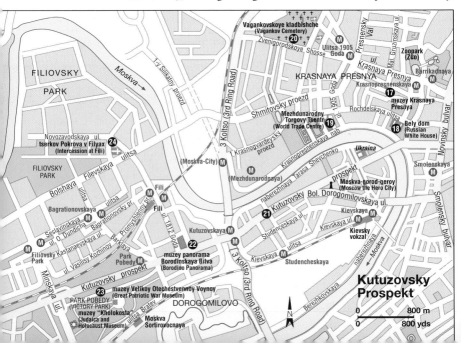

Immediately over the bridge from the city centre and on the right is the **Hotel Ukraina**, another of the seven Stalinist high-rises that carve out the city's skyline. Completed in 1957, it featured in the 1990 film *The Russia House*.

Where Dorogomilovskaya ulitsa meets Kutuzovsky prospekt, there is an **obelisk** dedicated to those who fought and died in World War II. On the right side of the road, the ornamented house at No. 26 was the city apartment of Leonid Brezhnev during his term as Secretary General of the Communist Party.

The war monuments continue as you drive away from the city centre. On the right is the **Battle of Borodino Panorama Museum ㉒** (*Muzey-panorama Borodinskaya Bitva*; 38 Kutuzovsky prospekt; tel: 148-9489; Tues–Sun 10am–6pm; closed last Thur of the month; admission charge). This contains a 115-metre (377-ft) circular painting depicting, in obsessive historical detail, one of the key battles of 1812. It was painted by Franz Rubo in 1912 and installed in this specially constructed, round building in 1962. Spectators stand on a raised podium in the centre to spot characters from Tolstoy's *War and Peace*. Not far from here, Kutuzovsky prospekt narrows, and the traffic snarls around the **Triumphal Arch**. Designed by Osip Bove, it is decorated with the coats of arms of the 48 Russian provinces *(guberniya)* and bas-reliefs of "The Expulsion of the French".

Victory Park

Just beyond the arch on the left-hand side of the road on Poklonnaya Gora is the vast **Victory Park ㉓** and **Central Museum of the Great Patriotic War** (*Park Pobedy* and *Tsentralny muzey Velikoy Otechestvennoy Voynoy*; 11 ulitsa Bratyev Fonchenko; tel: 142-4185; Tues–Sun 10am–6pm; closed last Thur of the month; admission charge to museum; English descriptions; English tours by appointment). The park is situated in the Poklonnaya Hills and has strong historical associations. In centuries past tsars would ride out to this hilltop to greet for-

Maps on page 140

'The Tragedy of Nations' *by Zurab Tsereteli in Victory Park.*

BELOW: Victory Park honours those who died in the Great Patriotic War (1941–5).

Maps on page 140

The name of Poklonnaya gora comes from the Russian word for "to pay obeisance", and visitors entering or leaving Moscow stopped here to "bow down" to the city before them. It could also refer to poklon, a kind of duty paid in feudal times for temporary residence in a principality. Most Russians now understand Poklonnaya Gora as "the Hill of Homage" to those who fought for victory in the Great Patriotic War.

BELOW: the Church of the Intercession at Fili.

eign delegations. Knowing this tradition, Napoleon waited in vain here for Russian noblemen to bring him the keys to the Kremlin. In 1983 the area was established as a park and museum dedicated to World War II. It is dominated by a 140-metre (460-ft) obelisk decorated by an angel of Victory and a sculpture of emaciated bronze figures called *The Tragedy of Nations*, all by Tsereteli *(see page 65)*. A church, mosque and synagogue were built to encourage religious observances.

The synagogue also has a small **Museum of Moscow Judaica and the Holocaust** (*Muzey Kholokosta*; tel: 148-1907; Tues–Thur and Sun 11am–5pm, Fri 11am–3pm), but the main attraction of the park is the **Central Museum of the Great Patriotic War**. Its main room, the Hall of Glory, depicts the course of the war; on the lower level, dioramas show the fiercest battles. Despite its solemn memories the site has become one of the city's most popular, filled on weekends with children climbing on the World War II weaponry and tanks, grandmothers with strollers, and teens rollerblading and flirting.

Baroque charms of Fili

Near by is a baroque masterpiece: the **Church of the Intercession at Fili ㉔** (*Tserkov Pokrova v Filyax*; 6 ulitsa Novozavodskaya; tel: 148-4552; Thur–Mon 11am–5.30pm, closed Tues, except for special excursions and last Fri of the month; admission charge; metro Fili, exit nearest the front of the train).

In the late 17th century the noble Naryshkin family commissioned estate and monastery churches that have become synonymous with Moscow baroque. This one is a pale, frothy wedding cake crowned by six golden domes: four semicircular apses form the main church on the upper floor, and the tiered style is reminiscent of both the early Russian "tent" churches and Western architectural forms.

The building has two churches: the church at ground level was stripped of ornamentation when it was closed in 1941 but its iconostasis has been recreated and it is open for weekend services.

Yet even during the waves of anti-religious campaigns in Soviet times, no one could destroy the interior of the church on the upper floor. One entire wall, from the plank wooden floor to the very top of the tent spire, is a nine-tiered iconostasis with myriad icons framed in heavily ornamented and gilded carved wood. At the very top, under the tip of the spire, is a wooden statue of the Crucifixion – a very unusual Western innovation in an Orthodox church. The icons, also more naturalistic in the Western style, are lit by shafts of sun streaming through the windows in the tent roof. The Naryshkin family and their royal guests sat in the gilded Tsar's Box suspended across from the iconostasis. ❏

RESTAURANTS

Correa's
32 ulitsa Bolshaya Gruzinskaya, Building 1. Metro: Barrikadnaya. Tel: 933-4684. Open: B, L & D daily. $$
Friendly, New York-style eatery serving good food at reasonable prices. Reservations essential.

Gandhara
15 ulitsa Rochdelskaya, building 7. Metro: Ulitsa 1905 Goda. Tel: 255-9959. Open: L & D daily. $$$
Airy and elegant, serving upmarket Pakistani cuisine with French and Russian influences. Try the seafood borscht.

Goodman Steak House
31 Novinsky bulvar. Metro: Barrikadnaya. Tel: 981-4941. Open: L & D daily. $$$
Features huge portions, highly praised pork chops and delicious lamb rack.

Gorki
3, 1-ya ulitsa Tverskaya-Yamskaya, building 1. Metro: Mayakovskaya. Tel: 775-2456. Open: 24 hrs daily. $$$
Plush dining hall with original 1950s Soviet Empire fittings. Well-executed Russian dishes, blandish Italian ones and a range of excellent desserts. Evening jazz.

Karetny Dvor
52 Povarskaya ulitsa. Metro: Barrikadnaya. Tel: 291-6376. Open: 24 hrs daily. $$
Cosy and reasonably priced Azeri restaurant serving unpretentious

food. Generous hunks of *shashlyk*. The menu is in Russian and bad English.

Malenkaya Yaponia
12a ulitsa Bolshaya Dorogomilovskaya. Metro: Kievskaya. Tel: 243-2133. Open: L & D daily. $$
Good value sushi. Also serves hot meals, salads and desserts.

Mario
17 ulitsa Klimashkina. Metro: Ulitsa 1905 Goda. Tel: 253-6505. Open: L & D daily. $$$$
Respected restaurant, favoured by the wealthy. Italian cuisine with creative meat and seafood dishes. Reservations and smart dress essential.

Pinocchio
4 Kutuzovsky prospekt, building 2. Metro: Kievskaya. Tel: 243-5688. Open: L & D daily. $$$$
Excellent but pricey Italian restaurant.

Scandinavia
7 Maly Palashevsky pereulok. Metro: Tverskaya. Tel: 200-4986. Open: L & D daily. $$$$
Good portions of modern European food, garden salads and grilled steaks. The outdoor café is ideal for drinks and snacks.

Shafran
12 Spiridonevsky pereulok, building 9. Metro: Tverskaya. Tel: 737-9500. Open: B, L & D daily. $$$
Lebanese food, with delicious mezes. Set lunch is an excellent option.

Shinok
2 ulitsa 1905 Goda. Metro: Ulitsa 1905 Goda. Tel: 255-0888. Open: 24 hrs daily. $$$
Quirky restaurant with Ukrainian menu. Try *okroshka* (cold *kvas* soup) and *pertsovka* (pepper vodka). Also serves excellent *vareniki* (dumplings).

Sindbad
14 Nikitsky bulvar. Metro: Arbatskaya. Tel: 291-7115. Open: L & D daily. $$
Middle Eastern restaurant ideal for a quick, cheap bite. Picturesque summer courtyard.

Starlite Diner
16 Bolshaya Sadovaya ulitsa. Metro: Mayakovskaya. Tel: 290-9638. Open: 24 hrs daily. $$
Generous portions of American food served in

a fair imitation of a 1950s-style diner. Great milkshakes.

Red Bar
23a naberezhnaya Taras Shevchenko. Metro: Kievskaya. Tel: 730-0808. Open: 6pm–3am. $$$$
Chic bar and restaurant on the 27th floor of the Moskva City Business Centre with a great view overlooking the White House and New Arbat. High prices, reservations essential.

PRICE CATEGORIES

Prices for three-course dinner per person with a glass of house wine:
$ = under $25
$$ = $25–40
$$$ = $40–60
$$$$ = more than $60

RIGHT: eating outside when the weather allows.

TVERSKAYA AND THE NORTHWEST

Shopping and family fun are the essence of this slice of the city. Following the "Tsar's Road" that leads towards St Petersburg, you pass through lively Pushkin Square and see the famous Moscow Art Theatre. Nearby attractions include a puppet theatre, doll museum and the Moscow Circus, plus the chance to take a plunge in the famous Sandunovsky Bathhouse

This chapter begins with a trip along Tverskaya ulitsa, from the shadow of the Kremlin to the sprawl of warehouse-sized shopping centres along the Outer Ring Road. We then follow the Boulevard Ring to the northeast with short excursions on Malaya and Bolshaya Dmitrovka ulitsas before a longer exploration of ulitsa Petrovka and Karetny Ryad, where shopping and the Upper Peter Monastery are the main attractions. Then it's on to Trubnaya ploshchad, the intersection of four picturesque boulevards where you can be pampered at the Sandunovsky Baths, before heading north to three classic Moscovite attractions: the Nikulina Circus, Durov's Circle and the Obrazstov Puppet Theatre.

The "Tsar's Road"

Moscow's main shopping street, its Fifth Avenue or Oxford Street, is **Tverskaya ulitsa ❶**. Built as a road to Tver – the nearest principality to Moscow at the time – it later grew in importance when Peter the Great established St Petersburg as his capital, becoming the main road connecting Russia's two principal cities. Tsars coming from St Petersburg arrived for coronations, holidays and official visits along Tverskaya, hence the name "Tsar's Road".

Tverskaya's appearance changed dramatically in the 1930s when the General Plan for Moscow's reconstruction called for the road to be widened from 18 metres (60 ft) to 60 metres (200 ft). Buildings were demolished or moved back, and the Stalinist neo-classical apartment houses and buildings that define the street were built around them. It is now a busy shopping district and civic centre. On public holidays, when closed to traffic, concerts are held outside the Mayor's office.

Map on page 146

LEFT: a summer's evening on Pushkin Square.
BELOW: Tverskaya ulitsa is the place to meet, shop and eat.

Exploring on foot

Starting at Okhotny Ryad metro, the most interesting stretch to walk is from the start of the street by the Historical Museum up to Pushkin Square. Here the main street and courtyards are lined with ethnic restaurants, foreign clothes shops and easy-going coffee houses.

On the western side of Tverskaya ulitsa (*see page 108*), a new 5-star hotel is going up where the 1970 "glass box" of the Intourist Hotel was torn down to public cheers. Nearly hidden by these covered construction walkways is the

The Central Telegraph Building was conceived as the central studio of Soviet radio.

elegant green-and-white **Yermolova Theatre** and, further up, the imposing 1927 **Central Telegraph Building** (*Tsentralny Telegraf*), marked by its distinctive, bulging globe.

On Tverskaya's eastern side, step through the arched gateway onto Georgievsky pereulok to glimpse the **Troyekurov Palace**, a lovely 17th-century boyar house behind the heavily guarded Duma building.

Moscow Arts Theatre

Further up Tverskaya, Kamergersky pereulok to the right is a pedestrianised street of restaurants and

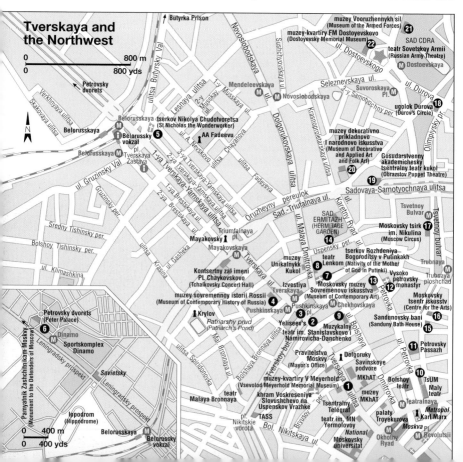

Map on page 146

cafés. On its northern side at No. 3 is the elegant *style moderne* **Moscow Arts Theatre** (MKhAT), one of Fyodor Shekhtel's master-pieces (1902). The sea theme in the 1903 sculpture over the right door, by A. Golubkin, reflects the seagull that became the theatre's emblem in honour of Chekhov's famous play.

The **MKhAT Museum** (*Muzey MKhATa im. A.P. Chekhova*; 3a Kamergersky pereulok; tel: 692-5187/692-8329; Wed–Sun 12–6pm; admission charge) has several halls filled with stage sets, old photos, dioramas and sketches of set deco-rations by celebrated Russian artists.

Before going back out onto Tver-skaya, step through the wrought-iron gates closest to the main street on the north side of Kamergersky pereulok; in the courtyard is the turreted and tiled **Savinskoye podvore**, a magnificent apartment block built in 1907 by the patri-archy. Though the façade is shabby, the huge apartments are being sold for nearly a million dollars each.

Further up Tverskaya on the east-ern side is a 1954 equestrian statue of Moscow's founder, **Prince Yuri Dolgoruky**, looking suitably heroic, opposite the red, classical-style Mayor's Office, built in 1782 by Kazakov for the Governor Generals of Moscow. In October 1993, when Yeltsin's government seemed about to be overthrown, it was a rallying point for the democratic forces.

Just past the Dolgoruky statue is the enormous **Moskva bookstore**, which has a reasonable stock of English-language paperbacks and art books.

Yeliseev's emporium

In the middle of the next block is **Yeliseev's ❷** (No. 14), a magnifi-cent *style moderne* food emporium with panelled shelves, chandeliers and elegant marble counters, once the mansion of Princess Volkon-skaya, famous for her literary soirées. It was bought by the Yeliseev family in 1898 and turned into Moscow's most fashionable food store. Even as Gastronom No. 1 during the Soviet period, it was always stocked with goods unavailable elsewhere.

Turn left just before Pushkin Square through the arches to Bol-shoy Gnezdnikovsky pereulok to see Moscow's first skyscraper at No. 10. The 10-storey *style moderne* **Nirnzee House** was built in 1913 with fine detailing both on the façade and in the lobby.

Pushkin Square

If Tverskaya is Moscow's Fifth Avenue or Oxford Street, then **Pushkin Square ❸** (*Pushkinskaya ploshchad*) is its Times or Leicester Square – lively, but a bit seedy. Located at the intersection of the Boulevard Ring with Tverskaya ulitsa, it's a place that makes nostal-gic Muscovites weep. Once an ele-gant open space surrounded by graceful buildings, churches and monastery walls, its garishly lit

Yeliseev's food emporium offers deli foods from all over the world.

BELOW: a mix of architectural styles in central Moscow.

On 31 January 1990, more than 30,000 Muscovites lined up at the city's first McDonald's, on Pushkin Square. It remains very popular.

RIGHT: the Yar's famous cabaret act.

buildings now include the world's largest McDonald's and a remarkably lurid casino.

All the same, the monument to Pushkin – installed in 1880 and moved to its present site in 1950 – is still a favourite meeting spot; at every hour of day and night you can see earnest men holding bouquets of flowers as they wait for their dates. The square is decorated when film festivals or premieres are held in the **Pushkin Movie Theatre**.

The square was also the site of pro-democratic rallies, because it was the centre of Moscow's newly liberal press, with *Izvestiya* on one side and the *Moscow News* on the other. The original **Izvestiya Building** is a fine example of Constructivism. Built in 1927 by Grigory Barkhin, it is a study in geometric forms with nothing to soften its angularity.

Northwest of Tverskoy bulvar at 21 Tverskaya ulitsa are the white lions immortalised by Alexander Pushkin in his poem *Evgeny Onegin*. They guard the entrances to the large red mansion which is the

Museum of Contemporary History of Russia ④ (*Muzey sovremennoy istorii Rossii*; 21 Tverskaya ulitsa; tel: 299-5458/299-6724; Tues–Sun 10am–6pm; closed last Fri of the month; admission charge). In 1831 it became the English Club *(see below)*, famously frequented by Russia's intelligentsia and celebrated in fiction. From 1924 until 1991 it was the Museum of the Revolution.

The new museum's exhibitions include a recreation of the English Club's famous library, an extensive collection of Soviet propaganda posters and bizarre home-made gifts presented to Stalin.

Pushkin Square to Belorussian station

North of Pushkin Square, Tverskaya is lined with upmarket European clothes shops, hotels and restaurants. The next square's name has reverted to the pre-Revolutionary Triumfalnaya ploshchad, but Muscovites still call it **Mayakovka**, because of both the 1958 statue of the poet Vladimir Mayakovsky

The English Club

In the 19th century, it was said that there were four milestones in a gentleman's life: birth, receiving a government rank, marriage, and membership of the English Club. This was a true gentlemen's club: no women allowed (even the floors were washed by men) and hence no dances or costume balls. Poets, writers, politicians, merchants, publishers and noblemen enjoyed evenings in the comfortable library, reading European newspapers and discussing politics without fear of police informers. In fact, it was said that Tsar Nicholas I regarded the club as a kind of barometer for the mood in the country and would regularly ask his advisers: "What do they say about it in Moscow at the English Club?" There were halls for card games, and in 1862 Lev Tolstoy lost 1,000 roubles to an army officer and was nearly blacklisted when he found himself short of cash; luckily, a kind-hearted publisher lent him the money. The Club's kitchen was renowned for its sumptuous meals. During the Soviet period, Russian readers salivated over a scene in *War and Peace* in which Count Rostov discusses a menu at the English Club, much of which no one had ever tasted.

(1893–1930), frozen mid-stride, and the avant-garde steel arches of the metro station bearing his name. Next to the monument is the famous **Tchaikovsky Concert Hall** (*Kontsertny zal imeni P.L. Chaykovskovo*; seating 1,600, it is the largest in Moscow, and home of the State Symphony Orchestra) and the **Satirical Theatre**. Behind them the ornamented Stalinist towers of the **Peking Hotel** rise over the square.

Contemporary art is on sale at the hip **Aidan Gallery** (22, 1-y Tverskaya-Yamskaya ulitsa, behind the black, unmarked door, 3rd floor; tel: 251-3734). Founded in 1992 as Russia's first private art gallery, it exhibits Russia's cutting-edge artists.

The last square before the Garden Ring overpass is **ploshchad Tverskaya Zastava**, the main ceremonial gate to the city, through which tsars entered from St Petersburg. A Triumphal Arch celebrating the routing of the French in 1812 stood here until 1936.

East of Tverskaya on **ulitsa Butyrsky Val** is an imposing Old Believers' church with an icon of *The Image of the Saviour Not Made by Human Hands* above the main portal. The church, dedicated to **St Nicholas the Wonderworker** ❺ (*Tserkov Nikolaya Chudotvoretsa*), was not completed until 1921, and remained open for 14 years. It later became the studio of Sergey Orlov, one of the sculptors of the statue to Yuri Dolgoruky *(see page 147)*, and in 1993 it was returned to the Old Believers.

Yar restaurant

On the other side of the overpass at Belorussian train station, Tverskaya becomes the main road out of the city, changing its name to **Leningradsky prospekt**. The grand Stalinist apartment buildings here include the last grande dame of Soviet hotels – the **Sovietsky**. In the 19th century the **Yar restaurant**, one of the most famous in Moscow, was on this site. Poets, writers and men about town would spend the night carousing and listening to gypsy music. By the mid-20th century it had become dilapidated, and in 1951 it was reconstituted into the present hotel. The Yar restaurant is still here, and the tradition of gypsy songs and dance continues at the Romen Gypsy Theatre in the hotel's concert hall.

Peter Palace and Beyond

Ten minutes' walk up the road, just past the **Dynamo soccer stadium**, is a miniature Kremlin in the round. This is **Peter Palace** ❻ (*Petrovsky dvorets*), built in 1775–82 under Catherine the Great by the architect Kazakov as a place for the imperial retinue on their way from St Petersburg to Moscow to rest and dress for their ceremonial entrance into the city. When Napoleon left the burning city in 1812, he stayed here.

In the 19th century the park behind the palace was famous. Full of

Map on page 146

In 2000 a bomb exploded in Pushkin Square underpass, killing dozens of pedestrians and kiosk traders. Neither the culprits nor their motivation were ever discovered. Fresh flowers are placed daily as a reminder by the entrance near the Actor's Gallery mall.

BELOW: soaking up the sun on Pushkin Square.

TsUM was once the favourite shopping centre for Moscow's wealthy, but has many more rivals today.

RIGHT: taking a break at TsUM.

dachas and country houses, it was a place for feckless young men to go riding, followed by an evening of gypsy music in the park restaurant or the Yar, or perhaps an evening at Voksal, the park theatre named after the Vauxhall Pleasure Gardens in London. Ambitious merchant families would bring their daughters for promenades in the square nicknamed "the bride fair". Only a small piece of the park remains.

Near Sokol metro, the **Triumph-Palace apartment building** towers 264 metres (866 ft) over the area – the tallest apartment house in Europe and what the developers call the "eighth Stalinist skyscraper".

The city of Moscow ends and Moscow *oblast* (province) begins 10 km (6 miles) from Peter Palace at the Outer Ring Road along and beyond which stretch department stores and malls. Near the turn-off to the Sheremetevo airport is the **Monument to the Defenders of Moscow** *(Pamyatnik zashchitnikam Moskvy)*. Three enormous tank traps mark the spot where the German

Army was stopped in its advance on the capital.

Malaya Dmitrovka

We now return to Pushkin Square. The boulevard that intersects Tverskaya here is **Strastnoy bulvar**, named after the Strastnoy monastery that once stood on Pushkin Square. A block to the east along Strastnoy bulvar, just past the Izvestiya Building, is **ulitsa Malaya Dmitrovka** and the lovely and ornately decorated **Church of the Nativity of the Mother of God in Putinki** **❼** *(tserkov Rozhdeniya Bogoroditsy v Putinkakh)*. This was the last tent church built in Moscow, in 1653. Patriarch Nikon banned the architectural style as inappropriate, because the thick walls needed to support the spires made the interiors small and cramped.

A few doors north of the church at No. 6 is the **Lenkom Theatre** **❽**, on the site of the elegant 1907 *style moderne* Merchants' Club. According to contemporary accounts this was a rowdy place with musical entertainment, theatrical perfor-

mances, dances and costume balls. It was briefly occupied after the Revolution by left-wing squatters and called the House of Anarchy, it later served as the first Communist University and is where Lenin addressed budding Communist leaders. The theatre was established here in 1938.

Near Lenkom, next to the chic Hotel Golden Apple, is the **Museum of Unique Dolls** (*Muzey unikalnykh kukol*; 9 ulitsa Malaya Dmitrovka; tel: 299-9385; daily 10am–6.30pm; free), opened in 1996 to house an extensive private collection of dolls from all over the world, with an emphasis on rare Russian dolls.

Bolshaya Dmitrovka

In the 19th century **ulitsa Bolshaya Dmitrovka**, which begins at Okhotny Ryad at the House of Unions and ends at the Boulevard Ring, was known as Club Street for the Noblemen's Assembly, Doctors' Club and first site of the Merchants' Club. Contemporaries complained about the stream of carriages dropping off well-to-do patrons and making the narrow street impassable. Today, lined with shops and cafés, it is clogged with weekday traffic heading for the **Prosecutor General's Offices** (No. 15, with impressive reliefs of Marx, Engels and Lenin) or the upper chamber of the Russian Parliament, the **Federation Council**, at No. 26.

About halfway down the street, the small pedestrian **Stoleshnikov pereulok** (Tablecloth Lane) leads east to ulitsa Petrovka. The lane is lined with upmarket boutiques and cafés. Further up Bolshaya Dmitrovka at No. 17 is the **Stanislavsky and Nemirovich Musical Theatre ❾**, founded in 1941 when Konstantin Stanislavsky's Bolshoy Theatre Opera Studio joined Nemirovich-Danchenko's Musical Studio of the Moscow Art Theatre. Rejecting opera

as "concerts in costumes", they introduced method acting into the opera repertoire. The building was an enormous 18th-century mansion belonging to the Saltykov family; part of the original is preserved in the foyers and the grand staircase. Renowned for its acoustics, the theatre began renovations in 2003 and is due to reopen.

Russia's first department store

Ulitsa Petrovka, which leads off between the Bolshoy and Maly theatres, takes its name from the monastery at the top of the street. Built up after the Neglinnaya River was funnelled underground, Petrovka was inhabited by well-to-do traders, craftsmen and carriage-makers. Start exploring the street from behind the Bolshoy Theatre. On the right is **TsUM ❿**, Russian acronym for Central Department Store. It was the country's first department store, opened by the Scottish firm of Muir and Mirrielees. The neo-Gothic pile was built in 1908 by Roman Klein, using revolutionary steel-and-concrete

Map on page 146

TIP

Across the street from the Lenkom Theatre, the Political Bookshop *(Politicheskaya Kniga)* on the corner of Nastasinsky pereulok has a nice selection of Soviet-era poster reproductions.

BELOW: for busy Muscovites there is no time "to stand and stare".

techniques. Chekhov and his family bought everything here, and the writer named his two farm dogs Muir and Mirrielees.

While middle-class shoppers are well served by TsUM, the more well-to-do head for the elegant **Petrovsky Passage** ⓫ at No. 10. This *style moderne* structure, built in 1903 as an elite arcade, has resumed its reputation for high prices despite the Revolutionary statues added in 1920.

Upper Peter Monastery

According to legend, Tsar Ivan I was passing a snow-covered hill, when suddenly the snow melted. Seeing it as a sign, he had a church built on the site, and by 1330 it was part of the **Upper Peter Monastery** ⓬ (*Vysoko-petrovsky monastyr*; daily 9am–8pm; free). The complex was rebuilt several times, notably by the Naryshkin family, who are buried here. A fine baroque bell tower leads to four churches, including the impressive **Church of the Icon of the Mother of God of Bogolyubovo** (*Bogolyubsky sobor*) at the entrance, and the **Church of**

The five domes of the Upper Peter Monastery.

the **Metropolitan Peter** (*Tserkov Petra-Metropolita*), built in 1517 by the Italian architect Alevesio Novo.

Across the street in a lovely 18th-century manor house is the **Moscow Museum of Contemporary Art** ⓭ (*Moskovsky muzey Sovremenovo iskusstva*; 25 ulitsa Petrovka; tel: 231-4405; Wed–Sun 12–8pm; closes Mon at 7pm; admission charge; English exhibit notes). Based on the private collection of Zurab Tsereteli and featuring rather more of his works than one might like, the museum is attempting to fill in the lost years of Soviet non-conformist art. There are only a few canvases of note by such artists as Oscar Ryabin and Anatoly Zverev. Early 20th-century art on the second floor includes works by Chagal, Kandinsky, Rodchenko and some truly excellent Malevich canvases. A kiosk by the entrance sells art books and contemporary artworks.

The Hermitage Gardens

Ulitsa Petrovka continues across the boulevard, with its plethora of cafés and restaurants, and becomes **ulitsa Karetny Ryad** (Carriage Row), named after carriage-makers who lived and worked here. The **Hermitage Gardens** ⓮ (*sad Ermitazh*) on the left is a well-kept pleasure garden with an illustrious history. It opened in 1894 with pavilions and theatres, including one in which the Lumiére brothers showed the first film in Russia and where the Moscow Art Theatre performed Chekhov's plays until their own theatre was completed. Filled with cafés, the garden is the venue of music festivals. The **New Opera** next door (3 ulitsa Karetny Ryad) stages a repertory of traditional and unconventional musical theatre.

Four boulevards

At the intersection of ulitsa Petrovka and the Boulevard Ring, Petrovsky bulvar slides gracefully downhill to

The Fate of 20th-Century Art

After the great avant-garde innovations of art during the Revolutionary period, officially sanctioned art in the USSR was Socialist Realism: glorified workers and peasants portrayed bringing peace and prosperity to the Soviet people *(see pages 26–7)*. "Non-formist" art (anything that was non-representational and did not conform to official canons) was banned from public exhibition, and non-conformist artists were persecuted, jailed, incarcerated in psychiatric hospitals or exiled. Between the 1960s and 1980s, many of the Soviet Union's greatest works of this underground art were sold to a handful of insightful private Western collectors; a few curators at the Tretyakov and other Russian museums used state funds to buy some works. The turning point came with the Sotheby auction of Russian contemporary art in 1988: a painting by an unknown artist, Grisha Bruskin, sold for more than $400,000. Suddenly "non-conformist" art was hot. But back in the USSR, when the Gorbachev reforms threw open the country's doors, many artists left with their works or signed exclusive contracts with foreign galleries. Several generations of contemporary art had disappeared from Russia.

the east amid lush greenery and pastel buildings. At the bottom of the hill four boulevards intersect: Petrovsky, Rozhdestvensky, Neglinnaya and Tsvetnoy. This is **Trubnaya ploshchad**, once a noisy, swampy square with The Crimea, Hell and other infamous taverns of cardsharps, crooks, swindlers, merchants and provincials looking for diversion. In the 19th century the green-and-white building on the corner of Petrovsky and Neglinnaya (No. 14), now a theatre, housed the Hermitage restaurant whose French chef, Olivier, invented the now ubiquitous Russian salad "Olivier".

Neglinnaya ulitsa stretches south from Trubnaya ploshchad to just above Theatre Square. One of the most important landmarks on the street owes its existence to the former Neglinnaya River. In 1806 an actor named Sandunov built a stone bathhouse by the river bank, at No. 14. In 1896 a complex of elegant buildings opened here, known as the **Sandunovsky Bathhouse** ⓮ (entrance is on Zvonarsky pereulok, on the right one block up; daily

8am–10pm). The men's side is lavishly decorated with columns and statues. The women's is smaller and less ornate, but elegant nevertheless *(see 'The Bathhouse' overleaf)*.

Also at No. 14, in one of the original bathhouse buildings, is the chic **Moscow Centre for the Arts** ⓰ *(Moskovsky tsentr iskusstv*; daily 11am–7pm; tel: 623-7863), run by a well-known Moscow collector, Marina Loshak. Her exhibitions of David Burliuk (the "father of Futurism") and David Sterenberg, both 1920s avant-garde artists, have attracted Moscow's artistic elite.

Animal pleasures

To the north of Trubnaya ploshchad is one of the city's most famous entertainments, **Moscow Circus** ⓱ *(Moskovsky tsirk im. Nikulina*; 13 Tsvetnoy bulvar; tel: 200-0668; ticket office open daily 11am–7pm with a lunch break on weekdays from 2–3pm and on weekends from 12.30–1.30pm). Founded in 1880, the circus became popular in the last century when Yuri Nikulin, a brilliant clown, singer and actor, made

Map on page 146

BELOW: Yuri Nikulin was a comedian loved by all. His jokes and anecdotes have become folklore.

The Bathhouse

Whether a simple village log house or an elegant city building, the bathhouse – *banya* – is a beloved tradition. Russians firmly believe that steaming cures a variety of ailments, rids the body of toxins, relieves stress and revives both body and soul. Many have a regular bath day with friends, chatting and drinking tea between the steam rooms. For women there are pampering massages, manicures and pedicures, for men beer and conversation.

Bring plastic slippers, shampoo, soap, hand cream, comb and brush. Bathhouses provide hairdryers and usually sell flip-flops, shampoo and bath gel or soap. Men and women have separate facilities. At the door, buy your ticket and ask for a sheet *(prostyn)*, towels *(polotensta)* and cloakroom *(khranenie)*. You might also buy a felt hat and a bough of branches, which are soaked in hot water to soften them so you can beat yourself to improve circulation.

Bathhouses have three sections: a changing room, often with separate cabins and banquettes, a washing room with marble benches and lined with shower stalls, and a steam room. City bathhouses usually have saunas (dry heat) and cold-water pools, as well as additional massage rooms, barber shops and hair salons.

After disrobing and checking in your valuables, wrap yourself in a sheet (or not, as you wish) and head for the steam room, a wood-lined room with a huge stove and tiered benches. Some announce "steam time", others let patrons handle the steam themselves. First rule for novices: sit on the bottom bench and cover your head with a towel or bathhouse hat, and your shoulders with a sheet. Only experienced bathers should sit on the top benches, where the temperature is highest. Second rule: no talking. Steaming is serious business.

The attendant will close the door, open the stove hatch and begin to ladle hot water on the red hot rocks. Usually there is a pause at some point, when the attendant will spray water mixed with aromatic oils on the ceiling or wave a towel to force the steam to descend. After more water is tossed on the rocks and everyone agrees the temperature is just right (which can be over 66°C/150°F), the stove door is closed, and everyone waits. After a minute the steam will descend like a blanket of fire (which is why your shoulders should be covered), and for several minutes you sit and sweat.

From the steam room, head straight for the cold water pool and plunge in. After 10 seconds of certainty that you are about to die, you receive a jolt of energy: your skin tingles and you think you could run a marathon. If the pool is too daunting, try taking a cool shower or pouring water over your head from one of the plastic tubs available. Once you're refreshed, you can go back into the steam room where, for a fee, you can lie on a bench and have an attendant pound you with birch branches. When you feel like jelly, it's time for water, tea or beer. The ritual is several steams interspersed with massages and, for women, other pampering.

When your skin is marbled and soft, it's time for a final shower. As you leave, the attendants will say *S lyokhim parom*, a hope that the steam was light and refreshing. ❏

LEFT: steam rooms are not for the faint-hearted.

it a national institution. For a fee you can have your picture taken in the lobby with a bear, chimpanzees (trained to give you a hug), leopards, panthers, pythons and sometimes a lion or tiger cub.

A kilometre and a half (one mile) to the north, across the Garden Ring Road, is another Moscow institution, **Durov's Circle** ⑱ (*ugolok Durova*; 4 ulitsa Durova; tel: 681-7222). The Durov family has been training animals since 1894, and performances are a delight.

For the full experience of the city's light-hearted entertainments, see an innovative and sophisticated show at the **Obrazstov Puppet Theatre** ⑲ (*Gosudarstvenny akademichesky tsentralny teatr kukol*; 3 Sadovaya-Samotyochnaya; tel: 299-3310). Every hour the little doors on the façade open and a puppet pops out. There is a Museum of Puppets in the theatre (tel: 299-5553).

The Ring Road and beyond

In a sprawling mansion off the Garden Ring Road where ulitsa Karetny Ryad ends is the **Museum of Dec-** **orative and Applied Art and Folk Art** ⑳ (*Muzey dekorativno-prikadnovo i narodnovo iskusstva*; 3 Delegatskaya ulitsa; tel: 609-0146/ 609-0167; Sat–Thur 10am–6pm; closed last Thur of the month; admission charge). It has an extensive collection of crafts, folk costumes and applied arts.

A few blocks beyond the Garden Ring Road near Dostoyevskaya metro station are the **Russian Army Theatre** and **Museum of the Armed Forces** ㉑ (*Muzey Vooruzhennykh sil*; 2 ulitsa Sovietskoy armii; tel: 681-6303; Wed–Sun 10am–5pm; admission charge). It tells the history of the armed forces from the 18th century to the present.

In a wing of what was the Mariinsky Hospital for the Indigent is the **Dostoyevsky Memorial Museum** ㉒ (*muzey-kvartiry F.M. Dostoyevskovo*; 2 ulitsa Dostoyevskovo; tel: 681-1085; Wed and Fri 2–6pm, Thur, Sat and Sun 11am–6pm, closed last day of month; admission charge). This 19th-century furnished apartment is where Fyodor, the son of a struggling doctor, grew up. ❑

Map on page 146

The clock at the Obrazstov Puppet Theatre has become its symbol. Every Russian would have seen puppet shows as a child, and every city has its own puppet theatre.

BELOW: selling newspapers tops up meagre pensions.

RESTAURANTS

Beloye Solntse Pustyni
29/14 ulitsa Neglinnaya.
Metro: Tsvetnoy Boulevard.
Tel: 209-7525. Open: L & D
daily. $$
An Uzbek restaurant with
a diorama of a marooned
ship, waitresses in full
Uzbek costume and
props from the 1970 film
White Sun of the Desert
after which it's named.
The menu is extensive,
and set meals include
unlimited access to the
salad bar. It shares a
building with Uzbekistan
(see opposite).

Bulvar
30/7 ulitsa Petrovka. Metro:
Chekhovskaya. Tel: 209-
6798. Open: L & D daily. $$$$
One of the city's most
exclusive restaurants,
with a lauded wine list.
Service is polite, if occa-

sionally pompous. Inven-
tive European cuisine is
exquisitely presented.
Reservations and smart
attire essential.

Café des Artistes
5/6 Kamergersky pereulok.
Metro: Teatralnaya. Tel: 692-
4042. Open: L & D daily. $$$$
A highly regarded, upmar-
ket restaurant on a
pedestrianised street of
eateries. Well executed,
expensive European cui-
sine. An excellently priced
luncheon set menu.
Pleasant outdoor summer
seating.

Café Pushkin
26a Tverskoy bulvar. Metro:
Tverskaya. Tel: 629-5590.
Open: 24 hrs daily (ground
floor only); L & D daily. $$$$
A Moscow classic serving
upmarket Russian food in
grand, 19th-century sur-

roundings. There is a
bustling ground-floor
dining hall and a more
sophisticated (and pricier)
upper level, with classical
quartet. Reservations are
essential.

Chaikhona No. 1
3 ulitsa Karetny Ryad.
Metro: Pushkinskaya. Tel:
782-6122. Open:
2pm–1am. $$$
This Uzbek café and
restaurant in the Her-
mitage Garden is perfect
for summer outdoor
lounging. In winter, try
restorative mugs of
gluwein after ice-skating
in the park. Small por-
tions of *shashlyks* and
other Uzbek fare are on
the pricey menu.

Galereya
27 ulitsa Petrovka. Metro:
Chekhovskaya. Tel: 937-
4544. Open: 24 hrs daily.
$$$$
Favoured by the newly
moneyed and those on
expense accounts, the
venue has excellent
European, Russian and
Japanese menus, but
expect small portions –
and large helpings of dis-
dain from the staff.
Reservations and smart
attire are essential.

Gogol
11 Stoleshnikov pereulok.
Metro: Okhotny Ryad. Tel:
514-0944. Open: 24 hrs
daily. $$
An inexpensive café and
restaurant favoured by a
bohemian-style crowd. A
basic Russian fare

includes soups, salads
and slightly greasy
mains, plus cheap
beer. The service is
indifferent; if you get
impatient, try the
standing shot bar. Large
concert stage and
bustling open courtyard
seating in the summer.

Goodman Steak House
23 ulitsa Tverskaya. Metro:
Pushkinskaya. Tel: 937-
5679. Open: L & D daily. $$$
A more central branch of
the upmarket American
steak house *(see page
143)*. Located down a
narrow alleyway just off
the main road.

Guilly's
6 Stoleshnikov pereulok.
Metro: Okhotny Ryad. Tel:
933-5521. Open: L & D daily.
$$$$
A favourite for prime
steaks. Situated in a cel-
lar that was once a
brothel, then a printing
house. Excellent
gourmet burgers and buf-
falo wings are served
alongside Russian food
and some seafood
dishes. Reservations
required.

Le Gâteau
23 ulitsa Tverskaya. Metro:
Tverskaya. Tel: 209-5020.
Open: B, L & D daily. $$
This stylish chain of
French-style cafés has a
chic interior with a
tempting counter of top-
notch pastries and
desserts. Expect also a
range of soups, salads
and mains – try the beef

Stroganov. Excellent-value daily set lunch.

Market

18 ulitsa Sadovaya-Samotyochnaya, building 1. Metro: Tsvetnoy Boulevard. Tel: 200-2905. Open: L & D daily. $$$

A cosy restaurant allowing a rare opportunity to inspect your food before it is cooked. Make a selection of fish, meat or vegetables from the iced, open display counters, then choose how you would like it prepared.

Na Melnitse

7 Tverskoy bulvar. Metro: Pushkinskaya. Tel: 290-3737. Open: L & D daily. $$$

Rustic wooden interior with watermill, fish pond, pheasants and tweeting birds. Excellent Russian food, this is a good place to sample *pirozhki* (filled savoury pastries) or try venison or Siberian dumplings with salmon and prawns. Attentive and helpful service.

Paname

7 Stoleshnikov pereulok, building 2. Metro: Chekhovskaya. Tel: 629-2412. Open: L & D daily. $$

A cosy French brasserie tucked in a basement. Friendly, occasionally erratic service. The menu has a good range of salads and mains, as well as French classics such as *andouillette* and sweetbreads. Has an extremely good value set lunch.

Paper Moon

17 ulitsa Petrovka. Metro: Teatralnaya. Tel: 980-7350. Open: L & D daily. $$$$

A branch of the chic international chain of Italian restaurants. The interior is elegant, the staff gracious and the ambience warm. Good portions of Italian salads, meat, seafood and dessert. The beef carpaccio never fails. For a more casual meal, the pizzas are excellent. Good wine list.

Seno

6 Kamergersky pereulok, building 1. Metro: Okhotny Ryad. Tel: 692-0452. Open: B, L & D daily. $

This inexpensive Russian restaurant is a good option for the budget- or time-conscious. Friendly staff. The self-service buffet offers an excellent range of salads and hot meals. Summer outdoor seating is ideal for a quick, cheap beer.

Uzbekistan

29/14 Neglinnaya ulitsa. Metro: Kuznetsky Most. Tel: 923-0585. Open: L & D daily. $$$

One of Moscow's oldest and most respected establishments, with a plush oriental-style interior. Traditional Uzbek cuisine, including coal-grilled *shashlyks*. Try a traditional *plov* (rice) and *laghman* (noodles). Belly dancing every evening and cock fighting on Mondays during which patrons can place bets.

Yakitoria

16 Ulitsa Petrovka. Metro: Chekhovskaya. Tel: 924-0609. Open: 11am–6am daily. $$$.

Good-quality, fresh sushi and sashimi. The dark-wood interior has an open sushi kitchen and a seated bar. Generally satisfactory service, although the doorman can be off-puttingly snooty. Reasonably priced, given its prime location. The comprehensive menu contains several assorted platters and a smattering of other Japanese dishes, including soups, rice and noodles.

Yar

32/2 Leningradsky prospekt. Metro: Dynamo. Tel: 960-2004. Open: D, daily. $$$$

Rasputin and Tolstoy ate in this classic restaurant in the Hotel Sovietsky. An excellent, Moulin-Rouge-like nightly cabaret performance. The menu is modern European – try the whole baked sea bass or the rabbit confit. Reservations essential.

Yolki-Palki

23 ulitsa Bolshaya Dmitrovka. Metro: Chekhovskaya. Tel: 200-0965. Open: L & D daily. $

A chain of cheap and cheerful Russian fast-food restaurants. All you want from the all-you-can-eat buffet.

PRICE CATEGORIES

Prices for three-course dinner per person with a glass of house wine:

$ = under $25
$$ = $25–40
$$$ = $40–60
$$$$ = more than $60

LEFT: Russia's answer to McDonald's.
RIGHT: traditional "fast food" has become popular.

LUBYANKA AND THE NORTH

Sense the power of the state in Lubyanka Square, site of
the headquarters of the KGB, and glimpse the world of
spies in the KGB Museum. Not far away is the fantastic
Futurist museum of Vladimir Mayakovsky. Further from
the centre is a museum to Russia's cosmonauts and the
delightful private theatre of the Ostankino Estate

This chapter begins at Lubyanka, the infamous headquarters of the KGB, and ends in Moscow's northern suburbs at the VVTs – a collage of golden fountains and buildings recalling Soviet ambitions. There are also two intimate convents and smart shopping on Kuznetsky Most. The highlights, however, are two intriguing museums: the experimental museum to Futurist poet Vladimir Mayakovsky, and the fascinating Memorial Museum of the Cosmonauts.

Lubyanka and the KGB

The word "Lubyanka" is indelibly associated with the square's main tenant: the Federal Security Service, formerly known as the KGB, who had their headquarters here. Before December 1917, **Lubyanskaya ploshchad** ❶ was a bustling trading area filled with carters and carriage drivers who plied their services with nothing more sinister than cheap taverns for the drivers. But the new Soviet power expropriated the Russia Insurance Company building, which dominates the square, for the secret police. They stripped its façade and built around and under the square to occupy most of the expanse. Before visiting the KGB Museum just off the square in Bolshaya Lubyanka, there are a couple of sites to note.

Opposite the KGB building is the enormous **Detsky Mir** ❷ (Children's World; 9am–9pm), opened here because one of the KGB's founders, "Iron" Felix Dzerzhinsky, had an interest in child welfare. The cavernous store still sells children's wares, and there is a charming carousel on the ground floor.

The **Polytechnic Museum** ❸ (*Politekhnichesky muzey*, 3/4 Novaya ploshchad; tel: 623-0756/925-0614; Tues–Sun 10am–6pm; closed the last Thur of the month; admission

Map
on page
161

LEFT: the Menshikov
Tower, one of
Moscow's finest
baroque buildings.
BELOW: a hotel door-
man with a black top
hat welcomes guests.

During "The Thaw" (1956–65) control over the arts was relaxed and the Polytechnic Museum played a big part in debates between those with a rationalist view of the world and those with a metaphorical view.

BELOW: Lubyanka, the former KGB headquarters, is now home to the Federal Security Service (FSB).

charge) is in the frothy building that fills an entire block on the southeast side of Lubyanskaya ploshchad. Established in 1872 by the Imperial Society of Amateur Naturalists, Anthropologists and Ethnographers, and located in a Russian Revival building completed five years later, the museum has an extensive collection of every kind of technological gadget, from writing quills to typewriters, timepieces to computers, TVs, robots and space equipment. It has also been the venue of liberal lectures, poetry readings and concerts.

In front of the museum is the **Monument to the Victims of the Totalitarian Regime**, a simple stone brought from the island monastery that became the Solovky prison camp in Russia's far north. Remembrance ceremonies are held at the monument on 30 October each year.

Foreigners can tour the fascinating **Museum of the KGB** (properly titled the Historical Demonstration Hall of the FSB of Russia) only through the Patriarshy Dom tour company *(see page 227)*. Located in the KGB Club,

an unmarked building on ulitsa Bolshaya Lubyanka, its entrance is to the left of the Seventh Continent food store. It was opened in 1984 under Andropov to educate trainees about the history of the service. Exhibits, which date back to Peter the Great, include spy paraphernalia – fake tree stumps, cameras the size of match sticks, etc – mostly taken from American and British agents. But there is also considerable attention paid to Stalinist repression during which 4 million citizens were incarcerated and a million executed, including many KGB officers.

The security service had several names and functions, finally settling on the KGB, which united what in the United States are the CIA, FBI and Secret Service. The current structure, the FSB (Federal Security Service) was headed by Vladimir Putin from 1998.

The pale-blue mansion just north of the KGB Museum on ulitsa Bolshaya Lubyanka – shrouded in construction nets at the time of writing – is the **Rostopchin House**, where the eponymous Governor General of

KGB Man or Monk?

Felix Dzerzhinsky (1877–1926) was born into a minor noble family and by 1895 was involved in revolutionary activities. He was a founder and head of the various incarnations of what would be known as the KGB until his death. The philosopher Nikolay Berdyaev, who was interrogated by him, wrote: "He made the impression of a person of conviction and sincerity. I don't think he was a bad person and wasn't even naturally cruel. He was a fanatic. You could tell by his eyes that he was obsessed… He had wanted to become a Catholic monk, and he transferred his fanatical faith to Communism".

Moscow lived. It was Rostopchin who ordered Moscow to be set ablaze when Napoleon and his army entered the city in 1812 *(see page 22)*.

Churches and monasteries

On the western side, just before ulitsa Bolshaya Lubyanka meets the Boulevard Ring, is the **Sretensky Monastery ❹**. Founded in 1397 and restored to the Church in 1994, it includes the **Church of the Icon of the Vladimir Mother of God** *(Tserkov Ikony Vladimirskoy Bogomateri)*, nestled in a peaceful garden behind the monastery's white stone fence decorated with tiles and icons. The icon is supposed to have invoked a vision of the Virgin Mary which convinced Tamerlane not to attack the city in 1395, and it has been one of Russia's most revered icons ever since.

At the top of Rozhdestvensky bulvar, where ulitsa Bolshaya Lubyanka crosses the Boulevard Ring to

become ulitsa Sretenka, sits the cosy white **Church of the Dormition of the Mother of God ❺** *(Tserkov Uspeniya Bogoroditsy)*, built in 1695 and rebuilt in 1902, with elaborate *kokoshniki* gables and a gold dome. An art gallery in the Soviet period, it is once again a church, its bare interior relieved by a fresco above the portal. The religious-looking statue across the street in the park is in fact **Nadezhda Krupskaya**, Lenin's wife.

The Boulevard Ring drops from Sretenskie vorota down a hill so steep that extra horses were once required to pull the trams up it. This stretch is Rozhdestvensky bulvar (Nativity Boulevard), which is named after the **Nativity of the Mother of God Convent ❻** *(Bogoroditse-Rozhdestveny monastyr*; daily 8am–8pm) whose fortified walls line its south side. The convent was founded in 1386 and was a place for unwanted wives, most

Capitalising on the past: missile- and dome-shaped vodka bottles.

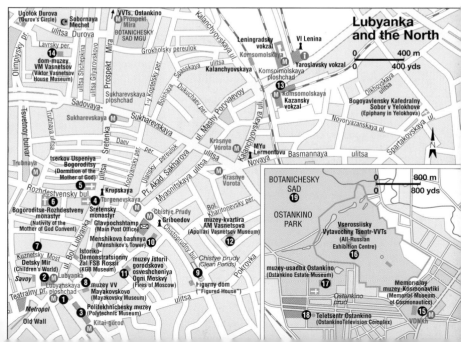

At the entrance to the Mayakovsky Museum, an excellent book and poster shop has a good collection of advertising and political posters and postcards from pre-Revolutionary days to the present.

RIGHT: Mayakovsky's avant-garde poetry and his tragic fate reflected the changes brought on by the Revolution.

famously the wife of Grand Prince Vasily III, Solomonia, who was sent to the nunnery for her inability to bear children, but gave birth soon after her arrival. She pretended the child had died and had him spirited away to the south, where he became a warlord. A grave containing a doll was found in the monastery in 1930. The convent is under reconstruction, but still tidy and peaceful. Most impressive is the 16th–18th century **Cathedral of the Nativity** *(sobor Rozhestva Bogoroditsy)*, a white stone church with clusters of gables.

"Smithy's Bridge"

Ulitsa Rozhestvenka leads south to Kuznetsky Most and past the pretty **Church of St Nicholas of the Bell-ringers** at No. 15 and the pale-green and tiled **Architectural Institute** at No. 9. The section of **Kuznetsky Most ❼** between Rozhdestvensky and Neglinnaya ulitsas is worth further exploration. This was once the "Smithy's Bridge", which crossed the Neglinnaya River until the water was shuttled underground in the early 19th century. Its paving blocks

were used to lay out Moscow's most aristocratic shopping street, filled with dozens of French fashion and jewellery shops that were so small that one writer said he felt like Gulliver among the Lilliputians. Kuznetsky Most has not reclaimed its former glory, but it's trying: Versace and Valentino have shops here, as does Fabergé (at No. 20).

Mayakovsky Museum

Myasnitskaya ulitsa, "Butcher's Street" is named after the meat stores that predominated here. It begins at the eastern corner of Lubyanskaya ploshchad. A monumental bust of Futurist poet Vladimir Mayakovsky peers from a portal in the **Mayakovsky Museum ❽** *(Muzey V.V. Mayakovskovo*; 3/6 Lubyansky proezd; tel: 921-9387; Fri–Tues 10am–5pm, Thur 1–8pm; closed last Fri of the month; admission and photo charges). Walk up to the fourth floor to the small room where Mayakovsky lived the last 11 years of his life, and where he shot himself in the heart on 14 April 1930. Then enter a maelstrom of

Vladimir Mayakovsky

Vladimir Mayakovsky (1893–1930) was one of Russia's most complex artistic figures. Born in Georgia, he came to Moscow in 1906 after the death of his father. A poet and playwright, he was part of the movement of avant-garde literary and artistic figures who embraced the Revolution, producing dozens of agit-prop (propaganda) posters for the Russian State Telegraph Agency, and Futurist poems that celebrated the new age. A poet of great sensibility and intelligence, he led a hopelessly convoluted love life. He fathered a daughter by an American he met while on a lecture tour, fell briefly in love with Tatiana Yakovleva, a Russian living in Paris who would eventually give birth to another writer, Francine du Plessix Gray, and marry Alexander Lieberman, the editorial director of all Condé Nast publications. At the end of his life, he was in love with Lilly Brik, the wife of one of his best friends, the critic Osip Brik, with whom he had founded the Dadaist journal *LEF*.

When he committed suicide in 1930, a fellow poet said that the man had been killing the poet throughout his life, and now the poet finally killed the man.

Constructivist and Futurist madness, which spirals down a ramp through twists of girders, displays of photographs piled willy-nilly around old furniture, Mayakovsky's hand-drawn posters, Constructivist drawings and models, manuscripts, letters, posters and photographs of his plays. The exhibitions are designed to plunge you into the dizzying days when Mayakovsky wrote the essay "A Slap in the Face of Public Taste", and the artistic and literary avant-garde thought they had overthrown Russia's moribund culture along with the tsar.

On Myasnitskaya ulitsa are two good bookshops, the Biblio Globus next to the museum and the John Parsons Bookshop at No. 20/1. The bright-blue baroque mansion behind the FSB building was once the town-house of the Saltykov-Chertikov family and will become a cultural centre in 2006. You can't miss the **Perlov Tea Shop** decorated in lavish fake Chinese style – supposedly to impress the Chinese Emperor on his state visit in 1893. Next to it on the right is the Moscow School of Painting, Sculpture and Architecture, founded in 1844. Mayakovsky was one of the students.

Myasnitskaya ulitsa meets the Boulevard Ring at Turgenevskaya ploshchad, with the modern **Lukoil Building** on one side, the **Main Post Office** (*Glavpochshtamp*) on the other, and a statue of the playwright **Alexander Griboyedov** in the centre.

Clean ponds

The broad park in the boulevard is called **Chistye Prudy** ❾ (Clean Ponds). Once called "Foul Ponds", because butchers on Myasnitskaya ulitsa dumped their waste here, in 1739 the ponds were cleaned and renamed, but only one remains. It is graced by swans in summer and ice-skaters in winter. This expensive

area is filled with cafés and restaurants serving wealthy residents and businesses.

It is a pleasant stroll along the park, but you may wish to take a detour into what was once the Armenian neighbourhood. Turn south on Archangelsky pereulok and you'll soon see the gold spire of the Church of the Archangel Gabriel (*Tserkov Arkhangela Gavriila*), commonly called **Menshikov's Tower** ❿ (*Menshikova bashnya*). It was completed in 1707 by Prince Menshikov, Peter the Great's close friend, in imitation of Western religious architecture. The archangel that once topped its salmon-pink tower was destroyed when the tower was struck by lightning. It was replaced with a more modest filial in 1780. In the courtyard is the Antioch Patriarch's Court.

In nearby Armyansky pereulok is the offbeat museum of lights called **The Fires of Moscow** ⓫ (*Muzey istorii gorodskovo osveshcheniya Ogni Moskvy*; 3/5 Armyansky pereulok, str.1, code 1; tel: 924-7374; daily 11am–5pm; admission charge; English room descriptions). The

A large collection of Mayakovsky's original artwork is on display amongst the chaos of his museum.

BELOW: the Perlov Tea Shop was decorated for a visit from the Emperor of China who never visited.

museum has lights and lamps from 1730 to the present, and the friendly staff runs unusual city light tours.

Outside the Boulevard Ring

The area beyond the Boulevard Ring holds some unique attractions, which are best reached via metro. East of Lermontovskaya ploshchad, two long blocks from Krasnye Vorota metro station, turn right on Furmanny pereulok and enter the quiet neighbourhood where the painter Apollary Vasnetsov lived for the last 30 years of his life, until 1933. The **Apollari Vasnetsov Museum** (*Muzey-kvartira A.M. Vasnetsova*; 6 Furmanny pereulok, apt 22; tel: 208-9045; Tues–Sun 11am–5pm; admission charge) displays his study and living room, with furniture he designed, and wonderful paintings and drawings of old Moscow.

Moscow's stations

"Three Station Square" is the popular name for **Komsolmolskaya ploshchad** ⓭, a mess of parking lots, dreary cafés and homeless people.

The three magnificent train stations here deserve a far better backdrop. Each reflects the city or country it serves: the **Leningrad station** (opened in 1851 by Tsar Nicholas I and his family) duplicates, in smaller form, the classical masterpiece of the Nicholas station in St Petersburg – there are countless television and film skits about drunken travellers unable to understand what city they are in. **Yaroslavl station**, a masterpiece of neo-Russian fantasy built in 1902 by Fyodor Shekhtel, mimics the walls and fortresses of Moscow and Yaroslavl. **Kazan Station**, built in 1926 by Alexander Shchusev, is reminiscent of Kazan's fortress walls. Between 1925 and 1927 Shchusev also designed and built the ornamented brick-and-stone Central House of Culture for Railway Workers across from Kazan station. It is one of Moscow's finest "worker's cultural centres".

Vasnetsov Museum and Prospekt Mira

The once important road leading to the Holy Trinity Monastery of St Sergius *(see page 200)* was built over by **Prospekt Mira** (Peace Avenue), the least pleasing of the Stalinist highways. However, not far north from Prospekt Mira metro station is a gem, the **House-Museum** of the artist **Viktor Vasnetsov** ⓮ (*dom-muzey V.M. Vasnetsova*; 13 pereulok Vasnetsova; tel: 681-1329; Wed–Sun 10am–6pm; closed last Thur of the month; admission charge).

Tucked amid a depressing conglomeration of rough tower blocks and tin garages is this small fairytale house designed by the prolific artist, architect and set designer Viktor Vasnetsov in 1894. It was was his home and studio until his death in 1926. The interior is decorated in an utterly charming late 19th-century Russian combination of *style moderne* and folk art.

South of the Olympic Stadium, Moscow's **main mosque** *(Sobornaya Mechet)* rises incongruously on pereulok Vypolzov.

Around VDNKh metro

In 1964 a huge space-rocket obelisk was erected at the intersection of Prospekt Mira and Ostankinsky pereulok in honour of Yuri Gagarin's first manned space mission on 12 April 1961. The rocket towers nearly 100 metres (330 ft) over the Alley of Cosmonauts, with busts of the USSR's first men and women in space and a statue to Konstantin Tsyolkovsky (1857–1913), the father of Russian cosmonautics. It also houses the **Memorial Museum of Cosmonautics** ⑮ *(Memorialny muzey-Kosmonavtiki;* 111 Prospekt Mira; tel: 683-7914; Tues–Sun 10am–6pm; closed last Fri of the month; admission, photo and video charges; English brochure; entrance is in end opposite rocket).

The largest part of the exhibition is devoted to Gagarin's flight. Be sure to note the first dogs in space, Belka and Strelka, who have been stuffed for posterity. Khrushchev gave Jacqueline Kennedy one of Strelka's puppies, so space-dog progeny may still be roaming the US.

The grand arches behind are the entrance to the All-Russian Exhibition Centre *(Vserossiisky Vytavochny Tsentr)* **VVTs** ⑯ (daily 9am–7pm, holidays 9am–8pm), which you walk to via a bustling market of CDs, DVDs and other items, which attract gaggles of teenagers. The exhibition centre was originally called the Exhibition of Economic Achievement (VDNKh) when it opened in 1959. Today the buildings, mosaics, statues and glorious fountain still comprise the country's finest collection of Socialist Realism statuary, but the halls that once displayed prize-winning pigs and bulky TV sets now house hundreds of mundane shops. At the time of writing, the monumental Worker and Peasant statue had been dismantled for repairs.

Only Pavilion 71 (directly north of the towered building) has a museum, the quirky **Ice Age Museum-Theatre** *(Muzey-teatr lednikovy period;* tel: 975-0913; 10am–6pm; admis-

Map on page 161

Soviet-era posters promoted the unity of workers "for peace, for people's democracy!"

BELOW: obelisks in honour of Yuri Gagarin, the first man in space.

Map
on page
161

In summer Ostankino holds early music concerts in the theatre, where you can hear every pluck of the lute and the softest whisper of the singer as you sit in 18th-century luxury. Leave time before your visit to wander through the romantic landscaped park.

BELOW: Trinity Church in Ostankino, dating from the 1680s.

sion and photo charges). Tots are thrilled by the skeletons and reconstructions of woolly mammoths and a furry rhinoceros.

Ostankino Estate

From the VVTs turn right on Ostankinsky pereulok and left on ulitsa Akademika Korolyova, following the small elevated monorail, and after a 20-minute walk among faceless estates, you'll come to one of Moscow's most delightful palaces, the **Ostankino Estate Museum** ⑰ (*Muzey-usadba Ostankino*; 5 1-ya ulitsa Ostankinskaya; tel: 683-4645; daily 18 May to 30 Sept 10am–6pm, with tours 10am–3pm and open visitation 3.30–6pm; museum is also closed when it rains or when the humidity is especially high; English-language room descriptions).

When Count Nikolay Sheremetev became bored with the old family manse at Kuskovo *(see page 191)*, he decided to remodel a neglected family estate in Ostankino. Passionate about theatre, he envisioned a Theatre Palace where guests would be both actors and spectators. The Theatre Palace, built from 1793 to 1797 and used for just four years, was meant for summer pleasures. In the luxurious Italian Pavilion (much of the rest of the museum is either under or awaiting repair) the count's guests would gather before the evening's opera or concert. This "theatre within a theatre" has a stage 22 metres (72 ft) deep and 17 metres (56 ft) wide that opens to a circular seating area, ringed by a balcony. The enormous columns could be moved to change scenes; wooden machines made the sounds of wind, thunder and rain (the last by tossing dried peas down a chute lined with curved metal blades).

Another part of the museum displays an exhibit of the dazzling and ingenious lighting fixtures that were essential to the theatricality of the count's entertainments.

Just past the palace stands the **Ostankino Television Complex** ⑱ – the production-and-broadcasting studios that were stormed in the second coup attempt of 1993 – and the 540-metre (1,770-ft) television tower. In August 2000 fire swept through the tower, but it is almost entirely repaired. The highlight is the Seventh Heaven restaurant at 350 metres (1,480 ft) that turns slowly to reveal 360 degrees of Moscow. It is expected to reopen in 2006.

If you walk past the TV centre to the end of ulitsa Akademika Korolyova and turn right on Botanicheskaya ulitsa, you will come to the main entrance to the **Botanical Gardens** ⑲ (*Botanichesky sad*, 4 ulitsa Botanicheskaya; tel: 619-5368 to arrange orangerie tours; gardens open all year during daylight; admission charge). The gardens have more than 16,000 types of flora, from the tropics to the tundra, all laid out in an artfully landscaped park. ❏

RESTAURANTS & BARS

Restaurants

Detsky Mir Cafe
5 Teatralny proezd. Metro: Lubyanka. Tel: 781-0950. Open: B, L & D daily. $
A Stalin-era cafeteria in the Detsky Mir toy store. Dumplings and ice-cream milkshakes are safe choices.

Dzhagannat Express
11 ulitsa Kuznetsky Most. Metro: Kuznetsky Most. Tel: 928-3580. Open: L & D daily. $$
One of the city's few vegetarian places. No smoking or alcohol. A wide range of Asian dishes. It also has a health-food store.

Loft
Lubyanskaya ploshchad. Metro: Lubyanka. Tel: 933-7713. Open: B, L & D daily. $$$
On the 6th floor of Nautilus Shopping Centre with an unobstructed view of Lubyanskaya ploshchad. Modern European menu.

Na Melnitse
24 Sadovaya-Spasskaya. Metro: Krasnye Vorota. Tel: 925-8890. Open: L & D daily. $$$
The original outlet of the deservedly popular Russian restaurant.

Nostalgie
12a Chistoprudny bulvar. Metro: Chistye Prudy. Tel: 925-7625. Open: L & D daily. $$$$
Celebrated for its extensive wine list and gourmet food, with a chic interior. The service is discreet. Expect creative modern French cuisine and a large bill. Reservations and smart attire essential.

Petrovich
24 ulitsa Myasnitskaya, building 3. Metro: Turgenevskaya. Tel: 923-0082. Open: L & D daily. $$$
Decorated to resemble a Brezhnev-era communal flat, it attracts a boisterous, alternative crowd. A surreal experience. Reservations are essential.

Planet Cosmos
150 Prospekt Mira. Metro: Prospekt Mira. Tel: 234-1000. Open: L & D daily. $$$
On the 25th floor of the Cosmos Hotel with impressive views. Unremarkable but palatable Russian and European cuisine.

Simple Pleasures
22/1 ulitsa Sretenka. Metro: Sukharevskaya. Tel: 207-1521. Open: L & D daily. $$
A modern American restaurant on its way to becoming a classic. With a laid-back bar area and summer terrace.

Vapiano
26 Prospekt Mira, building 1. Metro: Prospekt Mira. Tel: 937-8809. Open: L & D daily. $$
An affordable, casual Italian eatery for a low-key, relaxed meal. Good value set lunch on weekdays.

Vogue Café
7/9 ulitsa Kuznetsky Most. Metro: Kuznetsky Most. Tel: 923-1701. Open: B, L & D Mon–Fri, L & D Sat–Sun. $$$$
This is where the beautiful people come to sip cocktails and be admired. Excellent menu but portions are as petite as the female clientele.

Bars

Bungalo Bar
6/1 Zemlyanoi Val. Metro: Kurskaya. Tel: 916-2432. Open: B, L & D daily. $$
An unpretentious Ethiopian restaurant. Vegetarian food available. English-speaking staff.

Discreet Charm of the Bourgeoisie
24 ulitsa Bolshaya Lubyanka. Metro: Turgenevskaya. Tel: 923-0848. Open: 24 hrs daily. $$
Casual and lively, it is favoured by students and trendy twenty-somethings. Drinks are cheap.

Goa
8/2 Myasnitskaya ulitsa. Metro: Lubyanka. Tel: 504-4031. Open: L & D daily. $$$
A chic French-Indian restaurant and bar popular with young executives. Cosy seating areas are ideal for drinks in larger groups.

PRICE CATEGORIES

Prices for three-course dinner per person with a glass of house wine:
$ = under $25
$$ = $25–40
$$$ = $40–60
$$$$ = more than $60

RIGHT: beer is a drink of choice for early afternoons.

IVANOVSKAYA HILL TO TAGANKA

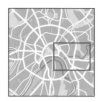

You can explore the quiet lanes and grand mansions of an area rich in places of worship and old monasteries. Here is the city's first Stalinist skyscraper and, by way of contrast, the Theatre on Taganka

Moscow's southeast section once had a reputation for debauchery and imprisonment. Now it is made up of quiet little lanes lined with old mansions, the city's oldest Stalinist skyscraper and one of its most experimental theatres.

The "Little Russia" quarter

BELOW: the apartments on Kotelnicheskoy naberezhnaya – one of the Stalin's "seven sisters".

This tour begins just south of the Polytechnic Museum (metro Kitaigorod, *see page 159*), where a large boulevard (called Lubyansky proezd on the eastern side and Staraya ploshchad on western side) slopes down past ulitsa Varvarka to the Moscow River.

The tree-shaded park in the centre of this boulevard is called the **Ilinsky Gardens ❶** (*Ilinskie sady*, named after the Ilinsky Gates that once stood at the end of the street Ilinka) and has monuments at each end. The bell-like monument across from the Polytechnic Museum is dedicated to the Russian soldiers who died in 1878 while defending the Bulgarian city of Plevna from the Turks.

At the bottom of the hill, on Slavyanskaya ploshchad, is the monument to Cyril and Methodius (*Kiril i Metody*), the monk-scholars who developed the Cyrillic alphabet to translate the Bible. Across from the statue is the bright little **Church of All Saints in Kulishkakh**, originally built to honour the dead of the battle of Kulikovo Fields in 1380.

Ulitsa Maroseyka runs to the east of the Polytechnic Museum and becomes ulitsa Pokrovka before it crosses the Boulevard Ring. The word Maroseyka is a corruption of the Russian word for "Little Russia", which – in the big Russian Empire – meant little Ukraine. In the 17th century the Ukrainian representative had his headquarters here in a bright-blue mansion at No. 17, now the **Belarus Embassy**, and the

area was inhabited by a mix of foreigners and local families. Maroseyka and Pokrovka ulitsas are now lined by a rather garish assortment of shops and restaurants, but the streets to the right that twist and curve down towards the river on Ivanovskaya Hill are filled with little churches and mansions.

Ivanovskaya Hill

The highlight of the area is a walk down **Kolpachny pereulok ❷** past four unique mansions on the left side: one Gothic (No. 5), the next bright blue-green baroque, the next a little pink classical jewel box and the last (No. 11) in *style moderne*. They were all built by wealthy traders in the 19th century as dwellings. *Kolpachny* means the street of hat-makers. *Khokhlovsky* means the street of Ukrainians, from the word *khokhol*, the characteristically Ukrainian long tuft of hair at the brow.

At the bottom of the hill, turn left up Khokhlovsky pereulok past the walled gardens and pistachio-coloured **Morozov Mansion** that was once owned by the Old Believer Morozova, and follow along two sharp bends, between which stands the **Trinity Church** *(Troitskaya tserkov)*, a magnificent example of Naryshkin baroque – and, just before it, an odd white warehouse building decorated with dark-red paint. This 17th-century dwelling was the archives of the Russian Foreign Service and, oddly enough, one of the favourite spots for Russia's golden artistic youth in the 19th century. Writers like Pushkin and Turgenev (and composers including Tchaikovsky) wiled away the hours here, plumbing the empire's ancient documents for raw material.

Ivanovskaya Hill has several landmarks to Moscow's non-Russian population. The yellow-and-white classical-style **Choral Synagogue ❸** *(Moskovskaya khoralnaya sinagoga)*

has been standing at 10 Bolshoy Spasoglinishchevsky pereulok for over 100 turbulent years.

On Starosadsky pereulok the beige-and-brown Gothic-style **Lutheran Church ❹** *(Lyuteranskaya obshchina)* is once again open at No. 7/10. Built in 1812 and then rebuilt between 1903 and 1905, it was the venue of a charity organ concert by Franz Liszt in 1843.

Beyond the Yauza

The last leg of the Boulevard Ring slopes gently down to the southeast from ulitsa Pokrovka to the Yauza River. From 1826 to 1923 this area was the labour market Khitrovka – a foul, swampy mass of tenement houses and taverns with names like "Transit Camp", "Siberia" and "Hard Labour", filled with prostitutes of every age and both genders, thieves, escaped convicts and murderers.

The area on the south side of the Yauza River was first settled by craftsmen that settled here so that the river would protect the city from any blaze that might be ignited as they worked. Today the community's

During the Soviet years the Choral Synagogue hosted Golda Meir in 1948, then the Ukrainian-born Ambassador of Israel.

BELOW: Moscow has a large and vibrant student population.

Founded in 1964, the tiny Theatre on Taganka produced dozens of plays that pushed up to – and sometimes over – the line of the politically and socially permissible.

little churches and lanes are dwarfed by the Stalinist skyscraper on the embankment, the first of the city's seven to be completed (1948– 52). This skyscraper is the **Kotelnicheskoy apartments** ❺ *(Dom na Kotelnicheskoy)*, once given to the Party's faithful but now sold in the high six digits.

Across the street on the same side of the Yauza is the **Foreign Literature Library** (a four-storeyed brick-and-glass office block) which houses the American Centre, British Council and French Cultural Centre (1 Nikoloyamskaya ulitsa).

Taganka

At the top of the hill (follow Yauzskaya ulitsa) is Taganskaya ploshchad, commonly called "Taganka" and named for the craftsmen who made *tagan*, iron stands that held cooking cauldrons. "Taganka" is a word rich in associations for Russians. From 1804 until the 1950s,

one of Moscow's most infamous prisons was located not far from here. The prison and the trials of Russians have been immortalised in dozens of folk songs still sung today by students and anyone sitting around the table with a guitar and an urge for liberty (and sentimentality).

In the 1960s, the spirit of Taganka was continued at the capital's most popular theatre, Yuri Lyubimov's **Theatre on Taganka** ❻. The most freedom-loving personality of the theatre was Vladimir Vysotsky (1938–80), a hard-drinking, hard-loving, raspy-voiced songwriter, singer and actor, whose songs were passed around the country on bootlegged tapes. When he died of a heart attack during the 1980 Moscow Olympics, over 10,000 people flocked to the theatre from all over the country.

Near by, there is a small **Museum to Vysotsky** ❼ *(Tsentr-muzey V.M. Vysotskovo*; 3 Nizhny Tagansky tupik; tel: 915-7578; Tues–

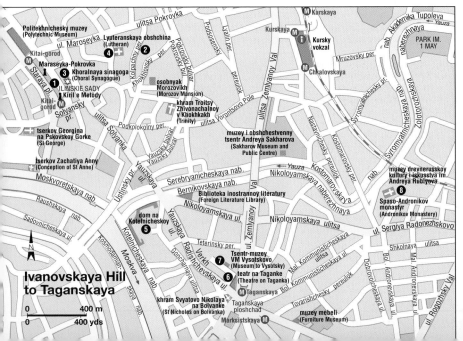

Ivanovskaya Hill to Taganskaya

Sat 11am–5.30pm; admission charge) just before you reach the square via Yauska ulitsa, with memorabilia, documents and photographs of his life in theatre, film and with his family.

In the square across from the theatre is the pretty brick and white **Church of St Nicholas on Bolvanka**, built in 1697–1712. Behind it is early baroque **Church of the Dormition of the Holy Mother of God in Gonchari**, built in 1654.

Andrey Rublyov Museum

Bolshaya Kommunisticheskaya ulitsa ends at Andronevskaya ploshchad, which is dominated by the robin's-egg-blue **Church of St Sergius of Radonezh in Rogozhkaya** settlement, built in the 18th and 19th centuries. Across the roundabout to the east is a square with a statue of Andrey Rublyov before the **Saviour-Andronikov Monastery** and **Andrey Rublyov Central Museum of Old Russian Art and Culture** ❽ (10 Andronevskaya ulitsa; Thur–Tues 11am–5.30pm; closed last Fri of the month; tel: 678-1467; admission and photo charges; brochure and some captions in English). Built in 1360, it is the oldest fortress-monastery extant in Moscow. Its thick white walls and towers topped by tent roofs (built in the 17th century) conceal a peaceful cloister, now dominated by two churches.

The three-tiered, airy **Church of the Archangel Michael** was built in the 17th and 18th centuries; it was finished with funds provided by the first wife of Peter the Great, Evdokiya Lophukhina, and serves as a crypt for the Lopukhin family.

Moscow's oldest stone church stands in the centre of the monastery, the **Cathedral of the Icon of the Saviour Not Made by Hands** (*Sobor Spasa Nerukotvornovo Obraza*). Built in the early 1400s with frescos (now lost) by Andrey Rublyov, who served and was interred in this monastery, the church was rebuilt many times, dismantled in the 1930s and painstakingly rebuilt to its original appearance. The museum displays a rich collection of icons, including the 13th century *Icon of the Saviour Not Made by Hands* that once graced the Cathedral. ❏

Not far from the square on Taganskaya ulitsa is the Furniture Museum 8 (Muzey mebeli; 13 ulitsa Taganskaya; tel: 912-5170; Tues–Sun 11am–6pm; admission charge). Housed in a gracious city mansion, the museum has recreated the interior of a late 18th to early 19th-century urban dwelling.

LEFT: curved arches *(kokoshniki)* are named after women's medieval headdresses.

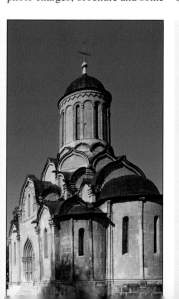

RESTAURANTS

Baklazhan
29 Nikoloyamskaya ulitsa, building 3. Metro: Marksistskaya. Tel: 915-3313. Open: L & D daily. $$
A good Georgian restaurant with fair prices. Cheerful service.

Dukhan Alaverdi
32 ulitsa Nizhegorodskaya, building 4. Metro: Taganskaya. Tel: 670-2811. Open: L & D daily. $$
Another good-value Georgian eatery. Try one of the generously portioned *shashlyks*.

Noyev Kovcheg
9 Maly Ivanovsky pereulok. Metro: Kitai-Gorod. Tel: 917-0717. Open: L & D daily. $$$
An Armenian restaurant considered by some to be the city's best ethnic dining experience.

Sem Pyatnits
6 ulitsa Vorontsovskaya. Metro: Taganskaya. Tel: 912-1218. Open: L & D daily. $$$
Intimate dining halls set in a 19th-century mansion. Classic Russian cuisine.

Verona
36/1 ulitsa Vorontsovskaya. Metro: Proletarskaya. Tel: 676-4150. Open: B, L & D daily. $$
Outstanding home-style Italian cuisine. Book in advance or be prepared to wait.

Price includes a three-course dinner for one and a glass of house wine.
$$$$ $60 and up, **$$$** under $60, **$$** under $40, **$** under $25.

BEYOND THE RIVER

Outside Moscow's walled city, the "Merchant Kings"
made the area south of the river their home. They
used their riches to build numerous churches
and to found the Tretyakov Gallery, the
world's finest collection of Russian art

The tongue of land to the south of the Moscow River is called Zamoskvoreche ("Beyond the Moscow River"). This low, boggy land was filled with the royal family's gardens and small settlements of sheep-herders, minters and smithies. Representatives of the Golden Horde lived along the road – now ulitsa Bolshaya Ordynka – that the princes took south to pay tribute to the Tatar khans. By the 16th century it had become the home of Ivan the Terrible's feared *oprichniki*. Later, musketeers, translators and Cossacks were billeted here to protect this vulnerable route from the south.

All that is left of these settlements are street names – although there is still a mosque on Bolshaya Tatarskaya ulitsa where the Golden Horde Tatars once lived. After the mutiny of the musketeers, Peter the Great cleared the area of armed men, and it became empty and neglected. In the 19th century merchants bought cheap land for their factories and homes, eventually taking over Zamoskvoreche and transforming it into a "separate country" of "Merchant Kings". One of these was Pavel Tretyakov, who built the Tretyakov Gallery to house his collection of Russian art. The area is also renowned for its

churches, mostly built by rich merchants, in gratitude for their good fortune or in atonement for their sins. They are set on quiet lanes lined with the merchant homes that weave among the four main thoroughfares of Zamoskvoreche: Pyatnitskaya, Bolshaya Ordynka, Polyanka and Yakimanka.

Bog Island

To combat flooding, the Drainage Canal (*Vodootvodny kanal*) was cut in 1783, creating a long island called

Map
on page
174

LEFT: Tsereteli's controversial statue of Peter the Great.
BELOW: crossing the Drainage Canal.

Children are the Victims of Adults' Vices *was donated to the city in 2001 by the artist, Mikhail Shemyakin.*

Bog Island *(Bolotny ostrov)*. It is joined to the "mainland" of the city by one foot and four road bridges. The Great Stone Bridge ends by the Kremlin's Borovitsky Gates. It was built in 1645 and has been renovated at least six times, most recently in 1938. The next crossing (off Red Square) is the Great Moscow River Bridge, built in 1872 (rebuilt 1938). Entering the island via these bridges gives great views of the Kremlin.

Bog Square

Over the Great Stone Bridge to the east is a park, **Bog Square ❶** *(Bolot naya ploshchad)* where in 1774 Yemelian Pugachev, a Cossack from the Don River who had organised an uprising, was beheaded and quartered. Today there is a statue of the Realist painter Ilya Repin (1844– 1940) in the square, and a statuary group called *Children Are the Victims of Adults'*

Vices by the émigré artist Mikhail Shemyakin.

West of the wide thoroughfare off the Great Stone Bridge is one of Moscow's most famous apartment houses, Government House, or the **House on the Embankment ❷** *(Dom na Naberezhnoy)*. Commissioned in the late 1920s for high Communist Party officials, it has more than 500 apartments and 24 entrances. Once home to hundreds of ministers, under Stalin's purges its residents began to disappear: over 700 officials and their families were arrested, executed or exiled. The house was immortalised in Yuri Trifonov's 1976 novel *The House on the Embankment.*

On the west side of the apartment house is the **Red October Chocolate Factory ❸** *(Krasny Oktyabr*; 4 Bersenevskaya naberezhnaya; tel: 696-3552; tours during the week in Russian by appoint-

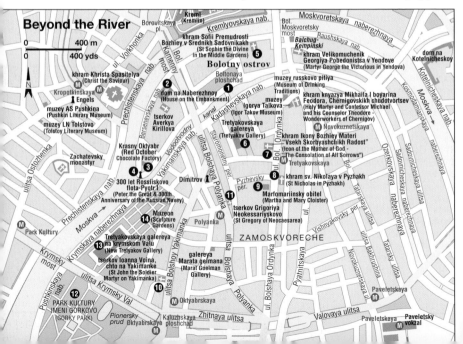

ment or through Patriarshy Dom, *see page 227*). Built by the young Berliner Theodore Einem and his partner Julius Heuss, in the mid-19th century, the factory still produces fine chocolates and other confectionery. Tours take you into the production halls to sample anything you wish off the assembly lines, including the bittersweet varieties of 80 percent pure cocoa butter. The factory has several shops about the city.

To the west of the Red October factory is Zurab Tsereteli's most controversial statue, the enormous **Monument to Peter the Great and the 300th Anniversary of the Russian Navy** ❹. Rumour has it that the sculpture was meant to be of Christopher Columbus but was changed to Peter the Great when New York City refused it. Cross the Tsereteli-designed footbridge to see the Cathedral of Christ the Saviour (*see page 120*), another Tsereteli commission.

Sophia Embankment

The riverbank between the Great Stone and Moscow River bridges is the **Sophia Embankment**, named after the church at No. 32. The house at No. 14 was built by architect Vasily Zalessky in 1893 and was famed for its Gothic interiors by Shekhtel. It was given to the British for their embassy in 1931, a decision Stalin rued: it annoyed him to see the Union flag from the Kremlin. In 2000 a new embassy opened and the mansion is now home to the British Ambassador.

At No. 32 is the **Church of St Sophia the Divine in the Middle Gardens** ❺ (*Khram Sofii Premudrosti Bozhiey v Srednikh Sadovnikakh*), tucked behind a grand bell tower that houses a small church. The pale-pink, ornamented tower was built in 1868; the stone church, decorated with *kokoshniki*,

delicate tiles and brickwork rising up to five cupolas of dark-green tiles, dates from 1682. Although under restoration, they are open for services.

Balchug

If you continue along the Sophia Embankment, just past the Moscow River Bridge is an area called Balchug, now home to the elegant Balchug-Kempinski Hotel. The word *balchug* meant "market" (which existed here centuries ago) or "mud" (which has existed here since time immemorial). Behind the hotel, on ulitsa Nizhnikh Sadovnikakh, is the dark-red 1653 **Church of the Martyr George the Victorious in Yendova** (*Khram Velikomuchenik Georgiya Pobedonistsa v Yendove*). The church is stunning, with a pyramid of *kokoshniki* rising to five domes and decorative stonework around the windows. The bell tower collapsed during a flood and was rebuilt in 1806 in a boxy classical style. The wooden cross commemorates the victims of the Gulag at

In 2003 the city approved a plan to develop Bog Island, evicting the factories and turning the buildings into a gallery and shops. Most people agree that the island, prime real estate opposite the Kremlin, needs development; but they fear the high-rises planned will overwhelm the narrow strip of land. Stay tuned. It may soon be reincarnated as Golden Island.

BELOW: the House on the Embankment, a former home of the Stalinist elite.

Pavel Tretyakov – founder of the eponymous gallery.

Solovky Monastery, with which the church is associated. The church is open for services.

Tretyakov Gallery

The main attraction of Zamosvoreche is the Tretyakov Gallery of Russian Art, more commonly called the "Tretyakovka". From Bog Island, cross the footbridge by Repin's statue to walk down pedestrianised Lavrushensky pereulok to the **Tretyakov Gallery ❻** (*Tretyakovskaya galereya*; 12 Lavrushinsky pereulok).

Most people start their visit to the gallery at **St Nicholas Church**.

To reach the church, follow the signs from the basement. The large Vladimir icon of the *Mother of God*, one of the most revered in Russia, stands in a special case to the left in front of the altar. It was created in Constantinople in 1100–30 and brought to Kiev and then Vladimir. This is the best-known of this type of image of "Tenderness" (*Umilenie*), with the Christ Child pressing against Mary's cheek. The sombre but emotional image in deep browns and gold conveys the universal love of mother and child. In 1395 the icon

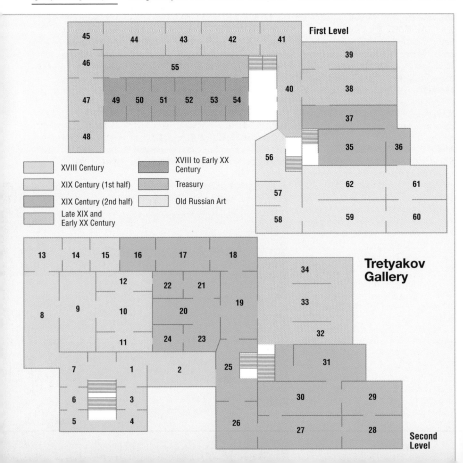

First Level

45 44 43 42 41
46
55
40
47 49 50 51 52 53 54
48

39
38
37
35 36

XVIII Century
XIX Century (1st half)
XIX Century (2nd half)
Late XIX and Early XX Century
XVIII to Early XX Century
Treasury
Old Russian Art

56
57
58

62 61
59 60

13 14 15 16 17 18
12
22 21
8 9 10 20
11
24 23
7 1 2 25
6 3
5 4
19
26

Tretyakov Gallery

34
33
32
31
30 29
27 28

Second Level

was carried in procession when Tamerlane was about to attack Moscow and, according to the legend, made the fearsome Khan change his mind and retreat from the city. Since then, the icon has been considered the patron and defender of Moscow and Russia.

18th-century art

Start on the upper floor with early secular Russian art, distinguished mainly by portraits and landscapes. **Hall 1** displays portraits painted by foreign artists in Russia; the 1728 portrait of a portly and self-satisfied Tsar Mikhail, the first Romanov tsar, is by Johann Wedekind. In **Hall 2** is a collection of sculpture by Fedot Shubin (1740–1805), considered Russia's finest master of busts. In **Hall 3** note the sketch for a portrait of Catherine the Great at her coronation by Aleksey Antropov (1716–95) and portraits by Fyodor Rokotov (1735–1808). The highlight of **Hall 4** is a rare 18th-century genre painting, *Celebrating the Marriage Contract,* by Mikhail Shibanov. *Portrait of an Unknown*

Woman in Peasant Dress by Ivan Argunov (1729–1802) captures the century's ideal of beauty.

Hall 5 is dedicated to Dmitry Levitsky (1735–1822), whose portraits are more psychologically revealing than those of his contemporaries. Landscape painting was not taught at the Academy of Arts until 1776, and **Hall 6** displays work by the master of this "new" genre, Fyodor Alekseev (1753–1824), renowned for his panoramic city views, such as the *Palace Embankment from the Peter and Paul Fortress in St Petersburg.* Paintings in **Hall 7** are from the turn of the 19th century, when Romanticism began to enter Russian art. A fine example is the *Portrait of Maria Lophukhina* (1797) by Vladimir Borovikovsky, in which his subject's beauty and haughtiness is caught against the background of idealised nature and romantic ruins.

Early 19th century

A portrait of Alexander Puskin, the famous poet, is on display in **Hall 8**. It was painted by Orest Kiprensky

Maps:
Area 174
Plan 176

TIP

The Tretyakov collection is designed to be seen chronologically, starting on the upper floor (signs in English point the way). Hall numbers above the doors refer to the rooms after the doorway, not the room you are in. The gallery is open Tues–Sun 10am–7.30pm; admission charges; English maps and audio guide available.

BELOW: from ancient icons to Realism – the Tretyakov represents Russian and Soviet art as it developed.

In Hall 16 note Konstantin Flavitsky's (1830–66) romantic rendering of the life of Princess Tarakanova, the illegitimate daughter of Empress Yelizaveta . In this version she is incarcerated in the Peter and Paul Fortress dungeon in St Petersburg, about to be drowned as flood waters fill her cell.

BELOW: *The Appearance of Christ to the People*, by A. Ivanov.

in 1827. In **Hall 9** note the *Portrait of the Writer Nikolay Gogol* by Fyodor Moller (1812–74) in a room dominated by the portraits of Karl Bryullov (1799–1852). The most popular portraitist of the time, Bryullov revolutionised the genre by painting his subjects in action. *The Rider* (1832) is a snapshot, catching the varied textures of horse, stone, earth and rider's dress.

Halls 10 and **12** are dedicated to Alexander Ivanov (1806–58) and his enormous canvas *The Appearance of Christ to the People*, which he worked on for nearly 20 years. The finest studies for this painting are on display in Hall 10. **Hall 11** exhibits more portraits of the early 19th century. **Hall 13** displays works by Vasily Tropinin (1776–1857), a former serf who portrayed his subjects with intimacy and informality. In **Hall 14** are works by Aleksey Venitsianov (1780–1847). His three famous landscapes – *In the Field*, *Spring* and *Haymaking* – exalt the Russian countryside. The next hall (**15**) exhibits works by Pavel Fedotov (1815–52). Note

the small canvas *The Major's Marriage Proposal*: a patriarchal merchant family caught at the moment when an unscrupulous suitor makes his case.

Critical Realism

By the second half of the 19th century, Russian artists began to rebel against the strictures of the Academy. In 1870, several artists formed the Society for Travelling Art Exhibits, commonly called The Wanderers. They sought to "bring art to the masses" and to portray the everyday life of common people with a critical social and political eye. Called "Ideological" or "Critical" Realism, it paralleled the great Realist Russian writers of the 19th century, particularly Lev Tolstoy, and was driven by social, religious and moral concerns, an interest in Russian history and a love for the land.

A striking example of Critical Realism in **Hall 16** is *Misalliance*, the wedding of a dowryless young woman and her ancient groom, by Vasily Pikurev (1832–90). **Hall 17** is devoted to Vasily Perov (1834–82), known for his depictions of the lives of the poor and downtrodden, such as *Troika* and *Village Walk of the Cross on Easter*. His portrait of writer Fyodor Dostoyevsky was commissioned by Pavel Tretyakov in 1872. **Halls 18** and **19** highlight Russian masters of landscapes and seascapes. In Hall 18 are works by Aleksey Savrosov (1830–97) and Fyodor Vasilev (1850–73). Despite Tretyakov's indifference to seascapes, he recognised the talents of Ivan Aivozovsky (1817–1900) and bought several canvases, now in Hall 19.

Paintings by Ivan Kramskoy (1837–87) are in **Hall 20**. One of the founders of the Wanderers, he is best-known for his portraits, including those of Pavel Tretyakov and

Lev Tolstoy. Kramskoy's finest painting is the *Unknown Woman*, a mysterious upper-class lady. **Hall 21** highlights the canvases of the Ukrainian painter Arkhip Kuindzhi (1842–1910). *After the Rain, Birch Grove* and *Ukrainian Night* anticipated Impressionism. Although he was unappreciated in his socially conscious era, he exerted a strong influence on post-Realist painters.

In **Hall 22** are other canvases outside the main trend of the late 19th century: works of the Academy painters Fyodor Bronnikov (1829–1902) and Stepan Bakalovich (1857–1947) and the sculptor Viktor Brodsky (1826–1904). **Halls 23** and **24** bring you back to the classic works of the Wanderers, such as *Fortune-Teller at the Village Wedding* by Vasily Maksimov (1844–1911), depicting a crone whispering to a disconcerted young bride. Genre paintings by other Wanderer artists, Vladimir Makovsky (1846–1920) and Illarion Pryashnikov (1840–94) are in Hall 24.

The large and airy **Hall 25** displays one of Russia's finest landscape artists, Ivan Shishkin (1832–98). The almost photographic detail of his brushwork is combined with lyricism in *Rain in the Oak Forest* and *Noon in the Moscow Countryside*, which are among Russians' most beloved depictions of their homeland.

Russian history and myth

Another hallmark of late 19th-century Russian art was the celebration of the past. **Hall 26** displays the wall-sized historical-mythological canvases of Viktor Vasnetsov (1848–1926), including *Three Bogatyrs* (Warriors) and *Ivan the Terrible*. The next hall (**27**) has works by the former naval officer Vasily Verashchagin (1842–1904), depicting his travels in India and Central Asia.

In **Hall 28**, canvases by Vasily Surikov (1848–1916) depict seminal moments in Russian history – *The Morning of the Execution of the Streltsy*, with an implacable Peter the Great on Red Square about to witness the execution of those who would have overthrown him, or *Boyarina Morozova*, a keen psychological portrayal of an unrepentant Old Believer being led away.

Halls 29 and **30** display the works of Ilya Repin (1844–1930), considered Russia's greatest Realist painter. You may be captivated by the drama in *Ivan the Great and His Son Ivan,* depicting the moment the tsar struck and killed his heir in anger, but don't overlook the smaller and subtler painting *They Didn't Expect Him*, which captures the moment a political exile unexpectedly returns home to his family. In **Hall 30**, you can't miss the giant *Coronation of Alexander III* by Repin, the only painting in the gallery commisioned by the tsar. **Hall 31** highlights works by Nikolay Ge (1831–94; also transliterated Gay or Ghe), a Realist painter closely associated with Lev Tolstoy (whose portrait he painted) and his social and religious concerns.

Plan on page 176

Studying a fresh take on a religious theme.

BELOW: Maxim Gorky in front of *The Three Bogatyrs*.

Breaking with Realism

With Mikhail Vrubel (1856–1910), a decisive break was made with Realism. **Hall 32** (up the stairs from Hall 31) exhibits some of his earlier works, including fine portraits, as well as the lyrical *Swan Princess*. **Hall 33** was designed to hold the enormous *Princess of Dreams*, executed for the Nizhni Novgorod train station and then reworked in the frieze of the Metropol Hotel. Note Vrubel's wonderful stained-glass panel in **Hall 34** along with works by Nikolay Roerich (1874–1947). The gallery has fine examples of his earlier paintings on old Russian themes, as well as later works from Asia.

After Russian Realism

The chronological tour continues on the ground floor in **Hall 35**, with the works of the Abramtsevo-circle painter, architect and set designer Vasily Polenov (1844–1927). Note the small canvas *A Moscow Courtyard*, which depicts the Church of the Transfiguration of the Saviour on the Sands. **Hall 36** displays landscapes and genre paintings by Vasily

The New Tretyakov Gallery, showing the gallery's modern collection, including excellent avant garde works, is on Krymsky Val (see page 185)

BELOW: *Girl with Peaches* by V. Serov is a portrait of the daughter of the founder of the Abramtsevo artists' colony.

Baksheev (1862–1958) and Nikolay Dubovsky (1859–1918), as well as a fine portrait of Anton Chekhov by Osip Braz (1872–1936).

Another favourite landscape artist, Isaak Levitan (1860–1900), is exhibited in **Hall 37**. A close friend of Anton Chekhov, Levitan's "emotional landscapes" such as *Evening Bells* and *Gold Autumn* cross the boundary into impression. **Hall 38** displays several canvases depicting historical Moscow by Apollinary Vasnetsov and *The Whirlwind* by Fillip Malyavin (1864–1940), in which dancing women disappear in a riot of red, blue and yellow skirts and shawls.

The works by Mikhail Nesterov (1862–1942), another of the Abramtsevo circle, are shown in **Hall 39**. Note the delicate colours and brushwork in the image of *The Vision of Young Varfolomey*, a depiction of the boy who would become St Sergius, founder of the Holy Trinity Monastery *(see page 200)*. **Halls 41** and **42** are devoted to the canvases of Valentin Serov (1865–1911), renowned for his lushly textural portraits of society figures, rendered with an eye to flatter but with a gentle irony. His luminous *Girl with Peaches*, painted at Abramtsevo, is in Hall 41.

Russian Impressionism reaches its apex in the paintings of Konstantin Korovin (1861–1939) in **Hall 43**. He emigrated after the Revolution and spent his last years in Paris, which he captured in such paintings as the *Boulevard des Capucines*. The highlight in **Hall 44** is the work of Zinaida Serebryakova (1884–1967), one of Russia's finest women painters; note her self-portrait *At the Dressing Table* and family portrait in *At Breakfast*. Also in Hall 44 are paintings by the Symbolist Viktor Borisov-Musatov (1870–1905). His dreamlike images express a concept of the musicality of art, similar to the composer Skriabin's notions of the "colours" of music.

The World of Art, founded by ballet impresario Sergey Diaghelev and painter Alexander Benois (1870–1960) is represented in **Hall 45**, with fine works by Benois, Leon Bakst (1866–1924) and Boris Kustodiev (1878–1927), such as *Moscow Tavern*. Another group, the Blue Rose Studio (named after an exhibition held in 1907), is shown in **Hall 46** with works by Nikolay Sapunov (1880–1912) and Martiros Saryan (1880–1972) that anticipate the great period of the Russian avant-garde. **Hall 47** exhibits sculptures by Sergey Konenkov (1874–1971).

Treasury and religious art

The Treasury room and excellent early religious art collection (Halls 56–61) are the last of the gallery's exhibition halls, and it's worth leaving time to see them.

The Treasury is in **Hall 55**. The museum's collection of precious gold- and silver-work ecclesiastical items include books, icons with frames encrusted with precious gemstones, as well as a small collection of secular objects.

The rare early religious art begins in **Hall 56**, the first of the five halls devoted to the subject. Here are early mosaics and icons from the time before the Tatar invasion. **Hall 57** displays icons from Rostov and Suzdal, including the fine *Mother of God Orants* from the early 1200s. The Novgorod and Pskov schools of the 13th to 15th centuries are represented in **Hall 58**. The Balkans and Theofan the Greek are exhibited in **Hall 59**; the icon of the *Transfiguration* and the *Don Mother of God* are particularly fine examples of the work of this icon painter.

Hall 60 displays the most brilliant icons in the Tretyakov collection, and indeed in the country: four astonishing icons painted by Andrey Rublyov (1360/70–1430s). Three of them, the *Apostle Paul*, the *Archangel Michael* and the *Saviour* are from the Cathedral in Zvenigorod and were discovered in a nearby barn in 1918. The fourth, the *Old Testament Trinity*, was taken from the Cathedral of the Dormition in the Holy Trinity Monastery of St Sergius. The graceful proportions, austere yet tender faces and del-

Plan on page 176

Andrey Rublyov's Trinity *is an unsurpassed masterpiece of icon painting.*

BELOW: an icon painter at work.

Looking at Icons

Icons were painted by a group of artists overseen by one master, who usually painted the faces, according to set patterns: proscribed ways of depicting the Mother of God or Saviour that had names, such as "Tenderness" or "In Thee Rejoiceth". They are painted in "reverse perspective" or from several points of view, and the images appear rather flat, with the most important figures largest. They depict time as simultaneous, not sequential. The impact of an icon is in the balance between this ritualised depiction and its emotional power. Some icons, called "miracle-working", are believed to have the power to heal or answer prayers.

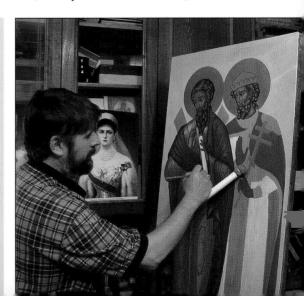

Oktyabrskaya ploshchad has one of Moscow's few remaining statues of Lenin.

icate, airy brushwork give these icons a luminous, emotional quality unmatched by any other icon painter. Dionysius (1430–*c.*1504) is represented by several icons, including *Christ Enthroned*, but even this master seems to pale next to Rublyov.

The final two halls (**61** and **62**) exhibit icons from the 16th and early 17th century. Of note is the unusual icon by Simon Ushakov (1626–86) called *The Tree of State of Muscovy*, which depicts the Moscow princes and tsars around the Vladimir *Mother of God* icon, establishing the religious legitimacy of the Russian throne and state power.

Beyond the gallery

At No. 21 ulitsa Bolshaya Ordynka, on the left just before Tretyakovskaya metro station, are the former **Dolgov Mansion** and, across the street at No. 20, the round yellow church built for this merchant family. **The Church of the Icon of the Mother of God "The Consolation of All Sorrows"** ❼ *(Khram ikony Bozhiey Materi "Vsekh Skorbyashchikh Radost")* was the work of Bazhenov, but all that remains of his original church after a fire is the bell tower (1790). Rebuilt in 1833 in the Empire style by Bove, it was closed from 1933 to 1948, but the interiors remained intact, including the church's icons.

On the right at No. 27a/28 is the delightful white stone **Church of St Nicholas in Pyzhakh** ❽ *(Khram sv. Nikolaya v Pyzhakh)*, built in the late 17th century by the musketeer regiment of Bogdan Pyzhov. The tent bell tower, ornamented with carving, cornices and recessed arches, is considered one of the finest in Moscow.

Across the street at No. 34 (accessed through a wrought-iron gate) is the **Martha and Mary Cloister** ❾ *(Marfomariinsky obitel)*, founded by the Grand Duchess Yelizaveta after her husband, Grand Duke Sergey, the uncle of Tsar Nicholas II, was killed by a terrorist bomb in 1905. She became a nun and used her vast fortune to build the cloister, which cared for the sick, elderly and poor. It was closed after the Revolution and used as a city clinic and art-restoration studio. Although the

cloister is again functioning, the city has yet to move the clinic, and the glorious **Church of the Intercession of the Mother of God** remains in the grip of the restoration studio. The church was built in 1908–12 by Aleksey Shchusev (who later went on to build Lenin's mausoleum). It ingeniously combines elements of the Novgorod and Pskov schools of church building with *style moderne*. Interior frescos painted by Mikhail Nesterov remain inaccessible.

Bolshaya Yakimanka

After crossing the Small Stone Bridge over the Drainage Canal, the road from Borovitskaya ploshchad splits : ulitsa Bolshaya Polyanka runs to the east and ulitsa Bolshaya Yakimanka leads to the west. In the centre is a statue to the first leader of the People's Republic of Bulgaria, Georgi Dimitrov (after whom Yakimanka was named from 1957 to 1993).

Yakimanka is a conflation of Joaquim and Anna, parents of the Virgin Mary, after whom a church here was named. Successive rounds of reconstruction have turned it into a joyless

street for walking, lined with elite apartment buildings and the President Hotel. The former **Igumov Mansion** on the north side was designed by Nikolay Pozdeev from Yaroslavl for the manufacturer Nikolay Igumov. It is now the residence of the French Ambassador; the new embassy is next door.

Across the street is the **Church of St John the Soldier Martyr on Yakimanka ❿** *(Tserkov Ioanna Voina, chto na Yakimanke)*. It was built on Peter the Great's initiative and based his own sketch. It honours the victory over the Swedes in Poltava. Completed in 1712, it is a fine example of baroque. Inside is the *Icon of the Saviour* that once graced the Saviour Gates to the Kremlin.

The intersection with the Garden Ring is called Kaluzhskaya ploshchad, though most Muscovites call it Oktyabrskaya after the metro station under the square. Once a huge market, the square is surrounded by state office buildings. A right along the Garden Ring leads to the New Tretyakov Gallery and Gorky Park *(see overleaf)*.

Maps:
Area 174
Plan 176

TIP

The two best streets for a stroll in Zamoskvoreche are ulitsa Bolshaya Ordynka and Pyatnitskaya ulitsa. Bolshaya Ordynka is quieter, with more architectural sights while Pyatnitskaya, from the Novokuznetskaya metro station to the bridge over the Drainage Canal, is lined with shops and cafes in pastel-coloured buildings.

BELOW: the bridge to Zamoskvoreche.

Bolshaya Polyanka

Bolshaya Polyanka (Great Meadow) has retained a few more charms than ulitsa Bolshaya Yakimanka, but it has also suffered from ill-conceived building booms. Still, the striking **Church of St Gregory of Neocaesarea**  *(Tserkov Grigoriya Neokessariyskovo)* at No. 29a is worth a glance. Commonly called the Red Church, it was commissioned by the spiritual advisor to tsar Aleksey in 1668–79 and built by Kremlin masters, including icon painters from the Ushakov school; the Tsar attended the dedication ceremony. Its decorative rows of *kokoshniki,* rising to five cupolas, tent bell tower and ornate white stone ornamentation, brighten an otherwise dull stretch of roadway.

Getting a new body at Gorky Park.

Krymsky Val

Another way to reach Zamoskvoreche from the centre of the city is to follow the Garden Ring Road past Park Kultury metro station and Krymsky Most to ulitsa Krymsky Val, southeast of Bog Island. This once marked the fortifications of the city on the route that led south to

BELOW: all the fun of the fair in Gorky Park.

Crimea (*Krym* in Russian), and is now associated with **Gorky Park**  *(Park Kultury imeni Gorkovo;* daily 10am–10pm in summer, 10am–9pm in winter; admission charge) on the right over the bridge and the New Tretyakov Gallery on the left.

The park was established in 1928 on the fairgrounds of the 1923 All-Russian Agriculture and Cottage Industry Exhibition. In Martin Cruz Smith's famous spy novel *Gorky Park*, three young people are murdered while ice-skating here. Skating still takes place every winter, when the park's network of paths are flooded and frozen and music blares from loudspeakers. In summer, the park is filled with families enjoying the roller-coaster and other attractions, including the Buran, the Soviet space shuttle that flew once.

The park is a traditional meeting place for veterans on 9 May, as well as for the Border Guards on 28 May and Air Force troops on the first Saturday in August. The young former military veterans take the opportunity to get drunk and rowdy, and the park is best avoided on these days.

The New Tretyakov

The **New Tretyakov Gallery** (*Gosudarstvennaya Tretyakovskaya Galereya na Krymskom Valu*; 10/14 Krymsky val; *for details see margin*) on ulitsa Krymsky Val houses the museum's collection of 20th-century art, including an excellent collection of avant-garde. It is on the top floor (up the main staircase past a model of Vladimir Tatlin's *Monument to the Third International* in the first-floor lobby). Most works are captioned in English, and the halls have extensive explanatory notes.

Halls 1 and **2** exhibit part of the museum's large collection of art by husband and wife painters Mikhail Larionov (1881–1964) and Natalia Goncharova (1881–1962), who were strongly influenced by both the icon and the *lubok*, a Russian folk drawing that often had inscribed texts or rhymes. Others are executed in a style they called Rayonism, in which images are fractured like rays of light through a prism. Note the fine *Nude* by Vladimir Tatlin and Primitivist canvases by the Georgian painter Niko Pirosmanashvili (1881–1962).

In **Halls 3–6** note the fine works by Robert Falk (1886–1958), particularly *Red Furniture*; Aristarkh Lentulov (1882–1943), whose works such as *Tverskoy Bulvar* expressed "colour dynamics"; Ilya Mashkov (1881–1944) and Pyotr Konchalovsky (1876–1958). **Hall 7** has notable works by Kuzma Petrov-Vodkin (1878–1939). *Bathing on a Red Horse, 1918 in Petrograd* (often called the *Petrograd Mother of God*) and *Girls on the Volga* take the composition, colours and images of iconography and transform them into paens to the Revolution. **Hall 9** has works by Blue Rose artists such as Pavel Kuznetsov (1878–1968) and paintings from several periods by Martiros Saryan. His bright 1957 *Yerevan Flowers* captures the movement's decorative emphasis.

Russian avant-garde

The treasure trove of the New Tretyakov Gallery is in **Halls 10–14**, which exhibit their fine collection of Russian avant-garde. There are a few works by Marc Chagall (1887–1985) and excellent canvases by Pavel Filonov (1883–1943), Vasily Kandinsky (1866–1944) and Kazimir Malevich (1878–1935), who went beyond Kandinsky with the first Russian paintings consisting solely of abstract geometrical elements. Vladimir Tatlin (1885–1953) developed this trend with his series of *Counter-Reliefs*. A torrent of work followed, with artists such as El Lisitsky (1890–1941), Alexander Rodchenko (1891–1956), Liubov Popova (1889–1924) and Olga Rozanova (1886–1918) taking Malevich's concept of Supremicism and pushing it further still. The Tretyakov has excellent paintings and graphics by these artists.

Towards Socialist Realism

Hall 15 plunges you back into the Realist tradition – already romanticised for Soviet consumption – with

Map on page 174

Opening times and information for the New Tretyakov on Krymsky Val: tel: 953-5223 for tours in English; daily 10am–7.30pm; closed Mon; admission charge; no photography; English audio guide for temporary exhibits; ATM, gift and books kiosks and café in entry lobby; access from metro Park Kultury and across the river or metro Oktyabrskaya; entrance to the museum is on the long side of the building.

BELOW: American street style is popular with young Russians.

works like Alexander Morovov's (1878–1951) *At the Volost Registry Office,* Georgy Ryazhsky's (1895–1952) *Chairwoman*, Yefim Cheptsov's (1874–1951) *Meeting of the Village Party Organisation* and Isaac Brodsky's portraits of Soviet heroes and leaders. Only in Konstantin Yuon's (1857–1958) *The New Planet* is the heroic image of the new world portrayed more expressively.

The spacious **Hall 16** gives an excellent sense of the wide variety of styles and subjects in the 1920s and 1930s, before Socialist Realism froze artistic expression. Note the Portrait of V.E. Meyerhold by Pyotr Williams (1902–1947) and the *Anniska* portrait by David Shterenberg (1881–1948). *Peasant Woman* by Vera Mukhina (1889–1853) was painted in 1927, 10 years before her monumental *Worker and Collective Farmer* became the symbol of Soviet art. Works by Alexander Labas (1900–83) and Alexander Tyshler (1889–1980) exhibit the lingering lyricism of the Impressionists. Some

Kandinsky led the avant-garde of the early 20th century with works like Improvisation *(1911).*

BELOW: *Children* by Kazimir Malevich, 1908.

of the finest works are by Alexander Deyneka (1899–1969), whose *Goalkeeper, At the Construction of New Factory Shops* and *Defence of Petrograd* glorified the Soviet state but maintained a style reminiscent of the great poster art of the avant-garde. Yuri Pimenov's (1903–77) *New Moscow* is lyrical and washed with light.

Halls 18 and **19** display graphics, watercolours and smaller works by these and other artists.

Note in **Hall 20** works by Antonina Safronova (1892–1966), Tatyana Mavrina (1902–96) and Boris Rybchenkov (1899–1994), members of the Group of 13 that promoted academic traditions, and Nikolay Kupreyanov (1894–1933), a member of the Four Arts Group that advocated a figurative reality. The Painter's Workshop Society artists are represented in **Hall 23** with fine works by Pavel Chelishchev (1898–1957). In **Hall 24** are works by Alexander Drevin (1889–1938), whose *Roe Deer* captures life in broad strokes and with an immediacy that countered prevailing styles. In the same hall are fine late works by Mikhail Nesterov and Nikolay Krymov (1884–1958), whose Realism is more intimate and less heroic than the dictates of Socialist Realism usually allowed.

Socialist Realist traditions

Halls 25 and **26** contain a number of canvases of Sergey Gerasimov (1885–1964), whose portraits of state leaders, particularly Joseph Stalin, are the apotheosis of Socialist Realism. **Hall 26** is dominated by the *Triumph of the Conquerors,* an enormous canvas by Mikhail Khmelko (1919–75), while *Letter from the Front* by Alexander Laktionov (1910–72) has remained one of the country's most beloved genre paintings. The artistic sensibilities of Arkady Plastov (1893–1972) were congruent with

Realism, but canvases such as *Hay-making* and *Spring* are fresh and heartfelt. The trauma of World War II was reflected in many works of the late 1940s and 1950s, including Yuri Neprintsev's (1909–96) *Resting After Battle* (**Hall 28**) and the triptych *Memory of the Dead* by Sergey Tutunov (1925–1999) in **Hall 30**.

Thaw to non-conformism

The last halls of the gallery, which exhibit art from the 1950s to the 1980s, is somewhat misleading: not all the art displayed here could be exhibited at the time. It is also odd now to look at the paintings of the so-called "austere style" that appeared during the "Thaw" and imagine how they could have elicited such passionate criticism. Works in **Hall 37** by Nikolay Andronov (1929–98) seem in keeping with the romantic image of "forging new lands" of the post-war era and owe much to Soviet poster art. Viktor Popkov's (1932–74) *Father's Greatcoat* seems artistically tame, and Pavel Nikonov's (b. 1930) *Geologists* barely breaks new artistic ground. Dmitry Zhilinsky's (b. 1927)

brightly coloured and poster-like *By the Sea: A Family* is a good example of the change in subject matter after Stalin's death.

There are a few smaller works and graphics in **Halls 32–5** by Anatoly Zverev (1931–86), Oleg Tselkov (b. 1934), Oscar Rabin (b. 1928) and Vladimir Yakovlev (1934–98), artists canonised as the trailblazers of "non-conformism". Works by Yuri Zlotnikov (b.1930) such as *Shop Window*, *White Pitcher and Plates: A Still Life with Venus by* Vladimir Veysberg (1924–85), and *Running in the Darkness* Dmitry Plavinsky (b. 1937) show the variety of post-war styles. Tatyana Nazarenko (b. 1944) is well represented with works such as *The Artist's Self-Portrait*. Natalya Nesterova's (b. 1944) paintings, such as *Gogol's House*, revert to a form of Primitivism heavily overlaid with the grotesque.

Sotsart and beyond

If many of these works seem weighed down by the gloom of the period of stagnation, **Hall 38** ends the gallery's collection on a playful and

Map on page 174

TIP

In front of the New Tretyakov is a craft-and-art fair, open weekends from about 10am until dark (or whenever the artists show up and decide to leave). It's also pleasant to walk along the Krymskaya Embankment by the river, where artists display and sell their canvases and drawings at weekends.

BELOW: a Socialist Realist sculpture combines classic proportions with Communist ideology.

Map
on page
174

*The haunting
composition at the
Sculptures Park
in honour of victims
of the Stalinist
regime.*

exuberant note. *Unofficial Russian Art*, by Viktor Pivovarov (b.1937), inscribed with the names of non-conformist leaders, is a jocular postmodernist homage to the text-decorated canvases of Larionov. Vitaly Komar (b. 1943), and Alexander Melamid (b. 1945), who did most of their mature work in New York in the 1980s and 1990s, developed "Sotsart" – wordplay on "socialist realism" and "pop art" – that both sentimentalised childhood memories of monumental canvases and poked fun at their memories and the art itself. Their work is represented, along with the illuminated *Marlboro-Malevich* by Alexander Kosolapov (b.1943), in which great art is branded like a pack of cigarettes. It is an apt end to this period of art, in which creativity and ideological "branding" fought a battle in the Soviet arts, leaving a rich, contradictory and glorious artistic legacy.

Street art

If you walk along the embankment towards the monument to Peter the Great, stop in the **Muzeon Sculpture Gardens** ⓭ on the right (*Muzeon*;

daily 9am–8pm; admission charge). The park appeared in 1991 when the city unceremoniously dumped Soviet monuments pulled down during and after the coup here. At first they were simply tossed in piles, but after a few years the government realised this was disrespectful to millions of citizens who believed in Soviet values. On the other hand, resurrecting the monuments would be disrespectful to those who had suffered in the Soviet period.

A compromise was made: a park was formed to show over 600 modern sculptures of all trends and schools. The Soviet monuments – Dzerzhinsky, Lenin, Stalin, Brezhnev busts, as well as an enormous Soviet emblem and giant letters spelling out "The USSR is the Bastion of Peace" – are in one area (closest to the New Tretyakov Gallery). They are on pedestals once again, but surrounded by sculptural images of the Stalinist repressions. It is a surreal place, with children dashing about among the bizarre collection of statues, families snacking in the cafés and grandmothers strolling and chatting. ❑

RESTAURANTS & BARS

Restaurants

Chaikhona No. 1
9 ulitsa Krymsky Val. Metro: Oktyabrskaya. Tel: 778-1756. Open: 2pm–1am daily. $$$
The Gorky Park branch of the Uzbek restaurant – ideal for summer lounging or winter warming.

Correa's
40 ulitsa Bolshaya Ordynka, building 2. Metro: Tretyakovskaya. Tel: 725-5878. Open: B, L & D daily. $$
An outlet of the charming New York-style café and restaurant. Reserve.

Dzhusto
5 Bolshoi Tolmachyovsky pereulok, building 9. Metro: Tretyakovskaya. Tel: 937-3750. Open: L & D daily. $$$
Stylish, minimalist Japanese restaurant with reasonable service. Food is well executed although not strictly traditional. Try the spicy tuna or Philadelphia rolls. Trendy evening lounge atmosphere with resident DJ.

El Gaucho
6/13 Zatsepsky Val. Metro: Paveletskaya. Tel: 953-2876. Open: L & D daily. $$$
Lively Argentinian restaurant with slabs of meat served sizzling on hot platters so you can cook your dinner to your exact preference. Also has seafood dishes and good service. Try to get a table away from the Latin ensemble.

Los Bandidos
7 ulitsa Bolshaya Ordynka. Metro: Tretyakovskaya. Tel: 953-0466. Open: L & D daily. $$$
Traditional Spanish cuisine at modern Moscow prices. Rustic interior, welcoming and efficient service, lively and convivial atmosphere. Good selection of Spanish wines. Book ahead.

Oblomov
5, 1-y Monetchikovsky pereulok. Metro: Paveletskaya. Tel: 953-6828. Open: 12pm–5am. $$$$
Traditional Russian cuisine with a few random extras, like rocket salad and beef carpaccio, served in a grand 19th-century mansion. The main dining halls are elegantly art deco with ambient low ceilings, while the private rooms are eastern-inspired. Pleasant summer veranda.

Ris I Ryba
2 ulitsa Serafimovicha. Metro: Borovitskaya. Tel: 959-4949. Open: 24 hrs daily. $$
All-you-can-eat conveyor-belt sushi bar. Decent if not entirely authentic food. Located above a mini-casino, which you have to enter to reach the restaurant.

Zhyoltoye More
27 ulitsa Bolshaya Polyanka. Metro: Polyanka. Tel: 953-9634. Open: L & D daily. $$$
A chic pan-Asian restaurant favoured by a young, professional crowd. Of the Chinese, Thai, Vietnamese and Japanese fare, the Japanese is the best, with a good range of *nigiri*, sashimi and rolls. A good church view from the open balcony.

Bars

Durdin
56 ulitsa Bolshaya Polyanka. Metro: Dobryninskaya. Tel: 953-5200. Open: L & D daily. $$
Stylish Russian microbrewery. Try a beer taster platter then *salo* (salted pork fat) and *voblya* (dried fish), both traditional and excellent beer snacks. Also serves beer cocktails, home-made vodka infusions and familiar starters and mains.

Pancho Villa
52 ulitsa Bolshaya Yakimanka. Metro: Oktyabrskaya. Tel: 238-7913. Open: 24 hrs daily. $$
Laid-back Mexican-themed bar and restaurant with a great vibe. Large portions of Tex-Mex cuisine, with excellent *burritos* and *fajitas*. Cheerful service and a large cocktail menu.

PRICE CATEGORIES

Prices for three-course dinner per person with a glass of house wine:
$ = under $25
$$ = $25–40
$$$ = $40–60
$$$$ = more than $60

RIGHT: lunchtime in the Balchug-Kempinski Hotel.

PARKS AND PALACES

Russia's nobility lavished time and energy on their country estates. Many now lie within a bus or metro ride of the city centre and make an excellent excursion – from the Vernisazh market and the ceramic collection at Kuskovo to the wooden buildings at Kolomenskoye and the ghostly ruins of Tsaritsyno

Just as today Muscovites clog the highways out of the city in the great Friday afternoon dacha exodus, centuries ago Russia's tsars and noble families rode out of the city to spend the summer at country palaces dedicated to art, theatre and the delights of nature. This "estate culture" is a separate chapter in Russian history: the greatest artists and architects of their day created magnificent palaces, pavilions and gardens where their patrons held week-long parties with dancing, theatre performances, endless meals in candlelit, silk-lined halls – and romance was encouraged in the moonlit gardens.

BELOW: the entrance to Vernisazh market.

Izmailovsky and Vernisazh

One of the city's oldest parks is the 332-hectare (820-acre) **Izmailovsky Park ❶** (17 Narodny prospekt; daily 10am–11pm, market best on Sat and Sun; metro station Izmailovsky Park, often called Partizanskaya), best-nown for its Vernisazh market.

The estate belonged to the Romanov family from the 16th century, but was most popular after 1663, when Tsar Aleksey built a wooden palace, church, theatre and glass factory. He turned the land into an experimental agricultural station with windmill, vineyards, menagerie and 20 well-stocked fish ponds.

Since the 1990s, Izmailovsky has been a weekend Mecca for shoppers at **Vernisazh ❷** (daily 10am–5.30 or 6pm; admission charge). Once an enormous, disorganised flea market selling everything from canning tops to pre-Revolutionary china, it is now organised into rows of booths under fake Russian wooden towers and turrets, with *shashlyk* stands, bio-toilets and trained bears at the main entrance.

Excellent bargains can be discovered past the touristy booths near the

entrance: table linen in bright colours, jewellery of amber and Russian semi-precious stones, thick angora sweaters and shawls, quilts and silk scarves, ceramics from Uzbekistan and an ever-changing assortment of handicrafts. The second tier has a fabulous rug market where you can still find carpets from the Caucasus coloured with natural dyes.

The upper level also has several rows of antiques and icons, where you can occasionally see serious collectors examining museum-quality items. Given the laws on exporting antiques, it's better just to look at this section and move on to the art exhibition and brightly coloured quilts flapping in the breeze. Remember to haggle.

To reach the old Izmailovsky estate, veer to the right, instead of following the path from the metro station to the Vernisazh, and then head in the direction of the market area, on the outside of the fence. On your right you'll see a pond with an island (reached by a small bridge) with what remains of the Romanov estate where Peter the Great spent much of his childhood. It was on the pond here that he learned to sail.

Here the **Church of the Intercession** ❸ (*Pokrovsky sobor*), completed in 1679, is a good example of Moscow baroque, with five black "scaled" domes and gables brightly ornamented with tiles. On its right are the brick remains of the **Bridge Tower**. On the other side of the estate is the white stone **Ceremonial Gate**, a main entrance flanked by two smaller gates and topped by a tent spire. If the architecture fails to impress you, just enjoy the 17th-century oasis of the little island.

Kuskovo and the Ceramics Museum

Vying with several other estates around Moscow for the title of the "Russian Versailles" is **Kuskovo** ❹

(2 ulitsa Yunosti; tel: 375-3131; Wed–Sun 10am–6pm; closed last Wed of the month, Oct–Apr museum closes at 4pm; admission charge; room descriptions and brochures in English; metro Ryazansky prospekt; from the city centre exit from the front of the train and take bus No. 133 or No. 208 six stops to the estate). Kuskovo was built by Count Pyotr Sheremetev *(see page 196)* in the late 18th century as a summer palace with French-style gardens.

After Pyotr's death, his son Nikolay focused his efforts on rebuilding their estate at Ostankino *(see page 166)*, and Kuskovo faded from the social life of the city. But in its heyday all Russia's nobility, including Catherine the Great, enjoyed its "countless delights and pleasures".

Today it is renowned as one of the best-preserved of Moscow's estate palaces, with an excellent collection of ceramics and porcelain – and as the site of the annual US Independence Day celebration, with hot dogs, hamburgers and fireworks.

The estate has more than 20 buildings artfully placed among the gar-

Map on page 192

Quaint and quirky fare for sale at the Vernisazh market.

BELOW: the estate of Kuskovo is often dubbed the "Russian Versailles".

Inside the wooden palace, you see the riches at the disposal of the old Russian nobility.

BELOW: the wooden palace is cleverly painted to resemble stone.

dens, including a **Dutch House**, the **Italian House**, **Hermitage** and the **Church of the Archangel Michael** (1738) – the oldest building on the grounds. Three of the buildings are open at present: the palace, grotto and the orangerie, which has the Ceramics Museum.

The **palace** was built by two serf architects, Argunov and Mironov, under Karl Blank in the neoclassical style with elements of baroque. The interior rooms open to the public include a ballroom, several sitting rooms and the bedroom – all have silk wallpaper, enormous glittering chandeliers, parquet floors and lush frescos depicting scenes from myths and antiquity.

The **grotto** is the most interesting structure on the estate. Built in 1761 by Argunov, it is designed to look like a baroque, highly stylised underwater cave.

The **orangerie** (1761–83) consists of a central pavilion flanked by airy glass galleries and small side pavilions. The central pavilion was used for concerts and dances, accompanied by musicians in the balcony. Now a **Ceramics Museum**, it displays china, porcelain and pottery from all over the world, with a particularly fine collection of Russian pieces from the 18th century.

Russian folk art at Kolomenskoye

You can explore four centuries of Russian art and history, see Russian folk crafts and traditions, and enjoy fairs and folk festivals on most weekends at **Kolomenskoye** ❺ (39 prospekt Andropova; tel: 115-2768; park compound daily 8am–10pm Apr–Oct, 8am–9pm Nov–Mar; museums Tues–Sun 10am–6pm; separate admission charges for the main museum, Peter the Great's cabin and the water tower can be purchased inside the compound in any ticket booth; photo and video

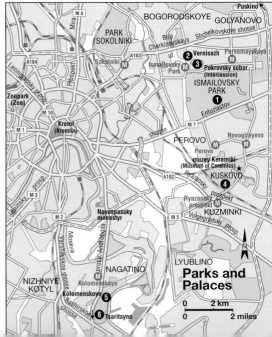

charges; English markers on the grounds, some English room descriptions and exhibit notes; metro Kolomenskoye). On the south side of the city overlooking the Moscow River, this is one of the oldest inhabited parts of greater Moscow, with settlement dating back more than 2,500 years. As a summer residence of the early Russian grand princes and tsars, it dates from the 14th century.

Ivan the Terrible had a palace here, and in the 17th century Tsar Aleksey built a wooden fantasy dubbed the Eighth Wonder of the World. It had an asymmetrical maze of 270 rooms and a front gate tower flanked by mechanical lions that "roared". When it became dilapidated Catherine the Great had it torn down and replaced by a four-storey palace, which was destroyed by the French in 1812. The final imperial palace, built by Alexander I, has also not survived.

In the Soviet period Kolomenskoye became a compound for wooden architecture and stone monuments brought from all over Russia. The few ancient churches and buildings that remain are set on a glorious hillside high above the Moscow River, with paths leading into ravines and woods and a spring reputed to have healing properties.

Touring the royal estate

Inside the main gate on the left is the **Church of the Icon of the Mother of God of Kazan** *(Tserkov Kazanskoy ikony Bozhiey materi)*, believed to have been built by Tsar Mikhail in 1644, with domes of deep lapis and dotted with enormous gold stars. In the small centre chapel, somewhat cramped by two enormous frescoed pillars, there is a copy of *The Mother of God of Kazan* icon, which miraculously helped the Russians rout the Polish invaders in 1612.

Beyond the church is the **Front Gate Museum**, once the main entrance to the estate, and the **brew house** *(Sytny dom)*, both of which house the **Treasures of Kolomenskoye Museum**. The brew house has an excellent collection of woodcarvings (the altar doors are astonishing in their ornamentation), tiles, ecclesiastical vestments and icons.

The second floor displays everyday objects, clothing and a tile fireplace (1899) by the artist Mikhail Vrubel that depicts the folk tale of Prince Volga and the peasant Mikula, in which the prince comes to appreciate the unsung labourer's work. The highlight of the museum is the exact model (scaled 40/1) that Catherine the Great had made of Tsar Alexei's fantastic wooden palace.

Just before the Front Gate Museum is a simple round stone podium called the **Petition Stone** in English, but more exactly translated as the "brow-beating stone". When petitioners came to the tsar, they "beat their brows" against the stone in deference (and presumably to ensure a positive response to their request). Behind the brew house is the **Stone Maiden**, an 11th- or 12th-century gravestone

Map on page 192

Kolomenskoye preserves four centuries of Russian art and history.

BELOW: the Saviour Gate entrance to Kolomenskoye.

from a Polovtsian burial ground. The stones are near a grove of oaks, reputedly planted by Peter the Great.

Church of the Ascension

The masterpiece of Kolomenskoye is the magnificent **Church of the Ascension** *(tserkov Vosneseniya Gospodnya)*, on the Unesco World Heritage list and a rival of St Basil's on Red Square in its beauty. It was built in 1532 by Tsar Vasily III as a votive church for the birth of a male heir (to become Ivan the Terrible). The church is a massive conical sliver of stone, with decorative rows of gables over the bays leading up to an octagonal drum and a tent-shaped spire soaring 62 metres (203 ft) above the river bank. Galleries round its base anchor it to the ground.

The church seems to borrow from Russian wooden architecture but includes elements of Western Gothic and Renaissance styles. There is some evidence that it was built by Pietro Solario, an Italian master who worked in the Kremlin. The interior of the church is surprisingly small. To support the towering spire the whitewashed walls are up to 3 metres (10 ft) thick, and the only lighting comes from the narrow windows in the octagonal drum and tent. There was no traditional sanctuary, but there was an iconostasis, and the walls may have originally been decorated with geometric designs.

On the gallery facing the river are remains of a stone throne, where, according to legend, Ivan the Terrible would sit to survey the river and countryside. The church is undergoing serious renovation, which is expected to be completed by 2008.

Wooden buildings

Several wooden structures were moved here from the northern part of Russia, including the **gateway tower** from the Nikolo-Korelsky monastery (18th century), a **mead brewery** from the town of Preobrazhenkoye and a **stockade tower** from Bratsk. On the path leading to the stockade is the massive **Boris Stone**, a 12th-century property marker carved with the cross and the inscription, "Lord, protect your servant Boris".

Another delight on the estate is the **cabin of Peter the Great**, where the tsar stayed while he was in the northern city of Arkhangelsk to supervise the building of the Novodvinsk fortress. As you crouch down to step into the low-ceilinged rooms, note the white tape on the wall opposite marking Peter the Great's height (2 metres/6 ft 7 in) and pity his two-month stay in what must have been extremely cramped conditions. The four-room cabin is simple and rustic, with hewn log walls, heavily carved furniture and benches and brightly coloured tile stoves.

Past the stockade tower is a path that leads down to a gully and then up a steep incline through the woods to the 16th-century **Church of the Beheading of St John the Baptist** *(Tserkov Useknoveniya glavi Ioanna*

Frescos followed the style of Byzantine cathedrals – with gold and red the prevalent colours.

BELOW: Tsaritsyno, "the tsarina's village". Have a break among picturesque ruins, lakes and forest paths.

Predteche), which may have been built by the same architects who designed St Basil's in Red Square.

The ghostly ruins of Tsaritsyno

One of the strangest of Moscow's urban estates is **Tsaritsyno** ❻ (1 ulitsa Dolskaya; tel: 321-0743; museums Wed–Sun 11am–6pm; closed last Wed of the month; tickets to the Small Palace, Opera House and the 2nd and 3rd Cavalier Pavilions purchased at the Opera House; metro Orekhovo or Tsaritsyno).

The village here, called Black Mud, was owned by several noble families until Catherine the Great took a fancy to it and bought it in 1775, renaming it "the tsarina's village". She commissioned Vasily Bazhenov to design the estate buildings and approved his plans for neo-Gothic palaces and pavilions.

Ten years later she returned, spent two hours surveying the buildings and demanded that they be torn down because "it would be impossible to live in them". For the past two centuries historians have speculated why she disliked the original buildings, citing everything from the decorative elements, which are suggestive of Masonic symbols, to the small, low-ceilinged rooms, lack of grand halls and impractical service and kitchen quarters. She commissioned Matvey Kazakov to redo the main palace, and before it was completed, lost interest altogether.

The estate has therefore been ghostly ruins for virtually all of its history. A 19th-century writer noted that the palace "reminds you of a huge crypt on a bier, surrounded by gigantic monks holding candles". It will remind the modern visitor of a ruined Gothic abbey. But not for long: in 2005 Mayor Luzhkov "traded" the former Lenin Museum, owned by the city, for Tsaritsyno, owned by the federal government,

and City Hall plans to build the palace according to Kazakov's revised blueprints.

Several of the Bazhenov pavilions have been restored. The two Cavalier pavilions *(Kavelerskie korpusy)* opposite the palace display permanent exhibitions about the estate and Catherine; the one closest to the Patterned Bridge screens a fascinating video reconstruction of the original Bazhenov structures.

Along a lane to the right of the palace (as one faces it) are the reconstructed **Small Palace** *(Maly dvorets)* and **Opera House** *(Operny dom)*, lovely light structures which display various temporary exhibitions. The pale-green **Church of the Icon of the Mother of God "Life-Bearing Source"**, which predated Catherine's purchase of the land (1722–60), is open for services.

The fun of Tsaritsyno is simply strolling among the ruins, along the brick and stone bridges covered with stars, crosses and other Gothic ornamentation, and enjoying the smells of the woods and the fresh air of the meadows. ❑

Russian Orthodox Church services are conducted facing the iconostasis.

RESTAURANTS

Druzhba
4 Novoslobodskaya ulitsa. Metro: Novoslobodskaya. Tel: 973-1234. Open: L & D daily. $$
Regarded by many to have the most authentic Chinese food in town. Efficient and cheerful service. The Szechwan menu has a wide range of meat, vegetable and tofu dishes. Generous portions – try the deep-fried sweet-and-sour pork, and for dessert, the battered and caramelised fruit.

Carré Blanc
19/2 Seleznyovskaya ulitsa. Metro: Novoslobodskaya. Tel: 258-4403. Open: L & D daily. $$$$

Elegant French dining, thought by some to be the city's finest. The bistro has daily specials and a more modest menu.

Sirena
15 Bolshaya Spasskaya ulitsa. Metro: Sukharevskaya. Tel: 208-0200. Open: L & D daily. $$$$
Pioneering seafood restaurant said to have fed Sting and Liza Minnelli. The glass floor has live sturgeon underneath. Try the *okroshka* (cold soup) or the mixed seafood in baking paper.

● ● ● ● ● ● ● ● ● ● ● ● ●
Price is for a three-course dinner for one and a glass of house wine. **$$$$** *$60 and up,* **$$$** *under $60,* **$$** *under $40,* **$** *under $25*

Map on page 192

AT HOME WITH THE COUNTS SHEREMETEV

The Sheremetev's Ostankino and Kuskovo estates were key in the rise of Moscow's estate culture and essential to the growth of the arts

The enormous iniquity of Russian society, which in part led to the Revolution, is clearly seen in the large estates of Moscow's nobility, its princes, boyars and royal favourites, who acquired property and land at the expense of the bonded serf peasantry. Some of the estates that can be seen around Moscow were modest mansions or artisitc communities. Others were vast enterprises with palaces, churches, pavilions, formal gardens, monuments, grottoes and even theatres; these estates, which were fully occupied in summer, played an important role in the developing cultural life of the city. Undoubtedly the most extravagant of them all belonged to the Sheremetev family.

The original benefactor of the family estates was Field Marshal Count Boris Sheremetev, who had received his grant of land from Peter the Great for bloody work against the Tatars and against the Swedes in the Baltic states. He also discovered in Latvia a 17-year-old serving girl called Martha who later became Peter the Great's wife, changing her name to Catherine. Boris's son, Pyotr, enlarged the estate at Kuskovo *(for details see page 191)* in an attempt to make it the Versailles of Russia. The well-preserved interior gives an excellent impression of the cultural pretensions of the upper nobility during the reign of Catherine the Great.

ABOVE: Pyotr Sheremetev's neoclassical palace was built in 1765–75 by Catherine the Great's favourite architect Karl Blank, aided by serf architects Fyodor Argunov and Aleksey Mironov who came as part of his wife's dowry. The interior culminates in a grand ballroom with a ceiling painting in praise of the Sheremetevs. The estate had a zoo and extensive formal gardens, and 20 of its original buildings remain. The estate was looted by the French in 1812, but remained the Sheremetevs' summer residence until 1918.
LEFT: a house on the Abramtsevo estate, which became Moscow's first artists' colony and gave rise to Russia's modern art movement. Based around the manor house of the writer Sergey Aksakov, it was used by Chekhov as the model for the decaying country estate in *The Cherry Orchard (see page 203).*

ABOVE: the palace at Kuskovo now houses a Ceramics and Porcelain Museum *(see page 192)*. Count Pyotr Sheremetev, a patron of the arts, had inherited the estate along with 200,000 serfs and added to the family fortune by marrying Countess Varvara Cherkasskaya, whose dowry included further serfs, estates and villages. Count Pyotr became the first nobleman to allow anyone not at work to walk through his grounds.

BELOW: the ruins of Tsaritsyno are a unique monument to a queen's capriciousness. Catherine the Great had taken a liking to a village owned by several noble families and had it rebuilt as "the tsarina's village". After 10 years she returned to look at the result, spent two hours criticising it, declared it impossible to live in and gave orders that it should be torn down *(see page 195)*.

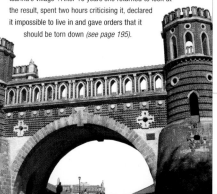

OSTANKINO'S DRAMATIC SECRET

The dowry of Pyotr Sheremetev's wife included the estate at Ostankino *(see page 166),* and it was here in 1792 that their son Nikolay undertook the construction of a much larger residence. He had inherited his father's passion for the theatre, had travelled widely in Europe and had performed in theatre and dance productions. Said to be twice as rich as any other noble Russian, he set up his own troupe of serfs, comprising 200 actors, singers and musicians, making Ostankino a "pantheon of the arts". One eight-year-old girl who joined the troupe was to become the brilliant actress Praskovia Zhemchugova. It was for her that Nikolay is said to have moved the theatre at Kuskovo to Ostankino, opening in 1795 with an opera of *The Capture of Ismail.* In 1801, when she was found to have tuberculosis, Nikolay secretly married her. Nikolay's "serf countess" was the scandal of high society, although such informal liaisons were common.

ABOVE: The luxurious theatre, still used as a venue for opera, ballet and concerts in the annual Sheremetev Season, is at the heart of the Ostankino estate. The two-storey palace in a capricious neoclassical form, with flanking wings, was built largely of wood and is attributed to a number of architects, including Giacomo Quarenghi and Francesco Camporesi, as well as Fyodor Argunov and Aleksey Mironov.

DAY TRIPS FROM MOSCOW

Major religious centres and delightful country estates are within striking distance of the city. On a day trip you can take in a stunning monastery or the museum-home of Tchaikovsky or Tolstoy. The finest towns of the Golden Ring, including Vladimir and Suzdal, are better appreciated with an overnight stay

PRECEDING PAGES: the domes of the Dormition Cathedral, Sergeev Posad. **BELOW:** young visitors at the monastery.

There is more than enough in Moscow to keep you busy, but you'll never truly understand the Russian character without exploring the treasure-laden countryside that all Muscovites – whether rich businessmen or widowed pensioners – retreat to as often as possible. Choose from the following destinations carefully. They can all be done in a day, but they will be full days. Picnics and patience are well rewarded when you are dependent on rural Russia's tourist infra-

structure, which is adequate but rarely luxurious.

Sergeev Posad Monastery

There is no more glorious sight than the white walls and gold domes rising above the town of Sergeev Posad, heralding the **Holy Trinity Monastery of St Sergius ❶** (*Sviato-Troitskaya Sergeeva Lavra*; tel: 254-05721; tours in English by appointment; suburban train from Yaroslavsky station and then a 20-minute walk up the hill to the monastery).

On a summer day the monastery is filled with unhurried activity: pilgrims paying reverence to the holy relics, young priests and their families enjoying the gardens, monks strolling along the tidy paths. But the monastery hasn't been frozen in time: you can see monks chatting on mobile phones and trainers peaking out from under seminarians' robes.

The monastery was founded in the 14th century by St Sergius of Radonezh. Born Varfolomey Kirillovich in 1314 to a wealthy boyar family, he began a life of prayer in the forest, soon drawing followers. After taking monastic vows, he became the *hegumen* (abbot) of the monastery he founded, which soon became the leading religious centre in Russia. His diplomatic missions

to Russia's principalities ensured the "gathering of the Rus" that led to the formation of the Russian state.

In 1550, after several Tatar raids, the monastery's first stone walls were built, and in 1618 these were raised to 10–14 metres (33–46 ft), with towers on the kilometre-long walls. After the Revolution the monastery was closed and many of its treasures plundered. Partially reopened in 1946 and made a museum, it was returned to the church in 1988.

Today there are about 300 monks, a divinity academy (the successor of the Russian-Greek-Latin Academy founded in 1687), a seminary and schools for choir masters and icon painters. The monastery is a *lavra*, an honorary title denoting special importance and service, conferred by Empress Yelizaveta in 1744.

Inside the monastery

You enter the monastery through the **Beautiful** or **Holy Gates**, with scenes from the life of St Sergius, and under the **Gate Church of St John the Baptist**, built in 1693. To the left is

the faceted and brightly painted Refectory *(Trapeznaya)*, from 1692.

Next to the Refectory against the south wall is the 1778 **Palace of Metropolitans**, which served as the residence of metropolitans and patriarchs from 1946 until 1988, when it was moved to Daniilovsky Monastery in Moscow.

Standing on the small square between the Refectory and the Palace of Metropolitans, you are surrounded by five magnificent churches and chapels under the great turquoise-and-white bell tower (built 1740–70).

Rising 88 metres (290 ft) in five tiers, the bell tower has 42 bells, including the largest in Russia (75 tons). In front of it is the delightful baroque **Chapel over the Well** *(Nadkladeznaya chasovnya)*, built over a spring that erupted in 1644 during renovations to the Cathedral of the Dormition. Next to it the spring burbles under the **Canopy Over the Cross** *(Sen nad krestom)*, with delicate columns and rich frescos.

The monastery's oldest church is the **Trinity Cathedral** *(Troitsky sobor)*, in front of the Palace of

A pilgrim collects holy water believed to have healing powers from the spring at the Chapel over the Well.

BELOW: St Sergius blessed Russian princes here before the war on the Tatars.

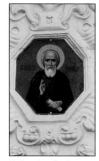

*St Sergius the Servant
(1314–92), founder
of the monastery.
His teachings and
example of humble
service defined
Russia's monastic
tradition.*

BELOW: a traditional
meal near the
monastery grounds.

Metropolitans. Built in 1425 to replace a wooden church over the grave of St Sergius, it is rather austere, with a single helmet cupola and little ornamentation; only the side chapel to Nikon, the abbot who succeeded St Sergius, adds a decorative note. The sense of height is achieved by a slight inward thrust of the walls as they rise. But the interior has perhaps the finest frescos and icons in Russia. The monk and brilliant icon painter Andrey Rublyov was asked to return to the monastery where he once served, and here he painted the *Old Testament Trinity*, considered the greatest masterpiece of icon-painting in Russia. The original is in the Tretyakov Gallery, but a copy and other icons by Rublyov and Daniil the Black fill the small church. In the Cathedral are the relics of St Sergius, and on most days there is a long line of pilgrims, waiting to view them.

Closer to the entrance gates stands the **Church of the Holy Spirit** (*Dukovskaya tserkov*), built in 1476 by architects from Pskov. Its three narrow bays rise up to the single cupola above the bell tower. The interior is the final resting place of several of the monastery's most revered abbots.

The largest church is the magnificent **Cathedral of the Dormition**, built in 1559–85 to replicate the church of the same name in the Kremlin. This church is considerably larger, with four azure-blue cupolas decorated with gold stars around the central gold cupola. Inside is an enormous five-tiered iconostasis with 76 icons; the icons and frescos were painted in 1684.

Two other churches on the monastery grounds are worth noting: the small baroque masterpiece of the **Church of the Smolensk Icon of Mother of God** (*tserkov Smolenskoy ikony Bozhiey Materi*), built in 1745, and the 17th-century tent-spired **Church of SS Zosima**

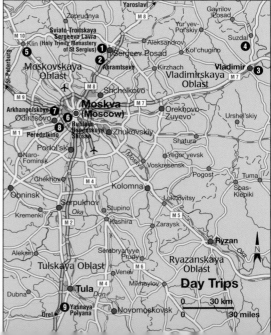

and **Savvaty** *(Khram prepodobnikh Zosimy i Savvatiya Solovetskikh)* that is part of the hospital wing.

The **Museum** *(Riznitsa)*, which is still under the auspices of the state, has an extraordinary collection of ecclesiastical vestments, vessels, gold- and jewel-encrusted Bible covers, embroidery and imperial gifts to the monastery. In the Tsar's Apartments is the monastery's teaching museum of icons.

Abramtsevo manor house

The first art colony in Russia was set up at **Abramtsevo ❷** (tel:8-254-32470; Wed–Sun 10am–5pm, closes at 4pm in winter; admission charge; suburban train from Yaroslavsky station to the Abramtsevo stop, exit and cross the tracks, turn left on the paved road to the museum) as a place to create, experiment and live close to nature surrounded by the inspiration of folk art.

It was founded by railway magnate and patron of the arts Savva Mamontov. In 1870 he bought the manor house of the writer Sergey Aksakov near Sergeev Posad, and invited Ilya Repin, Valentin Serov, Mikhail Vrubel, Konstantin Korovin, Mikhail Nesterov, Viktor Vasnetsov, Yelena and Vasily Polenov, and other artists and their families to spend summers here.

Mamantov left untouched much of Aksakov's manor house, which Chekhov used as the model for the decaying country estate in *The Cherry Orchard*. Inside, note the copy of the portrait *A Girl with Peaches* that Serov painted of Mamontov's daughter *(see page 180)*.

Today you can visit most of the buildings on the estate. Especially lovely is the fairy-tale *teremok* of wood that Ivan Ropet built as a bathhouse. Decorated with intricate carvings, a barrelled gable and a sharply pitched roof, the cosy interior is filled invitingly with wooden furniture.

The pride of the estate is the small **Church of the Saviour Not Made by Hands** that was built and decorated by the entire artistic circle in the style of Pskov and Novgorod churches. The icons were painted by Repin, Nesterov, Apollary Vasnetsov and Polenov. Viktor Vasnetsov designed the mosaic floor and Vrubel built the ceramic stove.

To keep the children happy, the two Vasnetsov brothers built the charming **Hut on Chicken Legs**. This is the house of the witch Baba Yaga in Russian fairy tales *(see page 53)*, which could turn on its legs when children ventured too close. The house is a sheer delight.

The Golden Ring

In the 1960s Soviet tourist agencies began to call the best-preserved of Russia's ancient cities near Moscow the Golden Ring. They were all important principalities or trading centres in the centuries before Russia existed as a state, and but for the whims of fate (and various Tatar invasions), any of them might have become the capital of this vast land.

Map on page 202

The artists at Abramtsevo built and decorated this 14th-century-style church in the 1870s.

BELOW:
a wooden house in Abramtsevo.

*Small provincial
towns and country
roads can be bleak
and quiet in winter.*

BELOW: early
Russian cathedrals
of Vladimir.

An overnight trip to Vladimir, or to the "White Monuments" of both Vladimir and Suzdal, is a beautiful break from Moscow's frenzied pace.

Vladimir

For centuries the political and cultural centre of the Russian lands was the city of **Vladimir ❸**, about 200 km (120 miles) to the east and slightly to the north of Moscow. Founded by the Kievan leader Vladimir Monomakh in 1108, it was the most powerful principality until the Tatars burned it to the ground in 1238. Vladimir Monomakh's son, Yuri Dolgoruky, went on to found a small fortress in Moscow, and Yuri's sons Andrey Bogoliubsky ("Godloving") and Vsevolod III (called "Of the Great Nest" having sired 12 sons) built some of the finest churches of the medieval period.

Start your tour at the **Golden Gates**, built in 1152–64 and modelled on Kiev's walls (which were, in turn, modelled on the walls of Constantinople). They are rather squat, but still majestic, combining a defence tower, triumphal arch and gateway church in one small structure. The **Museum** in the Gates has a diorama of the Tatar attack that gives a vivid sense of the city's bygone beauty and horrible destruction. Further along the earthen ramparts is the **Water Tower Museum**, with an exhibition of Old Vladimir.

The centrepiece of the city is **Cathedral Square**, on a high hill overlooking the Klyasma River. Here you can see the **Cathedral of Dormition** that was the model for the church of the same name in the Moscow Kremlin. It was built in 1158–89 and, after a fire, cleverly rebuilt to be much wider and higher. All the grand princes were crowned here until the 15th century. Some of the icons and frescos were painted by Andrey Rublyov and Daniil the Black; the original iconostasis was discovered in a nearby village and is now kept in the Tretyakov Gallery, but the frescos of the Last Judgement under the choir gallery and in the south gallery were done by these masters (1408).

The small **Cathedral of St Dmitry** is both a masterpiece of early Russian architecture and a mystery. Built in 1194–7, it is structurally austere, with three bays and a single helmet dome. But it is lavishly ornamented with a band arcading of saints and a profusion of bas-reliefs that puzzle specialists. They have been able to identify some of the Biblical and historical personages, but not the meaning of all the fantastical beasts and figures.

About 10 km (6 miles) to the northeast of the city is the village of **Bogoliubovo**, where Prince Andrey once had his palace and administrative buildings. The princely settlement is gone, but what has remained is the jewel in the crown of Russian medieval architecture, the **Church of the Intercession on the Nerl**. Accessible only by a stroll across an enormous field, the delicately pro-

portioned white church stands peacefully on the banks of the narrow Nerl River, reflected in the still waters. Built in one year (1165) when the river was on the other side of the structure, it stood on a high place faced by stone with stairs leading from the water to the church. Here the bas-reliefs are less profuse and more subtle than on the Cathedral of St Dmitry; the 20 women's faces still seem to offer intercession and protection to all who come here.

Suzdal

The "White Monuments" of Vladimir and Suzdal are on the Unesco World Heritage list. **Suzdal** ❹ is 35 km (25 miles) north of Vladimir. Tidy and neat, with geraniums on the windowsills of carved and brightly painted wooden houses, white-walled monasteries, meandering paths and brooks crossing fields – all redolent of the heady scent of apple blossoms in spring and as peaceful as down duvet in winter, when its churches and houses lie covered by pristine snow. You may be tempted to rush about the town trying to take in all 200 sites, but try instead to succumb to the slow pace and give yourself a full day or two just to wander about.

Suzdal was the centre of the principality until Prince Andrey moved it to Vladimir. Today there is hardly a single street that isn't graced by a church or lovely house, but the main sites are largely centred around the **kremlin**, the trading settlement (the *posad* area), the museum of wooden architecture and monasteries. The stone walls that once surrounded the **kremlin** were dismantled in the 18th century, but the earthen ramparts and moats are still visible.

The highlights of the former fortress are the **Cathedral of the Nativity of the Mother of God** (built 1222–5 and rebuilt several times since, with five blue domes dotted with gold stars and a particularly impressive portal), the **Metropolitan's Palace**, with its pillar-free "cross chamber" surpassing in size and grandeur even the Moscow Kremlin's chamber, and the **Historical Museum**. In the *posad* section of the town, you can shop at the stone

Map on page 202

The Cathedral of the Nativity of the Mother of God is the oldest building in Suzdal.

BELOW: the fairy-tale atmosphere of Suzdal is enhanced when snow covers its many churches and monasteries.

BELOW: a majestic dome in gold and azure reaches for the sky.
RIGHT: a windmill in Suzdal's Museum of Wooden Architecture.

trading arcade and marvel at the "summer" and "winter" churches remarkably preserved throughout the area. The summer churches were loftier and lighter, but freezing in the winter; next to them smaller churches were built with thick walls that maintained the warmth of the congregation. Fine examples are the summer **Church of St Lazarus** and winter **Church of St Antipus** on ulitsa Lenina. Be sure to visit the 18th-century **Likhonin merchant house**, recreated down to the bast shoes by the stove, and the lovely **Posad House**, the only surviving 17th-century dwelling in the town.

Across a wooden footbridge from the kremlin is the **Museum of Wooden Architecture**, where several wooden structures from different parts of the country have been reconstructed and placed next to Suzdal's existing buildings. Preservationists may squawk (the jumble of windmills, churches, houses and barns is far from a typical Russian village), but it's a delight to walk among them – and look inside them during the summer months – to see what life was like for the common folk in the 18th and 19th centuries.

Suzdal has two monasteries and two convents that are once again active, in whole or in part. The most interesting is the **Saviour-St Euphemius Monastery**, a fortress-monastery founded in 1352 on the high bank of the Kamenka River. Part of the monastery was made into a prison under Catherine the Great, and the prison wing contains reconstructed cells. The monasteries, churches and museums, including a nice collection of folk art, are open to visitors. And the view of the river and the white-walled **Convent of the Intercession** across a field on the other side is one of the most peaceful and serene in Russia.

Tchaikovsky country

The gentle hills, meandering rivers, woods and fields of **Klin 5** (about 90 km/60 miles northwest of Moscow) have inspired many artists who had estates in the area, including Tchaikovsky. First mentioned in the chronicles in 1190, Klin was a flourishing way station between the prin-

cipalities of Tver and Moscow. It was virtually destroyed under the reign of Ivan the Terrible, when his private security police, the *oprichniki*, went on a rampage against his purported enemies, and it was briefly occupied by the German army in World War II. Today the built-up city has few charms – except for the excellent Klinskoye beer, smoked hams and sausages.

Pyotr Tchaikovsky lived in several homes in and around Klin. After his death, his brother turned the last of these (where the composer lived between 1892 and 1893) into the **Tchaikovsky Museum** (*Dom-muzey P. I. Tchaikovskovo*; 48 ulitsa Tchaikovskovo; tel: 8-224-58196; Fri–Tues 10am–5pm; closed last Mon of the month; admission charge; English tours available by appointment; 1½ hours on bus No. 437 from metro station Rechnoy Vokzal or tours through Patriarshy Dom, *see page 227*). The large, pale-blue wooden house with white trim has preserved the composer's main living areas, and is filled with souvenirs from his travels and archives.

The airy living room is dominated by a Becker grand piano that is played twice a year, on his birthday (7 May) and on his memorial day (6 November). On 7 May, the honour goes to the winner of the Tchaikovsky Competition. The first laureate to play was Van Cliburn, who won the competition in 1958.

The heavily ornamented and panelled library and cosy bedroom, with Tchaikovsky's small slippers, are open to visitors, as are the gardens where he would stroll with his dogs every morning. In spring they are scented by the composer's favourite flowers – lilies of the valley. The concert hall built onto the house in the 1960s holds regular concerts.

The smartest dachas

During the Soviet period the countryside to the west of the city was traditionally the locale for Party dachas: gated communities with stone or wooden houses, large yards and all the modern conveniences. There is no industry, so the rivers and fields are still pristine, and the

Map on page 202

BELOW: dacha gardens are a matter of pride and are lovingly tended. Their produce is often pickled and preserved for winter.

THE DACHA

"**D**acha", from the verb "to give", originally meant a plot of land given to someone for service to the Empire. Over the years the dacha became a fixture of Russian life: even before the Revolution, middle-class families would spend the summer at a country house to enjoy swimming, mushroom- and berry-picking, bicycle trips and walks. During the Soviet period, the standard 600 sq. m plot was usually made into an enormous vegetable garden to grow easily stored root vegetables, and cucumbers and tomatoes for pickling. Today dacha settlements are being so modernised that they are moving towards becoming gated communities of elegant villas.

A team of British architects are heading a 3 billion-dollar project to create a millionaires' town in Rublyovo-Uspenskoye Shosse. The development will be heavily influenced by the architecture of Prague, Amsterdam and Munich, and will be almost twice the size of Monaco.

BELOW:
a former coronation site, the grand estate of Arkhangelskoye now houses a unique collection of art dating from the early 19th century.

roads are well tended to handle the traffic of official cars shuttling between state compounds and the city. The most exclusive area is along the **Rublyovo-Uspenskoye Shosse** ❻, a meandering two-lane highway that grinds to a halt twice a day when President Putin leaves or returns to his residence near the Moscow River.

In the 1990s Rublevo-Uspenskoye shosse became the hottest real estate in town. Residents privatised their spacious official dachas and sold them to New Russians; developers snapped up fallow collective farm lands and started building "cottage" communities – "cottage" being the Russian word for a four-storey stone house with turrets and towers, a six-car garage, swimming pool and tennis courts. Services followed: upscale shopping malls, chic restaurants, health clubs and, for a short time, the single most expensive farmer's market in the world, where a cup of strawberries sold for $10 and couture-clad *biznesmeny* jumped out of their Jeeps and

Mercedes to pick up 200 dollars' worth of sturgeon *shashlyk* for the grill on their way home. It was closed in 2004 for sanitary code violations.

State Folk Museum

Fitting perfectly into the Rublyovo-Uspenskoye atmosphere of ostentatious country living is the estate of **Arkhangelskoye** ❼ (*Gosudarstvenny Muzey-usadba Arkhangelskoye*; Ilinskoye shosse; tel: 797-5409; summer Tues– Sun 10am–5pm; closed last Fri of the month; winter closing hours 4pm; admission charge; metro station Tushinkskaya, then bus No. 549 to Arkhangelskoye stop or minibus No. 151 to Sanatorium stop).

This lovely land on a high bank of the Moscow River was owned by the princely Golitsyn family, but in 1810 it was bought by Nikolay Yusupov, said to be richer than the tsar himself. Nikolay invested hundreds of thousands of roubles to create his version of the Russian Versailles. He asked Rastrelli to design the **palace**, laid out French-

style gardens filled with pavilions and statuary, particularly lions, and built a 400-seat theatre and a number of cottage factories to provide glassware and china for the family.

He filled the house with his enormous library and an extraordinary art collection that included Velázquez, Raphael and David – the corner rooms had eight sides to display his art better. This pleasure estate was always filled with guests at week-long celebrations. It was also one of the sites for coronation celebrations; here Nicholas II and Alexandra were fêted.

After a generation of neglect, it was restored by Zinaida Yusupova in the late 19th and early 20th centuries. Although she had two sons (one of whom, Felix, murdered Rasputin in his St Petersburg palace), she willed the estate to the Russian Empire to be turned into a museum. Alas, her will was carried out by the Soviet government, which in 1937 dismantled some park buildings, including faux ruins in order to build a sanatorium in the grounds.

At present the palace is closed for much-needed renovations. But art exhibitions are still displayed in two of the estate buildings, and the beautiful park grounds can still be enjoyed. The tiny **Tea House** (*Chainy domik*) is a masterpiece of classical estate architecture, as is the **Yusupov Family Chapel and Crypt**, designed as a copy of St Petersburg's Kazan Cathedral on a small scale. Walk through the woods to the white **Church of Archangel Michael** (*Tserkov Mikhaila Arkhangela*), built in 1667: nestled in tall trees, its myriad *kokoshniki* gables rise to three "scaled" cupolas. Next to it is the grave of Zinaida's sister Tatiana, who died of typhus and was buried by the church beneath an angel monument.

Writers' village

The village of **Peredelkino** ❽ has existed since the 17th century, but only appeared on the cultural map in 1934 when Maxim Gorky suggested building a dacha community for writers here. The poet Yevgeny Yevtushenko, a long-time Peredelkino resident, suggests that Stalin agreed in order to keep a closer eye on the intelligentsia. Whatever the reason, since the 1930s Peredelkino's wooden houses tucked behind fences along quiet narrow lanes have been home to some of the USSR's and Russia's finest writers.

Pasternak's dacha

The poet and novelist Boris Pasternak (1890–1960) lived here from the 1930s until his death. He is best known in the West for his novel *Dr Zhivago*, which was published abroad in an Italian translation in 1957. Pasternak was awarded the Nobel Prize in 1958, but forced by the Soviet government to refuse it. In 1986 his dacha was made into the **Pasternak Dacha Museum** (*Dommuzey B.L. Pasternaka*; 3 ulitsa

To get to Peredelkino, west of Moscow, take the suburban train line from Kiev station to Peredelkino station; exit on the left towards the church; follow the main road up the hill, turn right on ulitsa Pavlenko for Pasternak's dacha and turn left on ulitsa Serafimovicha for the Chukovsky dacha.

BELOW: Nobel Prize winner Boris Pasternak at his desk in the dacha.

BELOW: Tolstoy at Yasnaya Polyana. Among his classic works is a book of morality tales for children.

Pavlenko, Peredelkino; tel: 934-5175; by appointment; admission charge). Its oval two-storey porch launches out into the yard as if the house were a ship about to sail into the fields. These fields, little changed, are the view Pasternak saw from his book-lined bedroom-study on the upper floor. The museum also exhibits the lower-floor main room, with walls filled with paintings by the poet's father, the painter Leonid Pasternak.

The Chukovsky dacha

Another extraordinary family of writers lived near Pasternak on ulitsa Serafimovicha: Korney Chukovsky (1882–1969) and his daughter Lydia (1907–96). A famed writer of children's books and verse, critic, translator and linguist, Korney Chukovsky endured periods of official disfavour during the Soviet era, but miraculously escaped arrest during the purges. His daughter, Lydia Chukovskaya, was spent time in jail for anti-Bolshevist activities. She is best-known for her memoirs and critical essays. Both father and daughter

took a final political risk in the 1960s when they let the dissident writer Alexander Solzhenitsyn live at their Peredelkino house before he was forced into exile abroad.

The house and children's library built by Korney Chukovsky next door have been lovingly preserved by Lydia's daughter as the **Chukovsky Dacha Museum** (*Dom-muzey K.I. Chukovskovo*, 3 ulitsa Serafimovicha; tel: 593-2670; Wed–Sun 10am–5pm; by appointment only; admission charge). The light rooms are filled with elegant pre-Revolutionary furniture, paintings, photos and mementoes of the family's literary life, spanning nearly a century from the Silver Age to the post-Soviet period.

Near Peredelkino train station is the charming salmon-coloured 17th-century **Transfiguration of the Saviour Cathedral** (*Khram Spaso-Preobrazheniya*), part of the Patriarch's Court. The Patriarch's summer residence is next to it. Pasternak, Chukovsky and the poet Arseny Tarkovsky (father of the filmmaker Andrey Tarkovsky) are buried in its lovely hillside cemetery.

Tolstoy's family home

In 1828 Lev Tolstoy was born at the estate of **Yasnaya Polyana ❾** (*Gosudarstvenny memorialny i prirodny zapovednik Muzey-usadba L.N. Tolstovo Yasnaya Polyana*; Tula oblast; tel: 8-751-35-425; May– Oct Tues–Sun 10am–4pm; Nov– Apr closes at 3pm, house closed last Wed of the month, Kuzminsky House closed last Thur of the month; admission charge; English-language tours by appointment).

He lived here for much of his life, writing his most acclaimed works, *War and Peace* and *Anna Karenina*, raising his enormous family, and beginning to put into practice his theories of social equality and simple Christian piety. The estate

belonged to Tolstoy's mother's family, the Volkonskys. His grandfather, Prince Nikolay Volkonsky, built a comfortable wooden house at the end of a long, shady drive *(Preshpek)*, a French park (called The Wedges), an English park (called the Lower Park) and a stone house (Kuzminsky House), which now displays Tolstoy's literary legacy and temporary exhibits.

After Tolstoy's death, his wife Sofia twice petitioned Nicholas II to make the estate a national preserve, but was refused. It was finally made a museum in 1921.

During World War II the German army occupied the house for 45 days, but the entire contents of the house had been evacuated in 110 crates to Tomsk before their invasion. In the 1990s Vladimir Tolstoy, the great-grandson of the writer, assumed directorship of the estate and museum, and is slowly turning it into a centre for Russian culture.

Thanks to Sofia Tolstoy's meticulous preservation of her husband's legacy, the comfortable house does not seem like a museum at all: it's as if the family just stepped out to hunt for mushrooms and will be back before lunch. Virtually the entire Volkonsky House is open to visitors, from the spacious hall on the upper floor where the family met for meals and entertained such distinguished literary guests as Anton Chekhov and Ivan Turgenev, to the "room under the eaves" that once served as Tolstoy's study.

Tolstoy's last study, where he worked for about 15 years, is exactly the way he left it, with books, photos and paintings, and a turtle bell he used to call his secretary. The sofa in this room belonged to his ancestors: the writer himself was born on it, as were his brother and sister, eight of his 13 children, and several grandchildren.

The contrast between Tolstoy's ascetic bedroom, with a narrow bed and simple furniture, and his wife's more luxurious sitting room and bedroom, filled with overstuffed chairs and knick-knacks, gives a good visual sense of the contrast between the spouses. ❏

Map on page 202

When Tolstoy was a child, his brother invented a story about the secret of happiness "written on a green twig buried by a path on the edge of a ravine". Tolstoy wrote in his will that he wished to be laid to rest in a wooden casket and buried "in the place of the green twig". The unmarked burial mound is deep in the woods, covered with grass in spring and summer, bright yellow leaves in autumn, and a thick shroud of snow in winter.

RESTAURANTS

Sergeev Posad

Russky Dvorik
134 Krasnoy Armii pereulok. Tel: 4-51-14. Open: L & D daily. $$
A traditional Russian restaurant popular with day-tripping tour groups. Cosy dining hall.

Trapeza na Makovtse
131 Krasnoy Armii pereulok. Tel: 4-11-01. Open: L & D daily. $$$
A more upmarket option with a grand dining hall. Traditional Russian menu, generous portions.

Golden Ring

La Forêt
8 Chigasovo, Rublyovo-Uspenskoye shosse. Tel: 935-8038. Open: L & D daily. $$$$
Rustic French food in a small country village. A red wood interior, with windows overlooking the nearby birch forest. Exquisitely presented French-style game and seafood dishes.

Prichal
2nd km of Ileinskoye Shosse. Tel: 418-4032. Open: L & D daily. $$$$
A chic restaurant, affiliated to the ultra-stylish Galereya. Italian, Japanese and Chinese menus. Reservations and smart attire required.

Russkaya Izba
1 ulitsa Naberezhnaya. Tel: 561-4244. Open: L & D daily. $$
Back-to-basics Russian restaurant, with a seasonal hunting menu. Try the homemade *kvas* and *mors*. Live balalaika and accordion music from Wednesdays to Sundays.

Tsarskaya Okhota
186a ulitsa Zhukovka. Tel: 418-7982. Open: L & D daily. $$$
Not for animal-lovers – expect antlers dangling from the beamed ceilings and animal skins draped over the wooden barstools. Friendly service from costumed waiters. A game-heavy menu, with hare, venison and a wide range of fish.

● ● ● ● ● ● ● ● ● ● ● ●
Price is for a three-course dinner for one and a glass of house wine. $$$$ $60 and up, $$$ under $60, $$ under $40, $ under $25

TRANSPORT

GETTING THERE AND GETTING AROUND

GETTING THERE

By Air

More than 30 international airlines connect Moscow with the rest of the world. Flights take around 9 hours from New York, 4 hours from London or Paris, 3 hours from Frankfurt, 2 hours from Stockholm, 6 hours from Delhi and 8 hours from Beijing.

British Airways and Aeroflot offer daily flights from London Heathrow, and the private Russian airline TransAero offers a direct, cheaper service from/to Gatwick. Numerous European carriers offer connections between British cities (and Dublin) to Moscow via their hub cities.

If you're coming from North America the only direct routes are from New York, Seattle, Washington DC, Los Angeles and Toronto with Delta, Air Canada or Aeroflot. There are no direct flights to Moscow from Australia or New Zealand.

Moscow has several air terminals, each servicing domestic and international locations. The main international terminal was Sheremetevo-2, located northwest of the city centre, but many airlines have relocated to the more modern international airport Domodedovo

in the south of the city. Visitors can expect a long wait when arriving at Sheremetevo-2. Things are generally a lot better at Domodedovo, although at the height of the summer season (July/August) you can expect large queues and delays everywhere. Exchange offices, duty-free stores, etc can be found at both airports.

Domestic flights leave from Sheremetevo-1 (a short bus ride away from Sheremetevo-2), Domodedovo and Vnukovo. When arriving for domestic flights, check in at least 40 minutes before take-off.

If you need assistance, contact:
Domodedovo
Tel: (495) 933-6666
Arrivals and departures can also be checked online at
www.domodedovo.ru
Sheremetevo-1
Tel: (495) 578-2372
Sheremetevo-2
(International Flights)
Tel: (495) 578-0901
Vnukovo
Tel: (495) 436-2414

By Rail

Within European Russia railways are the most important means of transport. Railways connect the largest Russian, Belorussian and Ukrainian cities (Moscow, St Petersburg, Kiev and Minsk) with

AIR SAFETY

Aeroflot has dramatically improved both its service and safety record in recent years. TransAero is a private company with a 100 percent safety record. There are, however, still many smaller airlines operating domestic flights with less than satisfactory service.

many Western European capitals – there are direct trains to cities such as Warsaw, Berlin and Budapest. Since June 2004 the *Jan Kiepura* has operated daily from Brussels to Moscow via Warsaw; journey time is just short of 37 hours (ie 1 day, 2 nights). Travellers can travel in comfortable first-class sleeping-cars, the pride of the Russian railways.

A popular rail route between the west and Russia is the Helsinki–St Petersburg line, which takes 8 hours. Helsinki–Moscow by standard train takes almost 17 hours. There is a high-speed train service from Moscow to St Petersburg which does the trip in 4½ hours and leaves daily from Leningradsky vokzal every morning at 6.30am.

The Trans-Siberian rail route can be used to access Moscow from the east; there are several trains every week from Beijing and Vladivostok. The 6- or 7-day journey demands an adventurous spirit and a willingness to spend a week on the train contemplating the endless Siberian landscapes. Food for the trip should be bought in advance since the buffet facilities at stations are pretty basic.

Railway stations

Of the nine railway stations in Moscow, the most important are:
Byelorussky vokzal, ploshchad Tverskaya Zastava; trains for Western Europe, Poland, Belarus and Lithuania.
Kievsky vokzal, ploshchad Kievskovo Vokzala; trains to Ukraine, Budapest, Prague and Bucharest.
Leningradsky vokzal, Komsomolskaya ploshchad 3; trains to Helsinki, Talinn, Novgorod, Murmansk, Tver and St Petersburg.
Rizhsky vokzal, Rizhskaya ploshchad; trains for Riga, Latvia.
Yaroslavsky vokzal, Komsomolskaya ploshchad 5, for the Trans-Siberian Express, Siberia and the Far East.

GETTING AROUND

To/from the Airports

Getting into the city centre from Sheremetevo-2 is no mean feat. Buses and minibuses will take you on a breakneck trip to either Rechnoy vokzal or Sokol station. From there you can access the metro to your destination. All of this is very inexpensive but not advisable for a first-time visitor – especially one who is not familiar with the Russian language. The best option is to arrange a transfer to your hotel prior to arrival. This normally costs between US$50–60 but will be secure and quick. Taxis start at US$100 but can be negotiated down to US$60. Be prepared to haggle.

Domodedevo is a far more accommodating airport. There is an express-train service which leaves hourly to Paveletsky vokzal from where you can connect with the metro system. Leave airport arrivals, turn left and walk to the end of the airport, the ticket office next to the train platform. Tickets must be paid for in roubles and cost about US$3.

AIRLINE OFFICES IN MOSCOW

Aeroflot
37/9 Leningradsky avenue
Tel: 753-5555
Fax: 155-6647
www.aeroflot.ru

Air Baltic
18/1 Malaya Pirogovskaya ulitsa, office 406
Tel: 786-6827
Fax: 242-9564
e-mail: airbaltic@continent.ru
www.airbaltic.lv

American Airlines
20 Sadovaya-Kudrinskaya ulitsa, office 207
Tel: 234-4074/75
Fax: 234-4079
e-mail: talav@comail.ru
www.aa.com

Austrian Airlines
5 Smolenskaya ulitsa
The Golden Ring Hotel
Tel: 995-0995
Fax: 725-2559
e-mail: auamow@aua.com
www.austrianairlines.ru

British Airways
Sheremetevo-2 Airport, 6th floor, office 601
Tel: 956-4676
Fax: 578-2936
23, 1-ya Tverskaya-Yamskaya ulitsa
Tel: 363-2525
Fax: 363-2505
www.britishairways.com

Delta Airlines
11 Gogolevsky bulvar, 2nd floor
Tel: 937-9090
Fax: 937-9091

Finnair
Sheremetevo-2 Airport, 6th floor, office 625
Tel: 578-2738
Fax: 961-2056
www.finnair.ru

Japan Air
5, 1-ya Tverskaya-Yamskaya ulitsa
Tel: 730-3070
Fax: 921-3294
www.jal-europe.com

KLM
33/1 Usacheva ulitsa, 3rd floor
Tel: 258-3600
Fax: 258-3606
e-mail: klm.russia@klm.com
www.klm.com

LOT (Polish Airlines)
26 Tverskoy bulvar
Tel: 629-5771/7388/8525
Fax: 629-8829
www.lot.com

Lufthansa
19, 1-ya Tverskaya-Yamskaya ulitsa
Sheraton Palace Hotel
Tel: 737-6405
18/1 Olimpiysky prospekt, Renaissance Hotel
Tel: 737-6400
Fax: 737-6401
e-mail: lufthansa@online.ru
www.lufthansa.ru

SAS (Scandinavia Airlines)
5, 1-ya Tverskaya-Yamskaya ulitsa
Tel: 775-4747
Fax: 730-4142
www.scandinavian.net

Swissair
2/3 Paveletskaya ploshchad
Tel: 937-7767
Fax: 937-7769
e-mail: moscow.townoffice@swiss.com
www.swiss.com

TransAero
3/4, 2-y Smolensky pereulok
Tel: 241-4800/7676
www.transaero.ru

Turkish Airlines
1/8 Kuznetsky Most
Tel: 692-1667/5121/4345
www.turkishairlines.com.tr

Orientation

Moscow's geography is organised in a series of concentric circles, which – like the rings of a tree – reflect the city's stages of growth

TRANSPORT

ACCOMMODATION

ACTIVITIES

A – Z

LANGUAGE

around the Kremlin in the centre. The city is bisected by the Moscow River, which winds through the city along with its tributaries. The old walls of Kitai-gorod once enclosed areas around Red Square down to the river. This division is now marked by Teatralny proezd and Lubyanka, Staraya and Novaya ploshchads.

The first ring built after Kitai-gorod was the White City, a protected residential district whose walls stretched in an arch along what is now the Boulevard Ring. This road, congested with traffic but with a boulevard of trees and gardens in the centre, was laid in the late 18th century when the White City walls were demolished. The final historic ring of the city is the Garden Ring, which replaced the old earthen ramparts of medieval times after the War of 1812. This is now little more than a massive motorway, but still marks the end of Moscow's city centre.

Outside the Garden Ring there are a few neighbourhoods of note. Krasnaya Presnaya is the area between the Moscow River and the Garden Ring to the west. Cross the Moscow River here to get to Fili. To the south lie Sparrow Hills and Moscow State University.

The big "tongue" which lies to the south of the Moscow River opposite the Kremlin is known as Zamoskvoreche (beyond the Moscow River) and has always been a separate entity to Moscow's walled city. East of Zamoskvoreche and south of the Yauza River is the area of Taganka.

Two more ring roads now encircle the city: the Third Transport Ring within the city and the Moscow Ring Road (called by the Russian abbreviation MKAD), which marks the outer limits of the city proper.

Public Transport

Metro

The quickest and most convenient form of transport in Moscow is the metro *(see map on inside back cover)*, which links the city centre with the suburbs and carries 9 million passengers a day.

Construction started before World War II, and the system is still expanding. At the last count there were 11 lines, 171 stations and 600 km (370 miles) of track. Not only is the service efficient but, from an architectural point of view, the stations are tourist attractions in their own right *(see pages 112–13)*.

The metro runs 6am–1am, and there are trains at approximately 3-minute intervals. The fares increase sharply every few

months, but still remain very cheap for foreigners (one journey costs about 50 US cents).

As efficient as the system is, it does have its quirks. Many stations have several exits, which are located hundreds of metres/yards away from one another. Luckily all exits are labelled with the streets and main attractions that are above you. However, most of these signs are still only in Russian.

To add to the confusion, when lines meet the "stations" for each line have a different name. The recently installed bilingual maps in all train carriages are of enormous benefit.

Commuter trains

Commuter trains *(Elektrichki)* serve Moscow's satellite towns. At train terminals serving long-distance locations, tickets are sold at the Prigorodnie Kassi. Tickets are sold according to the intended destination.

Trams, trolleybuses and buses

All of these forms of transport run from 5.30/6am to 1am, depending on the route. Tickets can be bought singly or in "books" in the underpasses next to metro stations. Some buses have recently introduced a system of mechanised entry (you place the ticket in the slot and the gate opens), which can considerably slow journey times at rush hours. On some trams/trolleybuses you pay the conductor. On others you pay the driver, passing the money through the hole in the glass, even while the bus is in motion. Failure to pay after one stop may lead to an encounter with the Moscow Travel Inspectors, burly guys who travel in pairs looking for fare dodgers (known as *zaytsi* – or "hares" – in Russian) to fine (about $3).

Taxis

There are two types of taxi: registered taxis are for personal use and run day and night; taxi-buses or *marshrutnye* taxis (small, fast mini vans) operate the same routes from 9am to 9pm from metro or mainline stations.

Marshrutnye can be flagged down anywhere on route. They don't take standing passengers, but they do get plenty of squashed ones. Only pay the flat fare that is marked on the window.

Moscow's registered taxis are usually yellow with a narrow chequered band round the sides. Most taxis are metered but there is no official tariff and fares vary considerably, so agree a price beforehand. It is safer, though not always cheaper, to get a hotel to book a cab for you.

Many private car owners operate an unofficial taxi service. To hail one, stand on the side of the road with your hand out. It helps to speak Russian, but by stating your destination and a price (US$3–6 for most places within the Garden Ring Road) you'll probably be understood. Follow two basic rules: never get into a cab that already has a passenger and never go with an unregistered cab driver who has approached you.

River trams

Between May and September you can travel up and down the Moskva River by boat. There are two routes: one runs from the International Trade Centre to the Novospassky Bridge, stopping every few minutes; the other leaves from the Kiev Railway Station Pier and goes to the Rowing Basin in Kuntsevo. They leave at 11.30am, 2.30 and 5.30pm. You can also take the Raketa hydrofoil from Gorky Park to the Novospassky Bridge.

Driving

Car rental

Several car-rental companies operate in Moscow, but you may feel most comfortable with the familiar Western companies which can be found at airports.

Petrol stations

Petrol stations are located all over the city. On the outskirts of the town they are found on main roads, but near the centre they tend to be hidden on side streets.

Accidents

Report all accidents to the DPC, Sadovaya 1 Samotechnaya ulitsa; tel: 02.

For a towing service and emergency repair, telephone ANGEL; tel: (495) 747-0022 (24 hours daily).

Insurance

To drive in Moscow it is advisable to take out additional Russian car insurance. Claims are paid only in the currency in which you pay for the policy. Contact Ingosstrakh, 12 Pyatnitskaya ulitsa; tel: (495) 956-5555.

Rules of the road

Rules of the road and road signs correspond in general to international standards. The basic rules, however, are worth mentioning.
• Traffic drives on the right.

• Don't drive after drinking or under the influence of drugs or medication.
• Drivers must have an international driving licence and documents verifying their right to drive the car. These papers must be in Russian and can be issued by Russian travel agents.
• Vehicles, except for those rented from official travel agencies, must carry the national registration code and have a national licence plate.
• The use of the horn is prohibited within city limits except in emergencies.
• The use of seat belts for the driver and front-seat passenger is compulsory.
• The speed limit in populated areas (marked by blue-coloured signs indicating "town") is 60 kph (37 mph); on most arterial roads the limit is 90 kph (55 mph). On highways different limits apply and these are shown on road signs.

On Foot

Despite Moscow's size, within the Garden Ring it is quite possible to get around on foot, especially if you break your journeys up into "chunks". Bicycling is not really an option; there are no cycle lanes in Moscow, and cyclists, while becoming more common, are still extremely rare.

Russian drivers are particularly reckless, and one should take great care when crossing the road.

GLOSSARY OF TERMS

shosse (sh.) = highway
ulitsa (ul.) = street
ploshchad (pl.) = square
pereulok (per.) = lane
naberezhnaya (nab.) = embankment
most = bridge
bulvar = boulevard

ACCOMMODATION

SOME THINGS TO CONSIDER BEFORE YOU BOOK THE ROOM

Choosing a Hotel

It's not easy to find a good room for a good price in Moscow. The demand for rooms exceeds the supply, so hotel guests often pay more than they would for a better room in other European capitals. In autumn 2005, the average cost of a night in a Moscow hotel was $225 and set to increase.

Moscow has never had enough hotel space, and Soviet-built hotels are being shut down one by one. Increasingly, the only options in the centre are the sterile hotels belonging to international chains.

You can receive a discount by booking rooms online. Try www.selectrussia.com, www.moscow-hotels.net and www.tripadvisor.com.

Private Accommodation

Because of the high prices and poor services, many independent travellers prefer to use agencies that offer short-term apartment rentals. It's not hard to find a centrally located apartment with good furnishings, satellite TV and internet for $100 per night.

When an agency's website says "Starting $80 per night", that's the price when renting for a few weeks. For a week's stay you'll pay about $110.

Some visa-support companies offer central apartments. Try www.apartmentsmoscow.co, run by Intelservice, or www.waytorussia.net; www.likehome.ru offers more than 100 apartments in the centre. If you're hoping to find accommodation in a specific neighbourhood, try here.

www.cityrealtyrussia.com and www.moscow-star.com (run by a boisterous American named Rick) both manage a few dozen apartments.

Real-estate companies that cater to expats also offer short-term rentals. They are more expensive – mostly starting at $150 per night – but you're guaranteed a clean stairwell and a quiet, modern elevator. Try www.beatrix.ru or www.intermark.ru.

Budget Lodgings

Shoestring travellers can find a bed in a hostel on the outskirts of Moscow for $15 a night; hostel contacts are given in the listings below. Stay anywhere cheaper and you'll be surrounded by workers from Central Asia in a dirty, bug-infested dormitory.

Several cheap hotels can be found in the north of the city, not far from the All-Russian Exhibition Centre (VVTs in Russian), formerly Exhibition of the People's Economic Achievements (VDNKh). A crotchety character who calls himself "Uncle Pasha" maintains www.cheap-moscow.com, which has a list of homestays starting at $50 per night and cheaper options.

Visas

Hotels are authorised by the Interior Ministry to issue visa invitations to their foreign guests. This invitation must then be submitted to the Russian consulate in your country of residence to obtain a visa. Upon arrival, your hotel will register your visa with the Interior Ministry. Visa support is free unless you cancel your reservation after receiving this service, in which case the hotel will charge a $50–100 fee to your credit card.

If you are renting an apartment, you will have to use the services of a visa-support agency. Rental companies will usually recommend one. They can also help with registration. Support and registration will each cost $30–60 dollars.

If you rent a room from an apartment owner, your host is unlikely to help with either visa support or registration.

ACCOMMODATION LISTINGS

CITY CENTRE

Hotels

Ararat Park Hyatt
4 Neglinnaya ulitsa
Metro: Okhotny Ryad
Tel: 783-1234
Fax: 783-1235 **$$$$**
www.moscow.park.hyatt.com
Named after the mountain in Armenia, the cuisine of which is served in a ground-floor restaurant. The bar and lounge on the top floor have an exquisite view of old Moscow's roofs. 220 rooms.

Golden Apple
11 ulitsa Malaya Dmitrovka
Metro: Pushkinskaya
Tel: 980-7000
Fax: 980-7001 **$$$**
www.goldenapple.ru
An aggressively trendy spot that claims to be Russia's only boutique

PRICE CATEGORIES

Price categories are for a double room without breakfast:
$ = under US$60
$$ = US$60–200
$$$ = US$200–300
$$$$ = over US$300

hotel. A different monochromatic scheme on each floor. Its restaurant is one of Moscow's best. 92 rooms.

**Golden Ring
(Zolotoe Koltso)**
5 Smolenskaya ulitsa
Metro: Smolenskaya
Tel: 725-0100
Fax: 725-0101 **$$$$**
www.hotel-goldenring.ru
A favourite of business travellers, Golden Ring is sparkling, efficient and tasteful. Rooms overlook the Moscow River, and the hotel is across the street from Arbat's entertainment. 293 rooms.

Marriott Courtyard
7 Voznesensky pereulok
Metro: Okhotny Ryad
Tel: 981-3300
Fax: 981-3301 **$$**
www.marriott.com
A historic façade with an airy glass atrium. Located on a quiet side street facing an Anglican church – a centre of expat-community life. 218 rooms.

Marriott Grand
26/1 Tverskaya ulitsa
Metro: Tverskaya
Tel: 937-0000

Fax: 937-0001 **$$$**
www.marriott.com
A stately hotel executed in Marriott's corporate style. Located on a busy stretch of Tverskaya ulitsa, with dozens of restaurants, bars and clubs near by. 375 rooms.

Metropol
1/4 Teatralny proyezd
Metro: Teatralnaya
Tel: 627-6000
Fax: 627-6010 **$$$$**
www.metropol-moscow.ru
An art deco palace with mosaics by proto-Modernist Mikhail Vrubel on its façade and each room with a different decoration. Buffet breakfast served in a lavish ballroom. 365 rooms.

**Royal Meridien
National**
15/1 Mokhovaya ulitsa
Metro: Okhotny Ryad
Tel: 258-7000
Fax: 258-7100 **$$$$**
www.lemeridien.com
With close-up views of the Kremlin walls and Manege Square, this luxury hotel is the closest you can get to Moscow's centre. Its spacious

rooms are furnished with antiques. 221 rooms.

Savoy
3 Rozhdestvenka ulitsa
Metro: Lubyanka
Tel: 620-8500
Fax: 230-2186 **$$$$**
www.savoy.ru
A distinguished, classical look attracts opera artists who sing at the nearby Bolshoy Theatre. Parquet floors and an art gallery. 84 rooms.

Hostel

Godzilla Hostel
6 Bolshoi Karetny pereulok
Metro: Pushkinskaya
Tel: 299-4223 **$**
www.godzillashostel.com
A centrally located, cheap hostel is rare. Common areas are clean but the rooms smell like backpackers. 10 rooms, with 2 to 8 bunks.

WEST AND EAST OF THE GARDEN RING

WEST

Hotels

Alexander Blok
12a Krasnopresnenskaya naberezhnaya
Metro: Ulitsa 1905 Goda
Tel: 255-9278

Fax: 253-9578 **$$**
A small hotel on a boat moored on the Moscow River. Each room is busily decorated; 24-hour casino and daily working nightclub also on the boat. 30 rooms.

Mezhdunarodnaya
12 Krasnopresnenskaya naberezhnaya

Metro: Barrikadnaya
Tel: 258-2122
Fax: 253-2501 **$$$$**
www.wtcmoscow.ru
Easy access to the Expocenter, Moscow's largest site for trade fairs, and the World Trade Centre make this hotel very popular for business travellers and

conference groups. 577 rooms.

Orlyonok
15 ulitsa Kosygina
Metro: Vorobyovy Gory
Tel: 939-8888
Fax: 939-8008 **$$**
www.hotel-orlyonok.ru
You'll need a taxi or bus to get anywhere – the hotel is not central and the metro is a long walk. But there's lots of entertainment on site: the basement has a casino, strip club and good Korean restaurants. 320 rooms.

Radisson SAS Slavyanskaya
2 ploshchad Yevropy
Metro: Kievskaya
Tel: 941-8028
Fax: 941-8000 **$$$$**
www.radissonsas.com
On the banks of the Moscow River, this

business-class hotel has sprawling premises that houses restaurants and cafés, lots of shopping and a gym. 410 rooms.

Tiflis
32 ulitsa Ostozhenka
Metro: Park Kultury
Tel: 733-9070
Fax: 203-3536 **$$$**
www.hoteltiflis.com
Small, handsome hotel in a neighbourhood populated by millionaires. Dark wood and red carpets give it grandeur. Attached to an excellent Georgian restaurant of the same name. Rooms with balconies overlook a courtyard with fountain. 66 rooms.

Yunost
34 Khamovnichesky val

Metro: Sportivnaya
Tel: 242-4860
Fax: 242-0284 **$$**
www.yunost-hotel.ru
A faceless hotel which raised its prices after renovations. Easy access to Luzhniki Stadium and Sportivnaya metro, but an otherwise boring neighbourhood. 120 rooms.

EAST

Hotels

G&R Asia Hostel
3/2 Zelenodolskaya
Metro: Ryazansky Prospekt
Tel: 378-0001
Fax: 378-2866 **$**
www.hostels.ru

Singles and doubles with shared baths on the 3rd to 5th floors of a shabby hotel on the outskirts of Moscow. Popular with travellers on their way to Beijing on the Trans-Siberian railroad.

Izmailovsky Complex
71 Izamailovskoye Shosse
Metro: Partizanskaya
Tel: 737-7000
Fax: 737-7070 **$**
www.izmailovo.ru
Monolithic slabs built for the 1980 Olympics. One of the cheapest hotels in the city. Popular among groups. Right next to the metro station, the centre is five stops away. Around 900 rooms, some undergoing renovation.

NORTH OF THE GARDEN RING

Hotels

Altai
41 Botanicheskaya ulitsa
Metro: Vladykino
Tel: 382-2797/956-8612
Fax: 956-8683/482-5621 **$**
e-mail: altayhotel@comail.ru
It looks small, but it sprawls in the back, offering renovated rooms and old ones for budget travelers. On a busy street. 400 rooms.

Baikal
15/1 Selskokhozyaistvennaya ulitsa
Metro: Botanichesky Sad
Tel: 189-7529
Fax: 189-8802 **$**
www.hotelbaikal.ru
In the lower-priced rooms, the tacky wallpaper and ratty carpets give the impression that nothing has changed since the Brezhnev era. 463 rooms.

Holiday Inn Lesnaya
15 Lesnaya ulitsa
Metro: Belorusskaya
Tel: 783-6500
Fax: 783-6501 **$$$**
www.holiday-inn.com
The hotel chain's first foray into Moscow has a classy red bar and elegant conference rooms with photographs of old Moscow. Near the top of Tverskaya ulitsa and busy Tverskaya Zastava. 154 rooms.

Kosmos
150 Prospekt Mira
Metro: VDNKh
Tel: 234-1000
Fax: 615-8880 **$$**
www.hotelcosmos.ru
This boomerang-shaped hotel has a casino, bowling alley and a theatre that hosts circus acts and folk ballets. A short walk from VDNKh, the

Stalinist park of delights. 1,623 rooms.

Marco Polo Presnja
9 Spiridonovsky pereulok
Metro: Mayakovskaya
Tel: 244-3631
Fax: 926-5402 **$$$$**
www.presnja.ru
Built to house British governesses in the early 20th century, it was the first joint-venture hotel in the *perestroika* period. The rooms are tasteful. The café, gym and massage parlour are frequented by local celebrities. 72 rooms.

Novotel Novoslobodskaya
23 Novoslobodskaya ulitsa
Metro: Mendeleyevskaya
Tel: 780-4000
Fax: 780-4001 **$$$**
www.novotel.com
This chain hotel has big conference rooms and a sterile feel. Outside the centre proper, but the

metro station is next door. 255 rooms.

Renaissance
18/1 Olimpiisky prospekt
Metro: Prospekt Mira
Tel: 931-9000
Fax: 931-9076 **$$$**
www.marriott.com
A Marriott property, with furnishings and amenities to match. It houses the Dome Cinema, which shows movies in English. 463 rooms.

Sheraton Palace Hotel
19, 1-ya Tverskaya-Yamskaya ulitsa
Metro: Mayakovskaya
Tel: 931-9700
Fax: 931-9703 **$$$$**

www.sheratonpalace.ru
The central location on Tverskaya ulitsa makes it easy to get around. The setting befits the brand. 204 rooms.

Tourist
17/2 Selskokhozyastvennaya ulitsa
Metro: Botanichesky Sad
Tel: 980-7391
Fax: 980-7398 **$**
www.hotelturist.com
A complex of seven boxy brick buildings around a quiet, leafy courtyard. Kind staff. Unrenovated areas have red-and-green carpet characteristic of Soviet hotels. Around

800 rooms, some under renovation or leased to Tramp *(see below)*.

Volga
2 Dokuchayev pereulok
Metro: Sukharevskaya
Tel: 783-9109
Fax: 783-9123 **$$**
www.hotel-volga.ru
Plain and clean rooms on a dull street not far from the Garden Ring and stations with trains to St Petersburg and Siberia. 231 rooms.

Hostels

Sherston Hostel
8 Gostinichny proyezd, building 1

Metro: Vladykino
Tel: 482-1306
Fax: 482-3190 **$**
www.sherston.ru
Unpretentious location between a commuter train station and the end of a trolleybus line. Unrenovated rooms are rented out to the hostel-going set. 445 rooms.

Tramp Hostel
17/2 Selskokhozyastvennaya ulitsa, Building 4
Metro: Botanichesky Sad
Tel: 187-5433
Fax: 551-2876 **$**
www.hostelling.ru
This organisation rents rooms from Hotel Tourist *(see above)*,

mostly in the un-renovated building, and resells them to backpackers.

Travellers' Guest House
50 Bolshaya Pereslavskaya ulitsa
Metro: Prospekt Mira
Tel: 631-4059
Fax: 680-7686 **$**
www.tgh.ru
On the 10th floor of an ugly white building in a residential area between three train stations and Pospekt Mira, a broad and busy avenue. $25 for a bunk in a 4- or 5-bed room, $60 for a double with shared bath.

BEYOND THE RIVER

Hotels

Academicheskaya
1 Donskaya ulitsa
Metro: Oktyabrskaya
Tel/fax: 959-8157 **$$**
www.maan.ru
Since renovations, prices have shot up at this hotel owned by the Russian Academy of Sciences. 230 rooms.

Baltschug-Kempinski
1 ulitsa Balchug
Metro: Novokuznetskaya
Tel: 230-6500
Fax: 230-6502 **$$$$**
www.kempinski-moscow.com
A hotel with imposing interiors and impressive views of the Kremlin and St Basil's

across the Moscow River. 230 rooms.

Katerina
6 Shlyuzovaya naberezhnaya
Metro: Paveletskaya
Tel: 933-0400
Fax: 795-2443 **$$$**
www.katerina.msk.ru
Lower-priced and more character than most hotels in its class. A cozy and colourful décor with Marc Chagall prints and fabric patterns influenced by his paintings. Views of Moscow River and monasteries. 119 rooms.

President
24 ulitsa Bolshaya Yakimanka
Metro: Polyanka
Tel: 239-3800
Fax: 239-3646 **$$$$**
www.president-hotel.ru
Built in 1982 to house members of the Communist Party, this hotel still has an officious atmosphere. Castro and Jiang Zemin were no doubt comforted by its ultra-high security. 208 rooms.

Sputnik
38 Leninsky prospekt
Metro: Leninsky Prospekt
Tel: 930-2287
Fax: 930-1988 **$$**
www.hotelsputnik.ru
Standard accommodation at reasonable prices, though a bit out of the way. It has a great Indian restaurants. 343 rooms.

Swissotel Krasnye Kholmy
52 Kosmodamianskaya naberezhnaya, Building 6
Metro: Paveletskaya
Tel: 787-9800
Fax: 787-9898 **$$$$**
www.swissotel.com
Swissotel's skyscraper transformed the city's skyline. Five-star amenities and a bar at the top with sweeping panoramas. In the same complex as the Moscow International House of Music. 235 rooms.

Uzkoe
3a Litovsky bulvar
Metro: Yasenevo
Tel: 427-0033

Fax: 427-5600 **$**
www.maan.ru
The location near the Bitsevsky woods park is green and quiet, but not convenient if you plan a lot of sightseeing – it's half an hour by metro from the centre. Otherwise quiet and relaxing. 104 rooms.

Warsaw (Varshava)
2 Leninsky prospekt
Metro: Oktyabrskaya
Tel: 238-1970
Fax: 238-9639 **$$**
e-mail: warsaw@sovintel.ru
A good location near Gorky Park and the New Tretyakov, but standard accommodation behind a drab monolithic exterior. Renovated in 2003. 100 rooms.

TRANSPORT

ACCOMMODATION

ACTIVITIES

A – Z

LANGUAGE

ACTIVITIES

THE ARTS, NIGHTLIFE, FESTIVALS, SHOPPING AND SPORTS

THE ARTS

Muscovites are proud of their city's vibrant cultural life. Russia's rigorous conservatories and ballet schools turn out enough performers to keep scores of stages lively. Most performances start at 7pm.

Circus

A night at the circus can be very entertaining, though some acts might offend animal-lovers. **The Great Moscow State Circus**, 7 prospekt Vernadskovo; metro: Universitet; tel: 930-0272; www.bolshoicircus.ru. The "New Circus" specialises in animal tricks – dancing bears, daredevil horseback riding – and clowns.
Nikulin Circus, 13 Tsvetnoy bulvar; metro: Tsvetnoy Bulvar; tel: 200-0668; www.circusnikulin.ru. Named after a well-known comedian, Yuri Nikulin, the "Old Circus" is renowned for its acrobats and illusionists.

Theatre

If you're not put off by the language barrier, Moscow offers excellent theatre.
Fomenko Studio, 30/32 Kutuzovsky prospekt; metro: Kutuzovskaya; tel: 249-1136;

www.fomenko.theatre.ru. Laboratory of a star director whose productions are fawned on by critics.
Lenkom, 6 ulitsa Malaya Dmitrovka; metro: Pushkinskaya; tel: 299-9668; www.lenkom.ru. Hits include the Soviet musical *Juno and Avos* and an Orthodox interpretation of *Jesus Christ Superstar*.
Maly Theatre, 1/6 Teatralnaya ploshchad; metro: Teatralnaya; tel: 623-2621; www.maly.ru. The heavyweight of Russian drama, with serious, intelligent stagings of 19th-century classics.
Moscow Art Theatre (MKhAT), 3 Kamergersky pereulok; metro: Okhotny Ryad; tel: 692-6748; www.theatre.ru/mhat. Where Chekhov premiered his plays, it now features a mix of old and new. Every year, American students stage some plays in English.
Moscow Theatre Yunovo Zritelya, 10 Mamonovksy pereulok; metro: Pushkinskaya; tel: 299-5360; www.theatre.ru/mtuz. Innovative productions – a vaudeville Chekhov, *Lady and the Lapdog* and *Dreams of Exile*, inspired by Marc Chagall.
Sovremnik Theatre, 19a Chistroprudny bulvar; metro Chistye Prudy; tel: 921-1790; www.sovremennik.ru. Founded a few years after Stalin's death by the group of young actors, the theatre developed a reputation for innovation, but in recent years it has grown more conservative.

Teatr.doc, 11–13 Tryokhprudny pereulok; metro: Pushkinskaya; tel: 233-4604; www.teatrdoc.ru. A hip theatre that focuses on new plays by young Russian playwrights.
Theatre na Yugo-Zapade, 125 prospekt Vernadskovo; metro: Yugozapadnaya; tel: 433-1191; www.teatr-uz.ru. A cramped space offering lively versions of *Hamlet*, *The Government Inspector* and other classics.
Theatre on Malaya Bronnaya, 4 Malaya Bronnaya ulitsa; metro Pushkinskaya; tel: 290-5093; www.mbronnaya.theatre.ru This fine, historic theatre is trying to inject new life in its repertoire by attracting younger actors and directors.
Theatre on Taganka Zemlyanoi val, 76; metro: Taganskaya; tel: 915-1217; www.taganka.theatre.ru. Founded by legendary director Yuri Liubimov, it suffered hard times when he emigrated during *perestroika*, but endures as one of the city's top theatres and innovatively adds elements of circus or carnival to make its shows compelling.

Opera and Ballet

Moscow has several opera theatres, and the wealth of singing talent means the quality of the soloists is excellent no matter where you go. However, in the smaller theatres, the chorus or orchestra may weaken the overall effect. But the main problem for local companies is finding a place to perform; by 2006, three groups await their stages to be repaired.

The main Bolshoy Theatre is due to reopen in early 2008. Its renowned opera and ballet companies meanwhile perform on the New Stage next door, where smaller dimensions mean new productions must be commissioned, giving art director Aleksey Ratmansky a chance to breathe life into the Bolshoy's stodgy repertoire.

The Stanislavsky Nemirovich-Danchenko musical theatre, also a fine spot for ballet and opera, is due to reopen following a fire. The Gelikon Opera is waiting for an extension to be constructed.

Bolshoy Theatre, 1 Teatralnaya ploshchad; metro: Teatralnaya; tel: 250-7317; www.bolshoi.ru. Russia's top theatre for opera and ballet. Though it's reaching out to explore 20th-century repertory like Shostakovich and Prokofiev and 21st-century direction, crowd-pleasers such as *Swan Lake* remain on the programme.

Boris Pokrovsky Chamber Musical Theatre, 17 Nikolskaya ulitsa; metro: Ploshchad Revoliutsii; tel: 929-1326. Led by a veteran director from the Bolshoy, this is quality small theatre.

Galina Vishnevskaya Centre for Opera, 25/1 ulitsa Ostozhenka; metro: Park Kultury; tel: 201-7703; www.opera-centre.ru. Concert performances of operas in a centre founded by the famous soprano.

Gelikon Opera, 19/16 Bolshaya Nikitskaya ulitsa; metro: Arbatskaya; tel: 290-6529; www.helikon.ru. The innovative productions are hit or miss. The theatre's gem is *Lady Macbeth of Mtsensk* by Shostakovich. Intimate setting in a former private theatre in a noble's estate.

Kremlin Ballet, Kremlin; metro: Alexandrovsky Sad; tel: 928-5232; www.gkd.ru. The company dances in the monstrous State Kremlin Palace.

New Ballet 25/2 Novaya Basmannaya ulitsa, Building 2; metro: Krasniye Vorota; tel: 261-7603. www.newballet.ru. A contemporary dance troupe that employs techniques adapted from pantomime and ballet.

Novaya Opera, 3 Karetny ryad (in the Hermitage Gardens); metro: Pushkinskaya; tel: 200-0868; www.novayaopera.ru. Founded by a renegade conductor from Stanislavsky and Nemirovich-Danchenko, this theatre is characterised by pared-down stagings, abridged scores and an outstanding chorus.

Operetta Theatre, 6 ulitsa Bolshaya Dmitrovka; metro: Teatralnaya; tel: 290-2557; www.mosoperetta.ru. Repetory of light opera by Lehar and Strauss to musicals like *The Hunchback of Notre-Dame*.

Stanislavsky and Nemirovich-Danchenko Musical Theatre, 17 ulitsa Bolshaya Dmitrovka; metro: Chekhovskaya; tel: 629-8388. Russian and Italian chestnuts competently put together. Performing at various venues around the city and country until its home theatre reopens.

Concerts

A number of top-flight symphony and chamber orchestras are based in Moscow. The Russian National Orchestra directed by Mikhail Pletnev is top of the heap. The Moscow Conservatory, with one hall for symphony concerts and two for chamber music, has the best acoustics and ambience of the city's major concert halls. Occasionally, various museums host recitals, for example, the annual December Nights series in the Pushkin Museum of Fine Arts.

Moscow Conservatory, 13 Bolshaya Nikitskaya ulitsa; metro: Arbatskaya; tel: 279-7412. The Great Hall has performances by star orchestras and soloists from Russia and beyond. The Small Hall and the Rakhmaninov Hall have chamber-music recitals.

Moscow International House of Music, 58 Kosmodamianskaya naberezhnaya; metro: Paveletskaya; tel: 730-4350; www.mmdm.ru. This rival to the Conservatory opened in 2002. The acoustics are a disappointment, and tickets more expensive than at the Conservatory.

State Kremlin Palace, 1 ulitsa Vozdvizhenka; metro: Alexandrovsky Sad; tel: 928-5232; www.gkd.ru. Built under Khrushchev to host Communist Party congresses, this arena now welcomes Western stars on their farewell tours and Russian popular singers.

Tchaikovsky Concert Hall, 4/31 Triumfalnaya ploshchad; metro: Mayakovskaya; tel: 299-3957. A spacious hall for symphony performances and occasional folk or pop concerts.

Cinema

Hollywood blockbusters dominate Moscow's cinemas, and almost all are dubbed. Only one theatre shows movies in the original language: the **Dome Cinema** (18/1 Olim-piisky prospekt; Renais- sance Hotel; metro: Prospekt Mira; tel: 931-9873; www.domecinema.ru).

A handful of theatres show undubbed art-house films.

35MM (47/24 ulitsa Pokrovka; metro: Krasniye Vorota; tel: 917-5492) shows European and Asian films with Russian subtitles. **Muzei Kino** (15 Druzhinnikovskaya ulitsa; metro: Krasnopresnenskaya; tel: 255-9057; www.museikino.ru), the cinema museum, on the premises of the massive Kinocentre, shows international classics. Usually foreign films are subtitled, but sometimes there is an irritating live translation. There are a couple of theatres that sometimes show British or American films subtitled in Russian; they are **Pyat Zvyozd** (25 ulitsa Bakhrushina; metro: Paveletskaya; tel: 916-9169; www.5zvezd.ru) and **Fitil** (12 Frunzenskaya naberezhnaya; metro: Park Kultury; tel: 246-8448).

The *Moscow Times* has daily listings of all films in English shown around the city.

TRANSPORT

ACCOMMODATION

ACTIVITIES

A – Z

LANGUAGE

WHAT'S ON LISTINGS

● The Friday issue of the *Moscow Times* (www.the-moscowtimes.com) carries listings of gigs and events through to the next Thursday.

● The *Exile* (www.exile.ru) also has listings, if you can handle the attitude and student humour. Nightlife listings are up to date and brutally honest.

● The *Element* (www.element moscow.ru) is an English-language entertainment weekly distributed free at restaurants and clubs. It writes articles praising its advertisers.

● In Russian, the best source of information is *Afisha* (www.afisha.ru).

NIGHTLIFE

Clubs are constantly opening and closing, as few can keep the interest of Moscow's fickle public for more than a year. Those listed below, however, have been around for several years and seem to have staying power.

If you look at local club listings, you'll notice the phrases "face control" and "dress code". This means the club does not charge an entry fee, but the doorman will turn away anyone who doesn't look ready to spend a lot inside.

Also note that many clubs claim to be open 24 hours or "until the last guest", but feel entitled to take a 2- or 4-hour "technical break" early in the morning.

Live Music

Clubs usually charge $5–10 for concerts, with the higher figure coming into effect when groups come from abroad.

16 Tons, 6/ 1 Presnensky Val; metro: Ulitsa 1905 Goda; tel: 253-5300; www.16tons.ru. The music-lovers who run the place

have an interesting programme of rock and electronica acts from Russia, Europe and the USA; small record store on the 2nd floor is staffed by passionate salesmen.

B2, 8 Bolshaya Sadovaya ulitsa; metro: Mayakovskaya; tel: 209-9909; www.b2club.ru. A mammoth club with a pool hall, jazz club, karaoke bar, sushi restaurant and a stage that hosts world-famous bands, though the abysmal sound system could make you regret paying $20 for entry. Open 24 hours.

Bilingua, 10/5 Krivokolenny pereulok; metro: Chistye Prudy; tel: 623-9660; www.bilinguaclub.ru. Upstairs is a restaurant with a stage for rock and alternative shows and poetry readings. Downstairs is a bookstore with a few tables for drinking coffee and musing, plus a shop with quirky clothes. Open 24 hours.

Dom, 24/4 Bolshoy Ovchinnikovsky pereulok; metro: Novokuznetskaya; tel: 953-7236; www.dom.com.ru. A gallery and club with avant-garde jazz, chamber music and video art programmes. The bohemian crowd appreciates the cheap beer and wine. The entrance is tucked in a courtyard. Concerts start at 7.30pm.

Gogol, 11 Stoleshnikov pereulok; metro: Kuznetsky Most; tel: 514-0944. Styled after a Soviet-era vodka bar, complete with vintage arcade games. The courtyard hosts bands on warm summer nights; in the winter it is a skating rink. Open 24 hours.

Nest of the Wood Grouse 22/12 Bolshaya Nikitskaya ulitsa; metro: Arbatskaya; tel: 291-9388. www.gnezdogluharya.ru Songwriters with guitars and poetic texts. Not as interesting if you can't understand the lyrics, though the simple accompaniment provides pleasant listening.

Tinkoff, 11 Protochny pereulok; metro: Smolenskaya; tel: 777-3300; www.tinkoff.ru. Microbrewery owned by the upmarket beer label serving delicious unfiltered

brews and occasionally hosting electronica and hip-hop acts. Open noon–2am.

Expat Bars

These are good places to meet compatriots who can share their opinions and tips about Moscow.
Doug & Marty's Boar House, 26 Zemlyanoi val; metro: Kurskaya; tel: 917-0150; www.boarhouse.ru. Crazy drink specials include three-for-one deals or $2 shots of absinthe and vodka (mixed). Open 24 hours.

Hard Rock Café, 44 ulitsa Arbat; metro: Smolenskaya; tel: 244-8970; www.hardrockcafe.ru. Memorabilia commemorating Russian rock stars. Drink until you buy a T-shirt. Open 24 hours.

Rock Vegas, 29/8 Pyatnitskaya ulitsa; metro: Tretyakovskaya; tel: 959-5333. A modestly decorated bar with live rock and blues, aimed at the expat set. 12pm–6am.

The Real McCoy, 1 Kudrinskaya ploshchad; metro: Barrikadnaya; tel: 255-4144; www.mccoy.ru. Wildly crowded and rowdy on weekends. 24 hours.

Yuppie Bars

A host of slick bars cater to Moscow's burgeoning yuppie population, pouring $8 *mojitos* to wash down rocket salads. The people-watching is great. Dress nicely or you might not get in.
30/7, 30/7 ulitsa Petrovka; metro: Pushkinskaya; tel: 209-5951. Hard to get inside on weekends, Big crowds and strict face control. Open 24 hours.

Courvoisier Café, 8/1 Malaya Sukharevskaya ploshchad; metro: Sukharevskaya; tel: 924-8242. Round-the-clock DJs and preening clientele in a beige café sponsored by the cognac company. Open 24 hours.

Maner, 5 ulitsa Petrovka (in the Berliner Haus business centre); metro: Kuznetsky Most; tel: 775-1959; www.maner.ru. Red-leather seats and a grey

interior evokes a decadent, pre-war Berlin feel to this bar and café. Open 10am–midnight, until 6am on weekends.

Just Bars

Poslednyaya Kaplya, 4/3 Strastnoy bulvar (go through the arch with the Venezia pizzeria sign); metro: Chekhovskaya; tel: 692-7549. There aren't many places in Moscow where you can go just to sit and have a drink. This dark, cosy basement bar is the best of them. Strong, expertly mixed drinks. Open noon–last guest.

Red Bar, 23a nabarezhnaya Tarasa Shevchenko (on the top floor); metro: Kievskaya; tel: 730-0808. An upscale bar with stunning views of Moscow, even from the gents'. Open 6pm–3am.

Jazz Bars

Forte, 18 Bolshaya Bronnaya ulitsa; metro: Tverskaya; tel: 202-8833; www.blues.ru/forte. A low-key jazz club with quality programming. Dark-wood panelling on the walls adds to the intimate atmosphere. Open 2pm–midnight.

Le Club, 21 Verkhnyaya Radishchevskaya ulitsa (in the building of Theatre na Taganke); metro: Taganskaya; tel: 915-1042; www.le-club.ru. Under saxophone great Igor Butman, the city's top jazz club flies in stars from the US. Cover charges are no less than $50. Open noon–last guest.

Sinyaya Ptitsa (Blue Bird), 23/15 ulitsa Malaya Dmitrovka; metro: Pushkinskaya; tel: 299-2225. Operating for 40 years, this club offers jazz from big bands to hybrids. Open noon–midnight.

Casinos

Casinos stay open 24 hours. Most require visitors to buy a certain amount of chips at the door – $50 is a common fee. On weekends you can catch concerts by Russian pop stars.

Arlekino, 15 Druzhinnikovskaya ulitsa; metro: Krasnopresnenskaya. Shares a gaudy entertainment complex with the Kinocentre and nightclub Infiniti.

Europa, 5 Bolshoy Putnikovsky pereulok; metro: Pushkinskaya; tel: 975-7484; www.clubeurope.ru. Europa asks high-rolling guests to buy $200 worth of chips to enter.

Metelitsa, 21 ulitsa Novy Arbat; metro: Smolenskaya; tel: 291-1130. One of the oldest.

Mirazh, 21/1 ulitsa Novy Arbat; metro: Smolenskaya; tel: 787-7501; www.casino-mirage.ru. Adjacent to Metelitsa, it does its part to make New Arbat a little strip of Las Vegas. Entrance is free.

Shangri-La, 2 Pushkinskaya ploshchad; metro: Pushkinskaya; tel: 209-6400; www.shangrila.ru. Ornate oriental decorations help detract from the Soviet-style Pushkin Cinema above.

FESTIVALS

Annual

For the most important holiday of the Orthodox Church, St Petersburg-based conductor Valery Gergiev comes south for the annual Moscow Easter

Festival (www.easterfestival.ru). Concerts of secular and sacred music are held around the city.

Every year in late June film buffs can check out the **Moscow International Film Festival** (www.miff.ru), which lasts for 10 days. Films from all corners of Europe and Asia are subtitled in English, and programmes are available in translation.

Biannual and Triennual

The **Chekhov International Theatre Festival** (www.chekhovfest.ru) occurs roughly every other summer and fills stages for the off-season with top international companies. Modern dance and experimental theatre helps to surmount language barriers.

The **International Tchaikovsky Competition** (www.tchaikovsky-competition.ru) awards fine young pianists, violinists, cellists and vocalists. Held once every four years.

SHOPPING

Art and Antiques

NB Gallery, 6/2 Sivtsev Vrazhek pereulok (ring 002 at the door for entry); metro: Kropotkinskaya; tel: 737-5298; e-mail: nbgallery@online.ru. Knowledgeable staff serve you tea and show you around their excellent collection of Realist, Impressionist and Expressionist Soviet painting.

Shishkin Gallery, 29/14 Neglinnaya ulitsa; metro: Tsvetnoy

TWELVE MAJOR RELIGIOUS FESTIVALS

The Orthodox calendar starts with the Nativity of the Mother of God (26 Aug in the Julian Calendar, 8 Sept in the contemporary calendar). After this comes: the Elevation of the True Cross (14/27 Sept); the Presentation of the Mother of God in the Temple (21 Nov/4 Dec); the Nativity of Christ (25 Dec/7 Jan); the Baptism of the Lord, or the Epiphany (6/19 Jan); the

Purification of the Mother of God (2/15 Feb); the Annunciation (25 Mar/7 Apr); the Entry of the Lord into Jerusalem (movable); Easter; the Ascension of the Lord; the Holy Trinity (on the 50th day after Easter, sometimes called "Pentecost"); the Transfiguration of the Saviour (6/19 Aug); and the Dormition of the Mother of God (15/28 Aug).

TRANSPORT

ACCOMMODATION

ACTIVITIES

A – Z

LANGUAGE

bulvar; tel: 200-5310; www.shishkin-gallery.ru. Paintings from pre-Revolutionary Wanderers to Socialist Realists. **Central House of Artists**, 10 Krymsky val; metro: Oktyabrskaya; tel: 238-9634; www.cha.ru. Fifty roubles entry to scores of antique salons, galleries and gift shops. Freely peruse landscapes and still lifes. Artists sell in rows outside the building and in the underground. In the same building as the New Tretyakov Gallery. Closed Mon. **ArtStrelka**, Bersenevskaya naberezhnaya; metro: Kropotkinskaya; www.artstrelka.ru. The cluster of galleries in the former garages of the Red October chocolate factory is a good place to get acquainted with the trends in Russian contemporary art. **Knigi**, 16 Bolshaya Nikitskaya ulitsa; metro: Pushkinskaya. Though the name means simply "books", it has all sorts of antiques.

Bookshops

The best selection in English is at **Anglia British Bookshop** (6 Vorotnikovsky pereulok; metro: Mayakovskaya; tel: 299-7766).

Bookberry (17/1 Nikitsky bulvar; metro: Arbatskaya; tel: 789-9187; www.bookberry.ru) is a plush bookstore with lots of magazines in English, and a used-book section with photo albums of Moscow and Russia. The most central shop is on 10 Kutuzovsky prospekt; metro: Kievskaya; tel: 243-3312.

Moskovsky Dom Knigi (8 Novy Arbat; metro: Arbatskaya; tel: 789-3591; www.mdk-arbat.ru) has science fiction and mysteries.

Bookstores in the **O.G.I.** chain have an appealing bohemian atmosphere, usually sharing the premises with cafés and clubs with live music and poetry readings. **Pir O.G.I.**, 19/2 Nikolskaya; metro: Ploshchad Revlyutsii; tel: 951-5827. **Proekt O.G.I.**, 8/12 Potapovsky pereulok, building 2.

There is also the **Library of Foreign Literature** (1 Nikoloyam-

skaya; metro: Taganskaya; tel: 915-3621; www.libfl.ru), but to access the American Center and British Council you need to fill out a form. The foyer has kiosks run by the **Library Bookshop**, which also has a store across the street at 4 Nikoloyamskaya; tel: 915-3284.

Clothes

Cox, 9/2 Maroseika; metro: Kitai-Gorod; tel: 921-6784; www.cox.ru. Daring fashions, plus unique gifts. **Galantereya O.G.I.**, inside Bilin-gua (see Live Music under Nightlife). T-shirts with slogans, hand-decorated bags, hippie tunics and punky jackets. **Marki**, 17/1 Pokrovka; metro: Chistye Prudy; tel: 916-5872. Well-made, understated women's clothing by local designers. **Spetsodezhda**, 50/2 Bolshaya Serpukhovskaya; metro: Serpukhovskaya; tel: 236-0173; www.vostok.ru. The name means "clothing for specialists", and the store is intended for blue-collar professionals, from waitresses to building workers, but the durable items, most under $15, look good enough to wear elsewhere.

Department Stores and Malls

Atrium, 33 Zemlyanoi val; metro: Kurskaya; tel: 970-1555; www.atrium.su. A three-storey mall with a multiplex and gaming centre on the top level. GUM, 3 Krasnaya ploshchad; metro: Ploshchad Revolyutsii; tel: 921-5762 or 929-3402. The grand architecture of the pre-Revolutionary department store never fails to impress, and its spaces are being snapped-up by high-end brands. **Okhotny Ryad**, 1 Manezhnaya ploshchad; metro: Okhotny Ryad; tel: 737-8449; www.or-tk.ru. Teenage girls overrun this three-storey underground mall under the Kremlin walls; stores target them. TsUM, 2 Petrovka; metro: Teatralnaya; tel: 692-1157; www.tsum.ru. A department store that has become a fashionista magnet.

Food Shops

Many Muscovites buy groceries at outdoor markets on the city outskirts. Closer to the centre are four indoor markets, where quality, presentation and prices are higher. A visit to any of these is a fun outing; vendors eagerly give free samples of pickled vegetables, sausage, cheese or honey. The largest is **Dorogomilovsky market** (10 Mozhaysky val; metro: Kievskaya), where top chefs go shopping.

The other three, similar in size and selection, are: **Rizhsky market** (94/96 Prospekt Mira; metro: Rizhskaya; **Danilovsky market** (74 Mytnaya ulitsa; metro: Tulskaya) and **Basmanny market** (47/1 Basmannaya ulitsa; metro: Baumanskaya).

Confael, 18 1st Tverskaya-Yamskaya; metro: Mayakovskaya; tel: 251-1555; www.confael.ru. A gourmet chocolate shop that makes sculptures to order. **Dom Myoda**, 5/10 Novokuznetskaya, building 1; metro: Tretyakovskaya; tel: 951-1012; www.dommeda.ru. Outlet of the National Union of Beekeepers. **Globus Gourmet** (22 Bolshaya Yakimanka; metro: Polyanka; tel: 995-2170) is an epicurean grocery store with affordable staples and a less affordable deli. **Kalinka-Stockmann**, 3 Smolenskaya ploshchad; metro: Smolenskaya; tel: 785-2500; www.stockmann.ru. At this grocery store you can find most things from your homeland, just don't expect to get them cheap. **Red October**, 6 Bersensevskaya naberezhnaya; metro: Kropotkinskaya (take the pedestrian bridge from the Church of Christ the Saviour). www.konfetki.ru. Outlet on the premises of this popular chocolate factory.

Gifts and Jewellery

Art Salon na Petrovka, 12 ulitsa Petrovka; metro: Teatralnaya; tel: 924-2654. Art and antique jewellery, fine decorations from glass and precious metals. Few items are under $100.

Byuro Nakhodok, 7/9 Smolensky bulvar; metro: Smolenskaya; tel: 244-7694. For clocks made out of everything from Melodiya records to caviar cans.

Russian Bronze, 8 Nikitsky bulvar; metro: Arbatskaya; tel: 202-3201; www.vel.ru. Statuettes, jewellery and bas-reliefs in pewter and bronze, made at studios in the shop. Another location at 20 Kuznetsky Most; metro: Kuznetsky Most; tel: 921-4793.

Russian Gallery na Vozdvizhenka, 5 ulitsa Vozdvizhenka; metro: Biblioteka im. Lenina. In the building of the Shchusev Architecture Museum. Eclectic collection of paintings, prints, antiques and quirky handmade handbags.

Markets

Vernisazh at Izmailovsky Park (metro: Partizanskaya; follow signs to the Vernisazh). The biggest souvenir market in Moscow, with rows of *matryoshka* dolls, fur hats and Soviet military paraphernalia. Pirated CDs and DVDs are at rock-bottom prices. Upstairs is a flea market. It may seem to be just junk, but antique dealers come early to find treasures. Admission 10 roubles.

Old Arbat (Metro: Arbatskaya or Smolenskaya). Antique and souvenir shops line the streets, and vendors set up stands on the cobblestones. Prices are higher than at the Izmailovsky Vernisazh. There are numerous street performers, many cafés, and architecture evocative of pre-Revolutionary Moscow. Street dealers have pelts, fur hats, *matryoshka* dolls, Soviet pilot caps and red banners with Lenin's profile. There are no price tags, and vendors may start out asking for three times what they expect to sell for, so haggle. Prices aren't set at all the shops, either. At **Souvenirs and Gifts** (21 and 41 Arbat; tel: 241-5710) salespeople may offer you a "discount" of up to 90

CUSTOMS

If you buy any paintings or antiques, you will need a certificate from the Ministry of Culture (7 Maly Gnezdikovsky pereulok; metro: Pushkinskaya) to present at customs when you leave the country. This is how "items of value to Russian culture" are prevented from leaving the country. Art galleries like NB and Shishkin will help you through the formalities for a fee; antique stores usually leave you to sort the paperwork yourself.

If you have questions, call Russian Customs, tel: 265-6628 or 208-2808.

percent. The starting prices there don't differ much from the average. Stores at the ends of the street tend to charge more than those in the middle. Thus, **Ivan Tsarevich** (4 Arbat; tel: 291-7076), attached to the inexpensive and hearty 3/9 Tsarstvo café, has higher prices than **Arbatskaya Lavitsa** (27 Arbat; tel: 290-5689), though the range and quality of goods are similar. Most stores offer painted platters, *matryoshka* dolls, blue-and-white Gzhel porcelain, amber jewellery, lacquer boxes and figurines. Arbatskaya Lavitsa, which has three floors, has an expanded selection of porcelain, lace and linens. Antique stores such as **Serebryany Ryad** (23 Arbat; tel: 291-7219; www.arbatantik.ru) sell silverware, samovars, clocks and figurines, nearly all of which need a certificate from the Ministry of Culture *(see above)* to bring out of the country. The stores do not provide assistance in this.

Gostiny Dvor (4 Ilinka; metro: Kitai-gorod). A shopping and exposition centre near GUM and Red Square. The entrances at the front lead to stores selling Russian-made goods, notably **Vologda Linens** (tel: 232-9463; www.linens.ru). It has clothing, tablecloths, sheets and napkins

– souvenirs with local colour. In the same row are an outlet of the cosmetics company **Novaya Zarya**, **Gusevskoi Crystal Factory** and **Infanta Fur Salon**.

Platform Mark is a shopping experience for the adventurous. Every Saturday and Sunday, a vacant lot on the edge of Moscow fills up with old men and women selling their belongings for $1 a piece. Lots of clothes, some in fine condition, and kitschy Soviet knick-knacks. Bus No. 685 from M. Altufyevo goes to the "Platform Mark" stop, or take a commuter train at Savyolovsky station (metro: Savyolovskaya). Make sure it is a stopping train otherwise it will bypass Mark.

Museum Shops

Museum gift shops are good places to buy souvenirs. You don't need admission to the museum to shop. The **State Historical Museum** on Red Square has high quality lacquerware and dolls. The **Tretyakov Gallery** has a wide selection of art books at a cost lower than most bookstores.

SPORT

Spectator Sports

In Russia a single sports club fields teams in several sports, which is why basketball, hockey and football teams all have the same name.

Basketball

Dynamo *(see address under Football)* is currently the strongest basketball team. CSKA also has a good basketball team that plays at CSKA's **Universal Sporting Complex** (39/ 1 Leningradsky prospekt; metro: Aeroport; www.cska.ru). The season runs from November to April.

Hockey

Champion hockey teams come from the provinces. CSKA,

Dynamo and Spartak field the local powerhouses. Each play at the sporting complexes of their respective clubs as listed below.

Skating

The large, modern **Krylatskoye Skating Centre** (Krylatskoye, Property 16; metro: Krylatskoye; tel: 141-7265; www.icepalace.ru) has hosted world speed-skating championships. Major figure-skating events are held at **Luzhniki** *(see Football)*, host of the 2005 World Figure-Skating Championships.

Active Sports

Chess

In Russia, chess is a sport. Serious enthusiasts regularly gather at a handful of clubs around the city for round-robin tournaments. These are not for beginners. Skills should overcome any language barrier. **Mikhail Botvinnik Central Chess Club**, 14 Gogolevsky bulvar; metro: Kropotkinskaya; tel: 291-8627. Sun at noon.

Oktyabrsky Chess Club, 35 ulitsa Bolshaya Yakimanka; metro: Oktyabrskaya; tel: 238-8824. Wed–Fri 4–8pm, and 3–7pm at weekends.

Tirgan Petrosyan Chess Club, 11/2 ulitsa Bolshaya Dmitrovka; metro: Oktyabrskaya; tel: 200-6550; www.chessmoscow.ru.

Ice-Skating

Skating is a great way to enjoy winter in Moscow. The ice rink at **Hermitage Gardens** (3 Karetny ryad; metro: Pushkinskaya) is centrally located and popular. Evenings are sponsored by Retro FM, which broadcasts oldies to entertain skaters. **Sokolniki Park** (1 Sokolnichesky val; metro: Sokolniki) has more of an alley than a rink. Bring your own skates to explore the kilometers of icy wooded paths. **Young Pioneers' Stadium** (31 Leningradsky prospekt; metro: Dynamo) has more space without venturing off the beaten path.

Rollerblading

Centre na Tulskoi 3 Kholodilny pereulok; metro: Tulskaya; tel:

771-6839; www.rollholl.ru. Experts who want to speed around and do tricks may find the youngsters who congregate here an obstacle, but it's a fun place, with pool tables, bowling alley and bar.

Victory Park (metro: Park Pobedy) is a favourite place to skate. **Adrenalin** (1 Chernyansky proyezd; metro: Medvedkovo; tel: 473-0005; www.skatepark.ru) is Moscow's Mecca for extreme skaters, with bowls and ramps.

Swimming

To use a pool you need a doctor's note in Russian saying that you have no skin diseases. If you have a doctor's note ready, try the pool at **Olimpiisky Stadium** (16 Olimpiisky prospekt; metro: Prospckt Mira; tel: 786-3203/786-3112; www.olimpik.ru). The outdoor heated pool at **Chaika** (Korobeinikov pereulok; metro: Park Kultury; tel: 202-0474) attracts French expats.

Tennis

Dynamo and Luzhniki *(see addresses below)* rent out courts to amateurs. **Sportkompleks**

FOOTBALL

Until the billionaire oligarch Roman Abramovich bought Chelsea in 2003, football was the last sport most people associated with Russia. Two years later CSKA became the first Russian club to lift a major European trophy, winning the UEFA Cup. Investment is now at an all-time high.

Attendances can still be low for less attractive matches. Torpedo's average gate is 3,000, and they play in the 80,000 capacity Luzhniki Stadium. For derbies and other important matches, however, attendances are high, and the atmosphere at these games (Lokomotiv vs CSKA, Spartak vs CSKA, any European games) is worth experiencing even if you are not a big football fan. The most modern stadium is Cherkizovsky,

with a 30,000 capacity, home to Lokomotiv Moscow, but regularly used by other teams (including the national side) for big matches.

The other two stadiums are the crumbling Dynamo Stadium (home to Dynamo, but also used by CSKA) and the 1980 Olympic stadium, Luzhniki (where both Spartak and Torpedo play).

Abramovich, who was born in Saratov, south of Moscow, in 1966 and made his money in Siberian oil, has promised to build Russia a 55,000-seat national stadium near the Botanical Gardens, but this won't be ready until 2007, at least.

Match details can be found in *Sovetskii Sport* or *Sport Express*. For English-speakers, the *Moscow Times* usually lists the games in advance.

Buying a Ticket

Tickets are cheap ($5–30), and for all but the biggest games can be bought on the day at ticket offices outside the stadium. Big games sell out quickly, and touts demand as much as five times a ticket's face value.

Matches are generally safe, the problems only occasionally occurring at the big derbies.

Stadiums

Dynamo Stadium, 36 Leningradskii prospekt; tel: 212-7092/212-3132 (tickets); metro: Dynamo.

Lokomotiv Stadium, 125 ulitsa Bolshaya Cherkizovskaya; tel: 161-9063; metro: Cherkizovskaya.

Luzhniki Stadium, 24 Luzhnetskaya Nab; tel: 201-0955; metro: Sportivnaya.

BATHHOUSES

The most famous of Moscow's bathhouses *(see page 154)* is Sandunovskie Bani, or Sanduny, where the men's section is decked in marble and gold. In most *banyas*, a 2-hour session costs $20 including use of towel and slippers. Birch branches and conical felt *banya* hats are extra.

Moskvich (46/15 Volgogradsky prospekt; metro: Tekstilshchiki; tel: 178-7126; www.skmmsk.ru) is a sporting centre for amateurs with indoor facilities for tennis, as well as figure-skating, curling, baseball, track and field, and football. The outdoor courts at **Chaika** (Korobeinikov pereulok; metro: Park Kultury; tel: 202-0474) are more expensive, but popular among expats.

SIGHTSEEING TOURS

The exception to the often overpriced and rather boring English-language tours offered by most Moscow operators is **Patriarshy Dom Tours** (6 Vspolny pereulok; inside school #1239; metro: Barrikadnaya; tel: 795-0927; www.russiatravel-pdtours.netfirms.com), which offers a full schedule of tours for all interest groups, from the Aviation Museum to architectural tours of small ancient cities near Moscow. They can also arrange individual tours if the ones in their regular schedule don't suit you.

If you plan in advance, it's possible to take a tour of the **Kristall Vodka Factory** (4 Samokatnaya ulitsa; metro: Kurskaya; tel: 749-4974; www.kristall.ru). The factory is state-owned, and you must first send a fax (362-3770) to the company director on behalf of your "organisation" requesting a date and time, and number of visitors. But it's interesting and concludes with a vodka-tasting. The cost is

Sandunovskie Bani, 14 Neglinnaya ulitsa; metro: Kuznetsky Most; tel: 928-4631; www.sanduny.ru.
Bani na Presne, 7/1 Stolyarny pereulok; metro: Barrikadnaya; tel: 253-8680.
Seleznyovskiye Bani, 15 Seleznyovskaya ulitsa; metro: Novoslobodskaya; tel: 978-7521.

30 euros, and you must bring a translator because the employees are only allowed to speak Russian.

CHILDREN

As Moscow's middle class grows and settles down, the city becomes more child-friendly. Playgrounds stand in courtyards, though the locals will raise eyebrows if English-speaking children jump in the sandpits with their kids. Along the Boulevard Ring there are public playgrounds, with rustic-looking swings and see-saws carved from wood. It's better to use these in the morning or afternoon, as they can become occupied with beer-guzzling youths in the evening.

Besides the circuses listed above, there are other venues that children will appreciate.
Durov Animal Theatre, 4 ulitsa

Durova; metro: Tsvetnoy Bulvar; tel: 631-3047/681-7222. The dynasty of top trainers is continued by Durov's elderly daughter.
Gorky Park, 9 Krymsky val; metro: Oktyabrskaya; tel: 237-8707. Roller-coasters, train rides and other amusement-park attractions in a pleasant setting on the bank of the Moscow River next to a wooded park.
Kuklyachov Cat Theatre, 25 Kutuzovsky prospekt; metro: Kutuzovskaya; tel: 249-2907. Yuri Kuklyachov's world-famous entourage of trained cats and clowns will please little cat-lovers.
Lel, 112 Prospekt Mira; metro: Alekseyevskaya; tel: 687-4207; www.lelik.ru. Clowns, mazes, slides and pools full of foam balls keep kids entertained. The entrance fee ($12 on weekdays, $20 on weekends) includes snacks and juice for kids. Adults get in free.
Natalya Sats Children's Musical Theatre, 5 prospekt Vernadskovo; metro: Universitet; tel: 930-7021; www.teatr-sats.ru. Operettas based on well-known fairy tales like *Thumbelina* for little kids and lighter versions of classic operas like *The Magic Flute* and *Evgeny Onegin* for adolescents.
Obraztsov Puppet Theatre, 3 Sadovaya-Samotechnaya; metro: Tsvetnoy Bulvary; tel: 299-5373; www.puppet.ru. Repertoire includes many familiar fairy tales so kids can follow along without knowledge of Russian.

BELOW: sightseeing on the Moscow River.

TRANSPORT

ACCOMMODATION

ACTIVITIES

A – Z

LANGUAGE

A – Z

A HANDY SUMMARY OF PRACTICAL INFORMATION, ARRANGED ALPHABETICALLY

A dmission Charges

Although technically against the law, many museums in Moscow continue to operate a system of dual pricing for Russians and foreigners. However, the prices are still not prohibitive and, in museums where there is no dual pricing system, nominal. International student discount cards are occasionally accepted as proof of identity where there is a system of student discounts. However, the cashiers sometimes only recognise those issued by Russian educational authorities.

B udgeting for Your Trip

Although Moscow has a real dearth of cheap, budget hotels, it is still worth hunting around for hotel rooms and not just taking the first thing your tourist agency offers you. In the latest rankings, Moscow was the third most expensive city in the world. While this may be true for visiting businesspeople, the fact that the average wage here is around US$500 a month is an indication of just how cheaply it is possible to get by in the Russian capital.

If you choose to stay in luxury 5-star hotels, eat in expensive restaurants, take taxis provided by your hotel etc, then you are not going to get much change out of $500 a day. However, by staying in cheaper hotels, eating in cafés and using the metro it is possible to get by on $30–100 a day, per person, depending on what you do on a particular day.

While the public transport system is very cheap (see the Getting Around section, page 213) you'll find that many museums, the Kremlin and most churches either forbid photography or slap a hefty charge for permission to use your camera.

C limate

Moscow has a continental climate, with cold, snowy winters and warm, humid summers. The first snowfall usually occurs in early November, and in most years the city is snow-covered until mid- to late March. In midwinter daytime temperatures are typically between -10 and -5°C (14–23°F), with the odd milder day around freezing point. Occasional Siberian spells bring temperatures below -20°C (-4°F). Spring is fairly short-lived, with large swings in temperature and some rainy weather. By the middle of June the weather is more settled, and by mid-August most days are warm or hot (typically 22–6°C/72–9°F) although heatwaves do occur, when it can be over 32°C (90°F) for days on end. North winds can also bring some very cool summer days, below 15°C (59°F). Rain is not uncommon in summer. Autumn tends to be cool and dry, as the days shorten from late August until the colder weather arrives in late October and the long winter starts again.

When to visit

Moscow offers two distinctive seasons for visitors. For those wanting to experience a real Russian winter – cold, but very beautiful – the middle of January to end of February is the best time to stay. The summers in Moscow are lovely, too, and the driest and warmest period is during June and July. Two periods worth avoiding are the beginning of May, when much of the city shuts down to take advantage of the month's two national holidays (the 1st and 9th). Russians also take a long break to celebrate the New Year.

What to wear

Russians, especially the younger generation, are fashion-conscious and often look down on "scruffy foreigners". However, that said, there is no reason to dress up for a visit to the Russian capital, unless you are planning to attend a formal event. Generally, in Moscow, wear whatever you would at home. Winter is another matter. Temperatures can reach -29°C (-20°F), and you should bring gloves, a good winter coat and thick waterproof shoes/boots.

Crime and Safety

Taking into account the size of Moscow and the low average salaries, the Russian capital is not as dangerous for visitors as might

be expected. However, while there is no need to become excessively cautious, taking the obvious precautions that you would in any large city (wearing a money belt etc) should ensure a trouble-free visit. If you are robbed you will probably require a police report to claim compensation from your insurance company.

Try not to draw attention to yourself, especially late at night on the metro. There have been a number of attacks on dark-skinned foreigners in recent years, and travellers should be particularly alert at night on public transport.

Apart from this, the only problem likely to be encountered is the police. Although it is forbidden for ordinary police officers to stop and check registration documents on the street, the police may well continue to do so, counting on the average tourist's ignorance of the law and lack of Russian language skills. Even if your papers are in order they will more than likely "find" a problem and demand an on the spot "fine". For the non-Russian speaker there is little that can be done about this. The best option is to refuse stubbornly, pleading incomprehension. Failing this, unfortunately, only a few dollars may help you to avoid a time-consuming and unpleasant visit to the local police station. It is therefore wise to carry your passport at all times to prevent these hassles, but never surrender it and always demand to see your consulate.

Customs Regulations

On entering Russia you will have to fill in a customs declaration form, stating how much currency you have and any valuables you may have with you (laptops, jewellery and mobile phones). Syringes must also be declared, and you will require a prescription to prove you need them. This form is then supposed to be stamped, but in reality the customs officials rarely bother doing so. However, if you have a large sum of money with you, (more than $3,000) which you

intend to take out of the country, it would be best to ask for your form to be stamped, as you may have problems with it when leaving.

Visitors are prohibited from importing and exporting weapons and ammunition (excluding approved fowling pieces and hunting tackle), drugs, syringes, antiques and works of art.

You are allowed to bring in any amount of foreign currency and personal property you do not intend to offer for sale on the territory of the Russian Federation. It's a good idea to keep receipts for expensive gifts and souvenirs to avoid interminable questions at customs. Duty-free allowances on tobacco and alcohol are as for all countries outside the EU.

When departing you are no longer required to declare any sums greater than $3,000. It is still worth filling out a declaration form even if you have less than this, as the rules change frequently. It may be worth checking with your airline/tourist agency before leaving. Customs officers are generally polite and reasonable, but you can expect a careful examination of all your luggage.

D isabled Travellers

Russia is a difficult place for disabled people, with many disabled Russians spending virtually their entire lives indoors. There are almost no facilities for the disabled (the metro, for example,

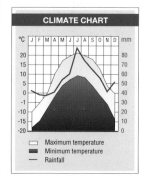

CLIMATE CHART

☐ Maximum temperature
■ Minimum temperature
— Rainfall

ELECTRICITY

Russia uses the continental-type, two-prong plug at AC220V.

would be virtually impossible to navigate in a wheelchair). For this reason, it is recommended that disabled travellers do not come to Moscow alone and think very hard about coming even if accompanied by an able-bodied person. Russia is an incredibly inconvenient place for the disabled traveller to visit.

 mbassies & Consulates

Embassies in Moscow

Most countries are represented in Moscow. Below is a list of some of the main embassies.
Australia
10A/2 Podkolokolny pereulok
Tel: (495) 956-6070
Metro:Kitai-gorod
Canada
23 Starokonyushenny pereulok
Tel: (495) 105-6000
Metro: Kropotkinskaya
Ireland
5 Grokholsy pereulok
Tel: (495) 937-5900
Metro: Prospekt Mira
United Kingdom
10 Sofiaskaya naberezhnaya
Tel: (495) 956-7200
Metro: Smolenskaya
USA
8 Bolshaya Devyanitskiy pereulok
Tel: (495) 728-5000
Metro: Barrikadnaya

Russian embassies

Australia
78 Canberra Avenue, Griffith, Canberra
Tel: 295-9033
Canada
285 Charlotte Street, Ottawa
Tel: 235-4341
Ireland
186 Orwell Road, Rathgar, Dublin
Tel: 492-3525
New Zealand
Carory, 57 Messines Road, Wellington

Tel: 476-6113
United Kingdom
5 & 13 Kensington Palace Gardens, London
Tel: (020) 7229-3628/9
United States
Embassy: 2650 Wisconsin Avenue NW, Washington, DC
Tel: 202-298 5700
Consulates: 2790 Green Street, San Francisco, CA
Tel: 415-928 6878
9 East 91st Street, New York, NY
Tel: 212-348 0926
2323 Westin Building, 2001 6th Avenue, Seattle, WA
Tel: 206-728 1910
1333 West Loop Street, Suite 1300, Houston, TX
Tel: 713-337 3300

Entry Requirements

Visitors to Russia must have a passport valid for six months from date of return and at least one blank page and a visa. The easiest way to obtain a visa is through a travel agent. A tourist visa is valid for a set number of days to a maximum of 30; the price varies depending on how quickly it is needed.

While getting a visa puts many people off a trip to Russia, it shouldn't. If you go with a package tour operator it will be no more inconvenient than getting your picture taken and filling in a form. Your agency will sort out all the details for you. If you are travelling independently, you can pay for an agency to obtain your visa. This, too, is pretty painless.

Changes to the visa are only possible in conjunction with a travel agent; any extension must

be negotiated after you arrive in Moscow. In order to obtain a visa the travel agency will require a valid passport, visa application form and three passport photographs.

Whether you apply individually to an embassy or through a travel agency, you should allow ample time, as it may take up to a month for the paperwork to be processed. In theory this period can be shortened to 48 hours if an applicant is a business traveller or if they have a written invitation (telex and fax are also accepted) from a Russian host, but things rarely work out this easily in practice. Technically, it is possible to obtain a Russian visa through the invitation of friends or relatives. In reality, however, the process is so torturous that the majority of visitors prefer to use an agency.

You should carry your passport and visa at all times while you are in Russia. Without it you might be prohibited entry to your hotel, your embassy and many other places.

Etiquette

Women visiting Russia should be aware that men in Russia are a lot more "old-fashioned" than men in the West, and should not be surprised if a male companion holds open doors, offers his hand when getting off buses etc. Men are also, usually, expected to foot the bill in restaurants on dates.

Apart from this, Russians expect you to take off your shoes when entering a private flat and whistling indoors is considered unlucky. Uniquely, museum

EMERGENCY NUMBERS

All Russian cities have the same emergency telephone numbers, which can be dialled free of charge from public telephones. Officials responding to these calls speak very little English, so a minimal knowledge of Russian may be

needed to make yourself understood.
Fire *(Pozharnaya okhrana)*: 01
Police *(Militsiya)*: 02
Ambulance *(Skoraya pomoshch)*: 03
Gas Emergency *(Sluzhba gaza)*: 04

guests are often asked to wear felt slippers *(tapochki)* when touring museums. It helps keep wooden floors clean and shiny.

It's also probably not worth getting into a discussion with most people about Chechnya – unless, that is, you enjoy long, heated arguments.

G ay & Lesbian Travellers

In the USSR, homosexuality between men was a crime (lesbianism was not even considered to exist). However, nowadays, in Moscow at least, there are a number of gay/lesbian clubs, whose addresses can be found in the English-language paper, the *Exile*. The general public remain negatively disposed towards homosexuality, although among the club-going youth attitudes are a lot softer, with lesbianism especially having taken on a certain chic of late, perhaps largely due to the lesbian pop group Tatu.

H ealth and Medical Care

Water

Although not as bad as in St Petersburg, it is still not a particularly good idea to drink water straight from the tap in Moscow. That said, it is OK in small doses (brushing teeth etc), and can be used for cooking. Cheap mineral and drinking water is available everywhere.

Medical services

Visitors from the US, Canada, European countries and Japan need no health certificate. It is a good idea to take your own medicines, although there are pharmacies selling foreign medicines where you can find most things you need. Emergency medical services for tourists are free of charge, but you will have to pay for drugs and in-patient treatment. Doctors at the major hotels speak foreign languages.The following hospitals offer Western levels of service, but charge accordingly:

**American Medical
Center Moscow**
1 Grokholsky pereulok
Tel: (495) 933-7700
Metro: Prospekt Mira
Includes dentistry.
Athens Medical Centre
6 Michurinsky prospekt
Tel: (495) 147-9322
**Russian–American Family
Medicine Center**
10, 2-y Tverskoy-Yamskoy
pereulok
Tel: (495) 250-0646
Metro: Mayakovskaya
The European Medical Centre
5 Spiridonievsky pereulok
Tel: (495) 933-6655
Metro: Tverskaya

Dentists

Dentists are available at the American and European Medical Centres *(see above).*
European Dental Centre
6/1, 1-y Nikoloschepovsky
pereulok
Tel: (495) 933-0002/6655
(24 hours)
Metro: Smolenskaya

Eye care

Lensmaster
Several offices throughout Moscow.
Tel: (495) 747-7367
www.lensmaster.ru
Optic Moscow Shop
30 Old Arbat
Tel: (495) 241-1577
Metro: Arbatskaya

Pharmacies

36.6 is a chain of good Western-style pharmacies in Moscow. It has branches throughout the city, mostly open Mon–Sat 10am–8pm, including: 25/9 ulitsa Tverskaya, 18/7 ulitsa Kuznetsky Most and 1146 Prospekt Mira.
**Pharmacy Central Enquiry
Office**
Tel: (495) 627-0561

I nternet

The internet now offers many sites on Moscow and Russia. The definitive guide to Moscow is

www.moscow-guide.ru, sponsored by the city government. This site provides a thorough list of what to do and where to go. For more detailed information on museums, check out www.museums.ru.

For news updates, you can read the *Moscow Times* at www.themoscowtimes.com, while one of the best sites dedicated to Russia (with extensive links) is www.russiatoday.com. www.eng.menu.ru is a good site for restaurants.

Internet cafés

Internet cafés open and close all the time and are not particularly hard to find, especially in the centre. Here are a few more established places.
British Council
1 Nikoloyamskaya ulitsa
Tel: (495) 234-0201
Metro: Kitai-gorod
Located in the library. Not many computers, but you can read English newspapers while waiting.
Kuznetsky Most Café
12 Kuznetsky Most
Tel: (495) 924-2140
Metro: Kuznetsky Most
Open 10am–midnight.
Netland
2 Rozhdestvenka ulitsa
Tel: (495) 781-0923
Metro: Lubyanka
Pool tables, table football and internet access.
Timeonline
Manezhnaya ploschad
Tel: (495) 363-0060
Metro: Okhotny Ryad/Teatralnaya
www.timeonline.ru
On the ground floor of the Oxhotny Ryad shopping complex, this is apparently the biggest internet café in Eastern Europe. Open 24 hours.

L eft Luggage

There are places to leave luggage – *Kameri khraneniya* – in train terminals and airports. This is also the name used for baggage checks in many museums. Be advised that pocket knives – no matter how small – are not allowed inside many buildings.

TRANSPORT
ACCOMMODATION
ACTIVITIES
A – Z
LANGUAGE

LOST PROPERTY

It is, unfortunately, extremely unlikely that you will ever see again anything you may lose in Moscow. However, should you be unlucky enough to lose something, you can try phoning the Lost Property Office situated at the metro station Universitet, tel: (495) 222-2085. There also exists a Lost Property Office for documents only – tel: (495) 200-9957.

M aps

Although in the USSR it was extremely hard to get hold of accurate maps, today they are available everywhere, and you can pick probably pick one up in your hotel.

Media

Newspapers/magazines

Kiosks located in major hotels carry the main western daily newspapers (usually one day late). The most important newspaper for any foreigner in Moscow is *The Moscow Times* (Tues–Sat; www.themoscowtimes.com). *Moscow News* (www.mn.ru/english) is an informative English-language weekly published in Moscow. Also available is the satirical the *Exile*, which has a good listings section (www.exile.ru). Russia's leading daily is *Kommersant*, which is controlled by the exiled Boris Berezovsky and reflects his mildly anti-government views. A recent competitor to *Kommersant* is the British-and-American-financed *Vedomosti*. Many Russians, however, find this paper boring. There are also popular tabloids such as *Argumenti i Fakti* and *Komsomolskaya Pravda*.

Radio

There are three official stations and several commercial stations in Moscow. One of the most popular is the French Radio Nostal-gie. Radio Moscow (107.0 FM) broadcasts news in English every hour on the hour.

Television

More than 40 satellite TV channels can now be received in Moscow with a TV and satellite dish. Many large hotels and even some restaurants offer CNN.

Money

Currency

The rouble is divided into 100 kopeks. There are 5, 10, 50, 100, 500 and 1,000 rouble banknotes. Counterfeits are common, and it can be difficult to spot a fake. Coins are 1, 2 and 5 roubles, as well as 1, 5, 10 and 50 kopeks.

Currency exchange

These can be found all over the city, including in hotels. Most deal exclusively in cash and major credit cards (eg Amex, Visa), but not usually travellers' cheques; to change these, try a bank. It's worth shopping around, as commission rates vary from 1–5 percent. You will sometimes be asked to present your passport and visa as well as your customs declaration where all your money transactions should be recorded, though this is often overlooked.

Credit cards

Most tourist-related businesses accept major credit cards: American Express, Diners Club, Visa, Eurocard and MasterCard. Cash dispensers are starting to appear on major streets in Moscow. If you have an Amex card you can use it at 21A Sadovokudrinskaya ulitsa and at Sovincenter (Mezhdunarodnaya Hotel), 12 Krasnoprenskaya naberezhnaya.
Lost Credit Cards
American Express: (495) 755-9001
Visa, **MasterCard**, **Diners Club**, **jcb**: (495) 580-9449

Black market

Avoid changing money on the street – the rates are rarely favourable and you are likely to be tricked or robbed. Although strictly illegal, you may be asked to pay in dollars for certain purchases, eg souvenirs bought from street vendors. You are within your rights to insist on payment in roubles, but it's probably best to play each situation by ear.

Tipping

Tipping is an accepted practice. Waiters, porters, taxi drivers, guides and interpreters have always appreciated tips. 10 percent is the accepted rule. Many restaurants add a service charge of 10–15 percent to your bill.

O pening Hours

In the centre of Moscow and around metro stations many shops open 24 hours. It is possible, if you look hard enough, to find anything at any one time. Most shops open from 10am to 8/9pm, often without lunch breaks. Banks and other organisations take breaks from 1–2pm or 2–3pm and usually stay open until 6/7pm.

Museums tend to open at 10am and close at 6pm. Hardly any are open on Monday, and most take one extra day off per month for "cleaning". They are also known to close for no particular reason and with no notice. Additionally, Moscow changes so quickly, it's difficult to obtain current information. Having said all that, you may find many small museums look closed – a big heavy door is shut tight, no lights are on, etc – but knock and you'll find they are very much open but just saving money on electricity and keeping out draughts.

P hotography

Photographic equipment is easily obtained, and there are quick film-developing services. There is a Kodak kiosk at the Passage Department Store, 10 Petrovka ulitsa, at GUM, 3 Red Square, and a Fuji Film Centre at 17 Novy Arbat ulitsa. Most hotels also sell photographic equipment. You should not take photographs of military installations. Some state and private buildings forbid photography for security reasons. Be cautious: ask your guide or interpreter. It is also technically illegal to take photos on the metro. This rule has almost always been overlooked in the past, but with the rise in terrorism it is sometimes enforced.

Postal Services

Post offices are usually open between 8am or 10am until about 7.45pm but, routine postal services are also available in larger hotels.

Not all post offices accept international mail above the size of a standard letter. Postal delivery is quite slow – it may take up to three weeks for a letter from Moscow to reach Western Europe, or a month to reach the US. Visitors wishing to send more valuable packages should use an international courier company *(see below)*.

Main post offices *(Glavpochshtamt)*: 26a ulitsa Myasnitskaya, open 8am–7.45pm, and 7 Tverskaya ulitsa, open 8am–10pm. The address of the international post office is 37 Varshavskoe shosse, open daily 9am–8pm.

Courier services

There are efficient international courier services available:

PUBLIC HOLIDAYS

Russia's public holidays were reorganised at the end of 2004. They are now as follows:

1–5 January	New Year holiday
7 January	Orthodox Christmas Day
23 February	Army Day
8 March	Women's Day
1 May	May Holiday
9 May	Victory Day
12 June	Independence Day
4 November	Unity Day

DHL
Express Centre 1-ya Tverskaya: 11 Yamskaya ulitsa
Tel: (495) 956-1000
Metro: Belorusskaya
31 Novinsky bulvar
Metro: Barrikadnaya
www.dhl.ru
Federal Express
17 Gogolsky bulvar
Tel: (495) 787-5555
Metro: Kropotkinskaya
www.fedex.com

Public Toilets

There are paid chemical toilets outside most metro stations. They are generally clean. Failing this, nip into one of the city's ubiquitous McDonalds.

R eligious Services

Russian Orthodox

Most churches are now open for services. The main Sunday service usually starts around 9am.
The Church of the Assumption
Novodevichy Convent,
1 Novodevichy proyezd
Metro: Borovitskaya
Trinity Cathedral
Daniilovsky Monastery,
Daniilovsky Val ulitsa

Anglican

St Andrew's Church
9 Voznesensky pereulok
Tel: (495) 143-3562

Baptist

Society of Evangelical Christian Baptists
3 Maly Vuzovsky pereulok
Tel: (495) 297-0568

Catholic

Chapel of Our Lady of Hope
7 Kutuzovsky prospekt
Tel: (495) 243-9621
Metro: Kutozovskaya

Jewish

Choral Synagogue
8 Bolshoy Spasoglinishchevsky pereulok
Tel: (495) 623-9697

Muslim

7 Vypolzov pereulok
Tel: (495) 281-3866
Metro: Prospekt Mira

Many former churches and religious meeting places are being reconverted to religious use. Information can be obtained from:
Moscow Patriarchate
5 Chistoprudny pereulok
Tel: (495) 201-3416
Religious Board of the Buddhists of Russia
49 Ostozhenka ulitsa
Tel: (495) 245-0930
Jewish Religious Community Council
10 Bolshoy Spasoglinishchevsky pereulok
Tel: (495) 925-4280
Muslim Religious Society
7 Vypolzov pereulok
Tel: (495) 281-4904

S tudent Travellers

Many places (museums etc) in Russia only recognise Russian student ID cards, although a lot depends on the cashier. Russia doesn't have any particularly good deals for students. Students are, the Russian view seems to be, foreigners, and little distinction is made between them and their wealthier compatriots.

T elephones

Calling from abroad

To call Moscow from abroad you must dial the country code, 7, followed by 495 – the area code for Moscow. Unless you have a special discount plan you will find calling Russia very expensive.

Calling abroad

For international calls, dial 8 +10 + the country code, followed by the area code (minus the initial 0) and finally the number.
Australia 61
UK 44
US and Canada 1

TIME ZONE

GMT plus 3 hours. Clocks switch to daylight-saving time at the same times as the UK.

Fax

All official institutions and major business representatives have a fax machine. Moscow has a public fax service at 7 Tverskaya ulitsa (tel: 495-924-9004) where you can register a number by which you can be reached if you plan to stay in the city for a long period. Any incoming message will be forwarded either by phone or by local mail. It is the only way to beat the slow mail service.

Public phones

If you need to make local calls, get a prepaid phone card. Avoid the old token phones, as most will just eat your token. For international calls, it's much cheaper to go to a call centre such as the one at the main post office on Tverskaya ulitsa. Every neighbourhood has a centre: ask at your hotel for more information.

Mobile phones

European phones will work in Moscow, but the American triband system will not. The cost for using a mobile phone from abroad is astronomical if you do not arrange a special tariff prior to your trip. If you are going to use a phone regularly and plan to stay for several weeks, look into buying a local mobile. This will cut your costs dramatically. MTS (www.mts.ru) and MegaFon (www.nwgsm.com) are two reliable local providers.

Tourist Information

Since the collapse of the state Intourist organisation, Moscow has suffered from a lack of a central, unified tourist information centre. English computer stands are due to appear on the streets in 2006. Meanwhile, use *The Moscow Times*, the internet and guidebooks.

Tour Operators

Today the city has dozens of tour operators offering all sorts of services, from hotel reservations, home stays, tickets for cultural events to trips on the Golden Ring.
Charisma Travel
20/1 Tvesrskaya ulitsa, office 34
Tel: (495) 209-7387
www.charismatravel.net
Metro: Tverskaya
Cultpohod
10 Mozhaiskoe shosse, 2nd floor, Office 200
Tel: (495) 258-0816
www.cultpohod.ru
Metro: Kutozovskaya
Steppes Travel
21/2 Trubinovskiy pereulok
Tel: (495) 290-6149
www.steppestravel.ru
Metro: Arbatskaya
Vesyolaya Planeta
58 ulitsa Shepkina, office 304,
Tel: (495) 924-7812
Metro: Sukharevskaya

Travel Agents

United Kingdom

Martin Randall Travel
10 Barley Mow Passage, London W4 4PH
Tel: (020) 8742-3355
www.martinrandall.com
Progressive Tours
12 Porchester Place, London W2 2BS
Tel: (020) 7262-1676
Regent Holidays UK Ltd
70 Piccadilly, London W1J 8HP
Tel: (0117) 921-1711
www.regent-holidays.co.uk
Russian National Tourist Office
15 John Street, Bristol BS1 2HR
Tel: (020) 7495 7570
www.visitrussia-org.uk

United States

Four Winds Travel
175 Fifth Avenue, New York, NY 10010

USEFUL NUMBERS

Information: *(Spravochnaya)*: 09.
Moscow city information: 05.
24-hr Information Centre: (495) 232-2232.
Time: 100.

Tel: 866-836 4145
Russian National Group
224 West 30th Street, New York, NY 10001
Tel: 646-473 2233
www.russia-travel.com

Useful Addresses

Chambers of Commerce

American Chamber of Commerce
7 ulitsa Dogorukovskaya, 14th floor
Tel: (495) 961-2141
www.amcham.ru
Metro: Tverskaya
British–Russian Chamber of Commerce
1904 World Trade Centre, 12 Krasnopresnenskaya naberezhnaya
Tel: (495) 937-8249
Moscow Chamber of Commerce
13 Malaya Dmitrovka
Tel: (495) 132-7510

What to Bring

Bring with you all prescribed medicines. It will also save time if you bring your own contraceptives, first-aid items, washing powder, special batteries for cameras, shavers and an umbrella.

In the winter you will also need waterproof shoes, a warm hat, scarf and gloves. Make sure you have photocopies of all documents, including your passport and visa. Dress as you would at home for sightseeing and formal dining.

WEIGHTS & MEASURES

Russia uses the metric system of weights and measures.

LANGUAGE

UNDERSTANDING RUSSIAN

The Alphabet

The first two columns show the printed letter in Russian upper and lower case. The third column shows how the Russian letters sound and the fourth column shows the name of the letter in Russian.

А	а	**a**, archaeology	**a**
Б	б	**b**, buddy	**be**
В	в	**v**, vow	**ve**
Г	г	**g**, glad	**ge**
Д	д	**d**, dot (tip of tongue close to the teeth, not the alveoli)	**de**
Е	е	**e**, get	**ye**
Ё	ё	**yo**, yoke	**yo**
Ж	ж	**zh**, composure	**zhe**
З	з	**z**, zest	**ze**
И	и	**i**, ink	**i**
Й	й	**j**, yes	**jot**
К	к	**k**, kind	**ka**
Л	л	**l**, life (but a bit harder)	**el'**
М	м	**m**, memory	**em**
Н	н	**n**, nut	**en**
О	о	**o**, optimum	**o**
П	п	**p**, party	**pe**
Р	р	**r** (rumbling – as in Italian; tip of tongue vibrating)	**er**
С	с	**s**, sound	**es**
Т	т	**t**, title (tip of tongue close to teeth)	**te**
У	у	**u**, nook	**u**
Ф	ф	**f**, flower	**ef**
Х	х	**kh**, hawk	**ha**
Ц	ц	**ts** (pronounced conjointly)	**tse**
Ч	ч	**ch**, charter	**che**
Ш	ш	**sh**, shy	**sha**
Щ	щ	**shch**	**shcha**
ъ		(the hard sign)	
Ы	ы	**y** (with tongue in same position as when pronouncing g, k)	**y**
ь		(the soft sign)	
Э	э	**e**, ensign	**e**
Ю	ю	**yu**, you	**yu**
Я	я	**ya**, yard	**ya**

Basics

I/we
ya/my
я/мы
You
ty (singular, informal)/
vy (plural, or formal singular)
ты /вы
He/she/they
on/aná/aní
он/она/они
My/mine
moy (object masculine)/*mayá* (object feminine)/*mayó* (neutral)/*maee* (plural)
мой/моя/моё/мои
Our/ours
nash/násha/náshe/náshy
наш/наша/наше/наши
Your/yours
tvoy etc (see My)
vash etc (see Our)
твой/ваш

His/her, hers/their, theirs
yevó/yeyó/íkh
его/её/их
Who?
keto?
Кто?
What?
shto?
Что?

Greetings

Hello!
zdrástvute (neutral)
Здравствуйте!
alo! (by telephone only)
Алло!
privyét! (informal)
Привет!
Good afternoon/good evening
dóbry den'/dobry vécher
Добрый день/Добрый вечер
Good morning/good night
dobroye útra/dobryo nóchi
(= Sleep well)
Доброе утро/Доброй ночи
Goodbye
dasvidáneye (neutral)
До свиданья
ciao! (informal)
Чао!
paká! (informal, literally "until")
Пока!
Good luck to you!
shchaslívo!
Счастливо!

What is your name?
kak vas (tebya) zavút?/
kak váshe ímya i ótchestvo?
(the second is formal)
Как вас (тебя) зовут?/
Как ваше имя и отчество?

My name is...I am...
menya zavut...ya...
Меня зовут...Я...

It's a pleasure to meet you
óchin' priyatno
Очень приятно

Good/excellent
kharashó/otlíchno
хорошо/отлично

Do you speak English?
vy gavaríte pa anglíski?
Вы говорите по-англи-
йски?

I don't understand/I didn't understand
ya ne panimáyu/ya ne pónyal
Я не понимаю/Я не понял

Repeat, please
pavtaríte pazhálusta
Повторите, пожалуйста

What do you call this?
kak éta nazyváetsa?
Как это называется?

How do you say...?
kak vy govaríti...?
Как вы говорите...?

Please/thank you (very much)
pazhálusta/spasíba (balshóye)
Пожалуйста/спасибо (большое)

Excuse me
izviníte
Извините

Getting Around

Where is the...?
gdye (nakhóditsa)...?
Где находится...?

toilet
tualyet
...туалет

bus station
aftóbusnaya stántsiya
...автобусная станция

bus stop
astanófka aftóbusa
...остановка автобуса

airport
airapórt
...аэропорт

railway station
vakzál/stántsiya (small towns)
...вокзал/станция

post office
póchta
...почта

police station
milítsiya
...милиция

ticket office
bilyétnaya kássa
...билетная касса

embassy/consulate
pasól'stvo/kónsul'stvo
...посольство/консульство

Where is there a...?
gdye zdes...?
Где здесь...?

currency exchange
abmén valyúty
...обмен валюты

pharmacy
aptyéka
...аптека

(good) hotel
(kharóshy) otél'
...(хороший) отель

restaurant
restorán
...ресторан

bar
bar
...бар

taxi stand
stayanka taksí
...стоянка такси

subway station
metró
...метро

news-stand
gazyétny kiósk
...газетный киоск

public telephone
telefón
...телефон

supermarket
universám
...универсам

department store
univermág
...универмаг

NUMBERS

1 *adín* один	**17** *semnátsat'* семнадцать	**300** *trísta* триста
2 *dva* два	**18** *vasemnátsat'* восемнад-цать	**400** *chityrista* четыреста
3 *tri* три	**19** *devetnátsat'* девятнад-цать	**500** *pitsót* пятьсот
4 *chityri* четыре	**20** *dvátsat'* двадцать	**600** *shessót* шестьсот
5 *pyat'* пять	**21** *dvatsat' adin* двадцать один	**700** *semsót* семьсот
6 *shest'* шесть	**30** *trítsat'* тридцать	**800** *vasemsót* восемьсот
7 *sem* семь	**40** *sórok* сорок	**900** *devitsót* девятьсот
8 *vósim* восемь	**50** *pidisyat* пятьдесят	**1,000** *tysicha* тысяча
9 *dévit'* девять	**60** *shez'disyat* шестьдесят	**2,000** *dve tysichi* две тысяч и
10 *désit'* десять	**70** *sémdisyat* семьдесят	**10,000** *désit' tysich* десятьтысяч
11 *adínatsat'* одиннадцать	**80** *vósemdisyat* восемьдесят	**100,000** *sto tysich* сто тысяч
12 *dvinátsat'* двенадцать	**90** *devinósta* девяносто	**1,000,000** *milión* миллион
13 *trinátsat'* тринадцать	**100** *sto* сто	**1,000,000,000** *miliárd* миллиард
14 *chityrnatsat'* четырнад-цать	**200** *dvés'ti* двести	
15 *pitnátsat'* пятнадцат'		
16 *shesnátsat'* шестнад-цать		

hospital
bal'nítsa
…больница
Do you have…?
u vas jest'…?
У вас есть…?
I (don't) want…
ya (ne) khachu…
Я (не) хочу…
I want to buy…
ya khochu kupít'…
Я хочу купить…
Where can I buy…?
gdye mozhno kupít'…?
Где можно купить…?
cigarettes
sigaréty
…сигареты
wine
vinó
…вино
film
fotoplyonku
…фотоплёнку
a ticket for…
bilyét na…
…билет на…
this
éta
…это
postcards/envelopes
otkrytki/konvérty
…открытки/конверты
a pen/a pencil
rúchku/karandásh
…ручку/карандаш
soap/shampoo
myla/shampún'
…мыло/шампунь
aspirin
aspirn
…аспирин
I need…
mne núzhno…
Мне нужно…
I need a doctor
mne núzhen dóktor
Мне нужен доктор
I need help
mne nuzhná pómashch'
Мне нужна помощь
car/plane/train/ship
mashina/samolyót/póezd/karábl'
машина/самолёт/поезд/корабль
A ticket to…
bilyét do…
билет до…

How can I get to…?
kak mozhno dobrátsa do…?
Как можно добраться до…?
Please, take me to…
pazhalusta otveszíte menya…
Пожалуйста, отвезите меня…
What is this place called?
kak nazyváetsa eta myésta?
Как называется это место?
Where are we?
gdye my?
Где мы?
Stop here
astanavíte zdes'
Остановите здесь
Please wait
padazhdíte pazhalusta
Подождите, пожалуйста
When does the train/plane leave?
kagdá atpravlyaitsa poezd/samolyot?

• вход/выход/входа нет
vkhot/vykhat/vkhóda nyet
entrance/exit/ no entrance
• Ж/М
dlya zhén'shchin/dlya mushchín
ladies/gentlemen (toilet)
• зал ожидания
zal ozhidániya
waiting hall
• занято/свободно
zányata/svabódno
occupied/free
• касса
kassa
booking office/cash desk
• медпункт
medpúnkt
medical services
• справочное бюро
správochnoye byuro
information
• вода для питья
vadá dlya pitya
drinking water
• вокзал
vakzál
terminal/railway station
• открыто/закрыто
otkryto/zakryto
open/closed

• опасно
opásna
danger
• продукты/гастроном
prodúkty/gastronóm
grocery store
• булочная/кондитерская
búlochnaya/kondítirskaya
bakery/confectionery
• столовая
stalóvaya
canteen
• самообслуживание
samaabslúzhivaniye
self-service
• баня/прачечная/химчистка
bánya/práchechnaya/khimchístka
bathhouse/laundry/dry cleaning
• книги
knígi
books
• мясо/птица
myása/ptítsa
meat/poultry
• овощи/фрукты
óvashchi/frúkty
green-grocery/fruits
• универмаг/универсам
univermág/universám
department store/ supermarket

Когда отправляется поезд/самолёт?
I want to check in my luggage
ya khochu sdat' bagázh
Я хочу сдать багаж
Where does this bus go?
kudá idyot étot aftóbus?
Куда идёт этот автобус?

How much does it cost?
skól'ka eta stóit?
Сколько это стоит?
That's very expensive
eta óchin' dóraga
Это очень дорого
A lot, many/a little, few
mnógo/mála
много/мало
It (doesn't) fits me
eta mne (ne) padkhódit
Это мне (не) подходит

At the Hotel

I have a reservation
u menya bron'
У меня бронь
I want to make a reservation
ya khochu zakazát' nomer
Я хочу заказать номер
A single/double room
odnamyéstny/dvukhmestny kómnatu
одноместный/двухмест-ный номер
key/suitcase/bag
klyuch/chimadán/súmka
ключ/чемодан/сумка

Eating Out

waiter/menu
afitsiánt/minyu
официант/меню
I want to order…
ya khochu zakazat'…
Я хочу заказать
breakfast/lunch/supper
záftrak/obyed/úzhin
завтрак/обед/ужин
mineral water/juice
minerál'naya vadá/sok
минеральная вода/сок
coffee/tea/beer
kófe/chai/píva
кофе/ чай/пиво
What do you have to drink (alcoholic)?
shto u vas jes't' vypit'?
Что у вас есть выпить?

ice cream/fruit/dessert
marózhenaya/frúkty/desért
мороженое/фрукты/десерт
salt/pepper/sugar
sol'/périts/sákhar
соль/перец/сахар
beef/pork/chicken/fish/shrimp
govyadina/svinína/kúritsa/ryba/krivyétki
говядина/свинина/курица/рыба/креветки
vegetables/rice/potatoes
óvashchi/ris/kartófil'
овощи/рис/картофель
bread/butter/eggs
khleb/máslo/yajtsa
хлеб/масло/яйца
soup/salad/sandwich/pizza
sup/salát/buterbrót/pitsa
суп/салат/бутерброд/пицца
a plate/a glass/a cup
taryélka/stakán/cháshka
тарелка/стакан/чашка
The bill, please
shchyot pazhalusta
Счёт, пожалуйста
Delicious/not good
vkúsna/ne vkúsna
вкусно/не вкусно

Money

I want to exchange currency (money)
ya khochu abmenyát' valyutu (déngi)
Я хочу обменять валюту (деньги)

Do you accept credit cards?
vy prinimáite kredítnie kártochki?
Вы принимаете кредитные карточки ?
Can you cash a travellers' cheque?
vy mózhyte obnalichit' darózhny chek?
Вы можете обналичить дорожный чек?
What is the exchange rate?
kakój kurs?
Какой курс?

Time

What time is it?
katóry chas?
Который час?
Just a moment, please
odnú minúti
Одну минуту
hour/day/week/month
chas/den'/nidélya/myésits
час/день/неделя/месяц
At what time?
v kakóe vrémya?
В какое время?
this/last/next week
eta/próshlaya/slyé-duyushchaya nidelya
эта/прошлая/следующая неделя
yesterday/today/tomorrow
vcherá/sivódnya/záftra
вчера/сегодня/завтра

FURTHER READING

History

1812: Napoleon's Fatal March on Moscow, by Adam Zamoyski (HarperPerennial, 2005).
A Traveller's Companion to Moscow, by Lawrence Kelly (Constable and Robinson, 2004).
History of Modern Russia, by Robert Service (Penguin, 2003).
History of Russian Architecture, by William Craft Brumfield (University of Washington Press 2004).
Ivan the Terrible, by Isabel de Madariaga (Yale University, 2005).
Lenin: a Biography, by Robert Service (Pan, 2002).

Natasha's Dance: A Cultural History of Russia, by Orlando Figes (Penguin, 2003).
The Russian Revolution, by Sheila Fitzpatrick (Oxford, 2001).
Stalin: The Court of the Red Tsar, by Simon Sebag-Montefiore (Weidenfeld & Nicholson, 2003).
Ten Days that Shook the World, by John Reed (Penguin, 1919).

Current Affairs

Black Earth: A Journey Through Russia After the Fall, by Andrew Meier (HarperPerennial, 2004).
Putin's Russia, by Anna Politkovskaya (Harvill Press, 2004).

Literature

Crime and Punishment, The Brothers Karamazov, The Devils, by Fyodor Dostoyevsky.
Dead Souls, Diary of a Madman and Other Stories, by Nikolay Gogol.
Doctor Zhivago, by Boris Pasternak.
Fathers and Sons, On The Eve, Sportsman's Sketches, by Ivan Turgenev.
Eloise in Moscow by Kay Thompson (Atheneum, 1959).
Lady with Lapdog and Other Stories, by Anton Chekhov.

MOSCOW STREET ATLAS

The key map shows the area of Moscow covered by the atlas section. An index of street names and places of interest shown on the maps can be found on the following pages. For each entry there is a page number and grid reference.

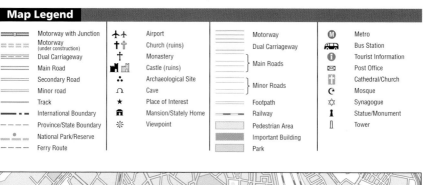

Map Legend

Motorway with Junction	✈ Airport	Motorway	Ⓜ	Metro
Motorway (under construction)	✝ Church (ruins)	Dual Carriageway	🚌	Bus Station
Dual Carriageway	✝ Monastery		❶	Tourist Information
Main Road	▦ Castle (ruins)	Main Roads	✉	Post Office
Secondary Road	∴ Archaeological Site		⛪	Cathedral/Church
Minor road	∩ Cave	Minor Roads	☾	Mosque
Track	★ Place of Interest	Footpath	✡	Synagogue
International Boundary	🏛 Mansion/Stately Home	Railway	🗽	Statue/Monument
Province/State Boundary	❋ Viewpoint	Pedestrian Area	⌷	Tower
National Park/Reserve		Important Building		
Ferry Route		Park		

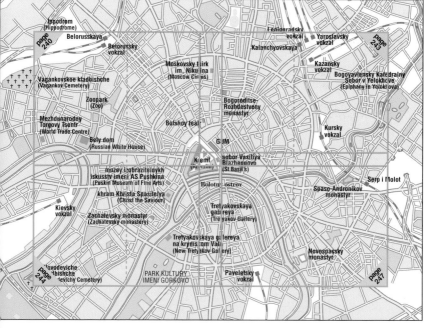

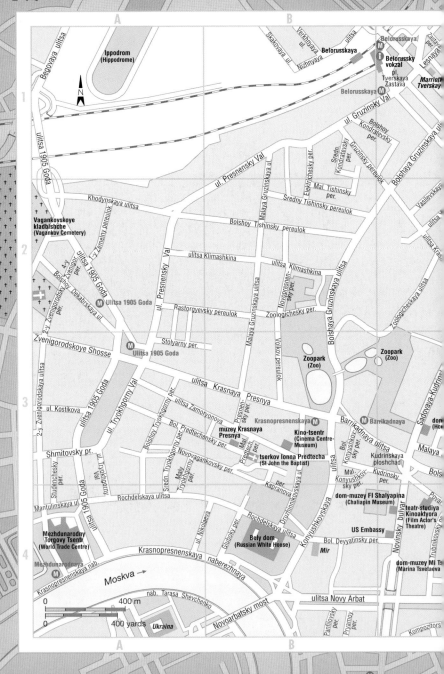

Ippodrom
(Hippodrome)

Begovaya ulitsa

Verkhnyaya ul.
Skakovaya ul.
Nizhnyaya ul.

Belorusskaya

Ⓜ **Belorusskaya**
ⓘ **Belorussky vokzal**
pl. Tverskaya Zastava
Ⓜ *Marriott Tverskaya*

Lesnaya

Belorusskaya

ul. Gruzinsky Val

Bolshoy Kondratevsky per.

Gruzinsky pereulok

Bolshaya Gruzinskaya

ulitsa 1905 Goda

Khodynskaya ulitsa

ul. Presnensky Val

Malaya Gruzinskaya ul.

Elektrichesky per.

Sredn. Kondratevsky per.

Mal. Tishinsky per.

Sredny Tishinsky pereulok

Bolshoy Tishinsky pereulok

Vasilevsky

Vagankovskoye kladbishche
(Vagankov Cemetery)

Zemelny pereulok
4-y Zvenigorodsky per.
Bolshoy Dekabrskaya ul.
2-y Zvenigorodsky per.

ulitsa 1905 Goda

ulitsa Klimashkina

ulitsa Klimashkina

Novopresnensky per.

Bolshaya Gruzinskaya ulitsa

Zoologichesky per.

Zoologicheskaya ulitsa

 Ⓜ **Ulitsa 1905 Goda**

ul. Presnensky Val

Rastorgyevsky pereulok

Malaya Gruzinskaya ulitsa

Volkov pereulok

Zvenigorodskoye Shosse

Ⓜ **Ulitsa 1905 Goda**

Stolyarny per.

**Zoopark
(Zoo)**

**Zoopark
(Zoo)**

2-y Zvenigorodskaya ulitsa

ulitsa 1905 Goda

ul. Tryokhgorny Val

ulitsa Krasnaya

Presnya

ulitsa Krasnaya Presnya

ul. Kostikova

ulitsa Zamoryonova

Presnensky per.

Ⓜ **Krasnopresnenskaya**

Ⓜ **Barrikadnaya**

Ⓜ **Barrikadnaya**

Sadovaya-Kudrins

don
(Ho

Bolshoy Tryokhgorny Val

Sredn. Tryokhgorny per.

Bol. Predtechensky per.

muzey Krasnaya Presnya

Mal. Predtech.

**Kino-tsentr
(Cinema Centre-Museum)**

Bol. Konyushkovsky per.

Kudrinskaya ulitsa

Malaya

Shmitovsky pr.

Novovagankovsky per.

**tserkov Ionna Predtecha
(St John the Baptist)**

Kudrinskaya ploshchad

Bols

Studenchesky per.

Malyy Tryokhgorny per.

per. Kapranova

Mal. Konyushkovsky per.

Kudrinsky per.

**dom-muzey FI Shalyapina
(Chaliapin Museum)**

**Teatr-studiya Kinoaktyora
(Film Actor's Theatre)**

Mantulinskaya ul.

Rochdelskaya ulitsa

Druzhinnikovskaya ulitsa

Konyushkovskaya

Novinsky bulvar

Trubnikovsky per.

**Mezhdunarodny Torgovy Tsentr
(World Trade Centre)**

ul. Nikolaeva

Glubokiy per.

Rochdelskaya ulitsa

**Bely dom
(Russian White House)**

Bol. Devyatinsky per.

US Embassy

Mir

**dom-muzey MI Ts
(Marina Tsvetaeva**

Ⓜ **Mezhdunarodnaya**

Krasnopresnenskaya naberezhnaya

Moskva →

Krasnopresnenskaya nab.

nab. Tarasa Shevchenko

ulitsa Novy Arbat

Pamfilovsky per.

Pryamoy per.

0 ──────── 400 m

0 ──────── 400 yards   *Ukraina*

Novoarbatsky most

Kompozitors

Ⓜ

A map of central Moscow showing numbered grid references A, B along the top and bottom, and 1, 2, 3, 4 along the sides.

Labels visible on the map:

ulitsa Durova
BOTANICHESKY SAD
Bol. Balkansky per.
Kalanchy
Grokholsky pereulok
Grokholsky pereulok
Zhivaryov per.
Koptelsky
Lavrsky per.
dom-muzey VM Vasnetsov (Viktor Vasnetsov House Museum)
Meshchanskaya ulitsa
ulitsa Shchepkina
ulitsa Gilyarovskovo
Prospekt Mira
Spasskaya ulitsa
Skornyazhny per.
Samotyochnaya prospekt
Olimpiysky prospekt
Troitskaya ul.
Samotyochnaya pl.
Sadovaya-Sukharevskaya ulitsa
Sukharevskaya ploshchad
Sukharevskaya
Tsvetnoy Bulvar
Moskovsky tsirk im. Nikulina (Moscow Circus)
Tsvetnoy bulvar
Sretensky tup.
Sadovaya-Spasskaya ulitsa
Bolshoy Karetny
Sretenka
Daev per.
Seliverstov per.
Kra
Mal. Sukharevsky per.
Bol. Sukharevsky per.
Mal. Sergievsky per.
Posledny per.
Bol. Golovin per.
Mal. Golovin per.
Pushkaryov per.
Uttansky pereulok
Prosvirin per.
Myasnitsky pr.
Vysoko petrovsky monastyr
Trubnaya
Bol. Sergievsky per.
ulitsa Prosvirin per.
Lukov per.
Kra
Petrovsky bulvar
Kolokolnikov per.
Tserkov Uspeniya Bogoroditsy (Dormition of the Mother of God)
Ashcheulov per.
Prospekt Akademika Sakharova
Myasnitskaya ulitsa
Bol. Golovin per.
Rybnikov per.
Bogoroditse-Rozhdestveny monastyr
Rozhdestvensky bulvar
Rozhdestvensky bulvar
Sretensky bulvar
Krupskaya
Moskovsky tsentr iskusstv (Centre for the Arts)
Nizhn. Kiselny per.
Sretensky monastyr (Sretensky Monastery)
Turgenevskaya
Bobrov per.
Chistye Prudy
Gusyatnikov per.
Rakhmanovsky per.
Sandunovsky bani (Sanduny Bath House)
Bol. Kiselny per.
Sreten. per.
Glavpochtamp (Main Post Office)
Griboedov
Petrovskiye liniye
Budapest
Sandunovsky per.
Varsonofevsky per.
Menshikova bashnya (Menshikov's Tower)
Chistoprudny bulvar
Marriott Royal
Petrovsky Passazh
Mily Lubyanka
Istoriko-Demonstratsionny Zal FSB Rossii (KGB Museum)
muzey istorii gorodskovo osveshcheniya Ogni Moskvy (Fires of Moscow)
Chistye prudy (Clean Ponds)
Kuznetsky
ulitsa Bolshaya Lubyanka
ulitsa Malaya Lubyanka
ul. Makarenk
TsUM
Kuznetsky Most
Pushechnaya ul.
Most
Furkasovsky per.
Figurny dom ("Figured House")
Bolshoy teatr (Bolshoy Theatre)
Savoy
Detsky Mir
muzey VV Mayakovskovo (Mayakovsky Museum)
ulitsa Pokrovka
Maly teatr (Maly Theatre)
Teatralnaya
Lubyanka
Lubyanskaya ploshchad
Teatralny proezd
Metropol
Moskva
Old Wall
muzey istorii goroda Moskvy (Museum of Moscow History)
Politekhnichesky muzey (Polytechnic Museum)
ul. Maroseyka
Lyuteranskaya obshchina (Lutheran)
Okhotny Ryad
muzey VI Lenina
Ploshchad Revolutsii
Zaikonospassky monastyr
Maroseyka-Pokrovka
Kitai-gorod
Khoralnaya sinagoga
osobnyak Morozovikh (Morozov Mansion)
Zhukov
Kazansky sobor (Kazan Cathedral)
Staraya pl.
Kitai-gorod
Gosudarstvenny istorichesky muzey (State Historical Museum)
Torgovaya palata (former Stock Exchange)
Krasnaya ploshchad
GUM
ILINSKIE SADY
Kiril e Metody
ulitsa Solyanka
khram T Zhivona v Khokh (Trinity)
mavzoley VI Lenina
Novy/Stary Gostiny dvor
muzey Palaty v Zaryade (Chambers in Zaryade)
tserkov Georgina na Pskovskoy Gorke (St George)
ul. Varvarka
Palaty starovo angliyskovo dvora (Old English Court)
Podkolokolny per.

0 ——— 400 m
0 ——— 400 yards

D   E

ingradsky vokzal

VI Lenina

Krasnoprudnaya ul.

ovskaya

Komsomolskaya

Yaroslavsky vokzal

Rusakovskaya estakada

Nizhnyaya Krasnoselskaya ulitsa

Olkhovskaya ulitsa

Baumanskaya ulitsa

Komsolmolskaya ploshchad

Komsomolskaya

Olkhovsky tup.

Olkhovsky per.

Olkhovskaya ulitsa

Bakuninskaya ulitsa

dskaya

Kazansky vokzal

Ryazansky proezd

Bogoyavlensky Kafedralny Sobor v Yelokhove
(Epiphany in Yelokhova)

ulitsa

ul. Fridrikha Engelsa

Baumanskaya

Yuzhny pr.

Novoryazanskaya ulitsa

Novoryazanskaya ulitsa

Spartakovskaya

Pletashkov

Ladozhskaya ulitsa

Kalanch. tup.

Basmanny pereulok

Ryazansky per.

Lefortovsky per.

Poslannikov per.

u montovu aya

Basmannaya

ulitsa

ul. A Lukyanova

Dobroslobodskaya ul.

Aptekarsky pereulok

Starokirochny per.

Baumanskaya ulitsa

Khomutovsky tupik

Staraya

Basmannaya

ulitsa

Tokmakov pereulok

Denisovsky pereulok

pereulok

Gardnerovsky per.

Brigadirsky

2-y Baumanskaya ulitsa

Basmanny tupik

Gorokhovsky pereulok

Mashkova ulitsa

sov Museum)

Maly Demidovsky per.

Bolshoi Demidovsky

Novokirochny per.

per.

Tekhnichesky per.

okrovka

ulitsa

Kazakova

ulitsa Kazakova

ulitsa Radio

Sadov. tup.

ulitsa Radio

ernogryazskaya ulitsa

Zemlyanoy Val

Puteysky tup.

Nizhny Susalny per.

Yelzavetinsky pereulok

Maly Kazyonny pereulok

Kurskaya

naberezhnaya Akademika Tupoleva

Bol. Kazyonny per.

Yauza

Yakovoapostolsky per.

Kurskaya

Kurskaya

Krasnokazarmennaya nab.

lok

Kursky vokzal

PARK IM. 1 MAY

Samokatnaya

Slobodskoi per.

Chkalovskaya

Mruzovsky per.

naberezhnaya

ulitsa

Volochaevskaya ulitsa

pereulok

ulitsa Zemlyanoy Val

Verkh. Syromyatnich.

4-y Syrom. per.

Syromyatnichesky pr.

Zolotorozhskaya nab.

Pole

Melnitsky per.

2-y Syromyat. nichesky per.

3-y Syrom. per.

Nizhnyaya Syromyatnicheskaya ul.

proezd

Obukha

Bol. Poluyaroslavsky per.

Poluyarl. nichesky per.

Syromyatnicheskaya nab.

Stroganovsky

D   E

1

2

3

4

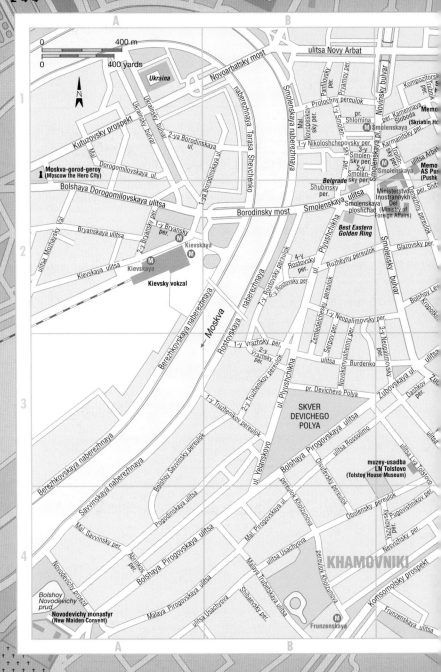

0 — 400 m
0 — 400 yards

N

Ukraina

ulitsa Novy Arbat

Novoarbatsky most

Smolenskaya naberezhnaya

Kutuzovsky prospekt

Ukrainsky bulvar

Mal. Dorogomilovskaya ul.

Moskva-gorod-geroy
(Moscow the Hero City)

Bolshaya Dorogomilovskaya ulitsa

2-ya Borodinskaya ul.

1-ya Borodinskaya ul.

naberezhnaya Tarasa Shevchenko

Bryanskaya ulitsa

1-y Bryansky per.

2-y Bryansky per.

Kievskaya

Kievskaya ulitsa

Kievskaya

Kievsky vokzal

ulitsa Mozhaisky

Berezhkovskaya naberezhnaya

Moskva

Rostovskaya naberezhnaya

Berezhkovskaya naberezhnaya

Savvinskaya naberezhnaya

Mal. Savvinsky per.

Novodevichy proezd

Bolshoy Novodevichy prud

Novodevichy monastyr
(New Maiden Convent)

Adrinos

Bolshoy Savvinsky pereulok

Pogodinskaya ulitsa

Bolshaya Pirogovskaya ulitsa

Malaya Pirogovskaya ulitsa

ulitsa Usachyova

1-y Yelanskovo

2-y Truzhenikov pereulok

1-y Truzhenikov pereulok

ul. Plyustchikha

pr. Devichevo Polya

1-y Vrazhsky per.

2-y Vrazhsky per.

Novokonyushenny pereulok

SKVER DEVICHEGO POLYA

Bolshaya Pirogovskaya ulitsa

Olsufievsky pereulok

Malaya Trubetskaya ulitsa

Shubaevsky per.

Panfilovsky per.

Pryamoi per.

Protochny pereulok

pr. Shlomina

Novopeskovsky per.

1-y Nikoloshchepovsky per.

Mal. Smolensky per.

3-y Smolensky per.

2-y Smolensky per.

1-y Smolensky per.

Shubinsky per.

Smolenskaya naberezhnaya

Borodinsky most

Smolenskaya ulitsa

Smolenskaya ploshchad

Novinsky bulvar

Kompozitorskaya

Trubn

Memo

(Skriabin H

Karmanitsky per.

Trollinsky per.

ulitsa Arbat

Smolenskaya

Memo
AS Pus
(Pushk

Belgrade

Ministerstvo
Inostrannykh
Del
(Ministry of
Foreign Affairs)

*Best Eastern
Golden Ring*

Plyustchikha

4-y Rostovsky per.

Ruzheyny pereulok

Glazovsky per.

Smolensky bulvar

Bolshoy Lev

Kropotk

1-y Rostovsky per.

6-y Rostovsky per.

Zemledelchesky per.

1-y Neopalimovsky per.

3-y Neopalimovsky per.

Serpov per.

Novokonyushenny per.

ulitsa Burdenko

Zubovskaya ul.

Dashkov per.

Zu

Bolshaya Pirogovskaya ulitsa

ulitsa Rossolimo

ulitsa Lva Tolstovo

**muzey-usadba
LN Tolstovo**
(Tolstoy House Museum)

Obolensky pereulok

pereulok Khaludzuna

Obo.

pr. Pugovishnikov per.

Nesvizhsky per.

Mstovsky per.

Yazkovsky per.

pereulok Khaludzuna

Komsomolsky prospekt

KHAMOVNIKI

Frunzenskaya ulitsa

Frunzenskaya

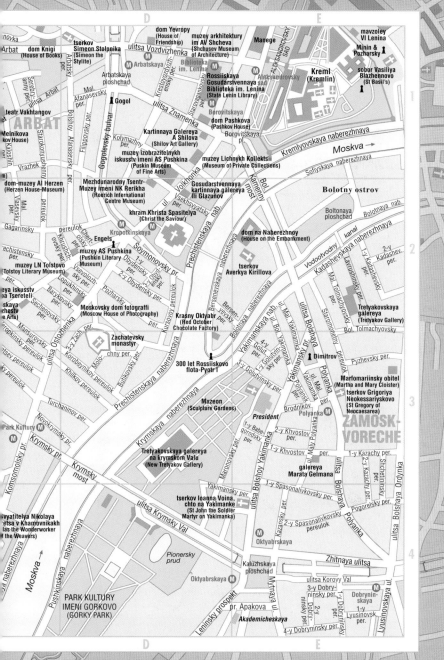

Arbat

dom Knigi
(House of Books)

tserkov
Simeon Stolpnika
(Simeon the
Stylite)

ulitsa Vozdvizhenka

dom Yevropy
(House of
Friendship)

muzey arkhitektury
im AV Shcheva
(Shchusev Museum
of Architecture)

Manege

Kreml
(Kremlin)

mavzoley
VI Lenina

Minin &
Pozharsky

sobor Vasiliya
Blazhennovo
(St Basil's)

Arbatskaya
ploshchad

Arbatskaya

Biblioteka
im. Lenina

Rossiiskaya
Gosudarstvennaya
Biblioteka im. Lenina
(State Lenin Library)

Aleksandrovsky
sad

ARBAT

teatr Vakhtangov

Melnikova
kov House)

Gogol

ulitsa Znamenka

Borovitskaya

dom Pashkova
(Pashkov House)

Borovitskaya.

Kremlyovskaya naberezhnaya

Moskva →

Kartinnaya Galereya
A Shilova
(Shilov Art Gallery)

muzey izobrazitelnykh
iskusstv imeni AS Pushkina
(Puskin Museum
of Fine Arts)

muzey Lichnykh Kollektsii
(Museum of Private Collections)

Sofiyskaya naberezhnaya

Bolotny ostrov

dom-muzey Al Herzen
(Herzen House-Museum)

Mezhdunarodny Tsentr-
Muzey imeni NK Rerikha
(Roerich International
Centre Museum)

Gosudarstvennaya
kartinnaya galereya
Ilii Glazunov

Boltonaya
ploshchad

Bolotnaya nab.

Gagarinsky

Engels

Kropotkinskaya

khram Khrista Spasitelya
(Christ the Saviour)

dom na Naberezhnoy
(House on the Embankment)

Vodootvodny   kanal

Kadashevskaya naberezhnaya

Kadashev.

muzey AS Pushkina
(Pushkin Literary
Museum)

tserkov
Averkya Kirillova

muzey LN Tolstovo
Tolstoy Literary Museum)

eya iskusstv
a Tsereteli

skaya
e Arts)

Moskovsky dom fotografii
(Moscow House of Photography)

Krasny Oktyabr
(Red October
Chocolate Factory)

Tretyakovskaya
galereya
(Tretyakov Gallery)

Bol. Tolmachyovsky

Dimitrov

Pyzhevsky per.

Zachatevsky
monastyr

300 let Rossiiskovo
flota-Pyotr I

Marfomariinsky obitel
(Martha and Mary Cloister)

tserkov Grigoriya
Neokessariyskovo
(St Gregory of
Neocaesarea)

Muzeon
(Sculpture Gardens)

President

Polyanka

ZAMOSK-
VORECHE

Park Kultury

Krymsky
most

Tretyakovskaya galereya
na krymskom Valu
(New Tretyakov Gallery)

galereya
Marata Gelmana

1-y Kazachy per.

2-y Kazachy per.

Komsomolsky pr.

Krymsky pr.

Krymsky Val

tserkov Ioanna Voina,
chto na Yakimanke
(St John the Soldier
Martyr on Yakimanka)

1-y Spasonalivkovsky per.

2-y Spasonalivkovsky
pereulok

Pogorelsky per.

 svyatitelya Nikolaya
etsa v Khamovnikakh
las the Wonderworker
the Weavers)

Oktyabrskaya

Pionersky
prud

Oktyabrskaya

Kaluzhskaya
ploshchad

ulitsa Korovy Val

Zhitnaya ulitsa

Dobrynin-
skaya

Moskva →

PARK KULTURY
IMENI GORKOVO
(GORKY PARK)

Leninsky prospekt

pr. Apakova

Akademicheskaya

3-y Dobry-
ninsky per.

Mytnaya ul.

1-y
Lyusinovsk.

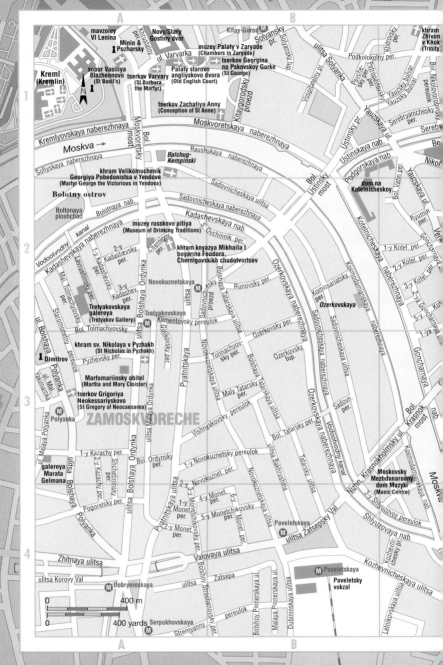

2 4 6

Kitay-Gorod

Novy/Stary
Gostiny dvor

mavzoley
VI Lenina

Minin &
Pozharsky

muzey Palaty v Zaryade
(Chambers in Zaryade)

ul. Varvarka

tserkov Georgina
na Pskovskoy Gorke
(St George)

khram
Zhivon
v Khok
(Trinity)

Kreml
(Kremlin)

sobor Vasiliya
Blazhennovo
(St Basil's)

tserkov Varvary
(St Barbara
the Martyr)

Palaty starovo
angliyskovo dvora
(Old English Court)

Podkolokolny per.

N

tserkov Zachatiya Anny
(Conception of St Anne)

Kremlyovskaya naberezhnaya

Moskvoretskaya naberezhnaya

Ustinsky nab.

dom na
Kotelnicheskoy

Moskva →

Moskvoretsky most

Sofiyskaya naberezhnaya

Raushskaya
naberezhnaya

Balchug-
Kempinski

Ustinskaya nab.

Podgorskaya nab.

khram Velikomuchenik
Georgiya Pobedonistsa v Yendove
(Martyr George the Victorious in Yendova)

Bolotny ostrov

Sadovnicheskaya ulitsa

Bol. Ustinsky most

Boltonaya
ploshchad

Boltonaya nab.

Sadovnicheskaya naberezhnaya

Kadashevskaya nab.

muzey russkovo pitiya
(Museum of Drinking Traditions)

Ovchinnik. per.

1-y Kotel. per.

Vodootvodny kanal

Kadashevskaya naberezhnaya

Chernigov.

2-y
Kadashevsky
per.

khram knyazya Mikhaila i
boyarina Feodora,
Chernigovskikh chudotvortsev

Ozerkovskaya naberezhnaya

Komissariatsky per.

Ozerkovskaya

Novokuznetskaya

Runovsky per.

3-y
Kadashev.
per.

Tretyakovskaya
galereya
(Tretyakov Gallery)

Bol. Tolmachovsky

tserkov sv. Nikolaya v Pyzhakh
(St Nicholas in Pyzhakh)

Klimentovsky pereulok

Ozerkovsky per.

Ozerkovsky
tup.

Dimitrov

Pyzhevsky per.

Marfomariinsky obitel
(Martha and Mary Cloister)

Tolmachyov-
sky per.

Maly Tatarsky
per.

tserkov Grigoriya
Neokessariyskovo
(St Gregory of Neocaesarea)

Sadovn.
per.

ZAMOSKVORECHE

Polyanka

Vishnyakovsky pereulok

Bol. Tatarsky per.

galereya
Marata
Gelmana

1-y Kazachy per.

1-y Novokuznetsky pereulok

2-y Kazachy per.

2-y Novokuznet. per.

Moskovsky
Mezhdunarodny
dom Muzyki
(Music Centre)

1-y
Monet.
per.

4-y Monet.
per.

5-y Monetchikovsky
per.

Paveletskaya

2-y Monet.
per.

Valovaya ulitsa

Zhitnaya ulitsa

Paveletskaya

ulitsa Korovy Val

ulitsa Zatsepa

Paveletsky
vokzal

Dobryninskaya

Kozhevnicheskaya ulitsa

0   400 m

0   400 yards

Serpukhovskaya

Stremyanny

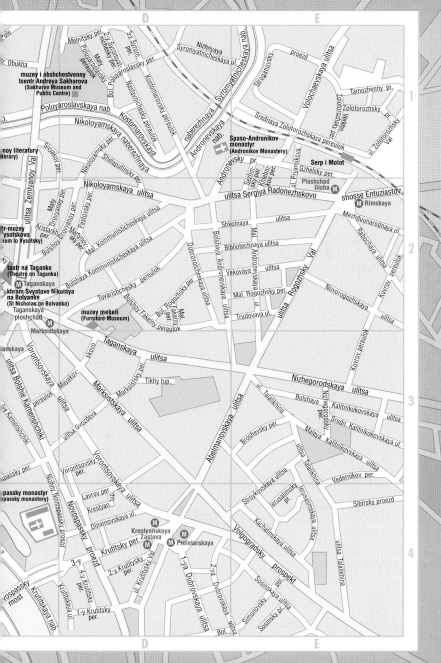

muzey i obshchestvenny
tsentr Andreya Sakharova
(Sakharov Museum and
Public Centre)

Melnitsky per.

3-J Strom. per.

2-J Syromat.
per.

Nizhnyaya
Syromyatnicheskaya ul.

Stroganovsky

proezd

Volochaevskaya ulitsa

Tamozhenny pr.

Bol. Polyarovslavsky
pereulok

Maly
Polyarovslavsky
per.

Nastavnichesky pereulok

Kostomarovsky pereulok

Zolotorozhsky
Val

Zolotorozhsky
pr.

r- Obukha

Poluyaroslavskaya nab.

Nikoloyamskaya naberezhnaya

naberezhnaya

Andronevskaya
nab.

Srednaya Zolotorozhskaya pereulok

Zolotorozhsky

ul. Zolotorozhsky Val

Kostomarovskaya

Shelaputinsky per.

Nikoloyamsky per.

Andronevsky pr.

Spaso-Andronikov
monastyr
(Andronikov Monastery)

Serp i Molot

noy literatury
brary)

Svyatov per.

ul. Zemlyanov Val

Maly

Drovyanov per.

Nikoloyamskaya ulitsa

Pestovsky per.

Bol. Polyarovslavsky per.

Sechin-
sky per.
Mal.
Khlebni-
kov per.

Gzhelsky per.

Ploshchad
Ilicha

ulitsa Sergiya Radonezhskovo

shosse Entuziastov

Rimskaya

r-muzey
ysotskovo
eum to Vysotsky)

Aristarkh.
per.

Bolshoy Drovyanov per.

Maylni-
sky per.

Mal. Kommunisticheskaya ulitsa

Shkolnaya

ulitsa

Mezhdunarodnaya ul.

Dobrovolcheskaya ulitsa

Bibliotechnaya ulitsa

Mal. Andronevskaya ulitsa

Rabochaya ulitsa

teatr na Taganke
(Theatre on Taganka)

Taganskaya

khram Svyatovo Nikolaya
na Bolvanke
(St Nicholas on Bolvanka)

Bolshaya Kommunisticheskaya ulitsa

Tovarishchesky pereulok

Vekovaya

ulitsa

Novorogozhskaya

Rogozhsky Val

Kovrov pereulok

Taganskaya
ploshchad

Marksistskaya

muzey mebeli
(Furniture Museum)

Bolshoy Fakelny per.

Bol. Rogozhsky per.

Mal. Rogozhsky per.

Mal.
Fakelny
per.

Trudovaya ul.

ulitsa

anskaya

Vorontsovskaya
pereulok

ulitsa Bolshie Kamenshchiki

skovo

Mayakov.
ulitsa

Taganskaya
ulitsa

Marksistskaya ulitsa

Marksistsky per.

Tikhy tup.

Nizhegorodskaya

ulitsa

Kovrov pereulok

ulitsa Gvozdeva

ul. Talalikhina

Bolshaya
Nizhegorodsky
per.

Kalitnikokovskaya
Sredn. Kalitnikokovskaya

ulitsa

ve Kamenshchiki

Nizhny Novospassky proezd

Vorontsovskaya ulitsa

Abelmanovskaya ulitsa

Broshevsky per.

Malaya Kalitnikovskaya ulitsa

Vedernikov. per.

passky monastyr
spassky monastery)

passky per.

Lavrov per.

Novospassky proezd

Krestyan.

Dinamovskaya ul.

Stroykovskaya ulitsa

Ierusalimsky
pr.

Ierusalimskaya ulitsa

Kachalinskaya ulitsa

Sibirsky proezd

ulitsa Talalikhina

Krestyanskaya
Zastava

Proletarskaya

Krutitsky per.

Volgogradsky prospekt

vospassky
most

Krutitskaya nab.

3-y
proezd

2-y Krutitsky
per.

4-y Krutitsky
per.

1-y Krutitsky
per.

1-ya Krutitskaya ul.

ul. Krutitsky Val

1-ya Dubrovskaya ulitsa

2-ya Dubrovskaya ulitsa

Sosinskaya ulitsa

Simonovsky
Sosinsky pr-zd

Bol.

STREET INDEX

ART & PHOTO CREDITS

AFP/Getty Images 32, 35, 36/37, 38
akg-images 178
akg-images/Erich Lessing 179
Paul Ancenay/Alamy 171L
Bogdanovich *back cover* CR, 21
Bridgeman Art Library 61, 180, 186
William Craft Brumfield 67
Sheldan Collins/Corbis 208
Contrast 59, 68R
Simon Crofts/Alamy 49
Culliganphoto/Alamy 187
Fritz Dressler 133, 165R, 207
Mary Evans Picture Library 48, 50L, 52
Alain Le Garsmeur 18, 210
Govorukhin 17, 19, 20, 31, 34, 101T
Gudenko 16, 124, 181T
Robert Harding Picture Library/Alamy 141T
Jurgens 22, 29, 176T
David King Collection 165T
Tom Le Bas 86T, 100, 106T, 109T, 126T, 133T, 149, 149T, 153, 190, 191T
Lebrecht Music and Arts Photo Library/Alamy 57
M. Timothy O'Keefe/Alamy 141
Iain Masterton/Alamy 179T, 188, 188T
Network Photographers 10/11, 101
Jeremy Nicholl/Alamy 154
Jeremy Nicholl/Katz 66
Novosti/TopFoto 33, 50R, 58, 177

Abraham Nowitz *back cover* BC, 1, 3BR, 6BL, 7TR, 7BL, 8B, 9T, 9BR, 9BL, 12/13, 14, 39, 41, 60, 68L, 72/73, 74/75, 78, 80, 86/87, 95, 117, 119, 120, 120T, 121, 122, 123, 123T, 126, 127, 128, 130, 135, 137, 138, 145, 150, 152T, 158, 161T, 162T, 165L, 166, 169T, 172, 175, 183, 185, 191, 192, 192T, 198/199, 200, 201T, 202T, 203T, 204, 204T, 205, 205T, 206L, 206R, 227
Richard Nowitz *back cover* CL, 2/3, 4T, 4B, 5T, 5B, 6T, 6BR, 7TL, 7BR, 8T, 40, 42L, 42R, 43, 44, 46, 47, 51, 53, 54, 55, 56, 69, 70, 71, 76/77, 81, 82T, 83, 84, 85, 85T, 87T, 88, 89L, 89R, 90, 91, 93, 94, 96, 96T, 97, 97T, 98T, 99, 99T, 100T, 102, 102T, 103T, 104, 105, 106, 107, 107T, 108, 109, 110, 111, 114, 115, 118T, 119T, 124T, 125, 129, 134, 136, 139, 143, 146T, 147, 147T, 148, 148T, 150T, 151,156, 157, 159, 160, 163, 164, 167, 168, 169, 173, 174T, 184, 184T, 189, 193, 193T, 194, 194T, 195T, 201, 202, 214, 216, 223
Pushkin Museum of Fine Arts 117T
RIA-Novosti 28, 139T, 142, 144, 155
Dmitry Shalganov/Corbis 131
John Spaull/Apa 98, 125T, 132T, 140T, 155T, 160T, 163T, 170T, 182T, 203

TopFoto 25, 94T, 162, 209
TopFoto/AP 30
TopFoto/HIP 24
TopFoto/Imageworks 181
Peter Turnley/Corbis 182
Roger-Viollet/TopFoto 23
Mark Wadlow/Russia & Eastern Images *back cover* TL
Neil Wilson 45

Picture Spreads

Pages 26/27: all images **David King Collection.**

Pages 64/65: AFP/Getty Images 65BR; **RIA-Novosti** 64TL, 65TR; **Abraham Nowitz** 64BR; **Richard Nowitz** 64/65, 65BL.

Pages 112/113: RIA-Novosti 112TL, 112BR, 112/113, 113TR, 113B; **Richard Nowitz** 112BL.

Pages 196/197: William Craft Brumfield 196BL, 197TR; **Abraham Nowitz** 196CR, 196/197, 197CR; **Richard Nowitz** 197BL.

Cartographic Editor: Zoë Goodwin
Map Production: Stephen Ramsay
©2006 Apa Publications GmbH & Co. Verlag KG, Singapore Branch

Book Production: Linton Donaldson and Mary Pickles

GENERAL INDEX

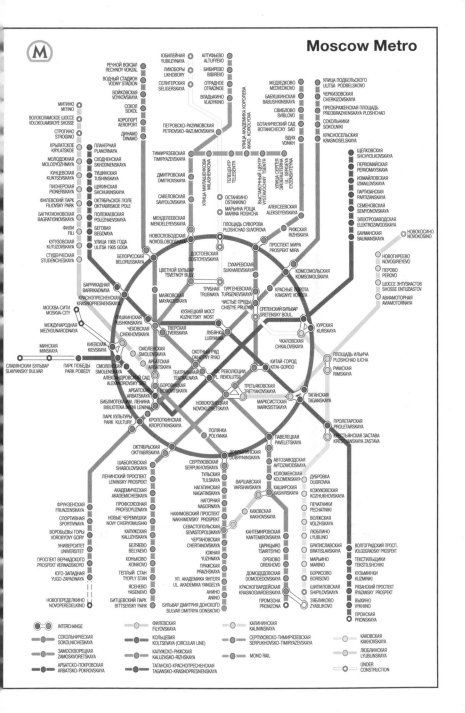